# ABSTRACT DESIGN IN AMERICAN QUILTS AT 50

1971–2021

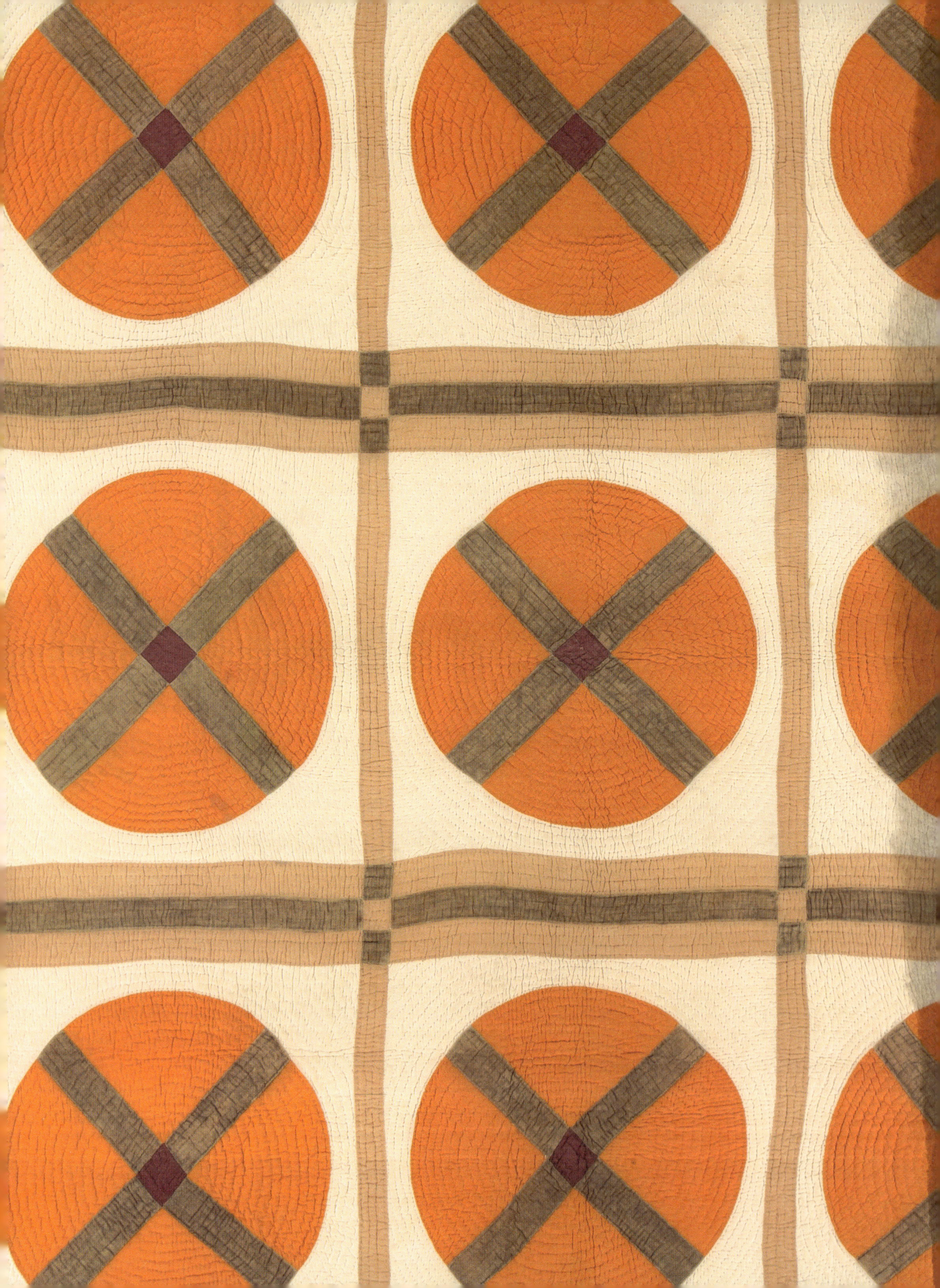

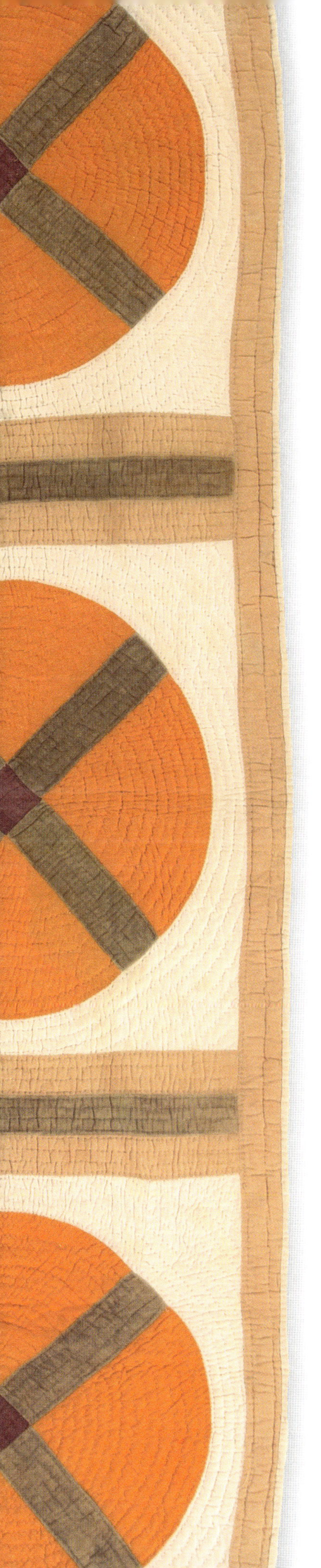

# ABSTRACT DESIGN IN AMERICAN QUILTS AT 50

## 1971–2021

EDITED BY MARIN F. HANSON

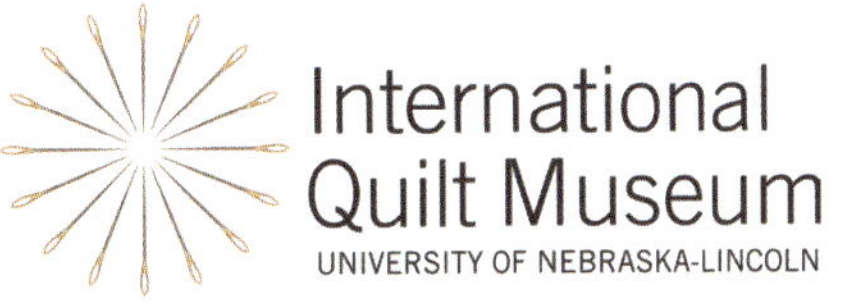

Publication of this catalog has been made possible through generous support from the Robert and Ardis James Foundation, Friends of the International Quilt Museum, and Anonymous.

This publication accompanies the International Quilt Museum's *Abstract Design in American Quilts at 50* exhibition series held between February 26, 2021, and September 4, 2021.



University of Nebraska-Lincoln
Lincoln, Nebraska 68583-0838
internationalquiltmuseum.org

UNIVERSITY OF Nebraska



ISBN: 978-1-7352784-2-1
Library of Congress Control Number: 2020948969

Production Services by

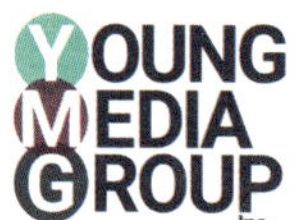


Cover images: *My Rob Peter to Pay Paul II* by Keiko Goke (2020, IQM, Gift of the Robert and Ardis James Foundation, 2020.052.0002) and Rob Peter to Pay Paul quilt (c. 1880–1900, IQM, Jonathan Holstein and Gail van der Hoof Collection, 2003.003.0017)

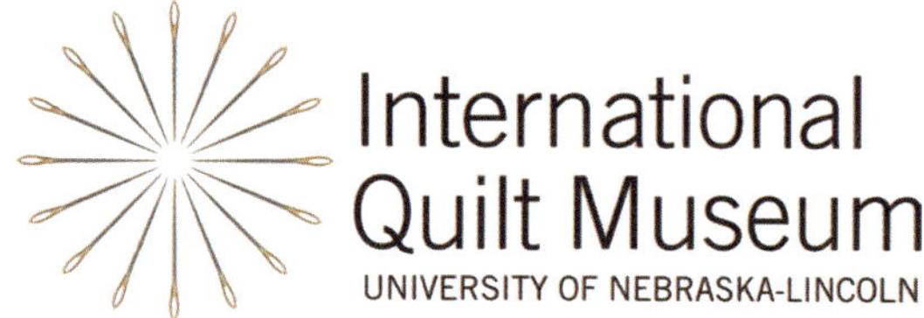

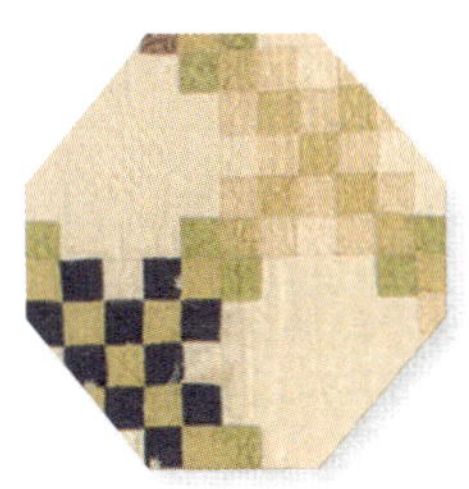

IN
MEMORY
OF

Gail van der Hoof
& Ardis Butler James

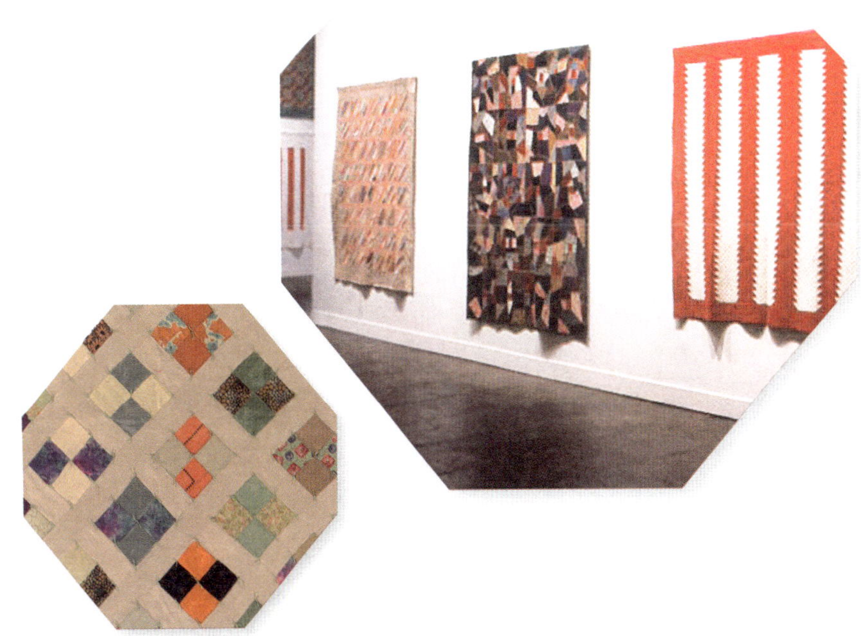

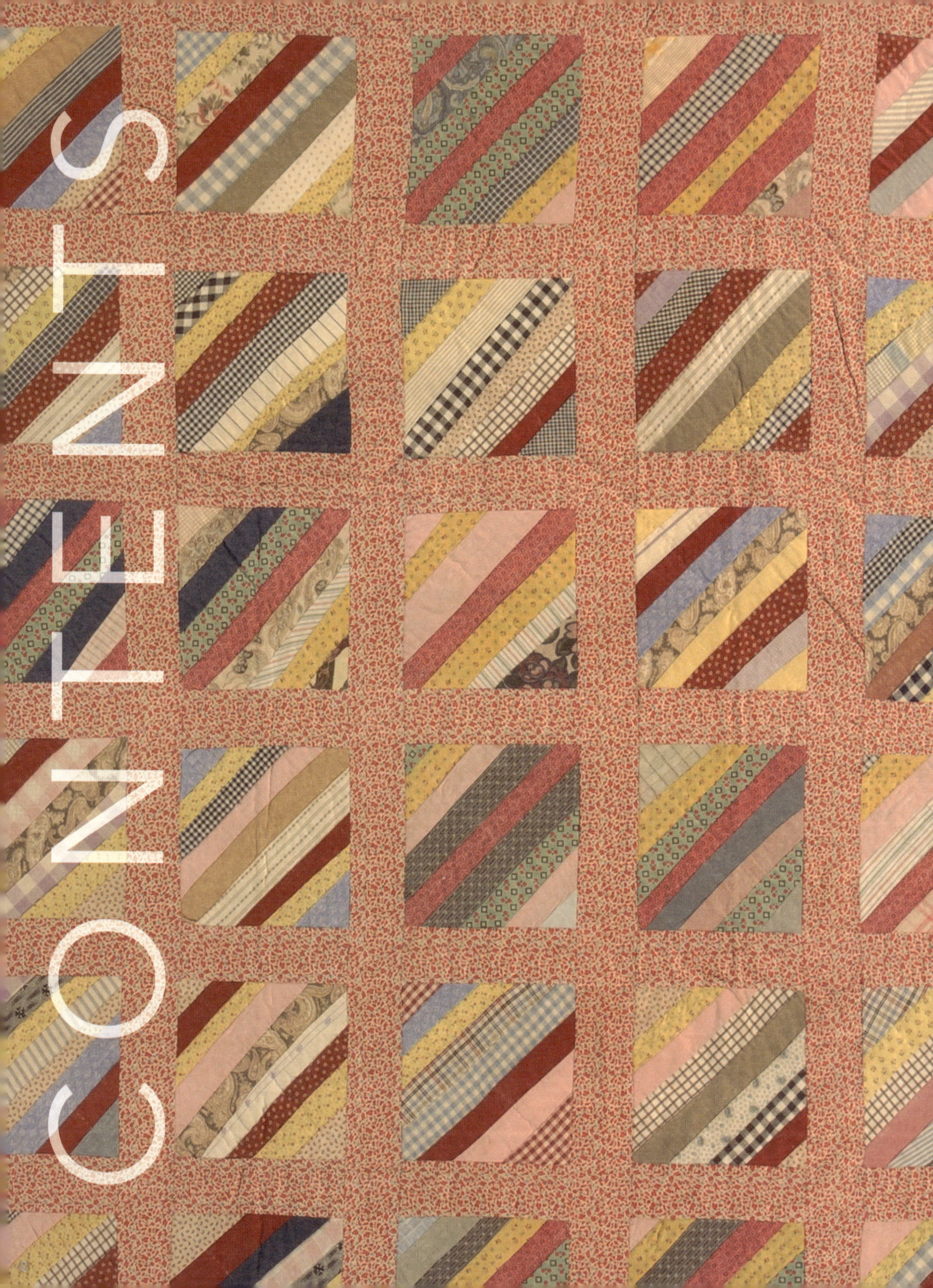

# CONTENTS

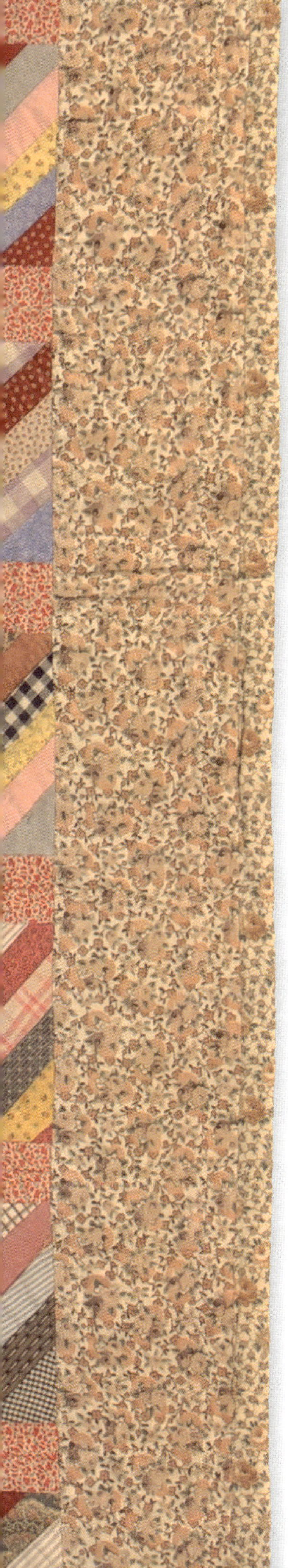

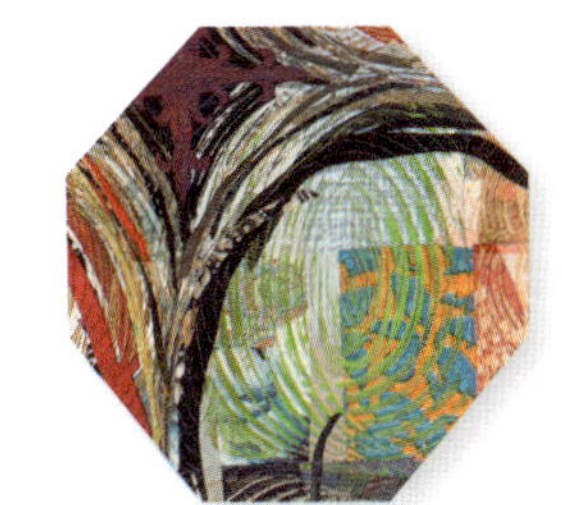



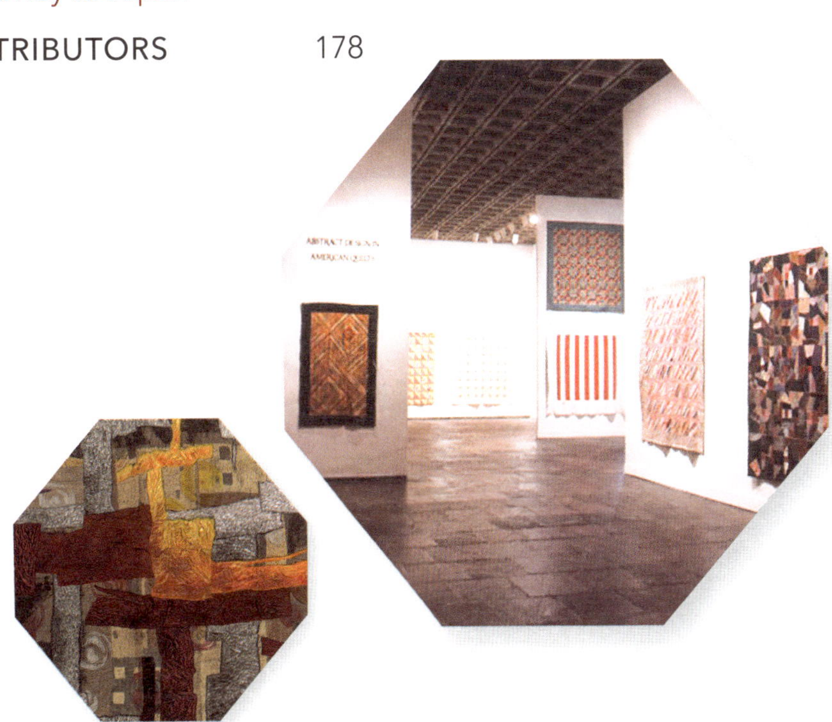

# FOREWORD

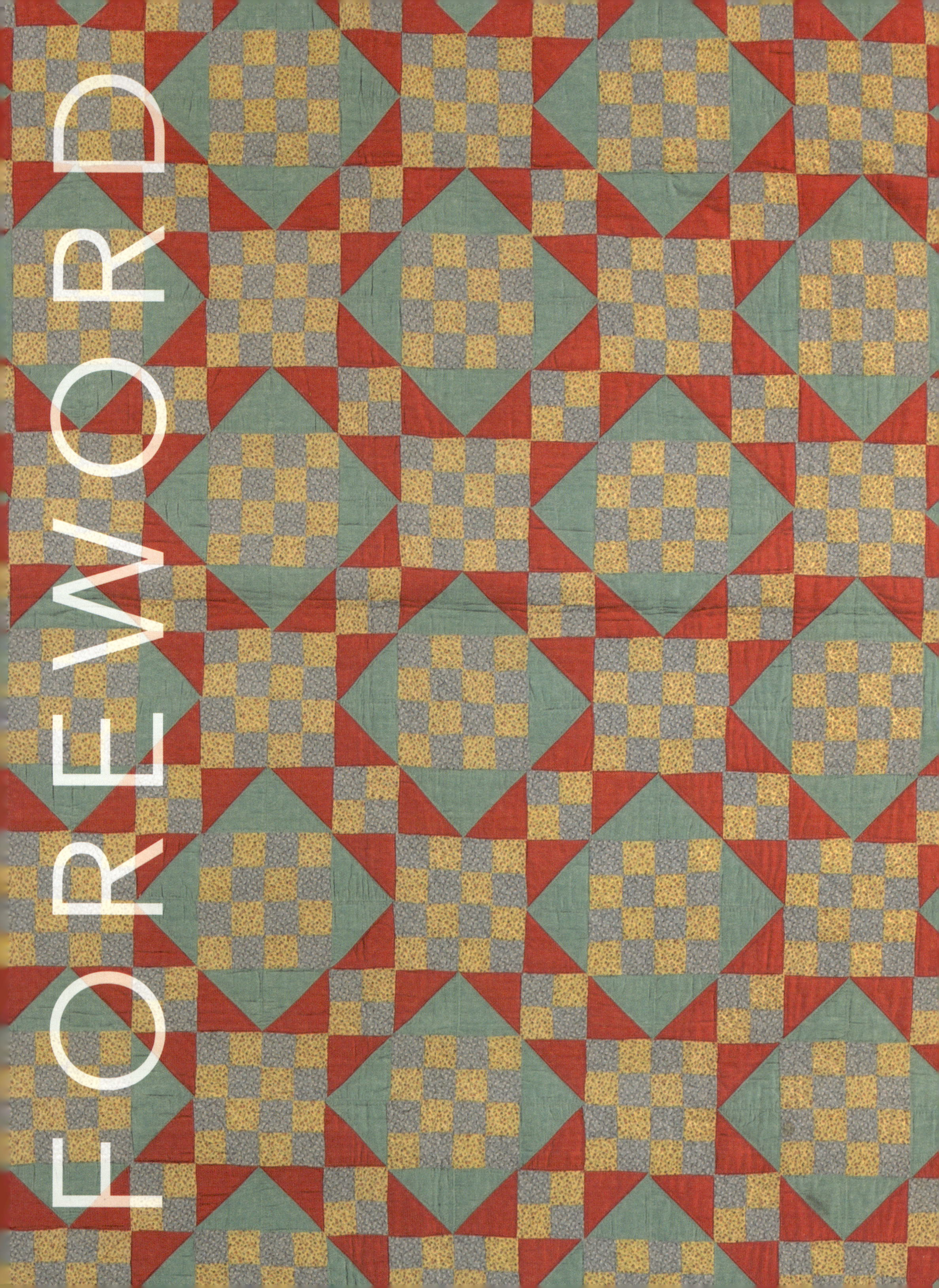

The International Quilt Museum is pleased to present this companion catalog to our *Abstract Design in American Quilts at 50* exhibition series.

The groundbreaking exhibition Jonathan Holstein and Gail van der Hoof curated for New York's Whitney Museum of American Art in 1971, *Abstract Design in American Quilts* (*ADAQ*), marked a significant moment in art, craft, and quilt history. It also went on, in various iterations, to travel the world for half a decade before finally settling into its enduring iconic status.

In 2003, the International Quilt Museum (IQM) was honored to receive the renowned Jonathan Holstein and Gail van der Hoof Collection, including the quilts exhibited at the Whitney. Since then, the IQM curators have looked forward to 2021, when we would celebrate the 50th anniversary of this seminal exhibition. As an academic museum, we felt compelled to both honor and reexamine *ADAQ*, not only installing the original Whitney quilts, but also producing parallel exhibitions that would explore other areas of significance to the evolution of the quilt revival of the last half-century plus.

Development of the exhibition series and catalog took place in unprecedentedly challenging times. As the exhibition team was working on content creation, the global COVID-19 pandemic arrived and interrupted normal curatorial processes, on all levels. Marin Hanson, co-curator of *Journey to Japan*, was slated to perform research and oral history interviews in Tokyo during spring 2020, but had to cancel her trip. Equally frustrating, many cultural institutions from which we hoped to obtain archival documents and images were closed, both in the United States and abroad. Like others worldwide and across all spectrums, we adjusted expectations and made necessary changes. In this light, we are especially grateful to the individuals and organizations who have partnered with us to financially support *Abstract Design in American Quilts at 50*, without whom these challenging times would have been even more difficult. The Robert and Ardis James Foundation, the Nebraska Arts Council/Nebraska Cultural Endowment, Friends of the International Quilt Museum, and other generous donors who provided research, exhibition, and publication funds.

One never knows the wide-ranging impact a single event can have or what the next pivotal moment will be as we look forward to the progression and transformation of quilts and quilt studies over the next 50 years.

Leslie C. Levy
Ardis & Robert James
Executive Director

# INTRODUCTION

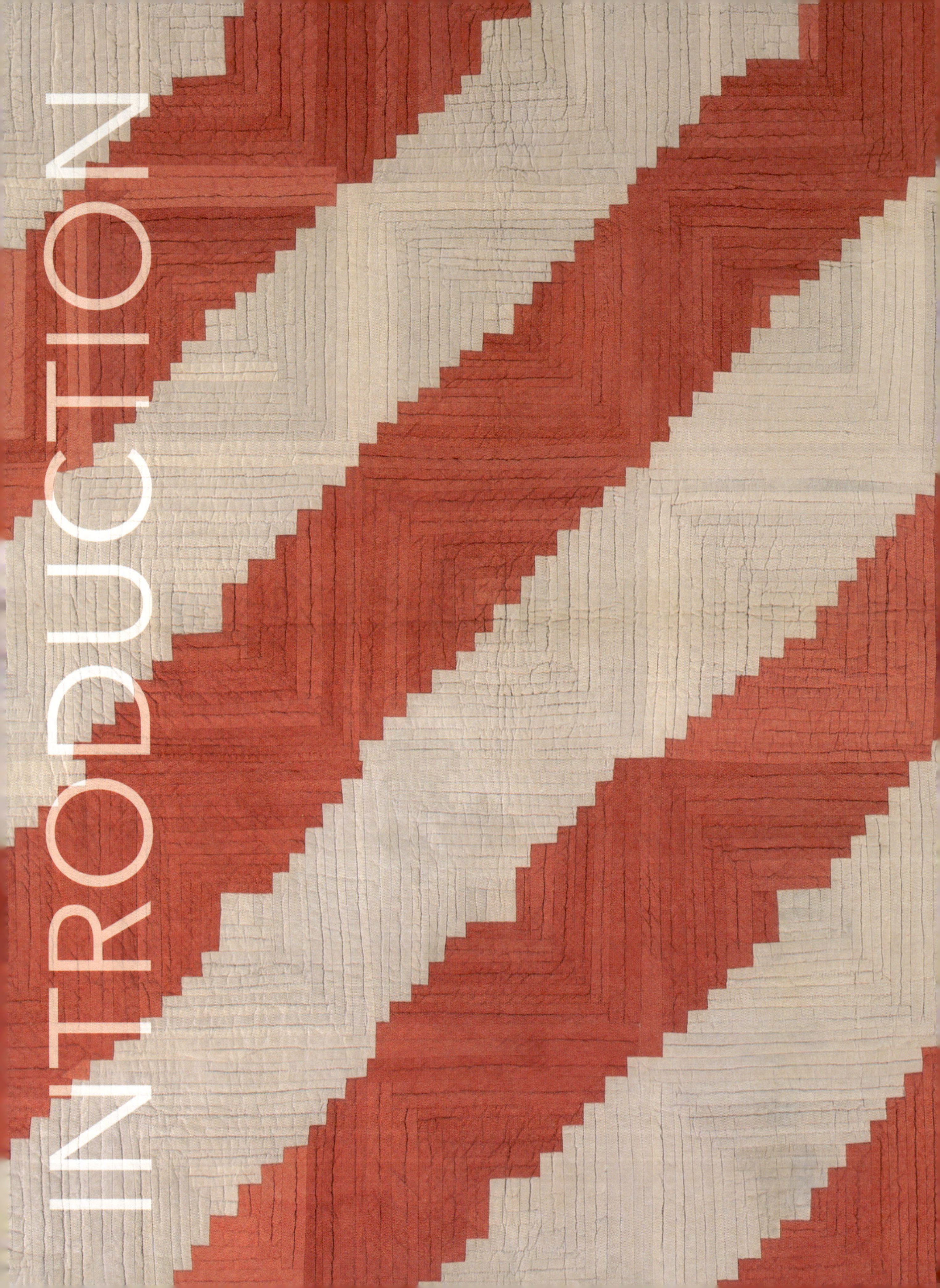

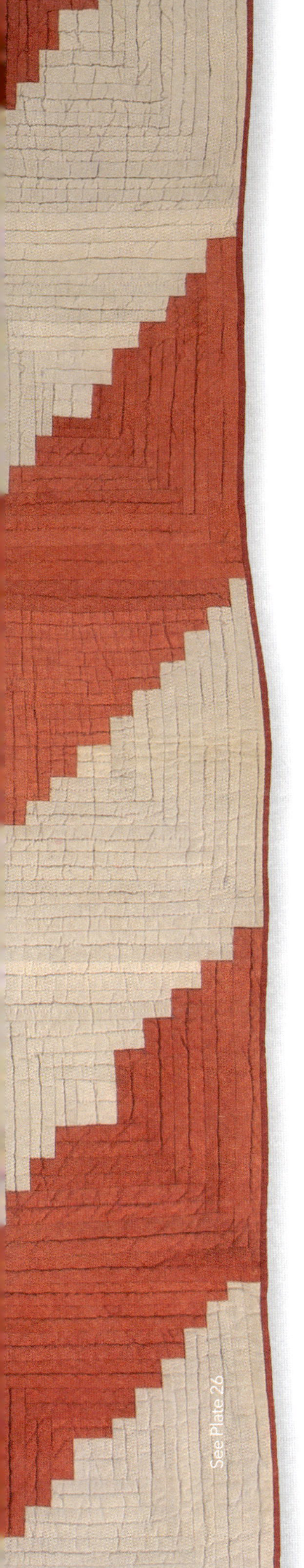

See Plate 26

*Abstract Design in American Quilts (ADAQ)*, an exhibition staged in 1971 at New York City's Whitney Museum of American Art, far exceeded the reach and impact its curators and hosts initially anticipated. A last-minute addition to the museum's July to mid-September schedule, *ADAQ* attracted unexpectedly large and enthusiastic numbers, quickly selling out its catalog and garnering praise from eminent art critics. As a result, the Whitney extended the exhibition's run by several weeks, meaning that "New Yorkers returning from their summer haunts would get a chance to see it"[1]—not just tourists and out-of-towners. By the time the exhibition closed in early October, the Smithsonian Institution's traveling exhibition program had contacted the collector-curators, Jonathan Holstein and Gail van der Hoof, about touring the quilts nationwide. *ADAQ* had made its mark and was beginning to take on a life of its own.

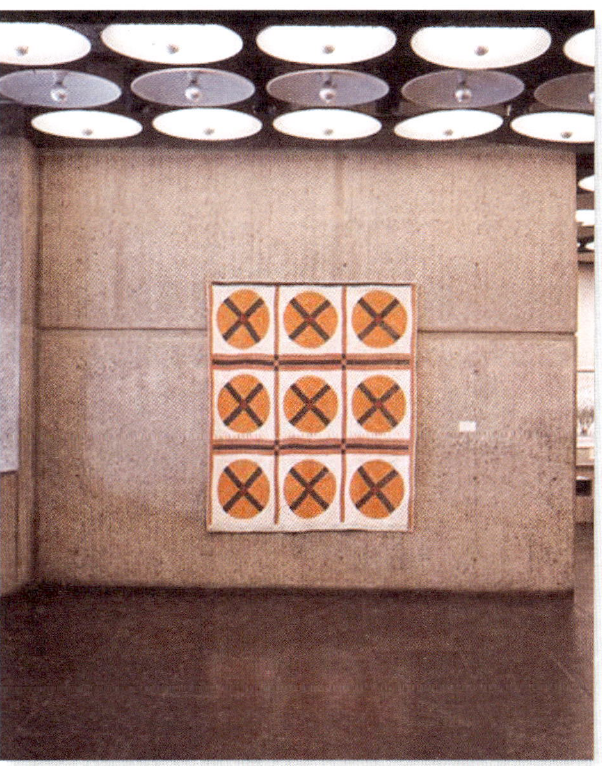

Installed in the Whitney Museum's lobby, this visually arresting *Circles and Crosses* quilt (Plate 59) welcomed visitors to *Abstract Design in American Quilts. Jonathan Holstein, Quilt Papers, Archives & Special Collections, University of Nebraska-Lincoln Libraries.*

---

[1] Jonathan Holstein, *Abstract Design in American Quilts: A Biography of an Exhibition* (Louisville, KY: Kentucky Quilt Project, 1991), 50.

*ADAQ* appeared in the right place at the right time. Although quilts had long been embedded in American life, they had rarely been seen in the country's cultural capital, let alone in one of its premier art museums. In the 50 years since it debuted at the Whitney, *ADAQ* has become a cultural phenomenon, a touchstone for scholars and laypeople alike when discussing issues related to art, folk art, craft, and textiles. The reasons for its initial success and enduring influence are varied, but alongside the exhibition's inherent qualities of visual appeal and novelty, *ADAQ* benefitted from a convergence of societal and cultural shifts. By the early 1970s, a series of civil rights and counter-culture movements, nostalgia for American colonial and pioneer history, and new paradigms in the fine art world had changed the ways people viewed and valued traditional folkways and folk art.

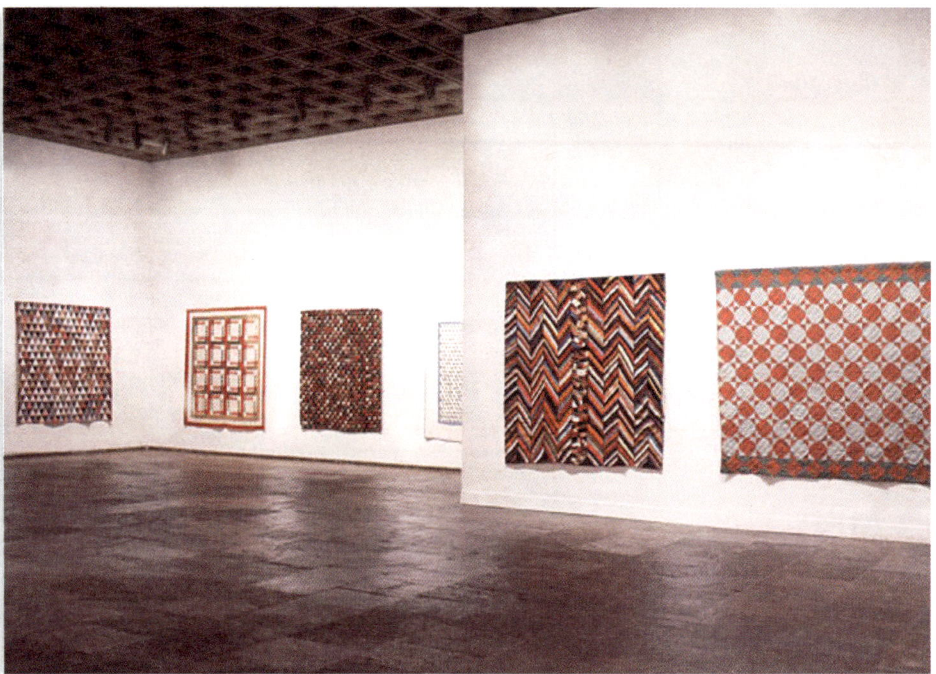

For some viewers, the Whitney's "white box" galleries transformed the *ADAQ* quilts into stand-ins for the abstract expressionist paintings more often displayed on the museum's walls. *Jonathan Holstein, Quilt Papers, Archives & Special Collections, University of Nebraska-Lincoln Libraries.*

The 1960s and early 1970s was a watershed era for the United States. The Civil Rights Movement that intensified in the mid-1950s, the Women's and anti-Vietnam War Movements beginning in the mid-'60s, and the Gay Liberation Movement beginning in the late-'60s had inalterably changed US social and cultural life, and yet activism of all kinds had been repeatedly met with suppressive government and military force. In this era of resistance to conventional power structures, interest in women's studies, women's history, and African-American and other area studies blossomed and brought attention to systemic inequalities in American society. Many Americans—especially younger people disillusioned with society's ills and the economic and ideological contributors to them—looked for better ways to live. Some gave up established modes of American life for a counter-cultural ideal that included seeking more peaceful and open relationships with themselves, others, and the earth. DIY (do it yourself) and back-to-the-land movements often incorporated handcrafting skills into their ethos.

The 1960s and '70s was also a time of deepening nostalgia for America's past and connection to one's heritage. A desire to establish a sense of rootedness and identity in their pasts drew many Americans to explore family genealogy, exemplified by Alex Haley's 1976 publication of *Roots*, the epic history of generations of a Black family in Africa and North America. Others brought the past into the present by embracing older folkways. Art historian Janet Berlo was among those who in the spirit of the age "[sought] out handmade, rural, and folk traditions and to emulate historical quilts as we sought to make new ones with our own hands."[2] Artists, too, referenced women's crafts, with Miriam Schapiro's "femmage"—mixed-media work that combines painting and traditional forms of needlework—forming a key part of the feminist Pattern and Decoration Movement. In broader society, quilts gained

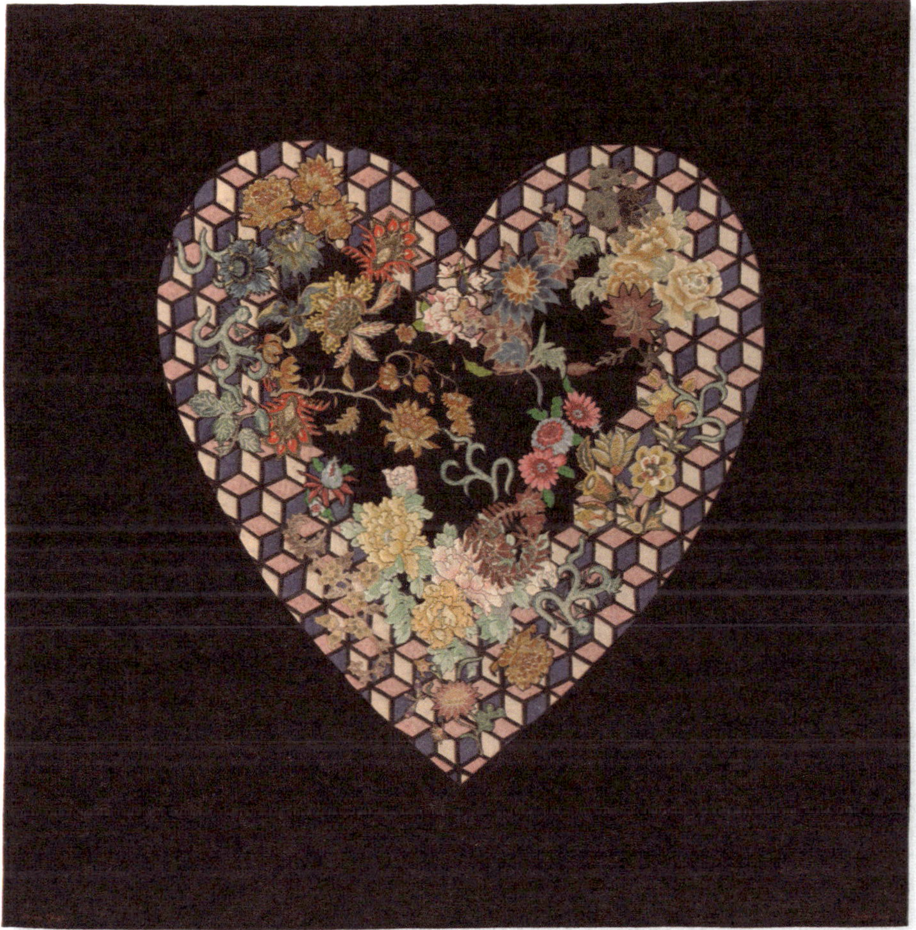

The *Phoenix Heart*, Miriam Schapiro and Marilyn Price, Indianapolis, Indiana, 1981, 82 x 82.75 in., gift of Altria Group, Inc., IQM 2019.032.0003. A collaboration between artist Miriam Schapiro and quiltmaker Marilyn Price, *The Phoenix Heart* was part of the multi-year project "The Artist and the Quilt" begun in 1975 as a celebration of the United Nations' International Women's Year.

increasing attention in the lead-up to the American Bicentennial, in part because they served as potent reminders of American ideals seemingly lost in the turmoil of the 1960s and early '70s. Berlo writes:

> … in the bicentennial year, women all across America, even those who might not embrace the language of feminism, identified themselves as sisters and granddaughters of this capacious matrilineage

[2] Janet Catherine Berlo, "'Acts of Pride, Desperation, and Necessity': Aesthetics, Social History, and American Quilts," in *Wild by Design: Two Hundred Years of Innovation and Artistry in American Quilts*, ed. Janet Catherine Berlo et al. (Seattle: University of Washington Press, 2003), 7.

of quilts who had long constructed an American artistic heritage with needle, thimble, and "scraps"—as the mythology would have it. [3]

For many, quilts symbolized the American values of thrift, perseverance, resilience, and artistry long associated with romantic visions of the nation's birth out of conflict and hardship. They also resonated with idealized notions of the nineteenth-century migrants who led the nation's westward expansion. [4]

Shifts in the status and estimation of folk art were also taking place. Folk art objects have long been valued as crafted, frequently functional items whose makers were intentional in selection of pattern, color, materials, and visual impact, even when this intentionality was understood rather than articulated (to quote folklorist Henry Glassie, "The lack of an aesthetic vocabulary does not prevent aesthetic operation").[5] They are rooted in a time, place, and visual vocabulary of a community. Art in this sense implies that the object is notable because of its embodiment of tradition and its skillful or imaginative execution. Under this rubric, many believe that folk art is not less worthy of esteem, even though it may not be recognized as art in the same sense that painting or sculpture is regarded by the established art world. That said, folk art has gone through waves of mainstream adulation, and in the 1960s and '70s it was seen as possessing, as art historian David Park Curry phrases it, a "reassuring formalism that helped artists slouch towards abstraction."[6] In other words, the formal visual qualities of folk art (including quilts), such as large planes of flat color, simple and economic line usage, and stylized/geometric (as opposed to realistic/naturalistic) depictions of form, were seen by some as precursors, facilitators, and/or complements to the abstract modernist artwork of the day.

*Abstract Design in American Quilts* was born amidst these interwoven aesthetic, historical,

Center Square, maker unidentified, probably made in Lancaster County, Pennsylvania, 1900–1920, 75 x 75 in., Jonathan Holstein and Gail van der Hoof Collection, IQM 2003.003.0082. Critics and observers have sometimes compared Amish quilts to mid-twentieth century Color Field paintings by artists such as Mark Rothko and Barnett Newman.



---

[3] Berlo, 7.

[4] Quilt scholarship has shown that until the Civil War, American quilts generally were made by the well-to-do and, in some cases, by those whom they employed or enslaved, and not from a need for thrift. Nevertheless, these associations have persisted to the present day. The late-nineteenth century democratization of quiltmaking (via the availability of cheaper, factory-made fabrics) meant that all sectors of society could participate, including westward migrants (pioneers), though generally quilt-making was practiced after settlement, not during the journey itself.

[5] Henry Glassie, "Folk Art," in *Material Culture Studies in America*, ed. Thomas J. Schlereth (Walnut Creek, Calif.: American Association for State and Local History and AltaMira Press, 1999).

[6] David Park Curry, "Slouching towards Abstraction," Smithsonian Studies in American Art 3, no. 1 (1989): 65.

social, and cultural threads. It immediately became another strand in the contextual cloth of the 1970s and beyond.

This volume accompanies the International Quilt Museum's 2021 exhibition series examining the half-century legacy of *ADAQ*. In 2003, the IQM became home to the 400-piece Jonathan Holstein and Gail van der Hoof Collection and, since then, the museum's curatorial team has been laying the groundwork for the creation of a 50-year *ADAQ* retrospective. Although the collection has figured prominently in a number of IQM exhibitions over the past 18 years, such as *American Quilts in the Modern Age: 1870–1940*, *The Collector's Eye*, and *Design Dynamics of Log Cabin Quilts*, we've always known that 2021 would be the big year, the year in which we would re-stage *ADAQ*. More than simply duplicating the original 61-piece installation, of which IQM has 59 quilts (see Plates 1–59), [7] we aimed to range more broadly and dig more deeply, examining *ADAQ* through a variety of lenses.

This is not the first time *ADAQ* has been revisited. An earlier assessment of the exhibition's impact occurred in 1991, on the occasion of its 20th anniversary. Collector-curator Jonathan Holstein teamed up with the Kentucky Quilt Project, led by Shelly Zegart and Eleanor Bingham Miller, to rehang *ADAQ* as part of its larger event, "Louisville Celebrates the American Quilt." The event consisted of a series of exhibitions and conferences held over several months and it has since become, like the 1971 exhibition

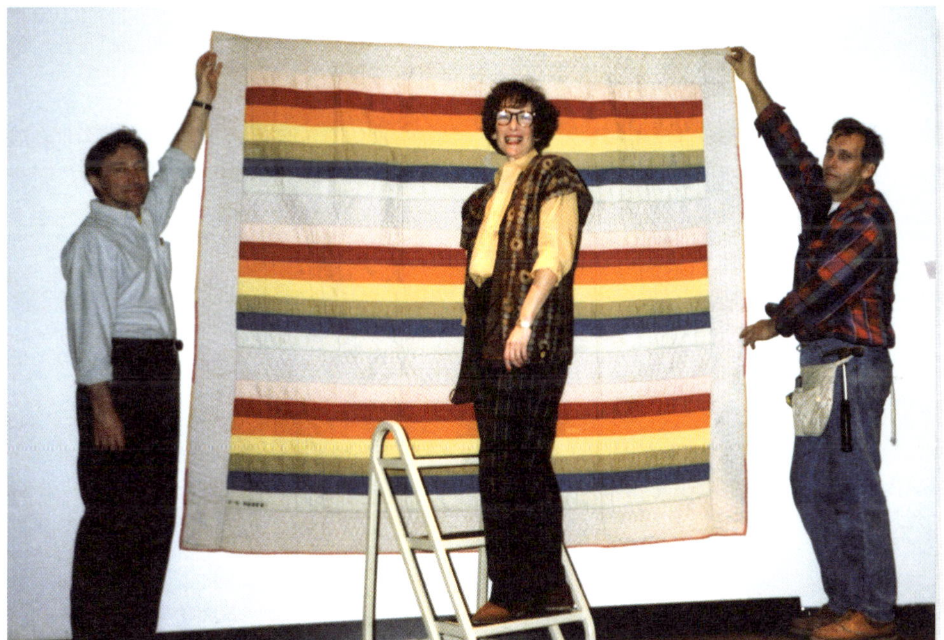

Jonathan Holstein (left) and Shelly Zegart (middle) worked closely with the Louisville Museum of History and Science staff to install the 20th anniversary rehanging of *Abstract Design in American Quilts*. *Jonathan Holstein, Quilt Papers, Archives & Special Collections, University of Nebraska-Lincoln Libraries*.



[7] The Jonathan Holstein and Gail van der Hoof Collection at the International Quilt Museum includes 58 of the 61 *ADAQ* Whitney quilts. Recently, a 59th Whitney quilt was donated to the IQM by Philip Holstein, from whom Holstein and van der Hoof had borrowed the quilt for the New York exhibition and several of its tours. Two Whitney quilts had already gone missing prior to the collection coming to the IQM. Many of the 61 Whitney quilts were included in the Smithsonian Institution Traveling Exhibition Service (SITES) exhibition (1973–1974), the European exhibitions (1972, 1975), and the Japan exhibitions (1975–1976), but were supplemented by other Holstein/van der Hoof quilts, also now in the IQM collection.

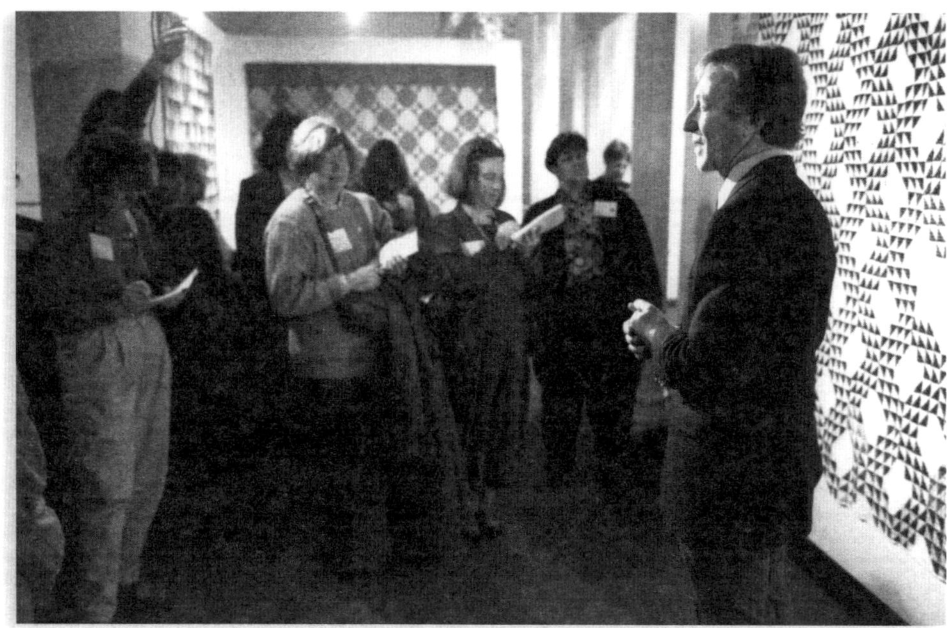

As part of the Kentucky Quilt Project's "Louisville Celebrates the Quilt" events in 1991, Jonathan Holstein gave a gallery talk among the reinstalled *Abstract Design in American Quilts. Jonathan Holstein, Quilt Papers, Archives & Special Collections, University of Nebraska-Lincoln Libraries.*

that inspired it, a benchmark for scholarly examinations of quilts and quilt history. In one of the project's volumes, *Abstract Design in American Quilts: A Biography of an Exhibition*, Holstein provides an absorbing and detailed account of the events leading up to the Whitney exhibition. He also narratively follows many of the threads that sprung from *ADAQ*'s unexpected and unqualified success. *A Biography of an Exhibition* is a "deep dive" into the events of 1971 and beyond, and serves as the ultimate chronicle of a defining moment in American quilt history.

The present volume does not delve as deeply as *A Biography of an Exhibition* into what happened in 1971 and shortly afterwards. Rather, it looks at how the exhibition became such a flashpoint—the contexts that framed its rapid rise in fame and the cultural currents that buoyed it along. Further, it examines how *ADAQ* changed the landscape for American quilts, both through widespread acclaim—the sheer might of positive publicity and word-of-mouth—and, in some cases, controversy. While *ADAQ* is rightly lauded as a groundbreaking exhibition, it also provided a conceptual foil, something for people to react to and/or against. [8] These reactions created expanded spaces in which to talk about quilts—as art, craft, women's work, collectible, commodity, etc. We owe a debt of gratitude not only to Holstein and van der Hoof, but to those who

---

[8] The initial and most famous critique came from feminist art historian Patricia Mainardi (Patricia Mainardi, "Quilts: The Great American Art," *The Feminist Art Journal* 2, no. 1 (January 1, 1973): 1, 18-23.), but for another roughly contemporary critique by a California feminist artist see: Patty Chase, "Quilt Making: Reclaiming Our Art," *Country Women*, no. 21 (September 1, 1976): 9-11. For later and perhaps more balanced discussions of *ADAQ*'s merits, demerits, and effects, see: Rachel Maines, "Review of 'The Muses' Stepchildren: American Folk Artists and Their Scholars'," *Woman's Art Journal* 2, no. 2 (1981): 63-67.; June Freeman, "The Discovery of the Commonplace or Establishment of an Elect: Intellectuals in the Contemporary Craftworld," *Journal of Design History* 2, no. 2/3 (1989): 61-75.; Susan E. Bernick, "A Quilt Is an Art Object When It Stands up like a Man," in *Quilt Culture: Tracing the Pattern*, ed. Cheryl B. Torsney and Judy Elsley (Columbia, Missouri: University of Missouri Press, 1994), 134-50.; Karin Elizabeth Peterson, "Discourse and Display: The Modern Eye, Entrepreneurship, and the Cultural Transformation of the Patch work Quilt," *Sociological Perspectives*, 2003.; Janneken Smucker, *Amish Quilts: Crafting an American Icon* (Johns Hopkins University Press, 2013).; and Jenni Sorkin, "Affinities in Abstraction: Textiles, Otherness, and Painting in the 1970s," in *Outliers and American Vanguard Art*, ed. Lynn Cooke (Washington, DC: National Gallery of Art, in association with the University of Chicago Press, 2018), 92-105.

followed and used *ADAQ* as a springboard from which they could dive into quilt history, women's history, craft theory, and beyond.

One of the primary critiques of *ADAQ* is that it removed quilts from their historical and gendered contexts. In our *Abstract Design in American Quilts at 50* exhibition, we are once again treating the quilts largely as an aesthetic grouping. We chose to do that in order to pay homage to the visual impact the Whitney exhibition had on many of its viewers—we wanted to repeat that optical "gut punch" for our visitors 50 years later. To address the decontextualization, however, we took other steps. One was to create an online resource as part of our "World Quilts" website (*worldquilts.quiltstudy.org*) for learning more about the exhibition and its quilts. Another was to curate three complementary exhibitions exploring the social, cultural, and global contexts surrounding *ADAQ*. The essays in this volume each have their own focus, while corresponding with one of the IQM exhibitions. [9]

To begin, in "*Abstract Design in American Quilts:* Looking Back," Jonathan Holstein offers some thoughts and reminiscences on the events of 1971 and the subsequent impact *ADAQ* had on his life. He outlines the path he and van der Hoof took to build their collection and the sometimes deliberate, sometimes serendipitous steps they made toward curating an exhibition for the Whitney. He also reminds us that his and van der Hoof's milieu was suffused with modern art: he says, "Our life in New York was centered on its art world of the time." Despite the curators' subsequent aesthetic approach to interpreting quilts in *ADAQ*, Holstein's allied interest in quilt history led him to conduct research, author books and articles, and lecture broadly on the topic. These activities would in turn influence budding quilt historians and quilt artists. His collecting activity, too, would bring him in contact with other quilt enthusiasts such as Robert and Ardis James, who went on to build the large and comprehensive collection that now forms the core of the International Quilt Museum's holdings. All along, as his essay reveals, Holstein's natural curiosity has driven him to keep studying, interpreting, and appreciating quilts, long after *ADAQ* first brought him and his partner, Gail van der Hoof, to widespread attention.

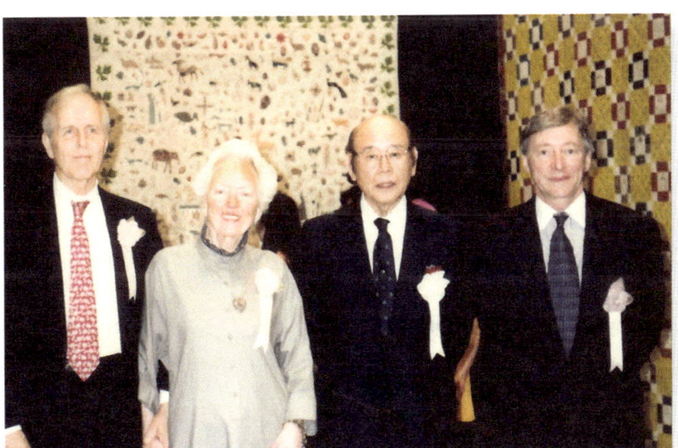

Collectors Robert and Ardis James, Nihon Vogue Corporation chairman Tadanobu Seto, and Jonathan Holstein posed in front of some of the James Collection quilts that were featured in Nihon Vogue's "World Quilt '98" exhibition in Tokyo. *Jonathan Holstein, Quilt Papers, Archives & Special Collections, University of Nebraska-Lincoln Libraries.*

In "*Abstract Design in American Quilts:* Looking Forward," Carolyn Ducey looks at how perceptions of quilts have changed since 1971 by outlining the evolution of the studio quilt genre over the past half century. As she points out, artists such as Jean Ray Laury and Radka Donnell had already begun exploring the artistic



[9] One important topic we were unable to cover in the current exhibition series and catalog is the impact of Holstein and van der Hoof exhibitions held at a number of venues in European cities, in 1972: Paris, France; Lausanne, Switzerland; Amsterdam, Netherlands; and Brussels, Belgium; and in 1975: Bristol and Manchester, England. We aim to include these exhibitions in future research and interpretive efforts.

potential of quilts well before New York's art elite embraced *ADAQ*. These vanguard quiltmakers influenced the next, most important wave of formally trained artists to embrace the quilt medium, among them Nancy Crow, Michael James, Therese May, and Pauline Burbidge. A critical mass of quilt art activity also led to the establishment of a number of organizations to support quilt artists, most of which still carry on their work today. Despite this seeming forward march of progress, the acceptance of quilts by fine art institutions has been spotty and cyclical. Major art museums and critics have embraced quilts at times—*ADAQ* and the mid-2000s Gee's Bend traveling exhibitions featuring quilts made by Black women from an isolated Alabama hamlet being two notable occasions—but ignored them at others. Today, it is the International Quilt Museum and a small cadre of quilt and textile museums and events that most consistently present the work of quilt artists.

The Whitney Museum's quick acceptance of Holstein and van der Hoof's exhibition proposal in April 1971 was likely primed by contemporary events in New York's museum and arts communities. In "New York Nexus," Sandra Sider examines the importance of New York's museums and galleries in promoting the acceptance of textile and fiber art in the fine art world, both before and after *Abstract Design in American Quilts*. A number of exhibitions in the 1960s and '70s promoted the idea that textiles could be displayed alongside paintings, prints, and sculpture. Many of the early leaders of what would become the studio art quilt movement saw these seminal exhibitions and were encouraged to pursue quiltmaking as their primary artistic medium. Among these artists were Michael Cummings, Patricia Malarcher, Paula Nadelstern, and Robin Schwalb, all of whom, among others, are represented with works in the *New York Nexus* exhibition, which accompanies *Abstract Design in American Quilts at 50* (see Plates 60–73).





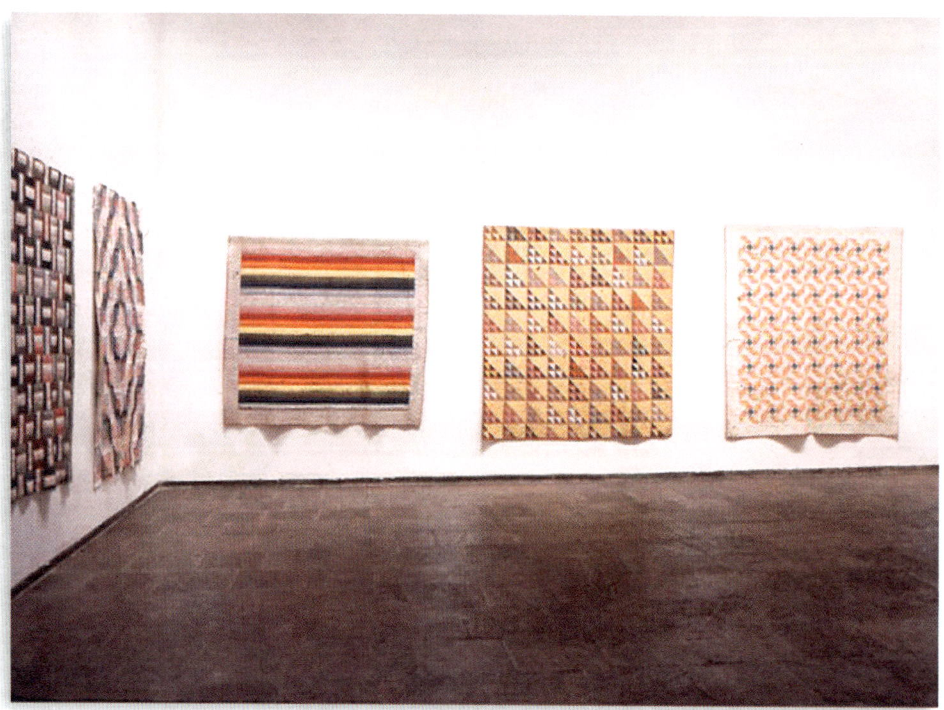

Several of the artists represented in the IQM exhibition *New York Nexus* visited the Whitney Museum of American Art's *Abstract Design in American Quilts* in 1971. *Jonathan Holstein, Quilt Papers, Archives & Special Collections, University of Nebraska-Lincoln Libraries.*

*ADAQ* was not simply a New York or fine art phenomenon, as Jonathan Gregory explains in "Raising the Profile." Quilts have been part of American folk culture for more than 200 years and are firmly rooted in diverse geographical regions and cultural groups. But by explicitly presenting quilts as art in New York, the country's cultural capital, Holstein, van der Hoof, and the Whitney Museum opened new spaces for the consideration and interpretation of quilts. Thereafter, quilts old and new were more frequently displayed and viewed as art. More than that, a market for antique and contemporary quilts emerged and grew in sophistication. Quilts gained recognition as a women's art form and as documents of women's lives past and present. Quilts also became objects of serious scholarly study and a dash to preserve these carriers of women's history spawned grassroots documentation efforts and contributed to establishment of numerous museums devoted to quilts. The reverberations of *ADAQ* were felt in multiple ways, complementing and building upon the quilt-related activity that had never disappeared in many corners of the country (see Plates 74–85).

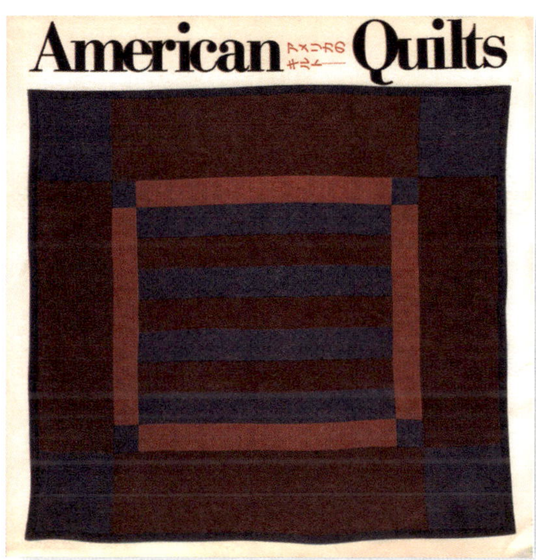


Holstein and van der Hoof's 1976 exhibition at Kyoto's Museum of Modern Art included several Lancaster County, Pennsylvania, Amish quilts like the one pictured here on the catalog cover. *Jonathan Holstein, Quilt Papers, Archives & Special Collections, University of Nebraska-Lincoln Libraries.*

Eventually, *ADAQ*'s reverberations affected more than New York museums, nascent studio quilt artists, and quiltmakers and enthusiasts across the US. As Marin Hanson and Nao Nomura recount in "Journey to Japan," *ADAQ*'s most far-flung trip was in 1975–1976, when an expanded version of the exhibition traveled to Tokyo and Kyoto. Inspired by the plentiful and positive media coverage the exhibition had received in the US and Europe, several Japanese museums and galleries invited Holstein and van der Hoof to tour the exhibition. Japan was in the midst of robust economic growth, and leisure time pursuits such as needlework were being promoted in both the governmental and private sectors. Combined with Japan's long-standing textile traditions and a general receptivity to American cultural influence, these phenomena led to an enthusiastic embrace of quiltmaking, which has continued in Japan to this day. The artists featured in the *Journey to Japan* exhibition were some of the earliest to adopt American-style quilt-making in that country and are among the most respected Japanese quilt artists and teachers today (see Plates 86–95). Several of them saw the Holstein and van der Hoof quilts in Tokyo or Kyoto and nearly all were familiar with the exhibition's Japan travel history. For *Journey to Japan*, each artist created a new work inspired by one of the original pieces in *ADAQ*, bringing our project full circle and demonstrating the enduring legacy of the exhibition that unexpectedly took New York by storm in the summer of 1971 and went on to influence quilt scholars, artists, makers, and enthusiasts around the world for the next 50 years.

Marin F. Hanson
Jonathan Gregory

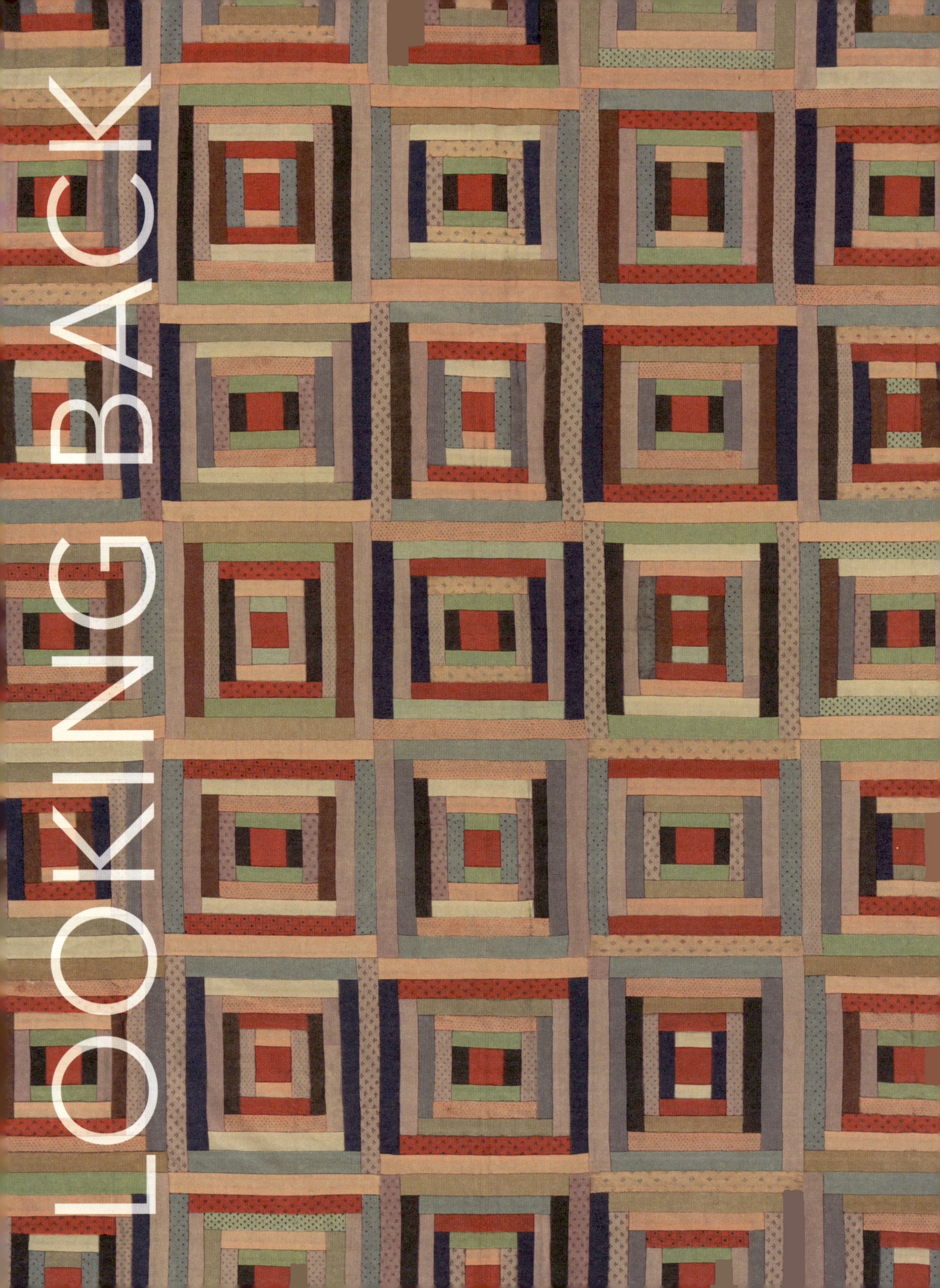
LOOKING BACK

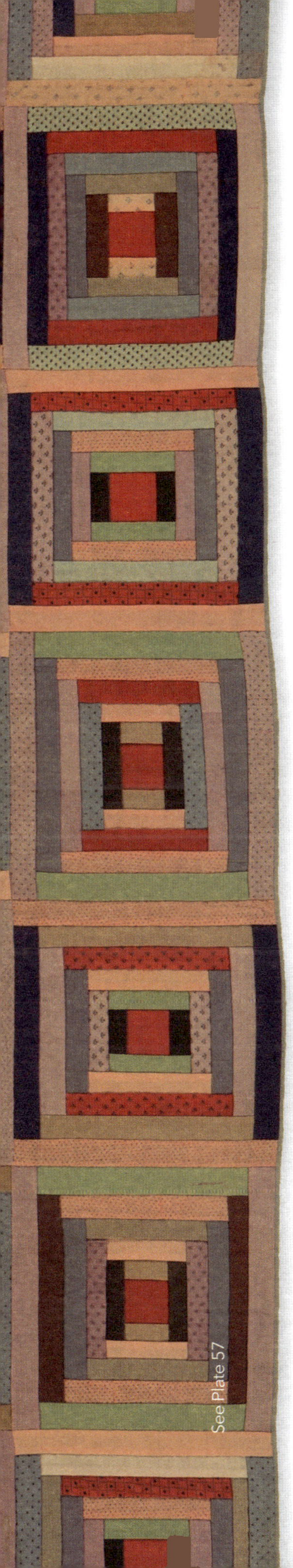


# JONATHAN HOLSTEIN

Writing about something that happened a half-century ago is daunting, especially if it has had a continuing presence in one's life, or in the world. In the case of the quilt exhibition Gail van der Hoof and I curated at the Whitney Museum in 1971, it has had both, which was not something we had anticipated. The exhibitions concerning it mounted by the International Quilt Museum (IQM) on *Abstract Design in American Quilts*' 50th anniversary, and this catalog that accompanies them, are thus a welcome chance to review how the universe of quilts looks half a century out from that moment.

Perhaps the most important thing to say at the start is that Gail and I came to quilts largely through art. I had a lifelong interest in art in general and American material culture, especially its more rural aspects and folk art in particular, and also a lifelong collecting (accumulating?) instinct. Gail had studied art in college and afterwards worked in fashion and design, which gave her an understanding of needlework. Our life in New York was centered on its art world. I was photographing art and artists for exhibitions, books, and catalogs, and she was making her beautiful beaded leather bags, a then-acclaimed fashion accessory. Our friends were largely from the art world, both those of the older generation such as Barnett and Annalee Newman, and the younger, such as Roy and Dorothy Lichtenstein. (We selected the quilts for the Whitney exhibition by spreading 90 or so out on the lawn surrounding the Lichtenstein's house in the Hamptons, standing on a roof walk and, with the help of Roy's two sons on the ground, moving them around until we had what was for us a satisfactory exhibition. It was a beautiful early summer day and a fabulous, if somewhat surreal, moment.)

Our discovery of pieced quilts—and it was that for us —occurred because we were indulging our mutual interest in folk art in Pennsylvania, one of its prime American sources, while visiting friends there on weekend escapes from the city. In the antique shops, indoor and outdoor antique markets, and house sales

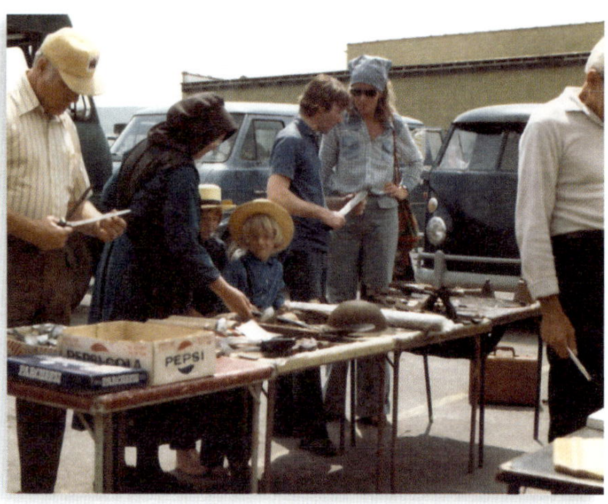

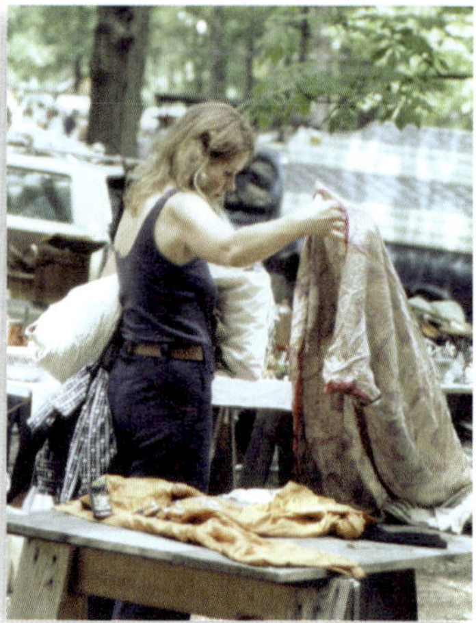

LEFT: Jonathan Holstein and Gail van der Hoof hunting for quilts at a typical Pennsylvania outdoor market in Belleville, Mifflin County, 1973. Next to them, an Amish mother and her two sons look at some implements. *Jonathan Holstein, Quilt Papers, Archives & Special Collections, University of Nebraska-Lincoln Libraries.* RIGHT: Gail van der Hoof examining textiles at a Pennsylvania outdoor antique market, early 1970s. *Jonathan Holstein, Quilt Papers, Archives & Special Collections, University of Nebraska-Lincoln Libraries.*





common in the southeastern counties of the state we were seeing piles of pieced quilts that were apparently of little interest to anyone, except perhaps those looking for colorful, inexpensive bed covers. I had grown up with plain bed quilts and the thicker covers some Americans call comforters. I had also seen quilts on display in American museums' period rooms, usually early, often appliqué examples (then considered "best"). Gail had learned about quiltmaking during her sojourn in Colorado, where we met. Mildly curious, we began to look through the piles, inadvertently developing the quick opening and folding movements we were later to practice many thousands of times. As we looked at scores of pieced quilts, we were amazed to see how many echoed aesthetically the modern abstract art we saw all around us in New York, in our friends' studios, in the galleries and museums here and abroad we had visited, and in the literature on modern art we had read. Once that intellectual link had been made, the hunt for both interesting quilts and knowledge about them was irresistible. We began to collect.

We would take our found treasures home, hang and photograph them, search for their patterns in the books available at the time, and puzzle over them in general. Two years of intense collecting and study convinced us that this was a distinct American phenomenon, its beginning in the Old World but its particular development in the New. It became clear that the powerful images we saw in many pieced quilts had preceded similar developments in modern abstract art, in some cases by a century or more, and that American women had accomplished it for the most part without any formal training in art, or considering themselves "artists" in the professional sense. Nor was that great body of work then generally recognized for its unique achievement. While there were some period books about quilts, pieced quilts received scant attention in the larger art world as significant American folk art. It was also clear to us that we should try to make this important accomplishment, its wonderful aesthetic content and its creators, more widely recognized and understood.

Intrigued with pieced quilts, we made a necessary decision to concentrate just on them as a distinct phenomenon within the larger field. We understood the place appliquéd pieces held in the overall American history of quilts, but realized we would not be able to

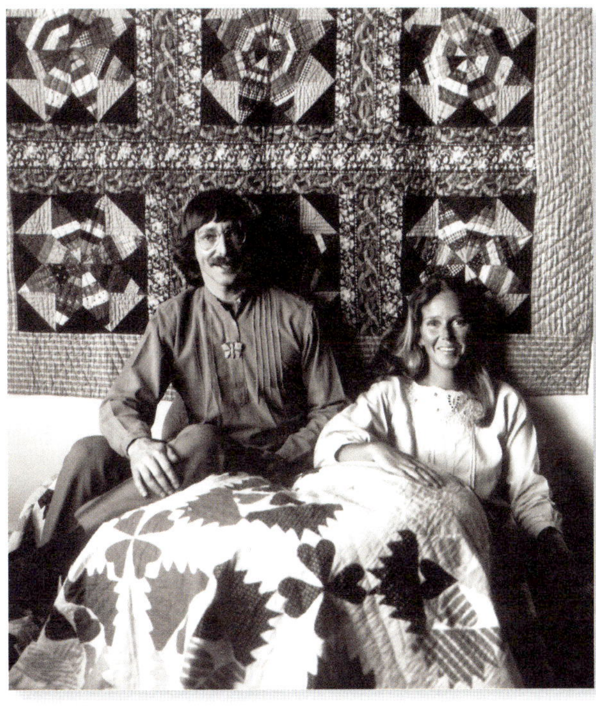

Jonathan Holstein and Gail van der Hoof in their New York Riverside Drive apartment with some of the quilts they had collected, 1972. *Jonathan Holstein, Quilt Papers, Archives & Special Collections, University of Nebraska-Lincoln Libraries. Photograph by: Horst P. Horst, House and Garden© Condé Nast.*

accomplish what we hoped if we did not concentrate solely on pieced examples, and what they particularly represented. The amazing proliferation of pieced quilts, with its extraordinary design developments, arose largely due to the flood of inexpensive cottons from English and American mills, plain and printed, colorful and colorfast, that became widely available after the mid-nineteenth century. (Those sturdy cottons also made laundering quilts less of a problem, increasing their popularity as bed covers.) The physical and intellectual talents had been there, awaiting only affordable raw materials for creation, and we were most interested in exploring what appeared to be a largely American phenomenon. One regret was that very few of the quilts we collected had any provenance, who had made them, where and when, so such information could not be included when they were exhibited. After several years of study we could at least assign them reasonable dates.



At the time we began to collect, there were many books and articles that supposedly recounted the history of American quilts. But, as we discovered, much of it was unreliable, often romantic and historically implausible. Several such notions I repeated in my first quilt catalog, a small one (16 pages) for the Whitney exhibition. Example: A number of the early books said American quiltmaking began of necessity, our thrifty, hardy ancestors needing warm bed covers so they used the scraps left over from clothes making to create quilts. At first, I believed and repeated it because it fit a national self-image. But it soon became clear it was erroneous, and I was fortunately able to correct it: The first American quilts were made in the homes of the well-to-do of expensive imported materials that the average housewife of the time could not afford, decorative covers that celebrated the traditional needlework skills expected of upper-class households and their economic positions. Once affordable, durable materials, especially cottons, arrived, as I have noted, American women did make many quilts as necessary bed covers rather than buying other available covers such as wool blankets.

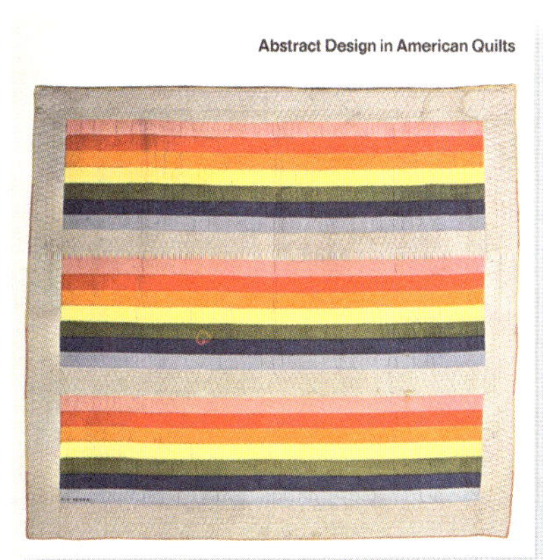


Catalog for the 1971 Whitney Museum of American Art exhibition, *Abstract Design in American Quilts*.

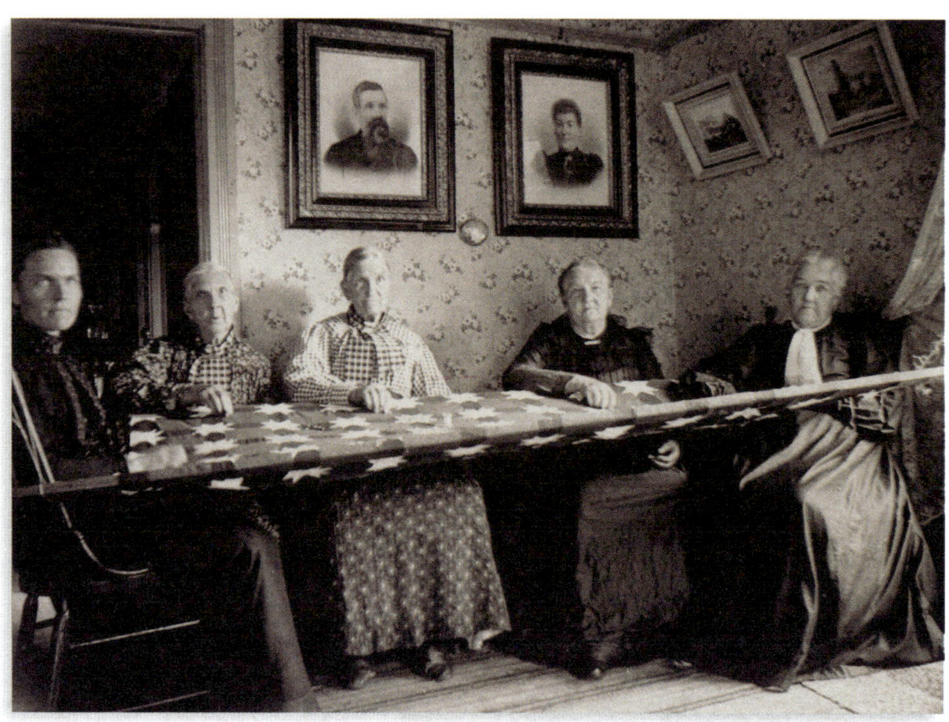

A quilting bee, circa 1880. *Images of American Quilts Archive*.

They were motivated to make quilts from a sense of frugality, fashion and, from many preserved records, fun. And yes, eventually some quilt tops were made from scraps left over from clothes making.

As our research progressed, we found that what we had first seen in the Eastern US had in fact occurred across the country, the skills, knowledge, and creative energy traveling west with settlers. I also saw interesting similarities between the ardent cultural phenomenon that had produced those remarkable creations and traditional communal art world scenes: the intense interactions we discovered that had existed among women creating their quilts, the private communications about patterns, the communal quilting bees that sometimes finished them and spread design knowledge, and the periodical publications devoted to women that offered illustrated quilt designs. I also noted the parallel we saw in the traditional art world: artists interacting socially and professionally and influenced by each other's work, accessing media devoted to new modes as such developed, and creating new visual structures as a consequence of such influences. Even the idea of training artists in the intricacies of creating different forms of art, and quiltmakers in the skills of needlework, forming designs, acquiring the necessary tools and raw materials, was a parallel. In sum, I see the development of pieced quilts as an art movement like any other. Additionally, as a technical consideration, it became apparent that an important aspect of the meteoric growth in quilt design had been the accommodating nature of the block style in which most of the quilts we collected had been made. That square shape lends itself easily to

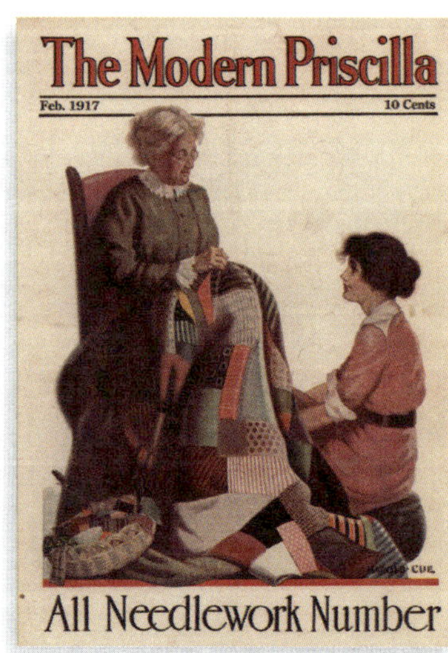


A 1917 issue of *The Modern Priscilla*, a women's periodical that typically presented sewing articles among its content.

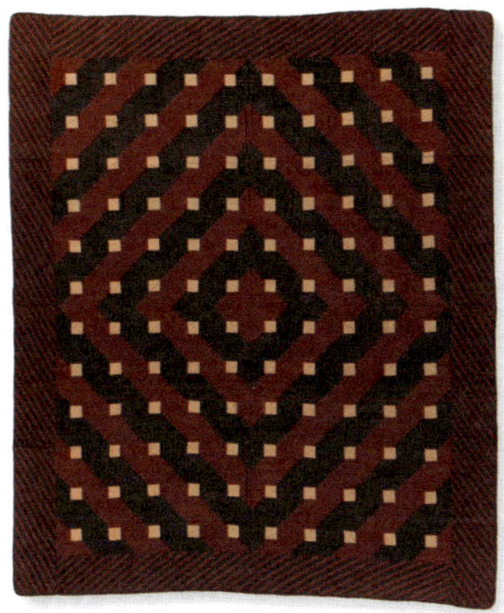

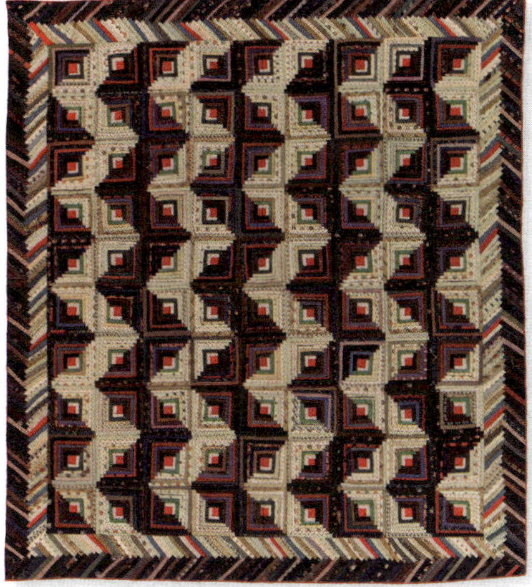

Log Cabin, Barn Raising setting, maker unidentified, possibly made in Pennsylvania, 1900–1920, 85 x 70.5 in., Holstein and van der Hoof Collection, IQM 2003.003.0158; Log Cabin, Streak of Lightning setting, maker unidentified, possibly made in Hagerstown, Maryland, or Franklin County, Pennsylvania, 1870–1890, 87 x 79 in., Ardis and Robert James Collection, IQM 1997.007.0825. Two pieced quilts from the IQM collection that used Log Cabin pattern blocks designed and arranged to achieve very different results, demonstrating the limitless aesthetic possibilities inherent in the square block format in which the majority of quilts were made.

both simple and intricate divisions. They can be done in the actual desired block size, the parts cut and used as templates for cutting material. And, it encourages and supports abstraction.

Once we had researched enough about pieced quilts to be comfortable with our view of them, we began to think of how we could bring that particular vision forward. An exhibition in a museum, but particularly a prominent art rather than a craft museum, seemed the best path. As it turned out, the exhibition's route to the Whitney was, fortunately, and unusually, fairly direct: We sought the advice of a friend, Diane Waldman, who was at that time a curator of the Guggenheim Museum in New York. She suggested that the Whitney might be open to such an exhibition, and she made an April appointment for us with its curator, Robert "Mac" Doty. The Whitney Museum of American Art, then the nation's premier museum of contemporary modern American art, had never done an exhibition of what was considered at the time utilitarian American folk art or the "decorative arts." Doty was interested and kind enough to present our proposal. We took a trip to Mexico and there received a telegram asking us to contact the Whitney. We returned to the US and there was a letter waiting for us dated the day after

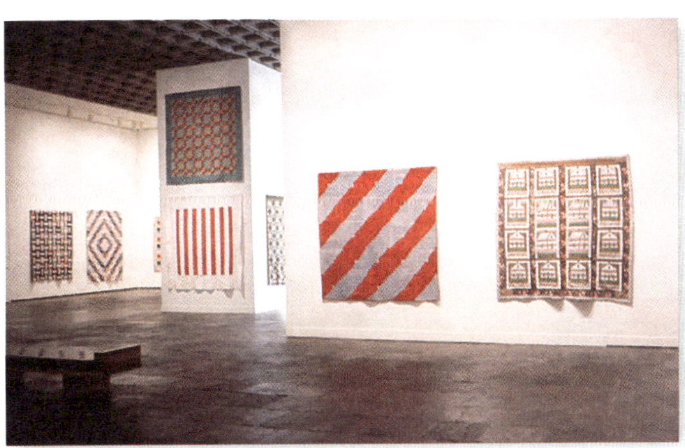

One unique element of the *Abstract Design in American Quilts* installation was the occasional stacking of quilts. *Jonathan Holstein, Quilt Papers, Archives & Special Collections, University of Nebraska-Lincoln Libraries.*

the Whitney had considered our proposal, asking if we could have an exhibition ready by July 1st. Of course we said yes, and it proceeded from there. Because of the enthusiastic public response and the positive publicity generated among New York's critics, the exhibition was extended two weeks beyond its initial closing date. *New York Times* writer Hilton Kramer, then the dean of New York art critics, wrote, to our immense surprise and relief, a long and laudatory review, *Art: Quilts Find a Place at the Whitney*, which set the tone for other critics' considerations. Other widely read critics also wrote complimentary reviews, and the publicity thus generated spread across the country. We began to get calls from heartland newspapers wondering what was going on. A number, especially from areas where quilts remained a traditional accessory in homes, had a similar question: Why are New Yorkers going crazy about quilts? We tried to give reasonable answers to what was a complicated issue, but most of the resulting articles we saw did not really get it. However, they did bring to the Whitney tourists and others, people who had never been there before and for whom modern art was not an interest.

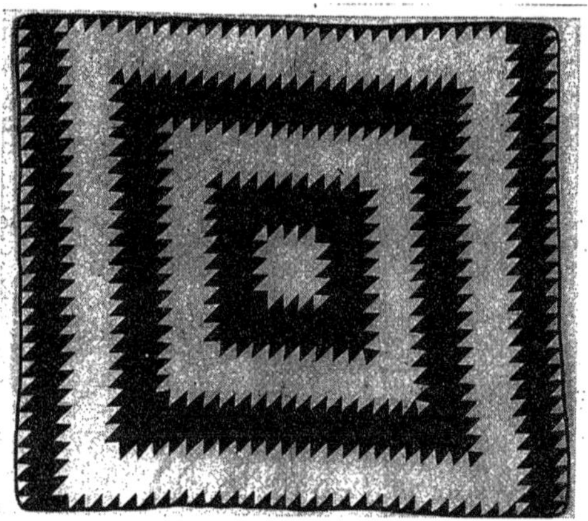

MASSACHUSETTS QUILT: "Sawtooth" on display at Whitney Museum of American Art

## Art: Quilts Find a Place at the Whitney

By HILTON KRAMER

The history of American art in the 19th century is still, as a general rule, written almost exclusively in terms of "high art"—that is, in terms of painting and sculpture created on the model of European precedents. Yet the question remains whether or not the native genius for visual expression found its most powerful expression in such forms. In many quarters the suspicion persists that the most authentic visual articulation of the American imagination in the last century is to be found in the so-called "minor" arts—especially in the visual crafts that had their origins in the workaday functions of regional life.

The exhibition called "Abstract Design in American Quilts," which opened this week at the Whitney Museum of American Art, Madison Avenue at 75th Street, lends unexpected support to this growing suspicion. The support is unexpected only because the Whitney has rarely condescended to acknowledge the "decorative arts," as they are called, as a significant contribution to American artistic achievements. One can only hope that the current exhibition, which is of an exceptionally high quality, signals a significant change of heart.

•

The quilts in this exhibition, drawn mostly from the 19th century, are on loan from the private collection of Jonathan Holstein and Gail van der Hoof, and Mr. Holstein has written a short but informative text for the Whitney's catalogue accompanying the exhibition. The quilts are all of the "pieced" variety—that is, they are composed of small, separate pieces of fabric, stitched together to conform to established patterns of the period. These patterns are, for the most part, rigidly geometrical in character, though a good deal of visual freedom is exercised in their execution.

What is so impressive, then, is not the originality of the designs—these designs were, in the most literal sense of the word, conventional—but the dazzling sensibility for color and visual construction that the execution of these designs, with their personal and regional variations, display with such appealing vigor. For a century or more preceding the self-conscious invention of pictorial abstraction in European painting, the anonymous quilt-makers of the American provinces created a remarkable succession of visual masterpieces that anticipated many of the forms that were later prized for their originality and courage.

•

The exhibition is, therefore, not only full of unusual visual pleasures, but it is the kind of exhibition that prompts us to rethink the relation of high art to what are customarily regarded as the lesser forms of visual expression. This is an issue that any serious historian of American art is going to have to come to terms with in future dealings with his subject, and one is grateful to the Whitney for pressing the issue upon us. One can hope, indeed, that this is the first of many such exhibitions.

Among the quilts, the esthetic quality is generally so high that it would be foolishly arbitrary to single out particular examples. For connoisseurs, the show will confirm what they already know—that this is one medium in which the American folk imagination excelled. For newcomers to the material, the show will be a stunning revelation.

Also on view at the Whitney just now is a very pleasant show of prints by John Sloan, marking the 100th anniversary of the artist's birth. Of particular interest, I think, are the scenes of New York life from the turn of the century—a reminder, if we needed one, of how New York has changed so drastically in a few short, devastating decades.

Art critic Hilton Kramer's review of *Abstract Design in American Quilts*, *The New York Times*, July 3, 1971. *Image courtesy of* The New York Times.

The Whitney exhibition is now considered an important component in encouraging the continuing revaluation of quilts and helping legitimize the ongoing acceptance of their exhibitions in art museums. For us, it was the first of many similar ones we went on to curate, with a mixture of the Whitney quilts and similar pieces drawn from our collection, along with significant additions such as Amish quilts as they came along. Over the next 10 years, more than 50 such exhibitions created from our collection were mounted in museums around the world, some curated by us, others by such vehicles as the Smithsonian Institution's Traveling Exhibition Service. Additionally, Gail and I singly or together lectured widely here and abroad, and I wrote about quilts in exhibition catalogs, articles, and a book. Some had particularly satisfying results: The 1972 exhibition we mounted for the then-new Renwick Gallery, the Smithsonian Institution's contemporary craft museum, while it had a wide variety of quilts, did have a good number of the Amish examples we had by then acquired, and several collectors

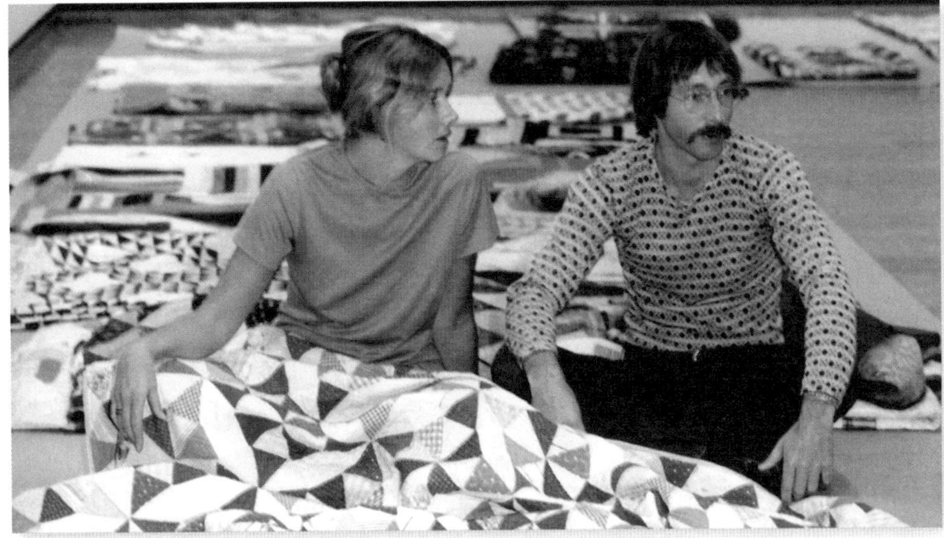

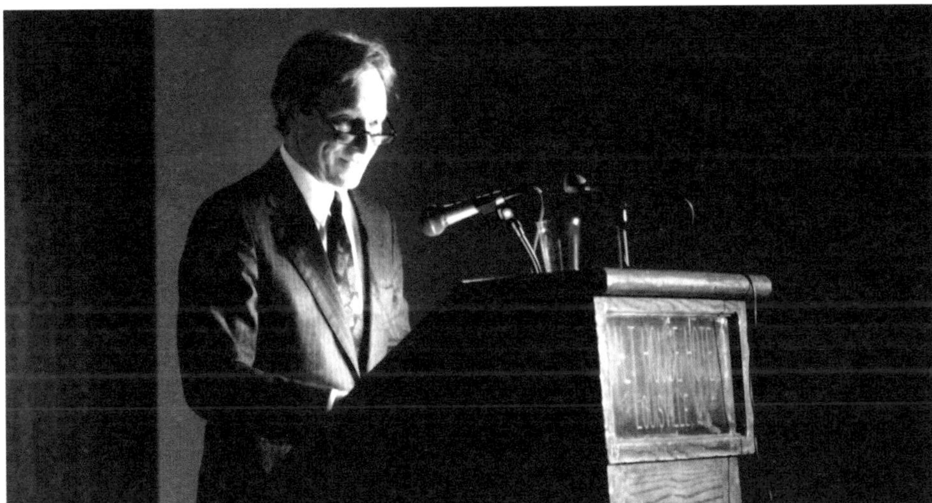

TOP: Holstein and van der Hoof preparing an exhibition at the Everson Museum of Art in Syracuse, New York, October 18, 1971, the first of many that followed the initial Whitney exhibition. *Jonathan Holstein, Quilt Papers, Archives & Special Collections, University of Nebraska-Lincoln Libraries. Photograph by Bob Brown.*
BOTTOM: Jonathan Holstein lecturing during *Louisville Celebrates the American Quilt*, November 1991–March 1992, whose many exhibitions included a remounting of the 1971 Whitney Museum of American art exhibition on its 20th anniversary. *Jonathan Holstein, Quilt Papers, Archives & Special Collections, University of Nebraska-Lincoln Libraries.*



who were introduced to them through it later formed important collections. That desire to share our romance with Amish quilts was fulfilled when we lent 30 examples to an exhibition service that traveled them for three years, 1979–1981.

As other countries became part of the adventure, we saw the beginnings of an awakening interest in their own quilt traditions (e.g. France, the Netherlands). It was not something we had anticipated, especially since in our initial discussions with museum curators in several of the countries, they averred they had had no significant quilt tradition, opinions which eventually proved to have been erroneous. Subsequently, we saw in other countries the beginnings of an interest in making quilts that has continued; Japan is a notable example. In that country, to which exhibitions of our quilts traveled in 1975–1976, it seemed a very short time before there were heavily attended public quilt expositions, guilds forming, sophisticated publications, master classes with students in the

Japanese tradition, and their enthusiastic acceptance of the form encouraged by a traditional regard for textiles as art. Japanese quilt artists are making powerful and interesting works, and I am pleasantly reminded of the profound impact Japanese aesthetics had on Western art beginning in the nineteenth century, an influence reflected in the quilt field by, for instance, the crazy quilt, its asymmetrical design, materials, and motifs (the ubiquitous fans) derived from Japanese art forms.

One predictable commercial result of the exhibitions was that some quilts became more of an art commodity. A number of folk and fine art dealers mounted exhibitions and offered quilts with designs of interest to those who were collecting modern art. This was particularly true for Amish quilts that could be hung in easy harmony with the work of such modern abstract painters as Josef Albers, to whose paintings they have often been compared.

Years later, as I continued my interest in collecting and researching quilts, I heard about a couple, Robert and Ardis James, who were forming an interesting collection, and I arranged a meeting with them. I found quickly enough that they were on a similar intellectual path to mine, trying to understand the whole of the field from the earliest to the most recent examples. While Gail and I had decided early on to limit our collecting largely to a single type of quilt while researching the rest, the Jameses began by collecting across the spectrum, including within the emerging movement of quilts made as art, starting with a piece by Michael James. Although we were aware of that movement and included quilts by pioneers Molly Upton and Susan Hoffman in our first Japanese exhibition, Gail and I had made our necessary initial decision to concentrate on traditional American pieced quilts, our aesthetic preference. Over the years, I remained focused on our first goal, the recognition of the aesthetic importance of traditional American pieced quilts and the achievement of the women who had made them. Both the Jameses and I recognized that while New York was at that point the world center of developing modern art, and while there were great encyclopedic and specialty museums in the city (traditional Western art and that of other cultures, folk art, modern art, tribal art), there was no single





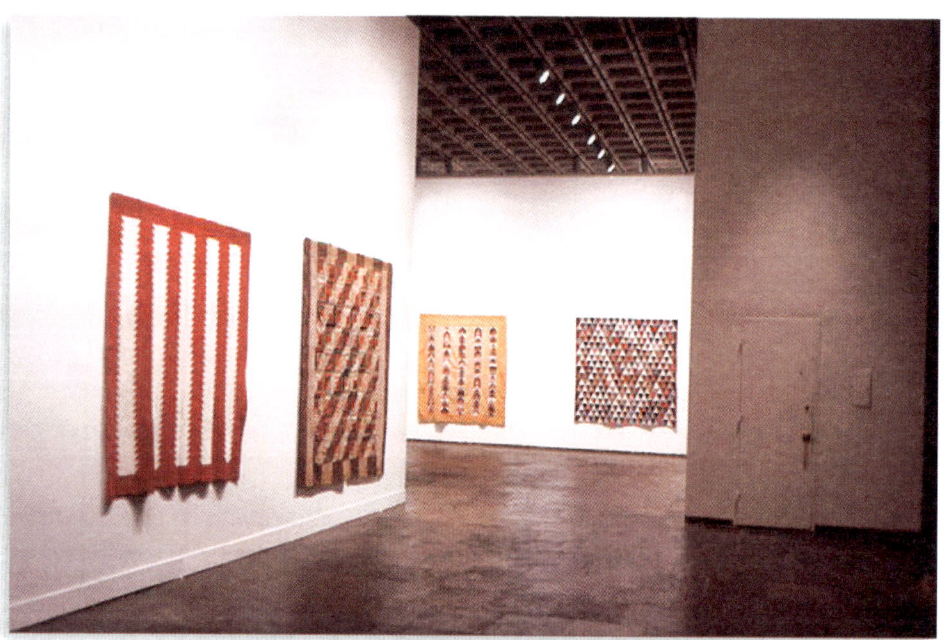

*Abstract Design in American Quilts* at the Whitney Museum of American Art, 1971. *Jonathan Holstein, Quilt Papers, Archives & Special Collections, University of Nebraska-Lincoln Libraries.*

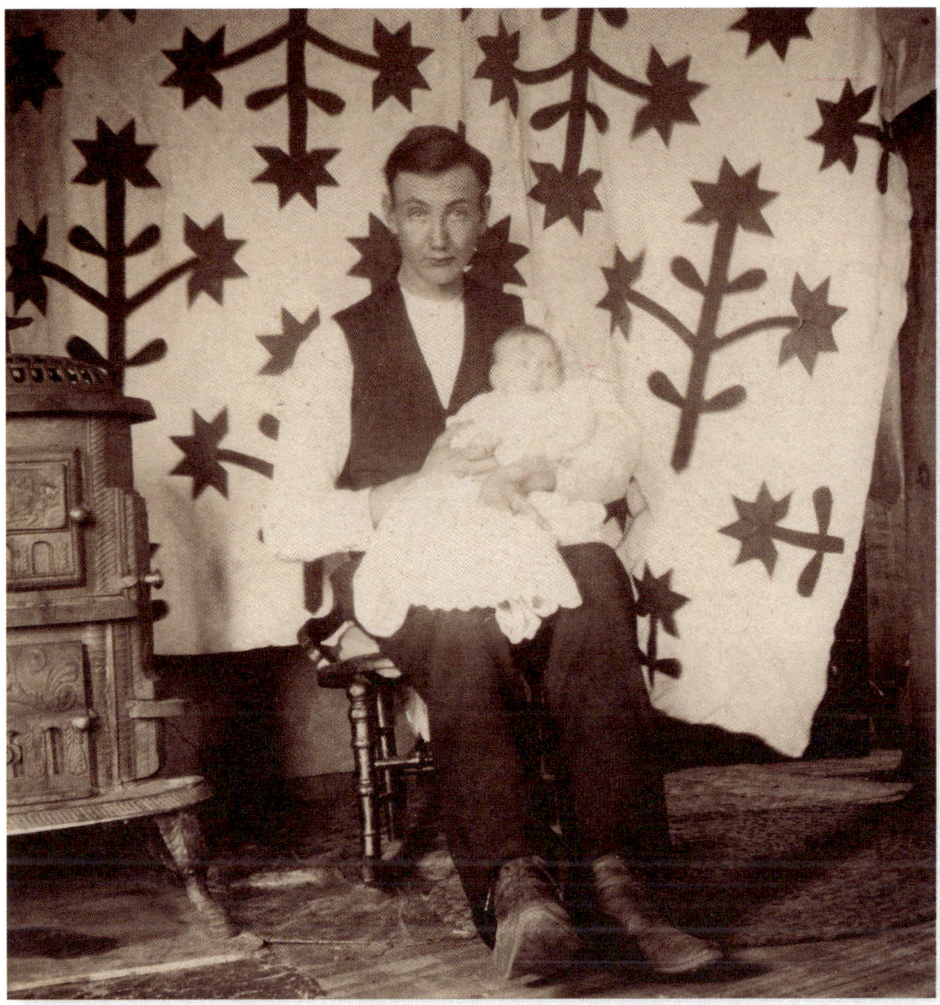

Man holding a baby, a large appliqué quilt used as a backdrop, circa 1890. *Images of American Quilts Archive*.



institution that would accord quilts the sort of lasting prominence they deserved. It was with this knowledge that the Jameses made their great decision to donate their collection to an academic institution in their native state, Nebraska, with the explicit goal of forming a quilt study center. Happily, this led to the eventual establishment of a museum, which has become the premier quilt museum in the world, with the most extensive collection of American quilts of all types, textiles made using quilting techniques from cultures around the globe, and an expanding major holding of works by leading international textile artists. I am of course gratified that our collection is safely housed there.

The Whitney exhibition has been credited with helping in the emergence of that "art quilt" phenomenon, artists using both basic quiltmaking techniques and those brought from other creative fields to make fabric paintings, many meant from the beginning for walls rather than beds. As it began, we saw quilts made in the basic traditional manner but in non-traditional patterns, the modern inception of using quilting techniques in a "painterly" manner. We jump to the present, and if one attends an international quilt exhibition now there will be everything from the most meticulous copies of early elaborate appliqué quilts to works that are hard to tell from modern paintings and that use many artistic techniques: dyeing, painting, printing, collage,

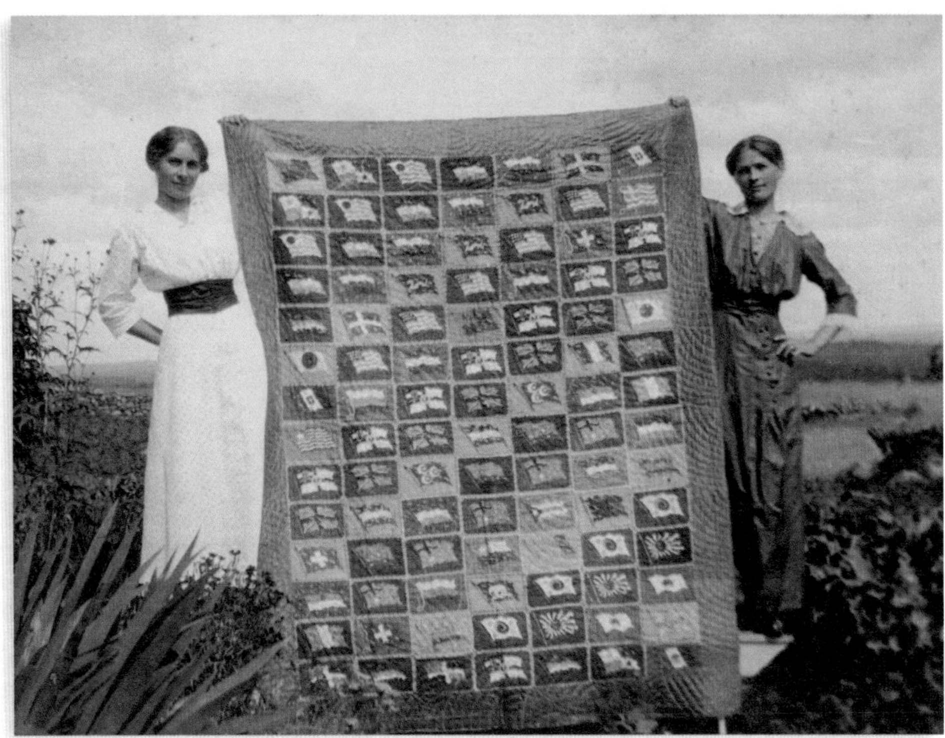

Two quiltmakers showing their tobacco silk Flags of All Nations quilt, circa 1915. *Images of American Quilts Archive*.

and materials antithetical to traditional quilt functions including paper, metal, and plastic. Some of the artists employ few or none of the traditional quilting techniques and, of course, their work looks nothing at all like the traditional textiles. Various terms have been created to describe the results, "art quilts," "studio quilts," but they should, I think, be thought of simply as art.

It is important here to remember that appreciation of quilts is by no means a new phenomenon. Quilts had important symbolic functions in an earlier America beyond their insulating abilities: In the nineteenth and twentieth centuries they were often displayed to demonstrate the domestic skills of the household's women, recording a family's history past and ongoing and significant community and national events. They were used to raise funds for charitable purposes ("tithing" quilts), displays of patriotism, and were carefully passed down in families. Such can be seen in early photographs of quilts proudly displayed on living and sitting room furniture, quilts used as backdrops for family photos, women proudly displaying their handiwork in and outside, even post-mortem photos where deceased children and adults were posed with beloved family quilts covering them. The one place where traditional quiltmakers could, and still do, test their skills against others were public fairs, particularly regional fairs that had competitions in every imaginable aspect of life, from farm animals to domestic skills. Women submitted their best quilts to be judged, and many were hung fully open, others folded and draped over stands—art shows, in effect. (And might I mention another art world parallel in those French salons in whose exhibitions contemporary art was shown and judged.) Now, of course, such events are outnumbered by the many occasional and annual quilt shows, regional and national, and global competitions devoted entirely to quilts that have proliferated over the last half-century, with significant participation and attendance. In truth those earlier ceremonial functions noted never completely vanished, and several returned prominently with such as the AIDS quilts and "Honor Quilts" made for and distributed by several organizations to veterans, honoring their military service, etc.

A similar sort of revival has happened with publications: In the late nineteenth and early twentieth centuries there were numerous periodicals designed specifically for women that carried quilt information including design patterns, and such also appeared in newspapers. Entrepreneurs, largely female, and companies offered quilt kits, some with pre-cut fabrics. There has now developed a very large array of sophisticated publications of all sorts devoted to people who make, study, or simply admire quilts. I note, also, the many flourishing quilt guilds that offer their members the companionship of like-minded enthusiasts and encourage the continuing creation of quilts, and the highly productive quilt study groups here and abroad. I am also mindful of the international coterie of quilt scholars who have over the past half-century vastly increased our knowledge, understanding, and appreciation of our common interest.

There is more to do: My current self-appointed task is to continue my research into beginnings, the history of the (ultimate) origins of our quilts. I feel quite certain it starts in the Middle East and comes to Europe with the Muslim occupation of Sicily, which brought cotton and silk cultivation and, I believe, the tradition and technical knowledge of quilting to the European continent. My search began with an early twentieth century Italian quilt that a resident of my small community brought to my office for me to see. It arrived in America with her immigrating grandmother in the early twentieth century and is now a treasured part of the IQM's collection. I was able to find similar ones in Italy on the Adriatic coast that support my notion, as do the very early silk quilts from Sicily that share significant features with those later ones. That moment was typical of the many unforeseen events that have fueled and enriched my half-century-plus attempt to understand our quilts, and, where I could, help others see them. Fortunately, I am still asked to curate an occasional museum exhibition, which enables me to continue exploring ways of demonstrating both the visual power and the vast range of cultural information inherent in pieced quilts.

I am, finally, grateful to my talented colleagues and friends at the International Quilt Museum who decided to celebrate this anniversary and worked successfully to make it happen under unexpectedly difficult circumstances.

Thank you.

In sum:
It has been for me
a great quilting *be*.

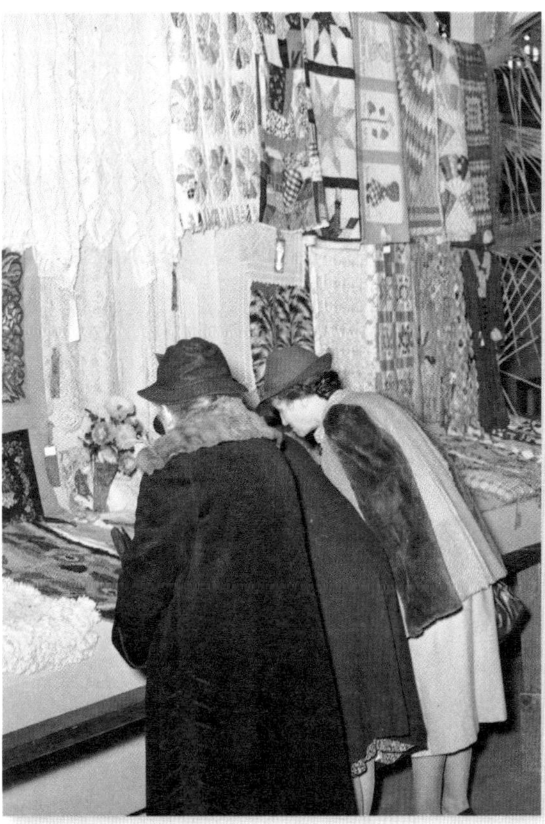

Women looking at the quilting and crocheting exhibit at Gonzales County Fair, Gonzales, Texas, 1939. *Library of Congress, Prints & Photographs Division, Farm Security Administration/Office of War Information Black-and-White Negatives.* Photograph by: Russell Lee.

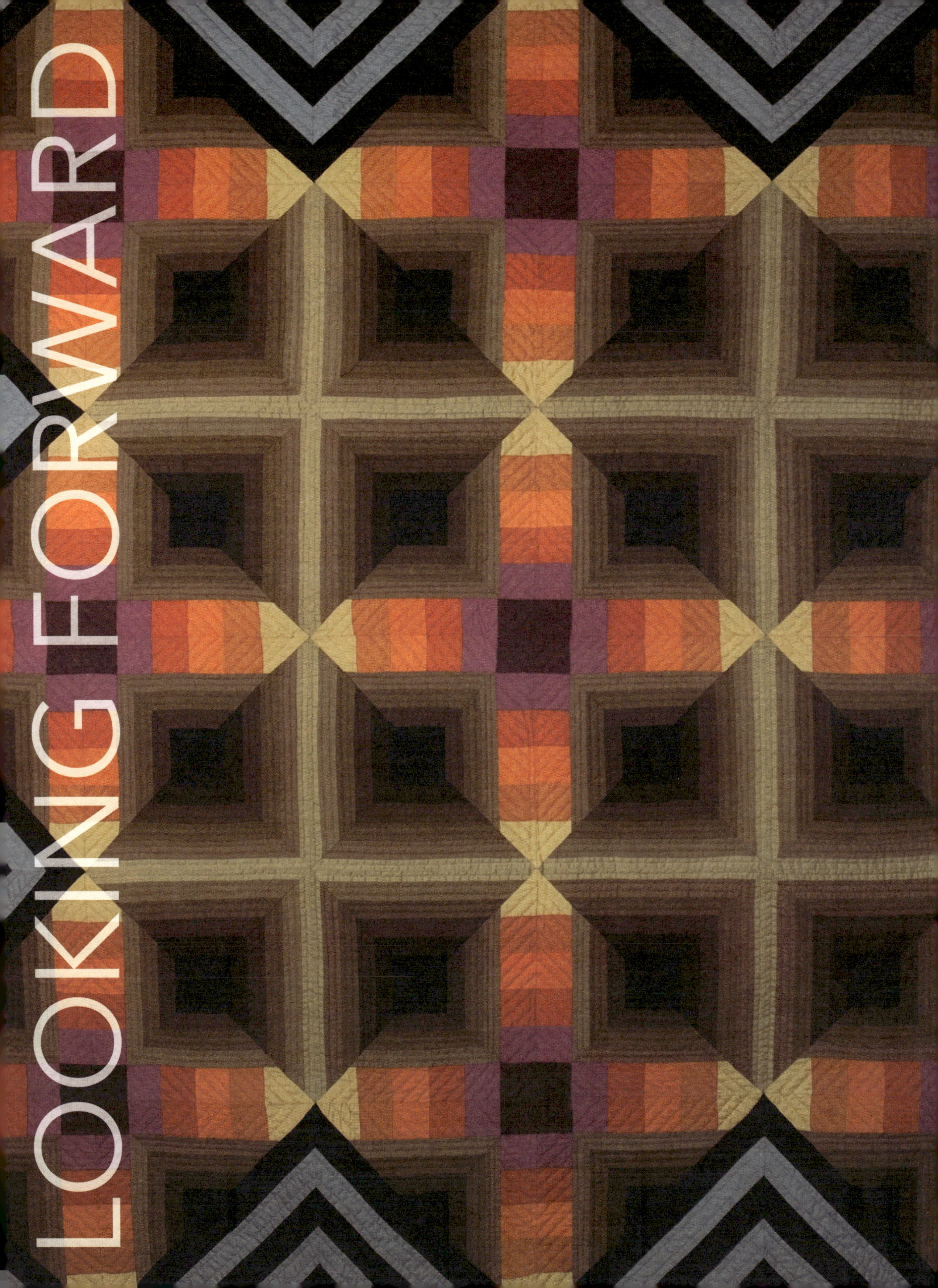
LOOKING FORWARD

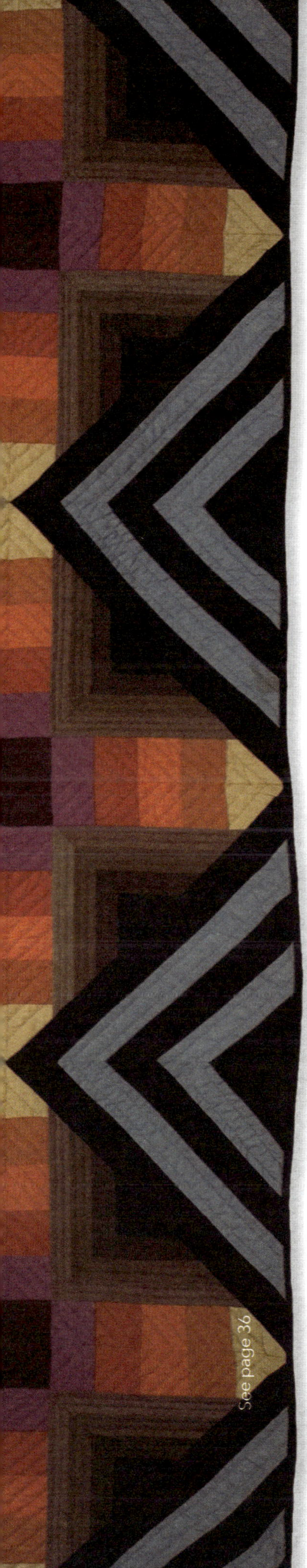

See page 36

# CAROLYN DUCEY

The Whitney Museum of American Art's 1971 exhibition *Abstract Design in American Quilts* (*ADAQ*) brought quilts to the forefront of the public's mind in a new and unexpected way. In a departure from standard presentations of textile folk art, exhibition curators Jonathan Holstein and Gail van der Hoof displayed traditional pieced quilts in one of the nation's foremost modern art museums. Thousands

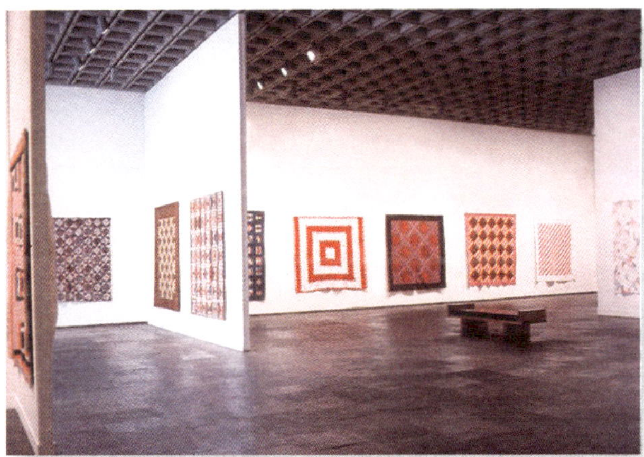

*Abstract Design in American Quilts* installed at the Whitney Museum of American Art, New York, New York, July 1–October 5, 1971. *Jonathan Holstein, Quilt Papers, Archives & Special Collections, University of Nebraska-Lincoln Libraries.*

of New Yorkers and tourists viewed antique textiles in galleries usually reserved for artists such as Picasso, Pollock, and Rothko. This radical approach shifted the perception of quilts in a number of ways: a much larger and broader audience was now aware of them; critics who had never before considered quilts hailed them as works of art; and artists who had begun exploring the quiltmaking medium saw that the quilt form was being taken seriously in America's cultural capital. This essay will look forward starting from 1971, outlining the evolution of quilts' status through the lens of the development, dissemination, and institutionalization of so-called "studio" or "art" quilts.

When the Whitney exhibition opened, visual similarities prompted viewers and reviewers to compare the quilts to the work more customarily seen on the museum's walls. For some, the quilts' repeated grid formats were reminiscent of Andy Warhol's pop art while for others, their expanses of saturated color bore resemblance to Kenneth Noland's color field paintings.[1] In the review that essentially put *ADAQ* on the map, *New York Times* art critic Hilton Kramer noted the quilts' visual resonance with modern abstract painting and credited their makers with developing sophisticated abstract forms well before painters did:

> For a century or more preceding the self-conscious invention of pictorial abstraction in European painting, the anonymous quilt-makers of the American provinces created a remarkable succession of visual masterpieces that anticipated many of the forms that were later prized for their originality and courage. [2]

Praise was also extended to the exhibition as a whole. Whitney curator Robert "Mac" Doty felt—as expressed 20 years later—that *ADAQ* had "established a new appreciation for an important segment of American art."[3] Lester Abelman of the *New York Daily News* opined that the Whitney had "given the homely quilt its artistic stamp of approval." [4] And the *New Yorker*'s Janet Malcolm marveled that, as demonstrated in *ADAQ*, "a quilt that looks merely homey lying at the foot of a bed may become a great work of abstract design when it is hung on an enormous white wall and regarded from a distance."[5] But many of the assessments were double-edged. Even when complimenting the exhibition, reviewers continued to describe quilts as "primitive" or "naive."[6] And while Kramer embraced the quilts as "native genius ... the most authentic of the American imagination in the last century," he also admitted that the dichotomy of the "High" arts—painting and sculpture—versus the "Minor" arts—those of the "workaday functions of regional life"—remained the dominant paradigm.[7] Thanks to *ADAQ*, quilts were now more visible to the public and more highly regarded among art critics. However, a dividing line still existed, albeit blurred. The questions remained: Were quilts fine art or folk art? Primitive or sophisticated? Did simply putting them on a gallery wall, as Janet Malcolm had suggested, transform them into "great work"?

Meanwhile, related discussions and developments in textile art were already underway in the US. The Newark Museum's 1965 *Optical Quilts* exhibition presented antique quilts as examples of optical illusion, "elicit[ing] the obvious comparisons between quilts and contemporary Op Art paintings."[8] And as outlined by Sandra Sider in this volume, New York hosted a number of cutting-edge art exhibitions around the same time as *ADAQ* that championed innovative approaches to textile art. Most relevant to this essay, a new generation of artists, many of whom saw these New York exhibitions,

---

[1] Although Holstein and van der Hoof themselves did not make these comparisons publicly during the Whitney exhibition (Holstein's essay for the Whitney catalog gave a brief overview of historical US quiltmaking), they made note of them privately. Additionally, Holstein pointed out these visual similarities shortly afterwards in his 1973 volume, *The Pieced Quilt: A North American Design Tradition* (see, for instance, Chapter 6, "The Skilled Hand, The Practiced Eye").

[2] Hilton Kramer, "Art: Quilts Find a Place at the Whitney," *The New York Times*, July 3, 1971, nytimes.com/1971/07/03/archives/art-quilts-find-a-place-at-the-whitney.html.

[3] Jonathan Holstein, *Abstract Design in American Quilts: A Biography of an Exhibition* (Louisville, KY: Kentucky Quilt Project, 1991), 43.

[4] Lester Abelman, "A Quilt Exhibit Uncovered at the Whitney," *New York Daily News*, July 4, 1971.

[5] Janet Malcolm, "On and Off the Avenue: About the House," *The New Yorker*, September 4, 1971, 60.

[6] John Gruen, *New York Magazine*, July 1971, as quoted in Holstein, *Abstract Design in American Quilts: A Biography of an Exhibition*, 50.

[7] Kramer, "Art: Quilts Find a Place at the Whitney."

[8] Nancy C. Bavor, "The California Art Quilt Revolution" (MA, University of Nebraska-Lincoln, 2011), 13, digitalcommons.unl.edu/cehsdiss.

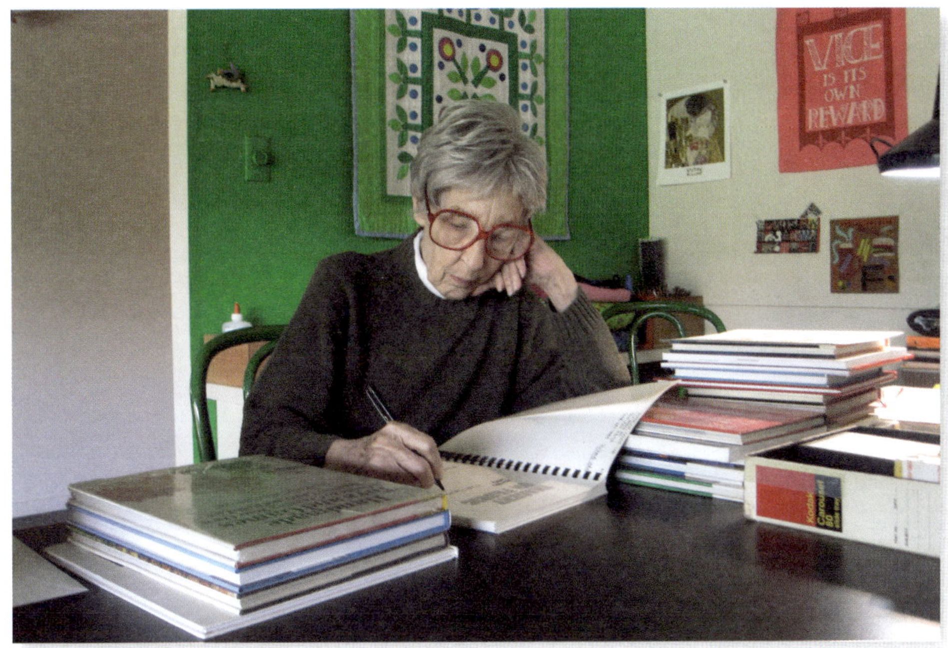


Artist Jean Ray Laury signs copies of her books at her home in Clovis, California, March 2010. *Photograph by: Carolyn Ducey.*

were developing a new genre of quilt—a style characterized by the artists' intention to remove any semblance of utility. Lacking a formal term, the quilts ultimately were identified as "studio" or "art" quilts.[9]

Artist Jean Ray Laury, a progenitor of the studio quilt movement, began making quilts as a graduate student at Stanford University in the 1950s. Her innovative, stylized approach to quiltmaking came to the attention of magazine editor Roxa Wright, who commissioned Laury in 1960 to design quilts for *House Beautiful*. Soon Laury began writing columns for a host of popular magazines and she authored more than 20 books, including *Quilts and Coverlets: A Contemporary Approach,* published in 1970. Artist Radka Donnell began to explore quiltmaking in the mid-1960s. She saw quilts as an expressive art form that links physical and symbolic meaning in their functional nature. Both artists influenced new quilters and remained actively involved in the movement, in which " . . . not only had lines between traditional and studio quilts softened but lines between decorative and fine arts had blurred."[10] Laury, whose work often was explicitly feminist and socially conscious, wrote: "By the time the life-altering '70s arrived, we were primed, and when the feminist movement flourished, we'd already tossed our aprons aside."[11]

Formally trained artists such as Nancy Crow, Therese May, and Michael James in the US and Pauline Burbidge in the UK began to explore quiltmaking in earnest in the



[9] Penny McMorris and Michael Kile, *The Art Quilt* (San Francisco: Quilt Digest Press, 1986), 23. Penny McMorris and Michael Kile devised the term "art quilt" in the 1980s. They wrote: " ... the art quilt is different from its predecessors: it is art for walls, not beds, created by artists abandoning media like painting, printmaking and ceramics to express themselves in original designs of cloth and thread." The IQM adopted the term "studio quilt" in 1998 to distinguish quilts in its collection made by individuals whose intent is to create artworks strictly for display. Neither "art quilt" nor "studio quilt," however, has been satisfactory for some artists, who feel the labels are cumbersome and, as the genre has gained recognition, simply refer to themselves as "artists."

[10] Bavor, "The California Art Quilt Revolution," 4.

[11] Jean Ray Laury, "My Journey through Quilting," *Quilter's Newsletter Magazine*, March 1, 2004.

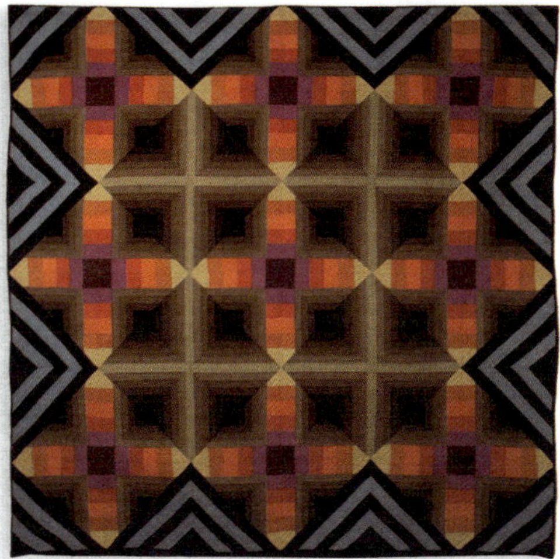
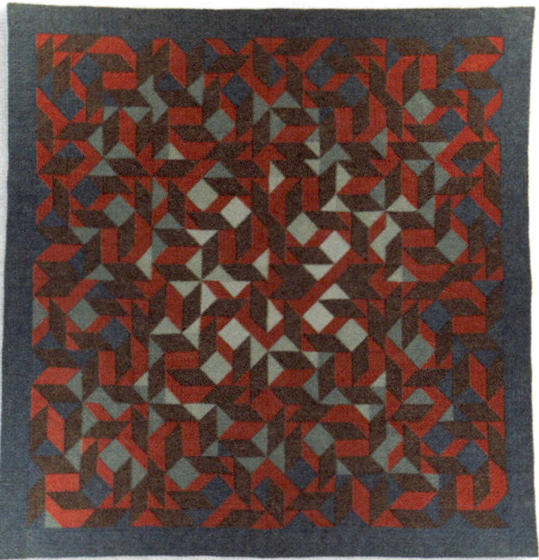

*Crosses*, Nancy Crow, Baltimore, Ohio, 1976, 93 x 94 in., Ardis and Robert James Collection, IQM 1997.007.1088; *Elaborated Tangram*, Michael James, Somerset, Massachusetts, 1976, 91.5 x 89.5 in., Ardis and Robert James Collection, IQM 1997.007.1012. Artists such as Nancy Crow and Michael James experimented with a variety of optical effects in their early quilts.





1970s. They chose textiles as their primary medium, appreciating that fabric gave them greater freedom to manipulate form as compared to painting or sculpture.[12] They approached quiltmaking through personal experience—having learned from a family member, or by self-teaching with contemporary books. Soon, however, they broke away from the use of traditional block formats and moved into expressing their artistic vision in new ways. They incorporated a variety of materials and techniques, including surface embellishment and textural stitching, and explored optical elements of light, dimension, and scale. Art curator Penny McMorris described this approach in the mid 1980s: " ... quiltmaking was, for the most part, dependent upon a catalog of established geometric and appliqué patterns. Now, however, trained artists are making one original design after another and ... manipulating the traditional geometric plan with a new vivacity."[13] The artists questioned the standard definition of quilts and expanded their work into new terrain.

People's overwhelming interest in all genres of quiltmaking in the 1970s led to the formation of a number of organizations, museums, and conferences with missions to promote quiltmaking.[14] Some focused solely on studio quilts, while others presented a wide range of styles and themes. Houston's International Quilt Festival, the largest annual quilt show in the US, debuted in 1975 with traditional and contemporary quilt exhibitions, retail sales, and classes. In 1977, the American Museum of Quilts and Related Arts (today the San Jose Museum of Quilts and Textiles), the first museum dedicated to quilts, opened in San Jose, California, " ... to increase the public's awareness, understanding, and appreciation of quilts and textiles as a form of artistic and cultural expression that people worldwide have practiced for thousands of years."[15] The year 1979 marked the first Quilt National exhibition, a juried show highlighting quilts, held at the Dairy Barn Art Center in Athens, Ohio. It was developed by artists Nancy Crow, Françoise Barnes, and Virginia Randles, who recognized the

---

[12] McMorris and Kile, *The Art Quilt*, 63.
[13] McMorris and Kile, 63.
[14] See Sandra Sider's essay in this volume.
[15] "Our Mission," San Jose Museum of Quilts & Textiles, accessed September 24, 2020, sjquiltmuseum.org/mission-history.

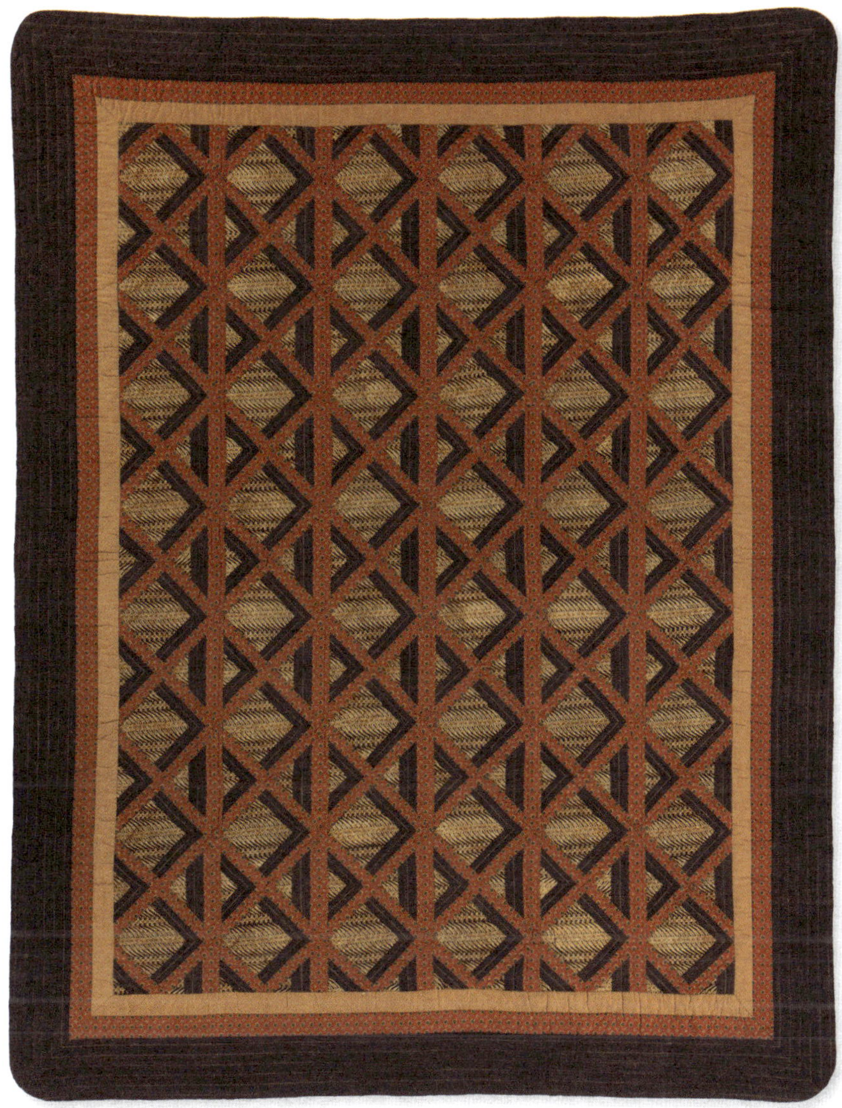



*The Norman Wall*, Judy Mathieson, Woodland Hills, California, 1977, 101.5 x 79.5 in., Quilt National Collection, IQM 2019.038.0001. Mathieson's *The Norman Wall* was shown in the 1979 inaugural exhibition of Quilt National in Athens, Ohio.

need for a showcase specifically for artists creating quilts for exhibition. Quilt National recently celebrated its 20th biennial exhibition and is recognized as one of the most significant venues today for quilt artists to show new work.

Among the plethora of 1970s publications focused on quilts, emerging quilt artists produced books that encouraged readers to take a new approach to making quilts. Beth and Jeffery Gutcheon in *The Perfect Patchwork Primer* (1973) and Michael James, in *The Quiltmaker's Handbook* (1978), taught traditional techniques while encouraging the creation of expressive and innovative quilts. The Gutcheons wrote, "We accept and respect what we have learned from our forebearers about How To Do It, then we use those lessons to push the traditional a step forward, to say something new about ourselves and our quiltmaking."[16] The Gutcheons quickly followed their first book with *The Quilt Design Workbook* in 1976, while James wrote a second edition

---

[16] Beth Richardson Gutcheon, Barbara Stockwell, and Jeffrey Gutcheon, *The Perfect Patchwork Primer* (Baltimore: Penguin Books, 1974), 22.

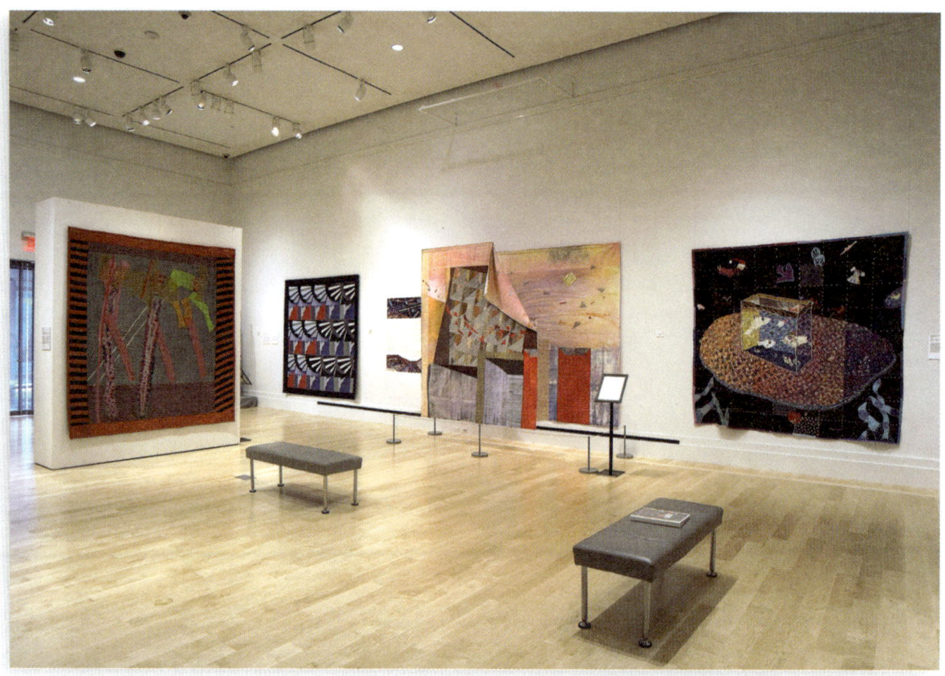

With the exhibition *Revisiting The Art Quilt* (2010), the IQM celebrated the 25th anniversary of the seminal exhibition *The Art Quilt*, which was staged at the Los Angeles Municipal Art Gallery in 1986.

of his *Handbook* in 1981. In addition to instructions, the books connected quilt artists with enthusiasts across the US and Europe, giving the artists a much-needed source of income and an audience to promote their individual approaches to quiltmaking. Innovative instructors also promoted new technical developments in quiltmaking, particularly in machine quilting, hand dyeing, and various stitching techniques, including embroidery and embellishment.

Innovative quilt production and exhibition continued to grow and flourish in the last decades of the twentieth century, thanks to a variety of individuals and organizations. *The Art Quilt*, a 1986 exhibition curated by Penny McMorris and Michael Kile, showcased work by 16 trailblazing leaders in the studio quilt genre. The curators invited the artists to "create the piece they'd always dreamt of making."[17] Some completed more than one piece for the exhibition. The resulting 25 quilts illustrated technical and aesthetic developments that distinguished studio quilts: abstract design, overlarge sizes (in contrast to typical bed sizes), specially designed wooden structures framing the work, layered or double-sided surfaces, copious embellishment, and machine quilting. Scholar and philanthropist Carolyn Mazloomi founded the Women of Color Quilters Network (WCQN) in 1985 to foster and preserve the art of quiltmaking among women of color. WCQN has shown the work of its members in critically acclaimed traveling exhibits including *Spirits of the Cloth: Contemporary African American Quilts, And Still We Rise: Race, Culture and Visual Conversation,* and *We Who Believe in Freedom.* The Visions Art Museum: Contemporary Quilts + Textiles (originally Quilt San Diego), was also founded in 1985 to promote contemporary quiltmaking. In 1989, artist Yvonne Porcella and a group of California artists founded

[17] Penny McMorris, "Revisiting the Art Quilt – Online Exhibition," International Quilt Museum, December 2010, internationalquiltmuseum.org/exhibition/revisiting-art-quilt.

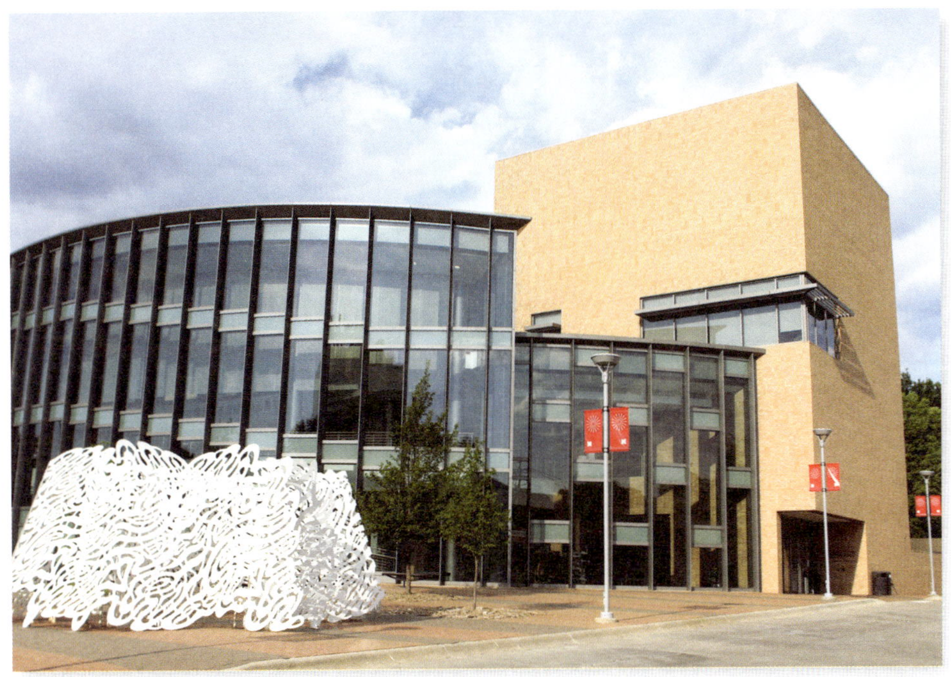

The International Quilt Museum, University of Nebraska-Lincoln, designed by Robert A.M. Stern.

Studio Art Quilt Associates (SAQA) to "create an organization to promote art quilts to major art publications, museums, and galleries, educate the public about art quilts, serve as a forum for the professional development of quilt artists and act as a resource for curators, dealers, consultants, teachers, students, and collectors."[18] Today SAQA has a global membership of more than 3,700 individuals and has developed more than 250 exhibitions. Quilt Surface Design Symposium (QSDS), a two-week event launched in 1990, offers a variety of class, workshop, and networking opportunities.



Quilt museums and study centers were founded in the 1980s and '90s, too, and have accumulated significant quilt collections, including the Great Lakes Quilt Center at Michigan State University (1984), the New England Quilt Museum (1987), Wisconsin Museum of Quilts and Fiber Arts (1988), the National Quilt Museum (1991), and the Pacific Northwest Quilt and Fiber Art Museum (1997). Founded in 1997, the International Quilt Museum, University of Nebraska-Lincoln, now holds approximately 700 studio quilts designated for display in its collection.

Studio quilts have also moved into a global realm. They are now being made, collected, and exhibited around the world. The Quilters' Guild of the British Isles (QGBI), an educational charity founded in 1979, collects and exhibits the work of contemporary makers in their location in York, England. In 1985, a subset of QGBI members created the group Quilt Art to provide a forum for artists who wished to experiment with studio work. The group now has members across Europe and in the US and it promotes new shows every two to three years. Studio quilts are exhibited at conferences around the world, including the Pour l'Amour du Fils (Nantes, France),

---

[18] "Our Story," Studio Art Quilt Associates, accessed September 24, 2020, saqa.com/about/our-story.

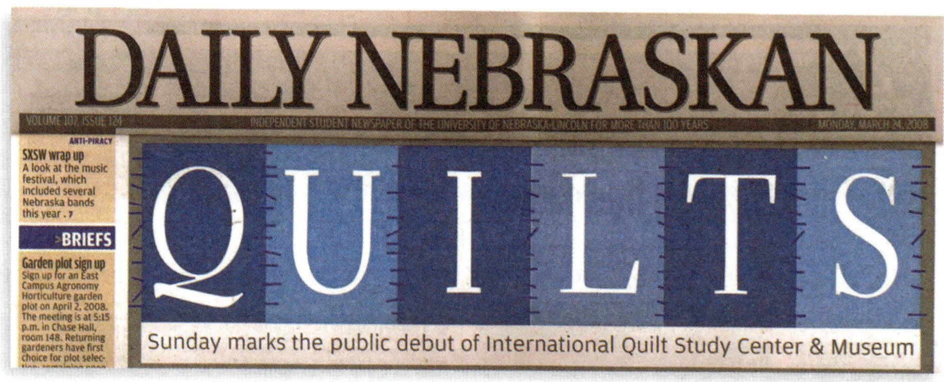

DAILY NEBRASKAN

VOLUME 107, ISSUE 124 INDEPENDENT STUDENT NEWSPAPER OF THE UNIVERSITY OF NEBRASKA-LINCOLN FOR MORE THAN 100 YEARS MONDAY, MARCH 24, 2008

ANTI-PIRACY

SXSW wrap up

A look at the music festival, which included several Nebraska bands this year . 7

>BRIEFS

Garden plot sign up

Sign up for an East Campus Agronomy Horticulture garden plot on April 2, 2008. The meeting is at 5:15 p.m. in Chase Hall, room 148. Returning gardeners have first choice for plot selec-

QUILTS

Sunday marks the public debut of International Quilt Study Center & Museum

Headline announcing the public opening of the International Quilt Study Center & Museum (now IQM), in UNL's *Daily Nebraskan* student newspaper, March 24, 2008.

European Patchwork Meeting (Alsace, France), the Festival of Quilts (Birmingham, England), the China International Patchwork Invitational Tournament & Patchwork Arts Show (Shenzhen, China), the Australasian Quilt Convention (Melbourne, Australia), the India International Quilt Festival (Chennai, India), and the largest quilt event worldwide: the Tokyo International Great Quilt Festival (Tokyo, Japan). In 2020, the Zhejiang Folk Art Quilt Museum opened in Shaoxing, China.

The latest genre of quiltmaking emerged 20 years ago as an outgrowth of twenty-first century "Do-It-Yourself" sensibilities and a renewed interest in handwork that was fueled in part by online resources and communities. Weeks Ringle and Bill Kerr co-founded the Modern Quilt Studio in 1999 to "rethink the possibilities of the American quilt."[19] In 2008, the online site *Fresh Modern Quilts* provided the first opportunity for interaction among self-described "modern" quiltmakers, and a year later, Alissa Haight Carlton and Latifah Saafir founded the Modern Quilt Guild (MQG). Members create quilts that blur the line between traditional and studio quilts, distinguished by use of "bold colors and prints, high contrast and graphic areas of solid color, improvisational piecing, minimalism, expansive negative space, and alternate grid work."[20] They now host an annual exhibition and conference, known as QuiltCon.

It is clear that in the 50 years since *ADAQ*, studio quilts continue to draw and inspire a large audience of makers, collectors, and admirers. But recognition, for both new and antique quilts, has been limited. In the fine art world today, quilts remain marginalized. Quilt artists struggle to find acceptance in major galleries and museums, and are celebrated primarily when they are "discovered" and viewed through the lens of the art establishment. Those who embrace quilts—the "insiders"—continue to attend exhibitions, take classes, purchase fabrics, and share their quilts, particularly in online forums. "Outsiders," however—those who have only an incidental relationship with quilts—still perceive them in narrow and stereotyped ways. This insider/outsider dichotomy is problematic and confounding for those who already appreciate quilts. As *Quiltfolk* magazine editor Mary Fons points out, "We like it when the other half notices what we know all day: Quilts matter, they are great, they have never gone anywhere," but, as she further asserts, "they aren't *going* anywhere, either ... ".[21]

---

[19] Weeks Ringle and Bill Kerr, "About Us," Modern Quilt Studio, accessed September 24, 2020, modernquiltstudio.com/about-us/.

[20] "Modern Quilting," Modern Quilt Guild, accessed October 11, 2020, mqg.memberclicks.net/modern- quilting.

[21] Mary Fons, "The Quiltdashians: Let Us Embrace Kim, Her Family, and Their Patchwork Ad Campaign," Mary Fons (blog), January 22, 2018, maryfons.com/2018/01/quiltdashians-let-us-embrace-kim-family-patchwork-ad-campaign/.

A set of twenty-first century exhibitions provides examples of the enduring "outsider" perception of quilts. *The Quilts of Gee's Bend* (2002) and its follow up, *Gee's Bend: the Architecture of the Quilt* (2006), were blockbuster exhibitions organized by the Museum of Fine Arts, Houston, featuring work by Black women from the remote rural community of Gee's Bend, Alabama.[22] Both exhibitions traveled extensively to major US art museums and brought quilts to the attention of large audiences. Reviewers described the quilts as "miraculous works of modern art" and as possessing "... composition that is more often associated with the inventiveness and power of the leading 20th century abstract painters than it is with textile-making."[23] More recently, the quilts in *Rosie Lee Tompkins: A Retrospective* (2020) at the Berkeley Art Museum and Pacific Film Archive were described in *The New York Times* as "crafted objects that [have] transcended quilting, with the power of painting," making them "canon-busting, and implicitly subversive" and "one of the century's major artistic accomplishments, giving quilt-making a radical new articulation and emotional urgency."[24] [25]

The reviews of the Gee's Bend and Rosie Lee Tompkins exhibitions are, in fact, similar to those of *ADAQ* decades earlier. The quilts are described positively—deservedly so—but are labeled "miraculous" and "canon-busting," implying they are unprecedented and radical, much in the same way the *ADAQ* quilts had been tagged "masterpieces" and "genius." Furthermore, their impact as visual objects is tied to their resemblance to painting—the fine art world's dominant medium. In reality, all of these quilts are part of longstanding, multi-generational needlework traditions formed by social, cultural, economic, and often gender- and race-influenced circumstances. They are not one-offs. They did not emerge suddenly, from a vacuum. The quilts in these exhibitions were given esteem not because of their complex place *in* the quilt world, but because of their appearance *outside* of it.

Unfortunately, as art historian Janet Koplos has recently noted, "One might think that the quilt could easily find a place in art galleries ... But the object ... [is] entangled in status restrictions." Quilts have come a long way toward mainstream and art world recognition, partly in thanks to awareness brought by the groundbreaking *ADAQ* exhibition, but status restrictions keep them on the fringes. Fifty years on from *Abstract Design in American Quilts*, we—insiders and outsiders both—must continue to work to remove these barriers. Great design and rich history can co-exist. Visually complex quilts can be made by artists who graduated from fine art programs and by those who learned from their community. Looking forward, we should aim to appreciate quilts in their fullness, noting their aesthetic strengths and varied contexts and saluting the many ways in which disparate quilts can be regarded as "great works."



---

[22] Quilts from this area were initially brought to nationwide attention in the 1960s with the formation of the Freedom Quilting Bee. For more information, see Nancy Callahan, "Freedom Quilting Bee," Encyclopedia of Alabama, August 8, 2008, encyclopediaofalabama.org/article/h-1628.

[23] Alvia Wardlaw, "The Quilts of Gee"s Bend," interview by Neal Conan, NPR, February 4, 2003, npr.org/templates/story/story.php?storyId=970364.

[24] Roberta Smith, "The Radical Quilting of Rosie Lee Tompkins," *The New York Times*, June 26, 2020, nytimes.com/interactive/2020/06/26/arts/design/rosie-lee-tompkins-quilts.html.

[25] The description of the quilts as "subversive" and "radical" has much to do with the improvisational style of the quilts, in other words, the fact that they were made largely without the strictures of traditional quilt patterns. The style is sometimes mistakenly attributed solely to African-American women, who, as outsiders of a different sort, are believed to be free to make quilts of an unrestrained, more artistic bent than those of mainstream makers. For a discussion of the local aesthetic of improvisation and asymmetry among Black and White quiltmakers see: Margaret Susan Roach, "The Traditional Quiltmaking of North Louisiana Women: Form, Function, and Meaning" (PhD, University of Texas at Austin, 1986), and Teri Klassen, *Tennessee Delta Quiltmaking* (University of Tennessee Press, 2017).

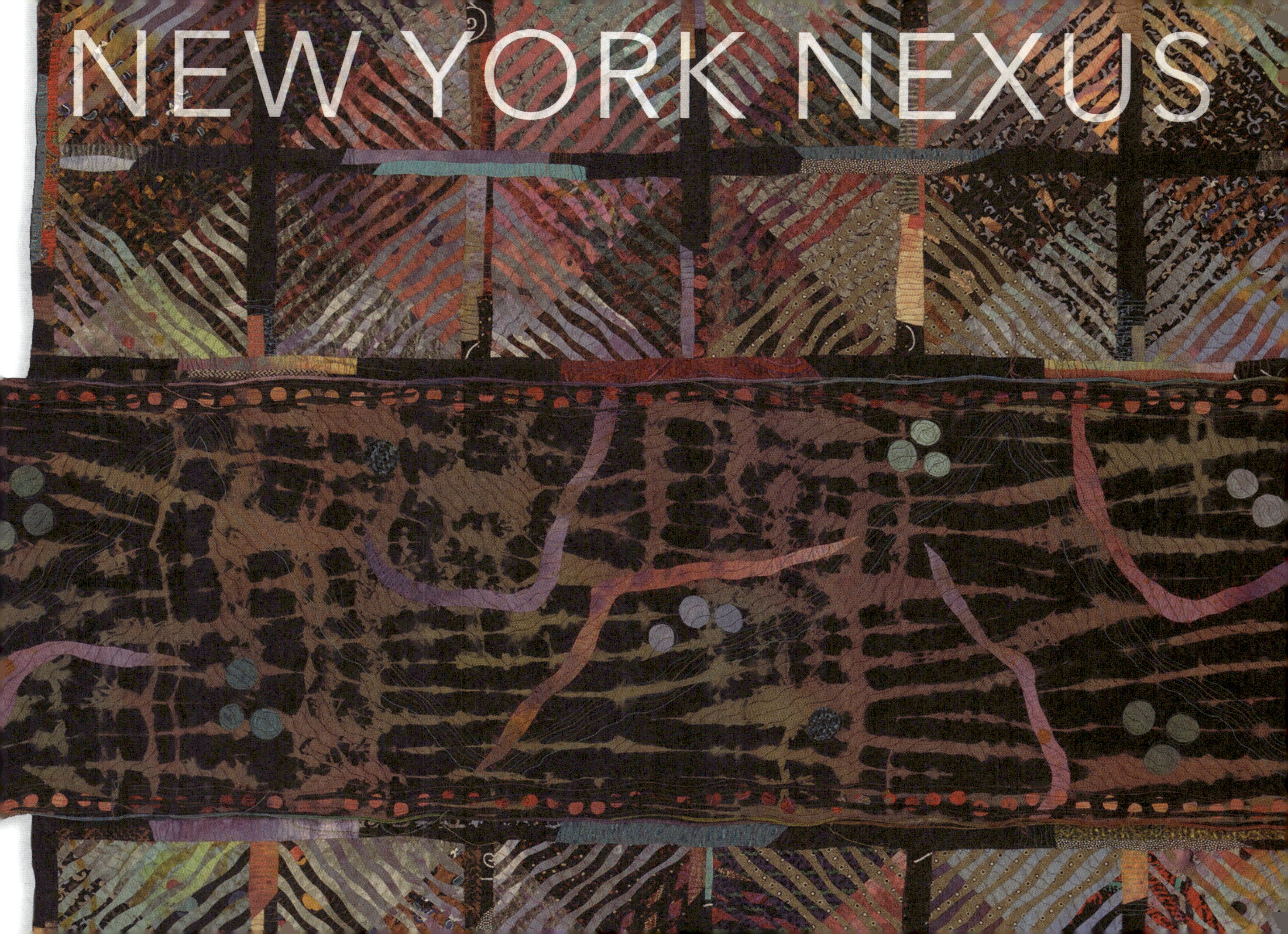
NEW YORK NEXUS

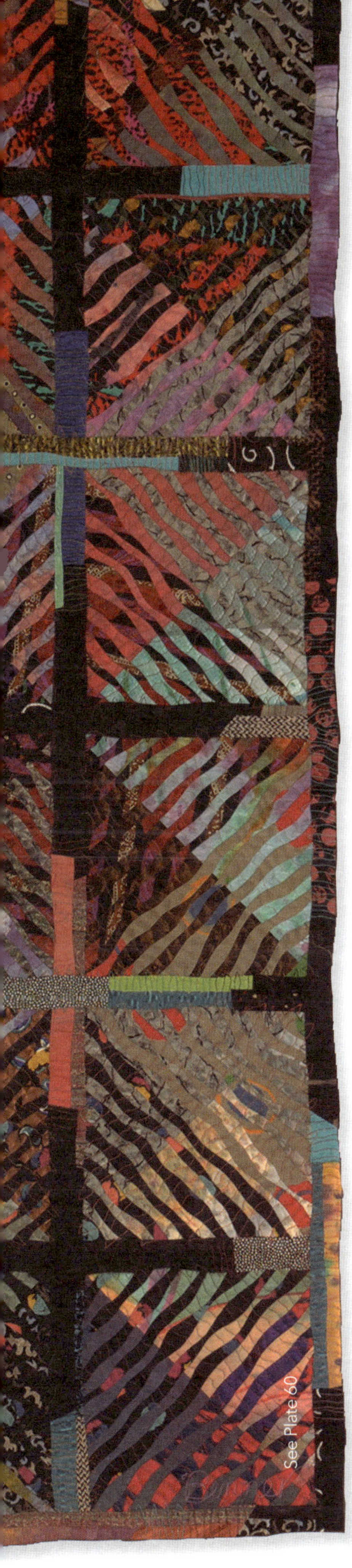
See Plate 60

# SANDRA SIDER

*New York Nexus* explores the instrumental role New York City played in the early stage of the Art Quilt Movement. Several exhibitions that originated or were conceived in New York during the 1970s, or that traveled to the city, directly influenced traditional quiltmakers as well as emerging artists working in various mediums—painting, printmaking, sculpture, collage, weaving, ceramics—who went on to become quilt artists. Although the term "art quilt" was not coined officially until the mid-1980s, dozens of artists were, in essence, creating art quilts in the 1970s, and a few of them much earlier.

As background, it is helpful to review what was happening in art museums in the years leading up to the 1970s. In the late 1950s, major museums across the country were preoccupied with exhibiting Abstract Expressionist art—paintings either textured with dramatic gestural movement or filled with great swaths of pigment in Color Field Painting. Then, in 1961, the Museum of Modern Art in New York presented an exhibition called *The Art of Assemblage*—galleries filled with all sorts of stuff, assembled together in a collage aesthetic. The materials even included a few textiles, such as floral needlepoint in a work by Arthur Dove, one of the earliest abstract painters in American art.

As was made clear in the exhibition catalog, "Assemblage is a new medium," derived from collage, and "the technique of collage has always been a threat to the approved media of oil painting, carving, and casting . . . [and] has added to art [a sort of] vernacular realism."[1] The same could be said of traditional quiltmaking, which is couched in a domestic and largely functional mode. This groundbreaking exhibition was seen nationally, touring to the Dallas Museum of Contemporary Art and the San Francisco Museum of

---

[1] William Chapin Seitz, *The Art of Assemblage* (New York: The Museum of Modern Art, distributed by Doubleday, 1961), 87.

Art, with some positive newspaper reviews. It was only a matter of time before quilt artists, as well as forward-thinking museum curators, would stride into the art world on the coattails of collage and fiber art—often under the aegis of "craft."

*Fabric Collage*, mounted in the spring of 1965 at the Museum of Contemporary Crafts in New York, had three sections: contemporary hangings, American quilts (all from the nineteenth century), and appliqués (molas, in reverse appliqué) from the San Blas islands of Panama, along with a catalog containing black-and-white illustrations. The contemporary hangings (including quilt-like objects) were by Alma Lesch, Marilyn Pappas, and others. All five works by Lesch and three by Pappas incorporated actual items of clothing, materials that later would appear in quilt art by other artists. In his introduction, curator Paul Smith stated, "The expressive possibilities of fabric—the seemingly endless variety of textures, colors, and tactile sensations—that we see in contemporary collage—parallel the innovations in contemporary art, particularly assemblage."[2]

Visitors to the show, who might have been expecting to see pleasant imagery of flowers and birds in the mola pieces, instead were presented with subjects more appropriate for Pop Art: cigarettes, Superman, and rockets, all executed in textiles. Quilters saw that a traditional folk medium could be subverted and transformed.

In the planning stages from 1966, a show titled *Wall Hangings* had a whirlwind tour of 11 cities in 1968, arriving in 1969 at the Museum of Modern Art (MoMA). There, it was installed, at curator Mildred Constantine's insistence, in the museum's first floor special exhibition galleries, rather than in the Department of Architecture and Design on a higher level in the building. *Wall Hangings* presented mostly woven works spotlighting "a new art form—not traditional flat tapestries, nor were they necessarily sculptural and dimensional, but they were new and bold."[3] This collection, installed on the ground floor, had excellent public exposure. Patricia Malarcher is among the quilt artists who consider this exhibition as a memorable experience.

Analogies can be seen between "developments in weaving [that] have caused us to revise our concepts of this craft and to view the work within the context of 20th-century art . . . "[4] and shifts in visual culture that caused quilts to be viewed by some as contemporary art by the early 1970s. Not the least of these was the extensive involvement of women as artists in both weaving and quiltmaking.

The now famous 1971 exhibition in New York City at the Whitney Museum of American Art, *Abstract Design in American Quilts (ADAQ)*, consisted of 61 antique pieces—including one quilt by an Amish maker—from the Jonathan Holstein and Gail van der Hoof collection. The expressive power of quilts on the white walls of a hallowed museum was an eye-opener for many visitors. Hilton Kramer, art critic for *The New York Times*, wrote in his review,

> The suspicion persists that the most authentic visual articulation of the American imagination in the last century is to be found in the so-called 'minor' arts–especially in the visual crafts that had their

---

[2] Paul J. Smith, *Fabric Collage* (New York: American Craftsmen's Council, Museum of Contemporary Crafts, 1965), 3.

[3] Jack Lenor Larsen, interview by Arline M. Fisch, Archives of American Art, and Smithsonian Institution, 6-8 February, 2004, aaa.si.edu/collections/interviews/oral-history-interview-jack-lenor-larsen13092#transcript.

[4] Mildred Constantine and Jack Lenor Larsen, *Wall Hangings* (New York: The Museum of Modern Art, 1969), np.

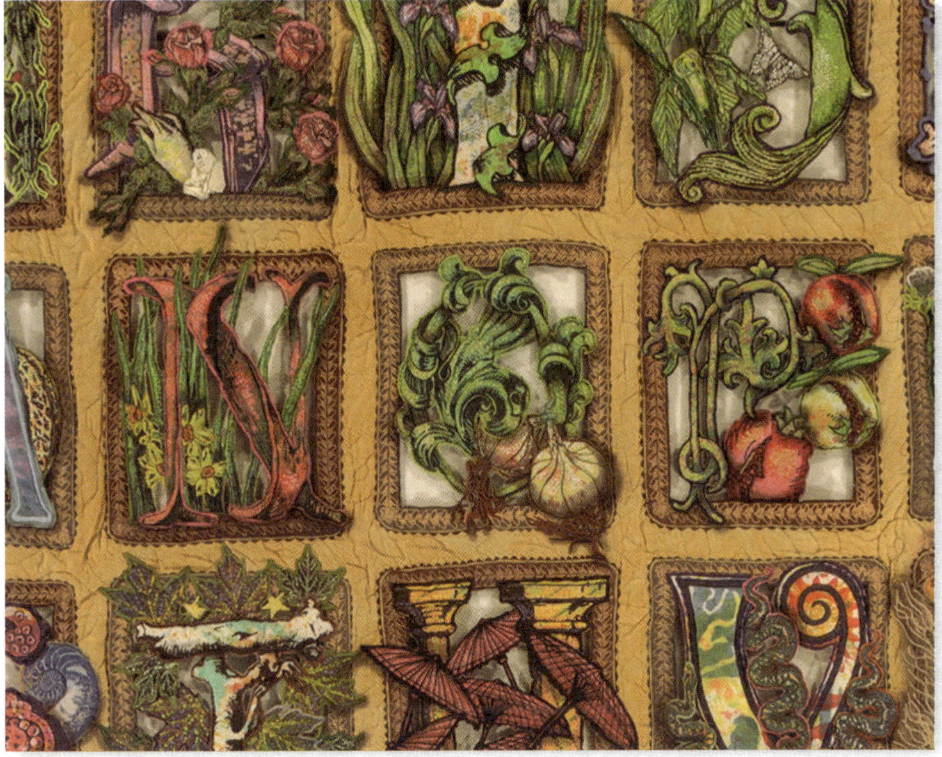

Detail from *A Riddling Tale* by M. Joan Lintault (See page 143, Plate 65)

> origins in the workaday functions of regional life. … For a century or more preceding the self-conscious invention of pictorial abstraction in European painting, the anonymous quilt makers of the American provinces created a remarkable succession of visual masterpieces that anticipated many of the forms that were later prized for their originality …[5]



The title of his review is "Art: Quilts Find a Place at the Whitney." Kramer's review closed with just a mention of another exhibition in the Whitney at the same time: "Also on view at the Whitney just now is a very pleasant show of prints by John Sloan, marking the 100th anniversary of the artist's birth."[6] Clearly, the antique quilts had captured his imagination.

The original exhibition traveled to three other art museums in the US after the Whitney and, in 1973 and 1974, the Smithsonian traveled selections from the exhibition to 21 venues in the United States. Holstein and van der Hoof created other similar exhibitions that traveled to four European countries in 1972, for which a separate catalog was printed. Sylvia Einstein, who later became a quilt artist, saw the exhibition in Switzerland, commenting that it was unlike anything she had ever seen. Among the artists with a new appreciation of quilts in a museum setting after visiting the exhibition were Michael Cummings, Radka Donnell, Beth Gutcheon, Marilyn Henrion, Joan Lintault, Paula Nadelstern, and Robin Schwalb (most of whom are represented in the International Quilt Museum exhibition this essay accompanies).

---

[5] Hilton Kramer, "Art: Quilts Find a Place at the Whitney," *The New York Times*, July 3, 1971, nytimes.com/1971/07/03/archives/art-quilts-find-a-place-at-the-whitney.html.
[6] Kramer.

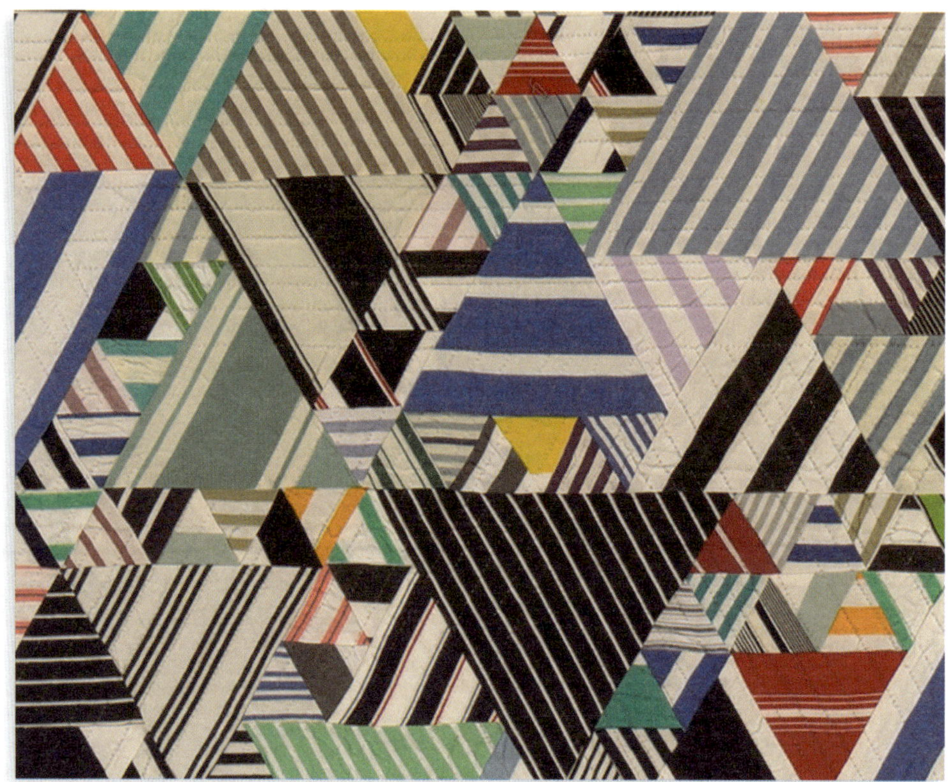

Detail from *Brighton Beach Memories* by Marilyn Henrion (See page 144, Plate 66)

The expressive power of Amish quilts was reinforced for artists in New York in 1973 by the first major gallery show of these works at the Schoellkopf gallery uptown on Madison Avenue, which specialized in American antiques and folk art. Rita Reif wrote a spectacular review for *The New York Times*, remarking that "unexpectedly, there is a passionate intensity, a play of vibrant color and a subtle wit that characterizes most of the 50 coverlets."[7] (The two young collectors curating the Whitney show had by 1972 acquired a significant number of Amish quilts, which they began to include in all of their later quilt exhibitions.) She also referred to the 1971 Whitney show as "the event that triggered widespread quilt collecting in this country," praising the exhibition's catalog as "a gem of a small, recently published volume (Viking, $5.95)."[8] Artists who could not see the quilts firsthand in an exhibition could experience them via this book and in subsequent catalogs, including foreign publications.

Also in 1973, the Museum of Contemporary Crafts in New York mounted *Sewn, Stitched & Stuffed*, with works created after 1969. Sandra Zimmerman, a noted gallerist in New York City, curated the exhibition. Artists included Lenore Davis and Joan Lintault, both of them becoming known during the early 1970s for their studio quilts, and Patricia Oleszko, whose use of zany humor in fiber art was notably original at the time. Quilting was among the techniques listed for several of the works. In her introduction to the catalog, Zimmerman emphasized the mixed-media nature of the art:

> Several techniques are often combined in the same work. Quilting, trapunto, and other types of sectional padding are used with

---

[7] Rita Reif, "Antiques: Amish Quilts Abound," *The New York Times*, July 14, 1973, nytimes.com/1973/07/14/archives/antiques-amish-quilts-abound-vibrant-color-and-wit-mark-patchworks.html.
[8] Reif.

> great innovation. Embroidery, appliqué, and stitchery are used as decoration and also become an integral part of the form and design of the work. Processes not usually associated with fabric, such as etching, photo silkscreen, watercolors, and blueprint photography on cloth are used here to enrich and expand the artist's statement.[9]

Her championing of this sort of work was prescient in that much of the quilt art of the latter 1970s and early 1980s featured mixed media, with several influential artists working in surface design processes and techniques.

Because the 1969 *Wall Hangings* catalog was rather brief, New York designer Jack Lenor Larsen and the MoMA curator with whom he was still working, Mildred Constantine, produced a book in 1973 titled *Beyond Craft: The Art Fabric* that caused a considerable stir in the press and led to a second show. The show opened at the San Francisco Museum of Art in 1981. *Beyond Craft: The Art Fabric* celebrated the "new freedom" being experienced by fiber artists—"the freedom to choose an aesthetic over a utilitarian need."[10] Although the exhibition consisted exclusively of fiber art along with textile art in the form of weaving, the same comment about aesthetics could be said of contemporary quilt art—especially by 1981.

In 1976, an exhibition titled *The New American Quilt* premiered in New York at the Museum of Contemporary Crafts, and I would have to say that this show gave *me* the courage to try new things in my own quilts, which mostly had followed traditional patterns up to that point, in step with my Appalachian heritage. Not only did this exhibition tour the country, it also had a provocative review by renowned art critic Lisa Hammel in *The New York Times*, describing how these quilt makers were "stretching the limits of the folk idiom through new processes and new techniques, new images and new ideas, until they have come out at the other end with something totally individual—the quilt transcendent."[11] Another reviewer coined the term "new-directions quilters," which (luckily) did not stick.[12]



Experimental quilters across the country were astonished by the exhibition, the first in a major museum to show contemporary, non-traditional quilts exclusively. Some of these makers actually had work *in* the exhibition, including Radka Donnell, Joan Lintault, Wenda von Weise, and Katherine Westphal.

The 1976 Great Quilt Contest, celebrating the US Bicentennial, was co-sponsored by the Museum of American Folk Art in New York. The 51 quilts selected out of more than 10,000 submitted ran the gamut of quilt styles, from stunning traditional pieced examples to avant-garde work. Nancy Erickson says that she first saw the possibilities of quilts as contemporary art after viewing the exhibition. It caused her to leave soft sculpture as her art medium and begin making quilts for the wall, or "flatties" as she called them. Teresa Barkley, whose *Denim Quilt* was in the show, said that it was her first piece that she considered a successful work of art. Embroidery designer and expert needleworker Erica Wilson's 1979 book *Quilts of America* documenting the exhibition caught the eye of many fledgling studio quilt artists across the country.

---

[9] Sandra R. Zimmerman, *Sewn, Stitched & Stuffed* (New York: American Crafts Council, Museum of Contemporary Crafts, 1973), 2.

[10] Mildred Constantine and Jack Lenor Larsen, *Beyond Craft: The Art Fabric* (New York: Kodansha International, 1986), 8.

[11] Lisa Hammel, "Quilts: A Folk Idiom That Has Come of Age," *The New York Times*, April 9, 1976, nytimes.com/1976/04/09/archives/quilts-a-folk-idiom-that-has-come-of-age.html.

[12] Jean Libman Block, "A Quilt Is Built," *Craft Horizons*, 1976, 31.

Returning to the beginning of this pivotal decade, in 1971, museums in New York had just gone through a year of extreme turmoil, beginning with a massive protest: the New York Artists' Strike Against Racism, Sexism, Repression, and War. The Vietnam War was very much in the news, racist repression continued in spite of the Civil Rights Movement, and the Women's Liberation Movement had definitely arrived. Artists withdrew their works from exhibitions, demonstrating inside and outside of arts institutions, with some 500 artists staging a sit-in on the steps of the Met. The Whitney had been especially targeted for its "whiteness" and "maleness," with activist artist Faith Ringgold leading some of the loudest protests during the 1969 Whitney Painting Biennial.

Then in 1971, the Whitney's exhibition *Contemporary Black Artists in America 1969–1971,* directed by a white curator, Robert "Mac" Doty, resulted in a media firestorm. The museum was trenchantly criticized for not involving Black curators and other people of color, and 15 of the 75 artists withdrew their works and put them on display elsewhere.[13] Whatever the state of mind of Doty while all this transpired, we might assume that he, as well as the Whitney administration, were looking in the spring of 1971 for an exhibition that might elicit somewhat better reactions from artists and the press—or at least nothing like the vehemence they had just experienced with the exhibition that closed in May.

The offer of an antique quilt exhibition that had the added attraction of remarkably expressive surfaces must have seemed like a godsend to Doty. Jonathan Holstein's meeting with Doty to propose a quilt exhibition happened in the midst of the virulent reviews condemning the Whitney in April of 1971. Although it turned out that some critics can't keep themselves from complaining, for the most part the quilt exhibition that opened in July was a stunningly redemptive success.

To contextualize *Abstract Design in American Quilts* within the Manhattan art scene at the time, one must consider what else was on view in major museums during the spring and summer of 1971. This helps to appreciate how startling it was to have antique quilts on display in the Whitney—and perhaps why arts reviewers became so excited about the exhibition.

Back in the 1970s, summer was viewed as the "down" season for museums and galleries in New York, when the glitterati left to spend the summer in beach houses or in the mountains, and tourists swooped into the city. Most museums pulled together exhibitions from their own collections. The art scene then was quite different from today, when museums are enticing visitors throughout the year via social media, offering an endless series of events.

During the spring and summer of 1971, the New York Cultural Center was displaying a half-scale photographic reproduction in color of Diego Rivera's monumental mural in the Hotel del Prado, Mexico City; photographs of Israel were on view at the Jewish Museum; the Museum of Contemporary Crafts was exhibiting tubular weavings by Jean Stamsta; visitors could learn a lot about Florentine painting and medieval ecclesiastical vestments at the Met; and the Museum of Modern Art gathered works, mostly about war, from its own collection by more than 140 artists to mount *The Artist as Adversary*. The Guggenheim, like the Whitney, found itself embroiled in a political controversy after the museum abruptly cancelled a Hans Haacke exhibition

---

[13] Grace Glueck, "15 of 75 Black Artists Leave As Whitney Exhibition Opens," *The New York Times*, April 6, 1971, nytimes.com/1971/04/06/archives/15-of-75-black-artists-leave-as-whitney-exhibition-opens.html.

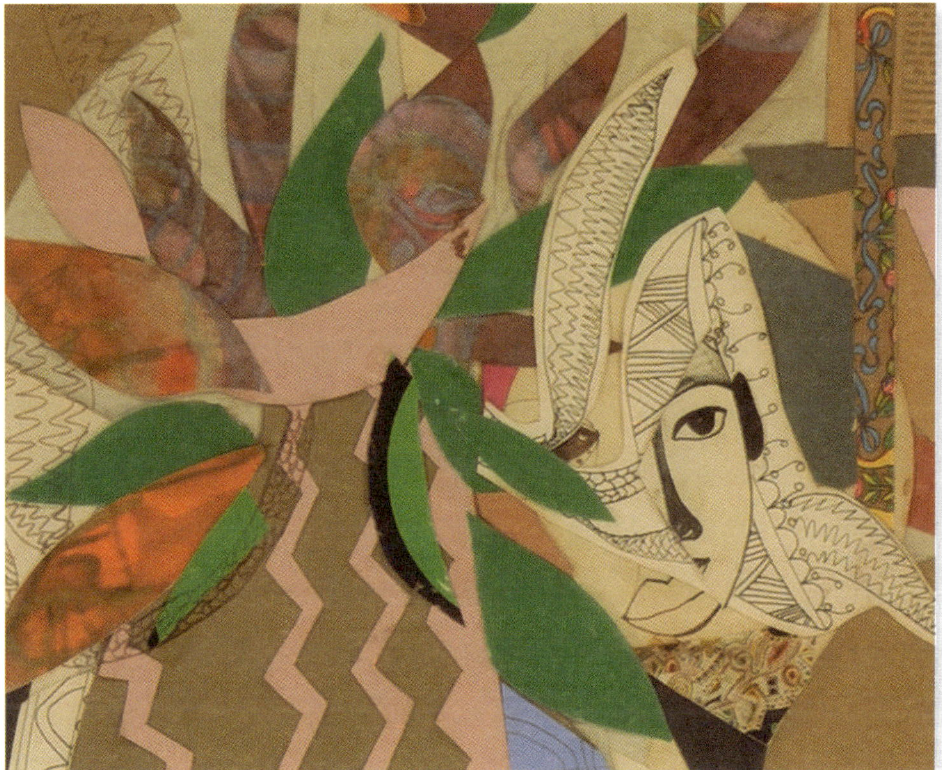

Detail from *Reflections* by Michael A. Cummings (See page 140, Plate 62)

scheduled to open in late April. Instead, the staff scrambled to create an exhibition titled *Collection and Acquisition 1971*, a sort of hodge-podge dating from post-Impressionism to the present.



On view at the Whitney in the spring of 1971 was a retrospective exhibition of pieces by Andy Warhol, including his cow wallpaper, in the very space where *ADAQ* would premier in early July. Art historian Barbara Rose in her *New York Magazine* review commented that the wallpaper made the museum look like a boutique. No one wrote that *ADAQ* made the museum look like a bedroom. A few weeks before the quilt exhibition opened, *Structure of Color 1969–1971* closed at the Whitney. In contrast with the extravagant praise of color in *ADAQ*, the general consensus about *Structure of Color* was that "the experience is rather like eating a large dish of sherbert—refreshing at first, and finally rather cloying."[14]

In her column "Art Notes" published in the July 4, 1971, edition of *The New York Times*, Grace Glueck summarized the main exhibitions being offered for the summer season, adding, "by way of lagniappe, there is also 'Abstract Designs [sic] in American Quilts,' a collection of some 60 'pieced' quilts, mostly 19th-century, acquired by two young collectors … ."[15] The word "lagniappe" is defined as "a little something extra, a bonus gift." Little did the Whitney realize the gift that the museum gave the world with their quilt exhibition.

---

[14] Hilton Kramer, "Miscellany Caps 'Structure of Color' Show," *The New York Times*, February 26, 1971, nytimes.com/1971/02/26/archives/miscellany-caps-structure-of-color-show.html.

[15] Grace Glueck, "Art Notes," *The New York Times*, July 4, 1971, nytimes.com/1971/07/04/archives/new-york-is-a-summer-art-fair.html.

# RAISING THE PROFILE

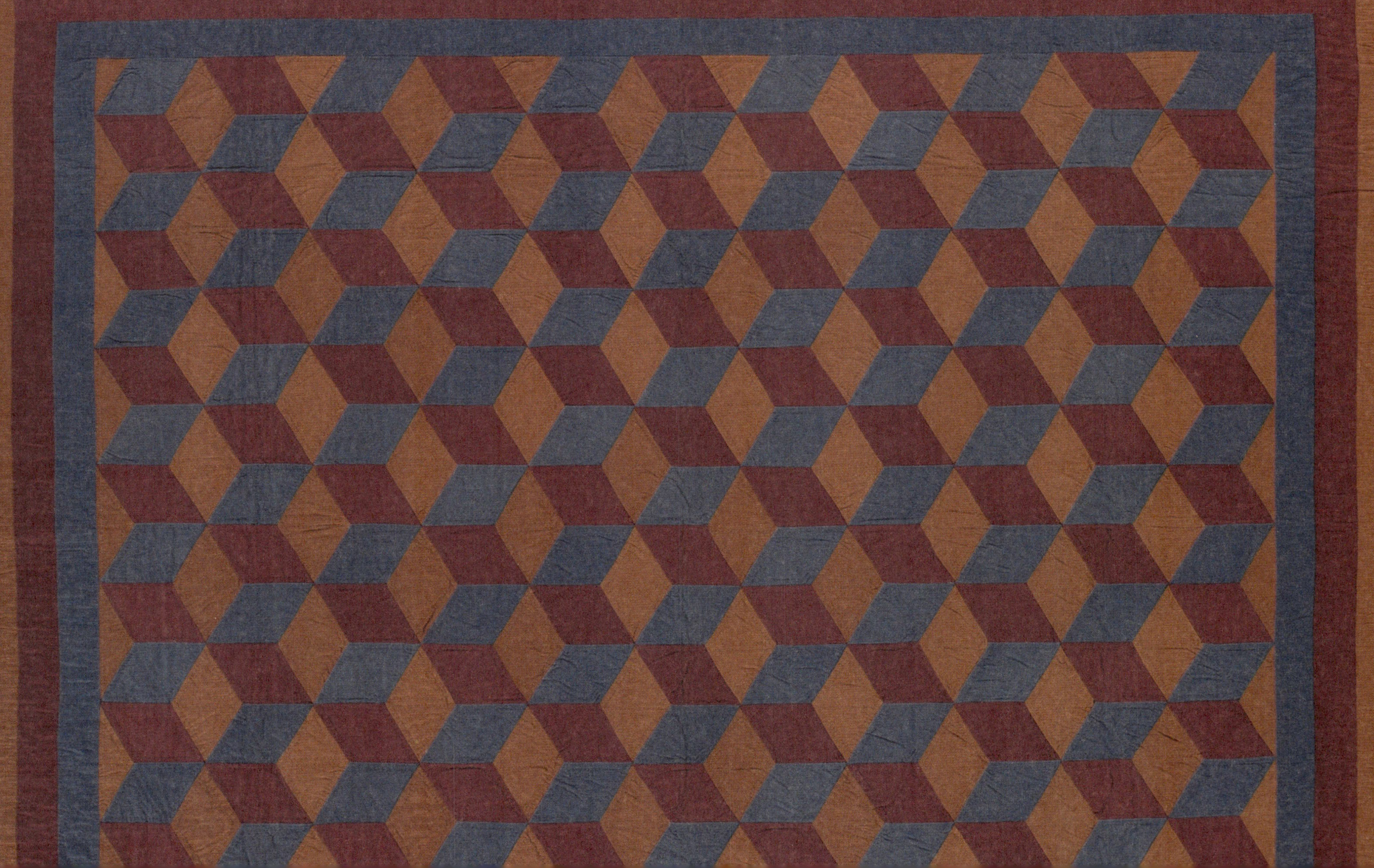

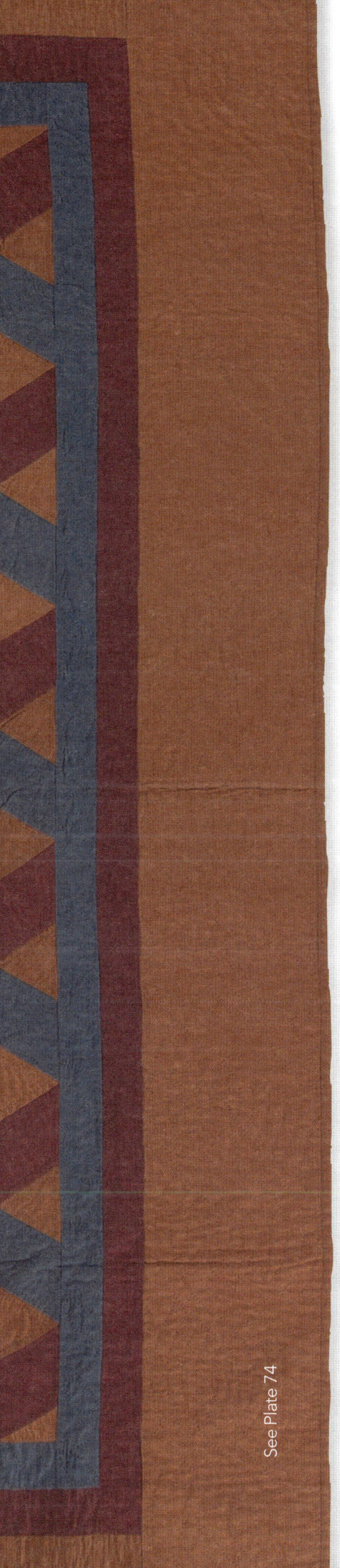

See Plate 74

# JONATHAN GREGORY

In 1973, Sally Garoutte, a co-curator with Joyce Gross of *Patch in Time*, an important exhibition in the West Coast quilt revival of the early 1970s,[1] wrote about a new profile for quilts:

> . . . there is beginning to be a fashionable movement connected with quilts, so that patchwork is not quite so "mere" as before. Now antique quilts, which can no longer be used, are being collected and shown in galleries "because of the way they work as paintings" (!) according to collector Jonathan Holstein.[2]

Holstein and his partner Gail van der Hoof's exhibition *Abstract Design in American Quilts (ADAQ)* at the Whitney Museum of American Art was one of the phenomena that raised the profile of quilts within American culture, where patchwork quilting traditions had flourished for at least 150 years. Garoutte continues:

> Quiltmaking is presently in an uneasy period of transition. There is a serious question whether this craft will turn into an art form and become functionally obsolete. There is a serious question as to what women themselves will do, in this age of search for liberation, with this craft. Will we try to "upgrade" it to an art form? Or will we be able to say that our work is as beautiful in use as it is in a gallery? [3]

We know, 50 years on, that quilts have evolved into an art form and also have persevered as beautiful and useful objects. But for Garoutte and anyone living at the time, the art museum was a relatively new space in which to view quilts, and exhibiting them in such a venue raised questions about quilts' future evolution.[4] This brief essay

---

1 Robin L. Rushbrook, "Sally Garoutte," The Quilters Hall of Fame, accessed July 29, 2020, quiltershalloffame.net/sally-garoutte/.

2 Sally Garoutte, "A Missing Patch in Time," *Quilter's Newsletter*, March 1973, 8–9.

3 Garoutte, 8–9.

4 Quiltmakers working in the first half of the twentieth century who had received art or design training, such as Bertha Stenge, Bertha Meckstroth, and Rose Kretsinger, applied their training self-consciously to create original and carefully designed and executed quilts. They might have displayed their quilts as art in art museums if the opportunity had been available to them. But as those not working in painting or sculpture those opportunities were meager, particularly for women.

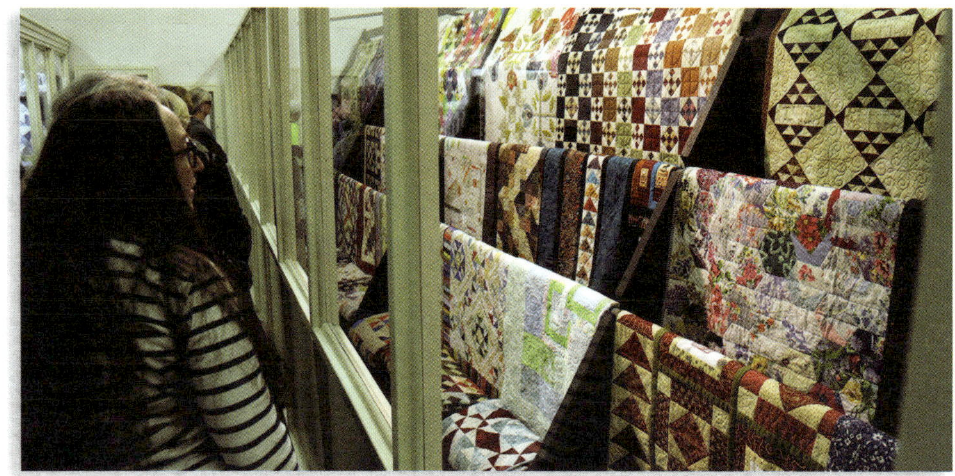

Quilts on view at the Creative Activities Building, Minnesota State Fair, Falcon Heights, Minnesota, 2018. Women were first invited to enter domestic products at agricultural fairs in the early 1800s. Quilts continue to be staples of Women's and Creative Arts divisions of state fairs today. *Courtesy of American Craft Council. Photograph by Bailey Aaland.*





cannot trace all the ways that an interpretation of quilts as art have influenced developments in quiltmaking of the last 50 years. It will, however, shed light on how quiltmakers and others responded to the raised profile of antique quilts and contemporary quilts made by DIY makers. The responses are evident in the realms of quilt display, engagement in quilt-related commerce, recognition of quiltmaking as an art form deeply connected to women's lives, and documentation and preservation of the history of quilts and quiltmaking.

## DISPLAY

When quiltmakers saw quilts on the walls of art museums, instead of in the halls of local or state agricultural fairs, they glimpsed a new space into which they could venture.[5] Garoutte noted that the bulk of the recent (1970s) quiltmaking activity—much of it only indirectly influenced by *ADAQ*—was a continuation of the long and evolving North American quiltmaking tradition. Throughout much of the region's quilt history, county and state fairs were a primary venue for display of citizens' agricultural and domestic production. These fairs also incorporated a process for assessing the aesthetics of the everyday object through evaluation by local judges.[6] Michael Marsden describes the process as,

> . . . not one of trying to achieve perfection, but rather one of trying to understand and apply the generally accepted standards by which to function well within a community. Yet within the frame of community standards, there is a spark of individuality that refuses to be sublimated and which, in turn, fuels interest and excitement.[7]

---

[5] There are exceptions. Quilts had been seen before in history museums, historic house museums, and museums of the decorative arts such as the Shelburne Museum and the Winterthur Museum. The Newark Museum, an institution of art, decorative art, and natural science installed *Quilts and Counterpanes in the Newark Museum* in 1948, and in 1965 mounted an exhibition that showed quilts' relationship to painting. (See Margaret E. White, *Quilts and Counterpanes in the Newark Museum*, Newark, New Jersey: The Newark Museum, 1948.) The Metropolitan Museum of Art in New York added to its quilt collection throughout the twentieth century.

[6] Greta Pratt and Karal Ann Marling, "Fairs: A Fixed Point on the Turning Wheel of Time," *American Art* 7, no. 2 (April 1, 1993): 24.

[7] Michael T. Marsden, "The County Fair as Celebration and Cultural Text," *Journal of American Culture* 33, no. 1 (March 2010): 27.

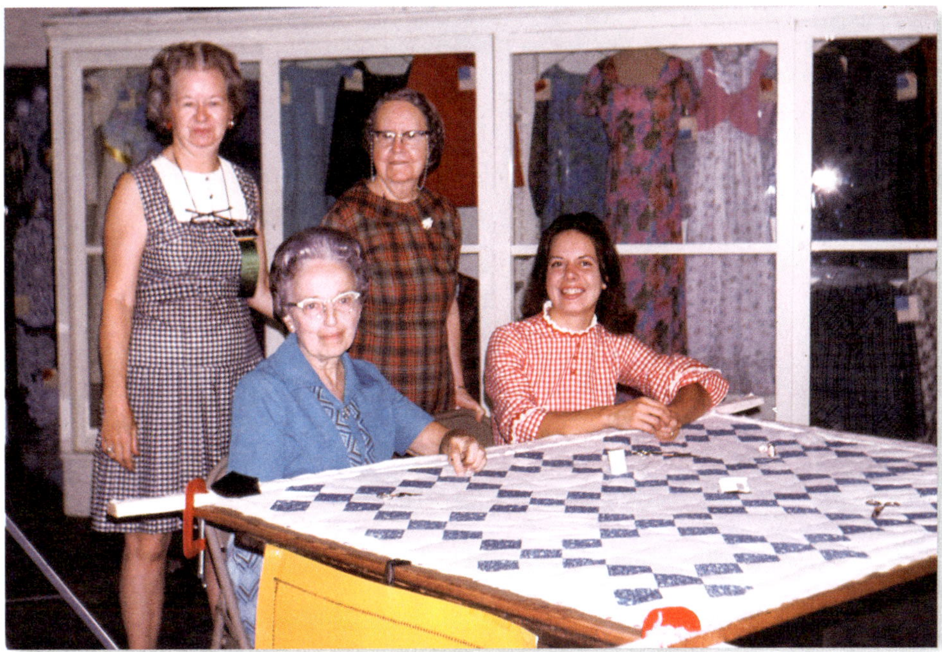

Quilting Demonstration, Nebraska State Fair, Lincoln Quilters Guild, Lincoln, Nebraska, circa 1970–75. "Old Tyme" quilting demonstrations at fairs and festivals began at least by the American Civil War. These women carried on the tradition at the Nebraska State Fair in the early 1970s. As art museums more frequently exhibited quilts in the 1970s and beyond, groups of quiltmakers readily accepted opportunities to demonstrate their traditional knowledge before the gaze of new audiences. Clockwise from upper left: Louise Howey, Isabelle Haight, Miriam Heacock, Unidentified. *Mary Ghormley, Quilt Papers, Archives & Special Collections, University of Nebraska-Lincoln.*



In these ways, as Marsden explains, the aesthetic standards of a community are developed and in some cases resisted.[8] Church quilting circles, family networks, and quilt clubs also provided a similar mechanism for sharing, displaying, and affirming innovation.

One movement of quiltmakers into the intersectional space between fine art and folk art/craft occurred at the Renwick Gallery in Washington, DC—the home of the Smithsonian American Art Museum's contemporary craft exhibitions—where the Holstein/van der Hoof Collection was installed from October 14, 1972, through January 9, 1973. During that period, the Renwick arranged 23 quilting demonstrations performed by individual quilters and members of quiltmaking groups in the Capital region.[9] These demonstrations were of enough consequence that *Quilter's Newsletter*, at the time North America's only quilt-specific periodical, founded in 1969, listed the dates and the names of quiltmakers and quiltmaking groups and the patterns of the quilts they were hand quilting in the gallery.

One of the Virginia women who demonstrated quilting at the Renwick, Hazel Carter, recalled the jolt of witnessing quilts displayed as artworks in a museum on the day she was there to quilt.

> I still remember stepping into the first room of quilts at the Renwick. The lights were not bright and each quilt had its own space. I stood

[8] Marsden, 27.

[9] Jonathan Holstein, *Abstract Design in American Quilts: A Biography of an Exhibition* (Louisville, KY: Kentucky Quilt Project, 1991), 76.

still and allowed my eyes to take in each quilt. I was overwhelmed! I had grown up with quilts; my mother and grandmother were great quilters. And at the time of the Renwick exhibit I had seen exhibits in other venues, but absolutely not in a museum setting ... I knew that I had to walk away from the exhibit area, quilt for a while, giving time to absorb what I had just observed ... Before leaving for the day, I took another look in the exhibit area. It took my breath away again. This was a whole new experience for me.[10]

A farther flung example demonstrates the penetration of quilts into a merged fine art/folk art space in cities far from the nation's cultural centers on the coasts. Mary Ghormley of Lincoln, Nebraska, had been a quiltmaker and antique quilt collector since the mid-1960s. She began holding quilt classes in her home in the early 1970s and with three other women organized the Lincoln Quilters Guild (LQG) in March 1973.[11] In July 1973, Ghormley attended the Smithsonian Institution's traveling exhibition of Holstein and van der Hoof's quilts, *The American Pieced Quilt*, at the University of Iowa Museum of Art in Iowa City. Inspired by seeing quilts hung in an academic art museum, Ghormley and the LQG convinced the Sheldon Art Gallery (now the Sheldon Museum of Art) at the University of Nebraska to host a quilt exhibition. The Sheldon vetted nearly 300 quilts for the exhibition, all from Nebraska museums or individual owners and makers. Those included, made in the 1840s through the 1970s, " ... were selected solely on their merits as works of art."[12] In the fall of 1974, the exhibition, *Quilts from Nebraska Collections*, set a new attendance record for the Gallery.[13]

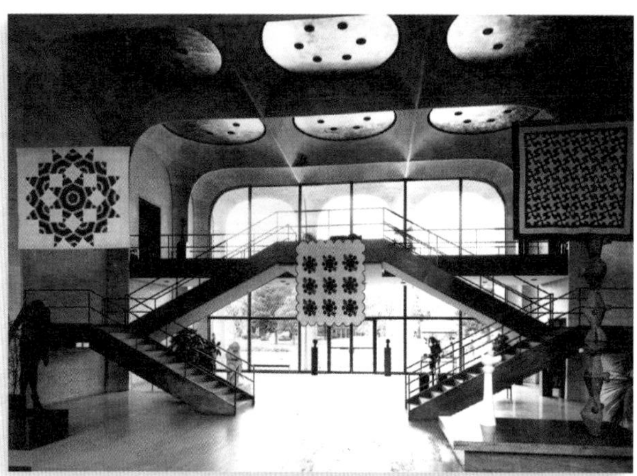

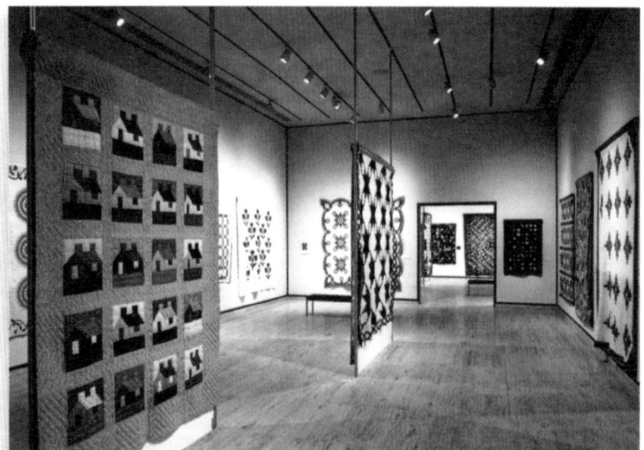

*Quilts from Nebraska Collections*, Sheldon Memorial Art Gallery, Lincoln, Nebraska, 1974. *Images courtesy of the Sheldon Museum of Art, University of Nebraska-Lincoln.*



---

[10] Hazel Carter, email to the author, September 30, 2020. Carter founded the Continental Quilting Congress in 1978 in Arlington, Virginia, an internationally attended convention that promoted the quilt as an art form. At the next year's Congress she established the Quilters Hall of Fame. Carter writes, "It had become apparent at the first convention that quilters were ignoring our quilting heritage. In 1979, we inducted six individuals to recognize 'their accomplishments, and thereby to establish documentation of a part of quilting history.'" See also "About" page, Quilters Hall of Fame website, quiltershalloffame.net/about-2/, accessed October 8, 2020.

[11] "About the Guild: History," Lincoln Quilters Guild, accessed July 19, 2020, lincolnquiltersguild.org/about/.

[12] *Quilts from Nebraska Collections: An Exhibition Presented in Collaboration with The Lincoln Quilters Guild* (exhibition catalog), Lincoln Nebraska: Sheldon Memorial Art Gallery, 1973.

[13] Mary Ghormley, Treasures of the Lincoln Quilters Guild, interview by The Corny Bunch, 1996.; Pat Hackley, interview by Jonathan Gregory, July 26, 2020.

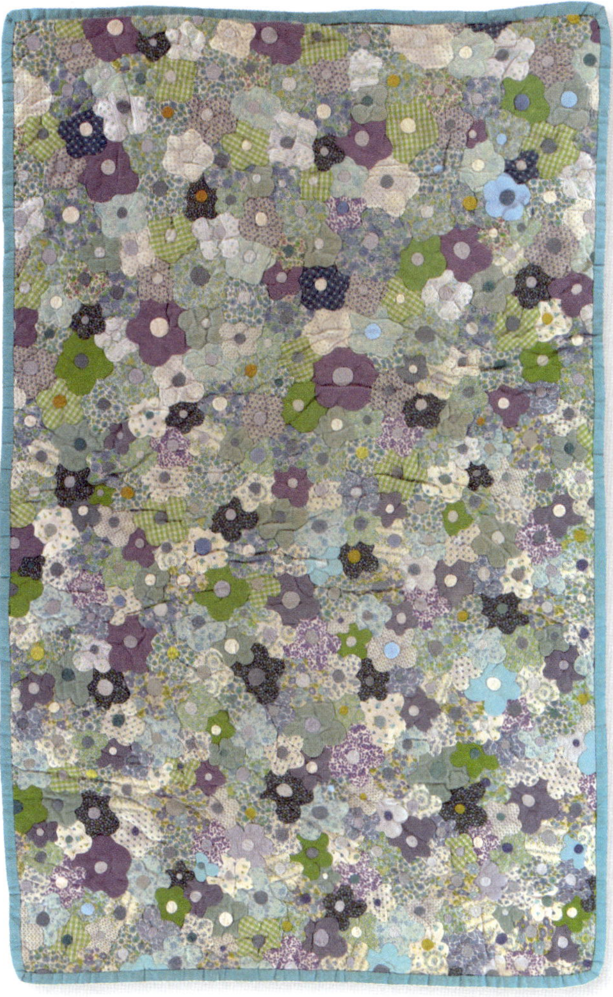

*Blue-Eyed Susans*, Margery Irvin, Lincoln, Nebraska, 1973, 92.5 x 58.5 in., collection of Susan Dinsmore. Irvin made this quilt for her daughter, Susan, reflecting the "flower power" look of the 1960s and '70s. It hung in *Quilts from Nebraska Collections* at the Sheldon Memorial Art Gallery in 1974.

## COMMERCE & COLLECTING

Bonnie Leman, editor of *Quilter's Newsletter*, begins an article on New York City antique dealers Kate and Joel Kopp in May 1972 by writing, "Thanks to a lot of publicity given to quilt shows and quilt-makers during the last year or two, quilts have become a hot item among dealers and collectors."[14] The attention Leman references includes *ADAQ* at the Whitney, other US and major European museums, and quilt-focused articles in national magazines.[15] The Kopps opened America Hurrah Antiques in Manhattan's Upper East Side in the late 1960s. They offered antique quilts, tops, and blocks from the day they opened. Leman quotes Kate Kopp in the article: "When you buy a good, old quilt you're getting a legitimate piece of 19th century art—and for $100 that's a steal."[16] Quilt historian Nancy Bavor emphasizes the importance of antique quilt dealers, particularly those in Manhattan: "New York dealers set trends, received lots of publicity and sold many of the most important quilts. But more significantly, they promoted the quilt as art."[17]

The market wasn't limited to antique quilts, however. When the Renwick hosted *ADAQ*, women from a Galax, Virginia, quilting group demonstrated quilting in the gallery and sold quilts in the gift shop.[18] The quilters and the Renwick both recognized the commercial opportunity created by having quilts hang in a national museum. So did



[14] Bonnie Leman, "America Hurrah," *Quilter's Newsletter*, May 1972, 9.
[15] Quilts were featured in national magazines with increasing frequency in the late 1960s. Examples include: "A Very Now Nostalgia," *American Home*, November 1969; Lois Bohlig and Richard Fitzgerald, "Patchwork Quilting Coming into Colorful Renaissance," *House Beautiful*, December 1968.
[16] Leman, "America Hurrah," 9.
[17] Nancy Bavor, "Knockers, Pickers, Movers, and Shakers: Quilt Dealers in America, 1970–2000," *Uncoverings* 35 (2014): 21, search.ebscohost.com/login.aspx?direct=true&profile=ehost&scope=site&authtype=crawler&jrnl=02770628&AN=110197726&h=dSotcTDSPO4l0ZZ5DqntcmCRtxx0miDSvdMhFuqzglTRVIXKB3SxKs7PG%2FElnmcJhAoVupmWWqcb%2FmPIX0hMAg%3D%3D&crl=c.
[18] Mary Ann Hedrick, "Galax Quilters Are a Capital Success," *RKE Times*, October 17, 1972.

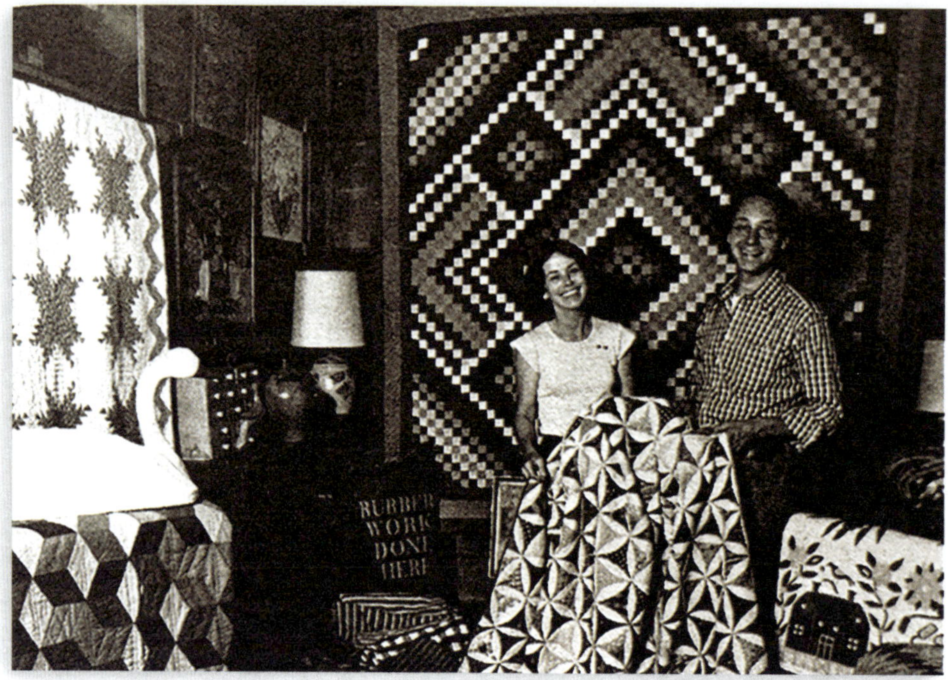


Kate and Joel Kopp at America Hurrah Antiques, Manhattan, New York, circa 1970–75. Because New York City was the cultural and business center of the country, dealers there, such as the Kopps and others, were most influential in raising the profile of quilts as art to collectors in the early 1970s. *Image courtesy of Kate and Joel Kopp.*

other quiltmakers whose communities possessed generations-long quilting traditions. The Freedom Quilting Bee, for example, a cooperative founded in 1966 by Black women in rural Alabama, sold quilts to famed New York decorator Sister Parrish for use in decorating her clients' homes. *Vogue* editor Diana Vreeland promoted its work in her influential fashion magazine. High-end department stores such as Bloomingdale's and Saks Fifth Avenue bought the cooperative's quilts for resale, and *The New York Times* covered the group and generated public interest in the women and their work.[19]

## QUILTS IN WOMEN'S LIVES

Visitors to the Whitney's *Abstract Design in American Quilts* did not find maker names on gallery labels. Very few of the quilts Holstein and van der Hoof found came with their histories. Additionally, their curatorial focus was on the quilts' powerful visual properties, which they felt had parallels to modern abstract art, and not their historical or social contexts. As has been noted elsewhere in this catalog, the quilts' aesthetic vigor convinced viewers and reviewers that the curatorial thesis was valid. *ADAQ*'s tour of major US and European museums as well as the Smithsonian's traveling exhibition *The American Pieced Quilt* to 21 US cities, and the widespread media coverage of quilts as art heightened their cultural profile and created space for a counter-message: quilts are documents that reveal the stories of women's lives.

Years earlier, Jean Ray Laury—a prolific author and a needlework contributor to *House Beautiful* and *Woman's Day*—had already opened the door to considering quilts from a variety of woman-centered perspectives. Laury made her first quilt in 1956 as a master's degree project in the fine art program at Stanford University. Called *Tom's Quilt* after her young son, she included the everyday objects of childhood that

---

[19] Nancy Callahan, "Freedom Quilting Bee," Encyclopedia of Alabama, August 8, 2008, encyclopediaofalabama.org/article/h-1628.

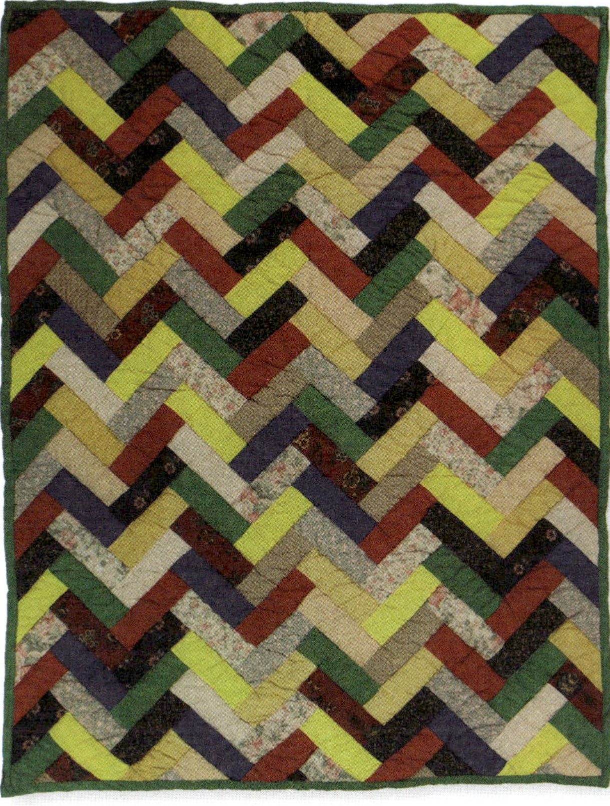

*Coat of Many Colors*, Lillie Major and Essie Young, Freedom Quilting Bee, Alberta, Alabama, circa 1980–1989, 49.25 x 39 in. *Gift of Pauline Woods and Amy Hislop, IQM 2010.040.0001*. The Freedom Quilting Bee cooperative emerged from the Civil Rights Movement in Wilcox County, Alabama, in 1966. The members' quilts were often traditional folk patterns, with variations dictated mostly by the materials at hand.

reflected his curiosity and interests. In her writing, Laury affirmed women's freedom to claim time and resources to express themselves creatively through art, whether they had chosen traditional roles as wives and mothers or as pursuers of a career or other non-domestic engagement. As the sociologist Colleen Hall-Patton writes, Laury, ". . . connected the concerns of everyday life with 'humble' materials and the 'simplicity, honesty, and direct freshness' found in Early American quilts and coverlets."[20] Later, when *ADAQ* ignited a debate about quilts' status as art, Laury had already made a space for women to both embrace the historical significance of quilts in women's lives and to creatively express their contemporary experience.[21]

In the years following the Whitney exhibition, critics and curators responded to what they saw as *ADAQ*'s decontextualization of quilts. One of the most vocal detractors, Patricia Mainardi, a feminist artist and art historian, penned a defense of quilts as women's art and included a critique aimed at Jonathan Holstein and *ADAQ* for using women's art to prop up male painting.[22] Other quilt collectors and enthusiasts rejected the exclusively visual *ADAQ* approach in favor of interpreting quilts through the lens of women's lived experience, from, as historian Janneken Smucker describes it, ". . . a social perspective of the relationship between object, maker, and user."[23] For example, Patricia Cooper and Norma Bradley Buferd saw *ADAQ* in New York City in 1971 and, ". . . recognized that the show signaled a renewed interest in quilts, especially quilts as an art form."[24] In 1972, they began collecting quilts from women in Texas and New Mexico for their own exhibition project. Through the process, as they explain,



[20] Jean Ray Laury, *Appliqué Stitchery*, (New York: Reinhold Publishing Co., 1966), 95, quoted in Colleen Hall-Patton, "Jean Ray Laury in the 1960s: Foremother of a Quilt Revival," *Uncoverings 2005*, 2005, 77.
[21] See Jean Ray Laury, *Quilts and Coverlets* (Van Nostrand Reinhold Company, 1970).
[22] See Carolyn Ducey's essay, "Abstract Design in American Quilts: Looking Forward," in this volume.
[23] Janneken Smucker, *Amish Quilts: Crafting an American Icon* (Johns Hopkins University Press, 2013). Smucker provides an engaging review of the 1970s debates involving differing interpretations of folk art, including quilts, from aesthetic, sociological, and feminist perspectives.
[24] P. Cooper and N. Buferd, *The Quilters: Women and Domestic Art*, Anchor (Doubleday, 1978), 15.

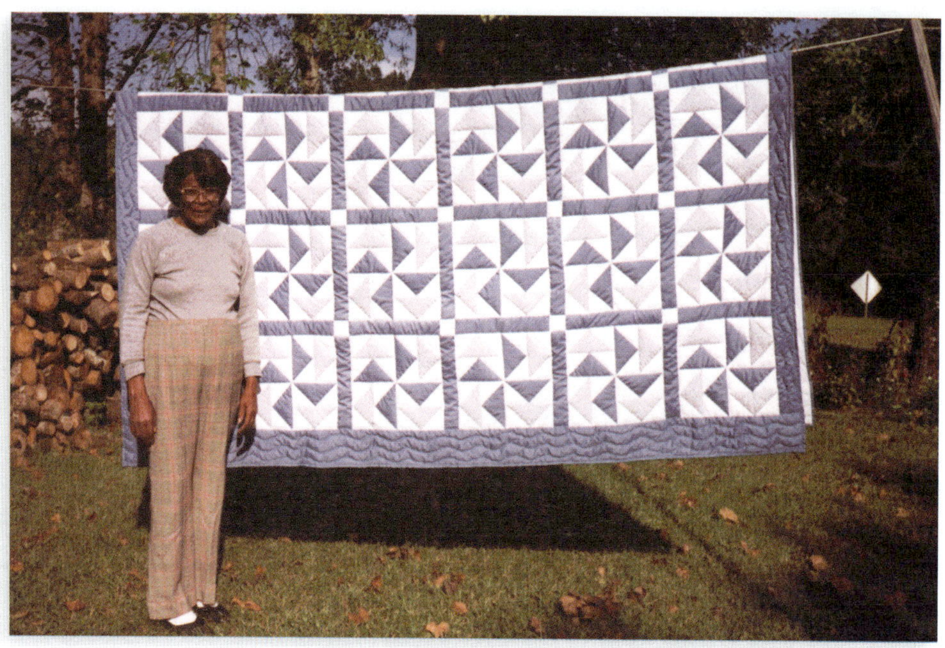

Polly Bennett, circa 1989. Polly Bennett, a member of the Freedom Quilting Bee cooperative, lived along the highway between Selma and Mobile, Alabama. As she finished a quilt, she advertised it by hanging it on her clothesline. *Gift of Pauline Woods and Amy Hislop, IQM archives.*

> We ... became so impressed with their wisdom and strength as individuals that we wanted to record what we could of their lives. Through them we came to know our grandmothers and mothers, and finally to know ourselves. Through long conversations, visits, shared work, we got a sense of our history we had not before experienced.[25]

Julie Silber and Linda Reuther, quilt collectors and dealers, and Pat Ferrero, a film-maker and professor at San Francisco State University, who also were responding to *ADAQ*, addressed the recent widespread recognition of quilts as aesthetic objects that had obscured their value as documents of every day experience. In the catalog accompanying their 1981 exhibition at the Oakland Museum, *American Quilts: A Handmade Legacy*, they write:

> We are learning that we can gain insights into the way in which ... women experienced their world by looking at the objects of their domestic live ... Our intention in this exhibit is to reconnect quilts to the lives of the people who made, used, and lived with them by suggesting the broad and multi-faceted contexts in which they were made. As James Deetz, historical archaeologist, states succinctly, "In the seemingly little and insignificant things that accumulate to create a lifetime, the essence of our existence is captured."[26]

With this exhibition, its catalog, and the accompanying documentary film series *Quilts in Women's Lives: Six Portraits*, they interpreted quilts by their role in the lives of the women who made and used them. The exhibition (and their previous small exhibition *Quilts in Women's Lives* in 1976) was a collage of the women's quilts and other hand-work, tools, images and excerpts from women's diaries, personal correspondence,

---

[25] Cooper and Buferd, 15.

[26] Pat Ferrero, Linda Reuther, and Julie Silber, "A Legacy of Hearts and Hands," in *American Quilts: A Handmade Legacy*, ed. L. Thomas Frye (Oakland Museum, 1981), 26.

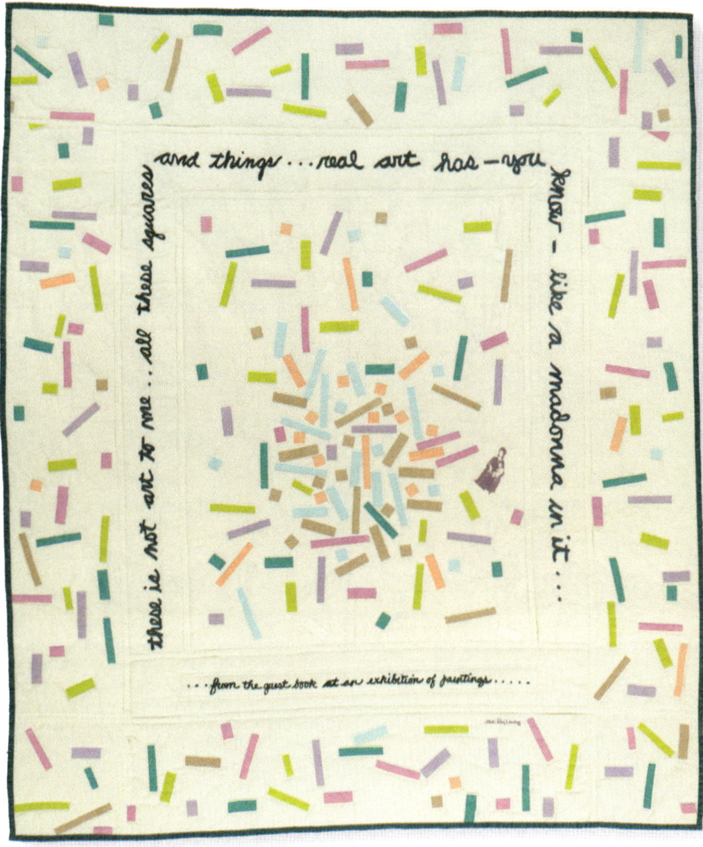


*These Is Not Art #1*, Jean Ray Laury (1928–2011), Clovis, California, 1984, 64.5 x 55.75 in. *Gift of Jean Ray Laury, IQM 2010.014.0035.* Jean Ray Laury discovered the quilt's text in a painting exhibition guest book. It evoked her sense of humor and her affirmation that women can be artists and quilts are art.

and biographies. Its thematic progression covered birth and infancy, childhood, education, puberty, marriage, family, friendship and community, religion, and death.[27]



## DOCUMENTATION & STUDY

Making connections between the historical and the contemporary, and between craft and art has characterized much of the academic and popular focus on quilts since the 1970s. A relatively new phenomenon, the 1960s and 1970s also saw a turn in historical study toward inclusiveness of women and gender, racial and ethnic histories, and the experience of ordinary people and the material objects embedded in their lives. Studies in these areas were directly linked to the contemporary foment of social progress for and among these groups. Quilt study emerged at the confluence of these streams.

Although critics such as *The New York Times'* Hilton Kramer lauded the extraordinary accomplishments of the anonymous nineteenth-century women who created the quilts in *ADAQ*, still, the makers were unknown. To prevent the perpetuation of quiltmakers' anonymity, women began grassroots quilt documentation projects in most US states, creating a photographic and documentary record of quilts and their makers. The first in this movement, and the model for the majority of those that have followed, is the Kentucky Quilt Project, begun in 1981. Its seminal idea originated with Bruce Mann, a quilt dealer in Louisville, who realized that the nineteenth century quilts he sold to collectors out of state were part of "Kentucky's artistic heritage." He saw the need to document, exhibit, and publish quilts as important pieces of Kentucky history before they were lost. Because of his untimely death, his friends Shelly Zegart, Eleanor

[27] L. Thomas Frye, ed., *American Quilts: A Handmade Legacy* (Oakland Museum, 1981), 26.

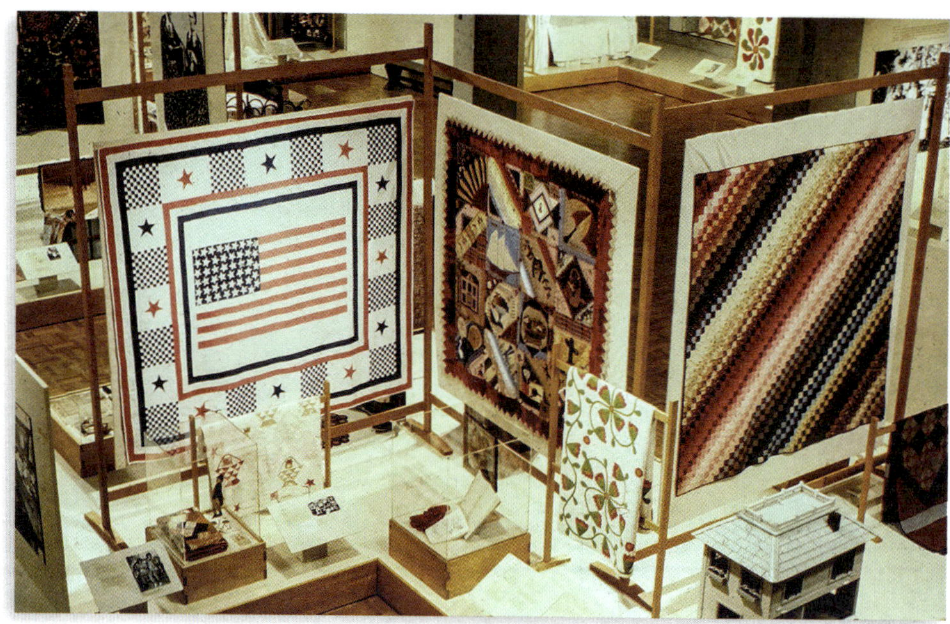

*American Quilts: A Handmade Legacy*, Oakland Museum, Oakland, California, 1981. In response to the decontextualization of quilts in *ADAQ*, scholars, artists, and curators asserted that quilts were properly understood through the contexts of women's experiences. *Quilts: A Handmade Legacy* is one exhibition that used *American Quilts* to document and provide material evidence of women's experiences. *Image courtesy of Julie Silber.*

Bingham Miller, and others led the project to reality.[28] Grassroots projects have documented approximately 200,000 quilts in private and institutional collections in the United States since 1981.[29] In her study of the books published from the primary research collected in state projects, quilt historian Christine Humphrey found that,

> The books tie the documentation of quilts to the study of women's history and women's stories by exploring them as gendered objects influenced by the contexts for making ... , the reasons for making them, and the meanings they have for their original owners ... , and by using them to provide a voice to the women who originally made them.[30]

The American Quilt Study Group, co-founded by Sally Garoutte and Joyce Gross, is devoted to interdisciplinary quilt study and has published a volume of research papers annually since 1980. Rounding out notable contributions to quilt study in the last 50 years are numerous book-length quilt studies published by museums, academics, and independent scholars on Black, Hawaiian, Native American, and Amish quilt traditions and numerous theses and dissertations, investigating quilts from many disciplinary perspectives.

## MIDDLE SPACES

The themes discussed in this essay have persisted throughout the years since 1971. Moreover, the cultural utility, presence, and meanings of quilts have endured and

---

[28] Jonathan Holstein and John Finley, *Kentucky Quilts 1800–1900* (Louisville, Kentucky: The Kentucky Quilt Project, Inc, 1982), 15–17.

[29] Christine Humphrey, "Coffee Table Books or Serious Reference Works? A Critical Analysis of the Quilt Documentation Project Books" (PhD, University of Nebraska-Lincoln, 2015), 4, search-proquest-com.libproxy.unl.edu/docview/1712387163?accountid=8116.

[30] Humphrey, 182.

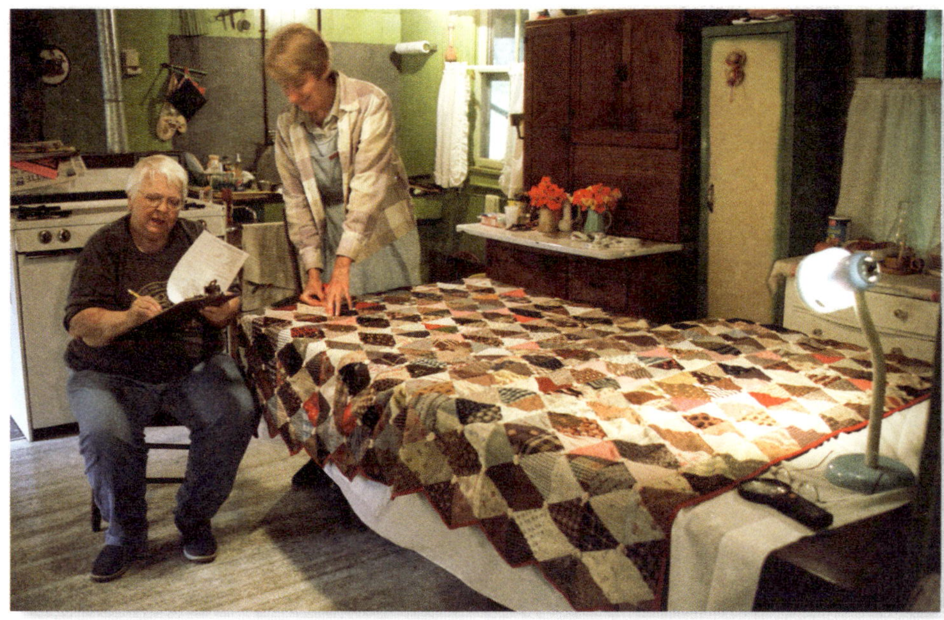

Quilt Documentation, Cummington, Massachusetts, September 2004. Beginning in 1982, grassroots organizers have sponsored quilt documentation projects in nearly every US state and in other English-speaking countries. Volunteers have held documentation events at museums, libraries, businesses, and even in kitchens. Left to right: Marjorie Childers and Jan Dreschler. *Courtesy of the Massachusetts Quilt Documentation Project. Photograph by Jane Crutchfield.*

expanded. As one scholar states, quilts are "multi-vocal," and defy fitting into clean categories as art or craft.[31] Quilts as items for display and commerce, as documents of women's life cycles, and as objects worthy of documentation and study have not stayed in their own lanes. For example, the International Quilt Museum's (IQM) founding collection, built and donated by Ardis and Robert James, exemplifies the value they saw in antique American quilts and quilts by contemporary artists. The IQM displays its diverse and growing collections in themed exhibitions, variously interpreted as women's history, art, and ethnographic objects. The museum collects in interaction with dealers, collectors, and quiltmakers or their descendants. And it devotes several days each year to quilt documentation for the public, and curators engage in study of quiltmakers, quilts, and the contexts that inform interpretation for our audiences. Other organizations and events, such as specialty museums,[32] quilt markets, festivals, and guild shows are active in multiple ways, too, as are quilt media companies, small businesses, bloggers, and social media influencers. In summary, there has been little quiet in the spaces opened by the raised profile of quilts, all of which have expanded since the moment *Abstract Design in American Quilts* opened for the world to see one hot New York day in 1971.



---

[31] Karin Elizabeth Peterson, "Discourse and Display: The Modern Eye, Entrepreneurship, and the Cultural Transformation of the Patchwork Quilt," *Sociological Perspectives*, 2003, 480, doi.org/10.1525/sop.2003.46.4.461.

[32] A number of specialty museums focused on quilts and related textile arts have been founded since 1971. American Museum of Quilts and Related Arts (now the San Jose Museum of Quilt and Textiles), San Jose, California, 1977; New England Quilt Museum, Lowell, Massachusetts, 1987; Rocky Mountain Quilt Museum, Golden, Colorado, 1990; Museum of the American Quilters Society (now National Quilt Museum,) Paducah, Kentucky, 1991; Virginia Quilt Museum, Harrisonburg, Virginia, 1995; La Conner Quilt Museum, La Conner, Washington (today's Pacific Northwest Quilt & Fiber Arts Museum), 1997; International Quilt Study Center, University of Nebraska, Lincoln, 1997 (now International Quilt Museum, 2008); Texas Quilt Museum, La Grange, 2010; Wisconsin Museum of Quilts & Fiber Arts, Cedarburg, 2011; and Iowa Quilt Museum, Winterset, 2016.

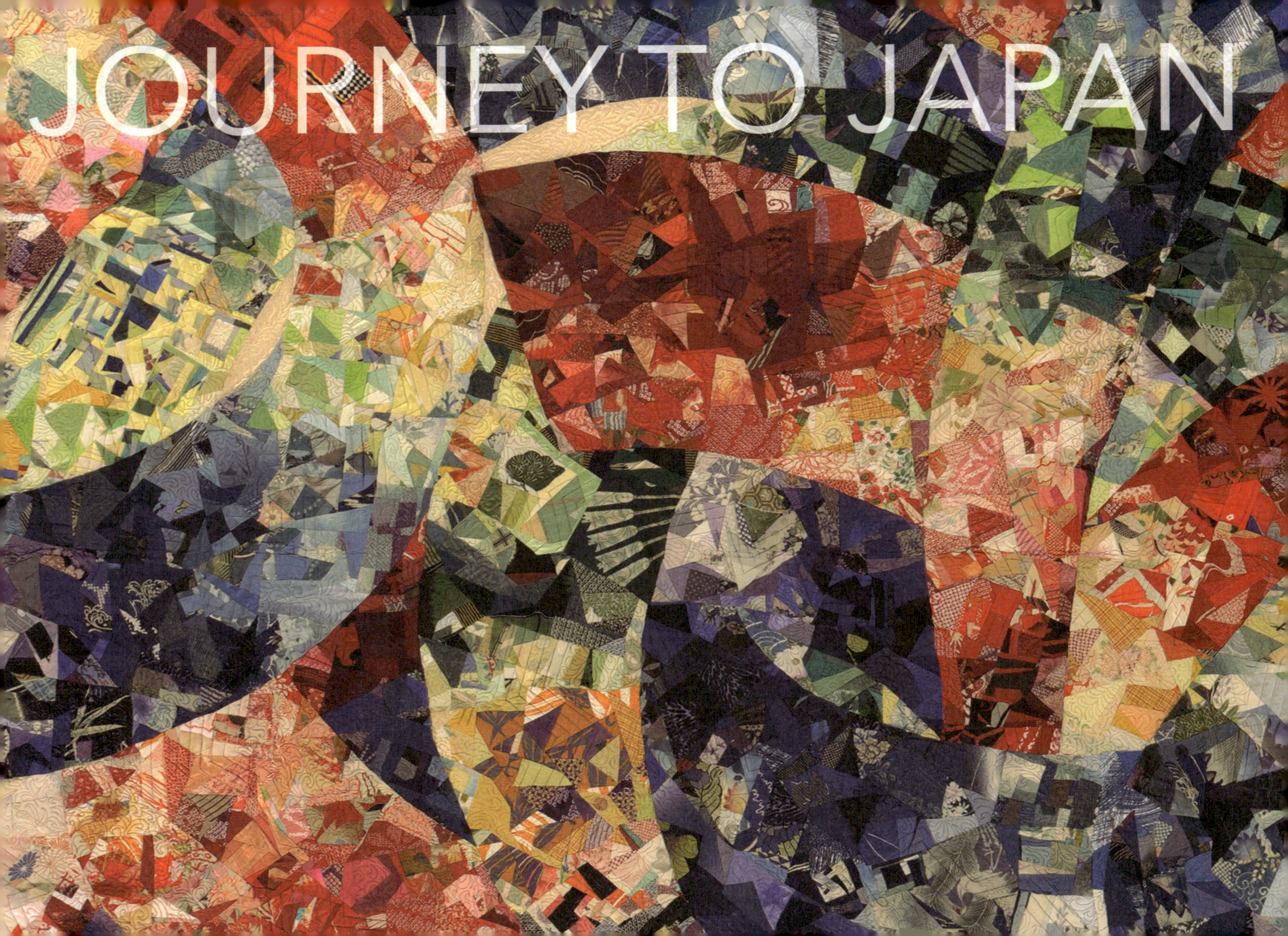
JOURNEY TO JAPAN

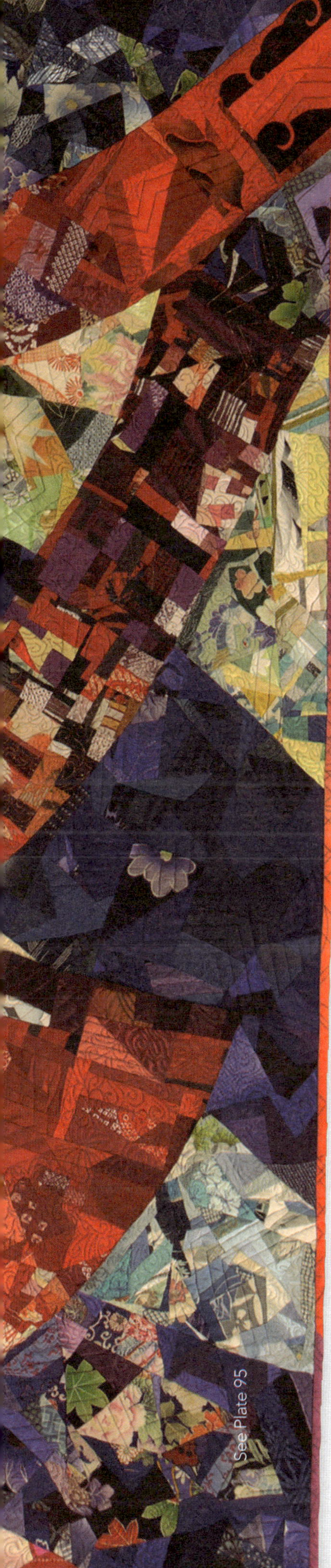
See Plate 95

# MARIN F. HANSON & NAO NOMURA

After the Whitney's 1971 surprise summer hit closed, venues around the world requested to borrow *Abstract Design in American Quilts* (*ADAQ*). Between 1972 and 1975, Holstein and van der Hoof sent iterations of the exhibition to museums around the US and to Europe, where the antique pieced quilts delighted their enthusiastic hosts and audiences.[1] The quilts' most distant trip, however, was to Japan in 1975–1976. It was a journey that would produce reverberations in both Japan and the US for the next several decades.

## HISTORICAL QUILTING & PATCHWORK IN JAPAN

Japan has a long and illustrious history of textile art, often centered on high-end materials and techniques. Silk, embroidery, and resist-dyeing (most famously, *shibori* and *katazome*) graced the clothing and furnishings of aristocrats and merchants for centuries

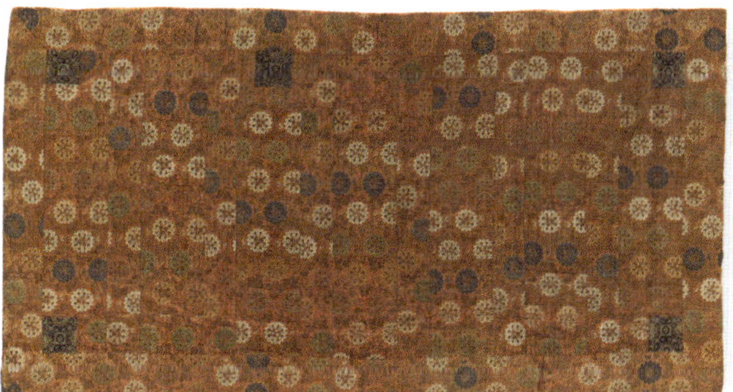

Buddhist priest's robe (*kesa*), probably made in Japan, circa 1800–1850, 45 x 87 in., on permanent loan from UNL Lentz Center of Asian Art, IQM 2014.024.0003. Because they are often made of pieces cut almost entirely from a single fabric, the patchwork columns in *kesa* robes can be extremely subtle.

---

[1] For more about the European tour of *ADAQ*, see Jonathan Holstein, *Abstract Design in American Quilts: A Biography of an Exhibition* (Louisville, KY: Kentucky Quilt Project, 1991), chap. 4.

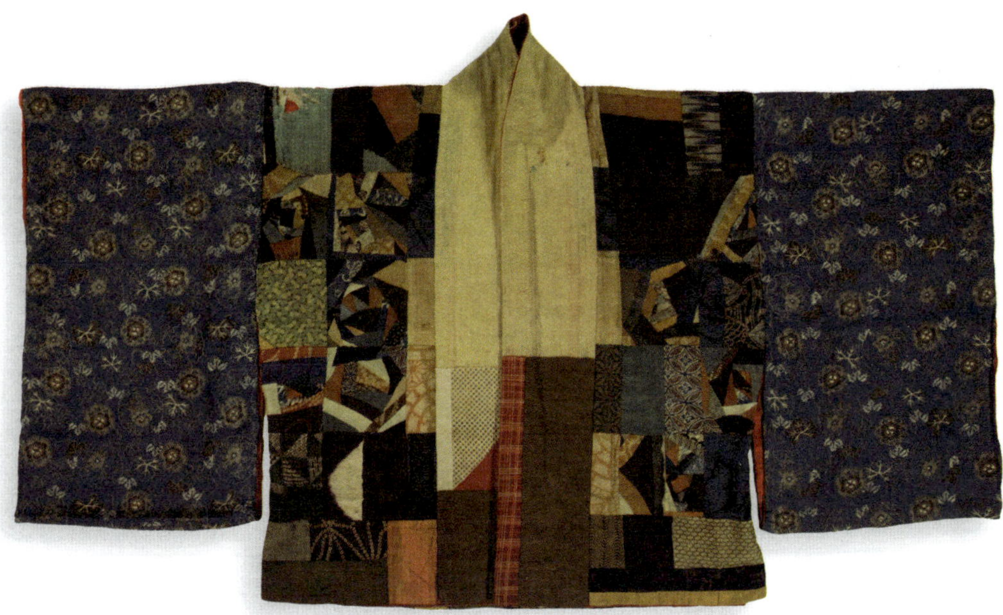

Half under-kimono (*han juban*), made in Japan, circa 1850–1870, 24.25 x 48 in., IQM 2009.043.0001. Patchwork in Japan often bore the connotation of frugality—a highly honored quality in both Buddhism and Japanese society, generally.

and were considered forms of high art. For the lower classes, humbler fabrics such as cotton and ramie and methods like patchwork and quilting provided protection and decoration.

In many Asian cultures, particularly those with strong Buddhist influence, patchwork is viewed as an expression of humility and poverty. Patchwork robes worn by Buddhist priests (*kasaya* in India, *jiasha* in China, and *kesa* in Japan) were intended to reflect the wearer's rejection of material wealth. In actuality, they were frequently made from expensive silk brocade fabrics, donated by wealthy benefactors to curry favor with powerful Buddhist temples, and became "sumptuous pious ornaments for the faith."[2] Nevertheless, in many cases, patchwork retained the unassuming nature of its Buddhist roots. In Japan, it was used to make bags for carrying rice offerings to temples and shrines (*komebukuro*) and to construct under-kimono (*juban*). In rural and working communities, damage to indigo-dyed clothing was repeatedly patched in a process called *boro* until their original surfaces became entirely obscured.

Quilting also was a traditional Japanese textile technique, perhaps most famously appearing in protective wear such as firemen's jackets. In eighteenth- and nineteenth-century Edo (now Tokyo), fires were an ever-present danger. The city's wood-clad and paper-glazed houses frequently caught fire, and local fire brigades battled the flames. Firefighters soaked their heavily *sashiko*-stitched (quilted) jackets and helmets with water for protection. They frequently also marked the indigo-dyed jackets' outer panels with crests and writing to identify their unit and rank.

---

[2] John E. Vollmer, *Silks for Thrones and Altars: Chinese Costumes and Textiles from the Liao through the Qing Dynasty* (Paris: Myrna Myers Gallery, 2004), 114.

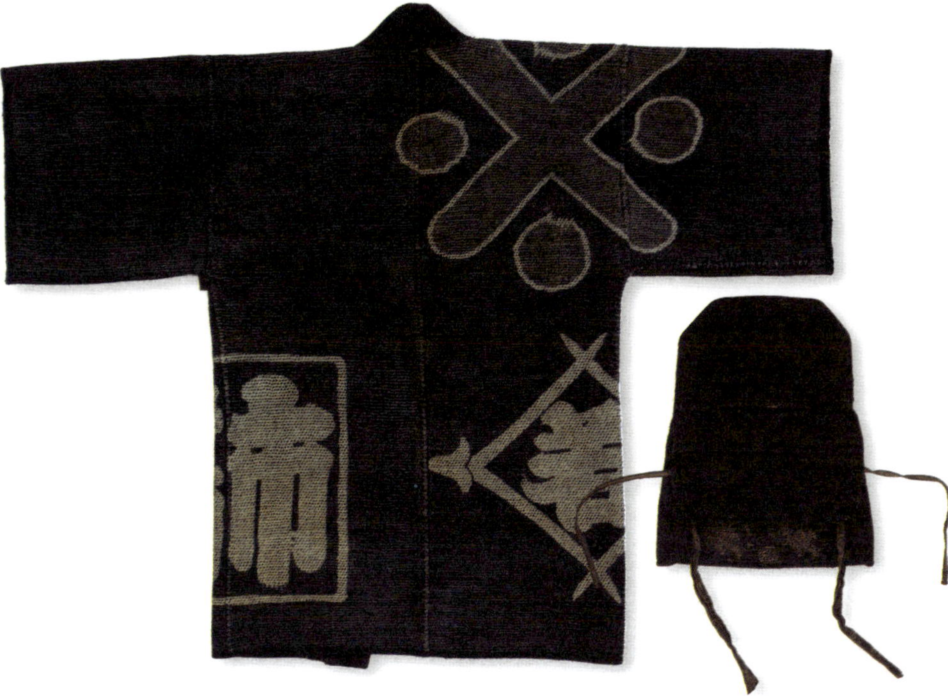

Firefighter's Coat (*hikeshi hanten*) and Helmet, made in Japan, Meiji period (1868–1912), 34 x 47.7 in. (coat), 18 x 15 in. (hat), IQM 2009.016.0001, 2015.058.0008. Firefighters soaked their quilted (*sashiko*) clothing with water to protect themselves. Large writing and symbols on a coat were used to identify the individual firefighter and his firefighting company.

## THE GROWTH OF LEISURE TIME & AMERICAN CULTURAL INFLUENCE

Although some began transforming needlework into a pastime in Meiji-era (late nineteenth century) Japan, sewing was primarily a practical or professional skill prior to World War II. Within a few decades, however, it had largely become a hobby. The reasons for this evolution are varied.

Following the devastation of WWII[3] and the subsequent Allied occupation (1945–1952), Japan quickly turned its situation around, rebuilding its infrastructure and developing and modernizing its economy. The 1950s and 1960s saw rapid manufacturing growth, with production of consumer and electronic goods becoming a mainstay of the national economy. Although many in the US and Europe remember mid-century products bearing the words "Made in Japan," exports represented only about 10% of the gross national product; in other words, "domestic consumers were the most important force behind the rapid growth in the 1950s, 1960s, and early 1970s."[4] Japan's reputation for having a "workaholic" labor force sprang from this era of economic expansion, but it was an image the government, in its desire to emulate and/or compete with Western powers, was eager to counteract. Japan's leaders aimed to become a "lifestyle superpower" (*seikatsu taikoku*)—an economically

[3] Not only had Hiroshima and Nagasaki been destroyed by the dropping of the atomic bomb on August 6 and 9, 1945, but Japan's capital, Tokyo, had been firebombed five months earlier, leveling huge swaths of the city and killing as many as 100,000 people. John Ismay, "'We Hated What We Were Doing': Veterans Recall Firebombing Japan," *The New York Times*, March 9, 2020, nytimes.com/2020/03/09/magazine/we-hated-what-we-were-doing-veterans-recall-firebombing-japan.html.

[4] Gary D. Allinson, *The Columbia Guide to Modern Japanese History* (Columbia University Press, 1999), 87.

developed nation whose citizens could afford to participate in a wide range of leisure activities. They created policies to encourage time off from work and even established a dedicated think tank in 1972, the Leisure Development Center (*Yoka Kaihatsu Senta*).[5] Promoting tourism, sports, and hobbies—including handicrafts—was part of these efforts.

This changing social environment was also influenced by globally ubiquitous American culture. Following the Allied occupation, the United States was viewed enviously by many Japanese as rich, glamorous, and exciting. By the 1970s, however, Japan had largely reached economic parity with US and "'America' had by then become not so much a symbol by which people were fascinated but an artifact which people would repeatedly consume."[6] Consuming American culture meant listening to rock 'n' roll, going to Tokyo Disneyland (which opened in 1983), and watching television shows like "Little House on the Prairie" (1974–1983, first broadcast in Japan in 1975). The latter also was the vehicle by which some nascent quiltmakers became enamored of American quilts, after seeing Ma Ingalls's patchwork bed covers in numerous episodes.[7] Like many in the US, they fell under the spell of the "mythic West," a romanticized version of the American pioneer era that offered an escape from the busyness of modern life.[8] It was in this atmosphere of burgeoning interest in handicrafts and in American folk culture that *Abstract Design in American Quilts* embarked upon its journey to Japan.

## JOURNEY TO JAPAN

In November 1974, Holstein and van der Hoof received requests from two Japanese institutions to borrow *ADAQ*. One was from the Shiseido Cosmetics company, which wanted a blockbuster exhibition to inaugurate the gallery space in their newly rebuilt flagship store in Tokyo's toniest district, Ginza. Their agent wrote that their visitors "will be delighted to see some authentic quilting works done more than [a century] ago."[9] The other request was from the Museum of Modern Art, Kyoto (MoMAK), one of Japan's four national modern art museums, which was hoping to obtain an "attractive show of American folk art appropriate for the US bicentennial year."[10] The stature of these two institutions[11] is evidence of the attention the Holstein/van der Hoof collection had garnered since 1971, not just in the US but globally.

Several articles about *Abstract Design in American Quilts* had appeared in Japanese publications after the show's New York City debut, including one by Kazuko

[5] David Richard Leheny, *The Rules of Play: National Identity and the Shaping of Japanese Leisure* (Cornell University Press, 2003).

[6] Shunya Yoshimi, "Consuming 'America': From Symbol to System," in *Consumption in Asia* (Routledge, 2002), 210.

[7] Teresa Duryea Wong, *Japanese Contemporary Quilts and Quilters: The Story of an American Import*, 2015, 15.

[8] See also Hisayo Ogushi, "Little House in the Far East: The American Frontier Spirit and Japanese Girls' Comics," *Japanese Journal of American Studies* 27 (2016): 21–44. for the ways in which the *Little House* books and television series influenced *shojo manga* (comics for girls).

[9] Keiko Hirayama to Jonathan Holstein, Jonathan Holstein, Quilt Papers (MS-0305), November 26, 1974, Archives and Special Collections, University of Nebraska-Lincoln Libraries.

[10] William D. Miller and US Embassy to Jonathan Holstein, Jonathan Holstein, Quilt Papers (MS-0305), November 26, 1974, Archives & Special Collections, University of Nebraska-Lincoln Libraries.

[11] The Shiseido Company was founded in 1872 and in 1919 they established the Shiseido Gallery, which claims to be the oldest art gallery in Japan. It has a reputation for showcasing both eminent and emerging Japanese and international artists and designers. Established as a national museum in 1967, the Museum of Modern Art, Kyoto focuses on twentieth and twenty-first century national and international artwork, with a special emphasis on the Kansai (western Japan) region.

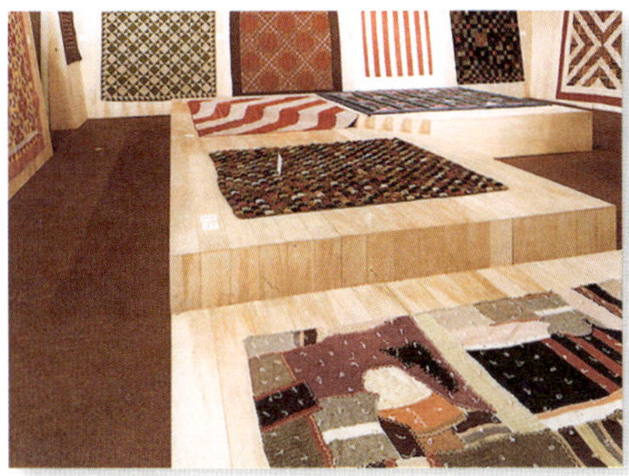

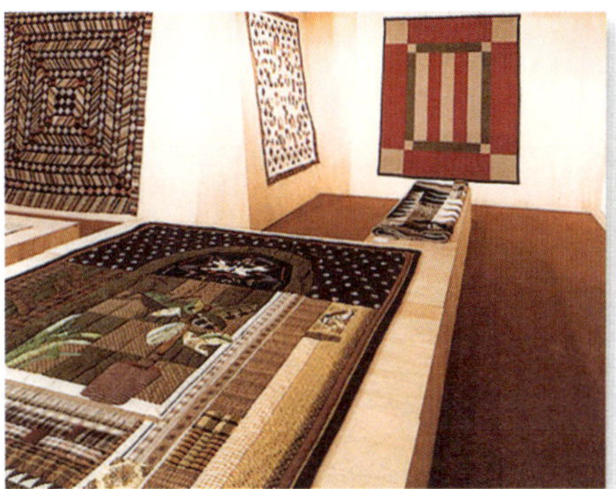

LEFT: *American Pieced Quilts* was hosted by the Shiseido Gallery in 1975 at their newly re-built flagship store in Tokyo. The gallery was established in 1919. *Jonathan Holstein, Quilt Papers, Archives & Special Collections, University of Nebraska-Lincoln Libraries.* RIGHT: The Shiseido Gallery's *American Pieced Quilts* included quilts by American artists Susan Hoffman (foreground) and Molly Upton (folded in background), representing perhaps the first appearance of "art quilts" in Japan. *Jonathan Holstein, Quilt Papers, Archives & Special Collections, University of Nebraska-Lincoln Libraries.*

Yamakawa[12] in the July 14, 1972, edition of the lifestyle magazine, *Kurashi no Techo* (*Living Handbook*). Yamakawa interviewed Holstein in Paris during *ADAQ*'s tenure at the Musée des Arts Décoratifs. She was surprised by Holstein's appearance, apparently anticipating someone older and more conservative: "My expectation for 'American collector' and 'quilt collector' did not match the young man in blue jeans standing in front of me."[13] Holstein's startling appearance notwithstanding, Yamakawa (later Masui) was impressed by *ADAQ* and happily agreed to act as go-between when Shiseido set out to obtain the quilts for an exhibition to be titled *American Pieced Quilts* and held March 2–25, 1975. The request from MoMAK, on the other hand, was facilitated by the American Embassy, whose American Center in Kyoto co-sponsored the MoMAK exhibition (July 4–August 8, 1976, titled *American Quilts*) and also displayed a small group of the quilts at their facility in the summer of 1975, between the Shiseido and MoMAK exhibitions.[14]

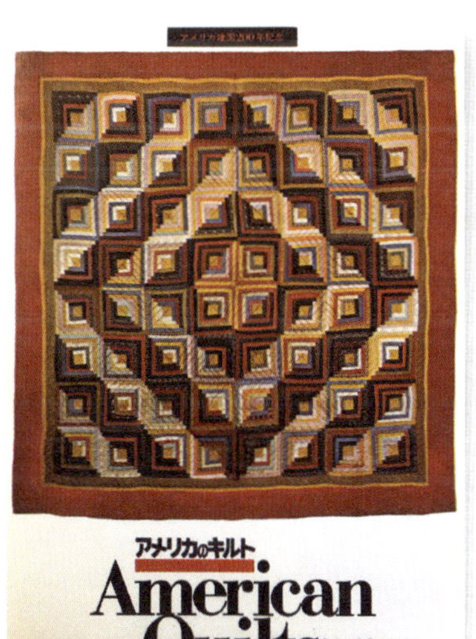


Kyoto's 1976 exhibition of the Holstein/van der Hoof collection, *American Quilts*, at The National Museum of Modern Art, was purposely scheduled to coincide with the American Bicentennial. *Jonathan Holstein, Quilt Papers, Archives & Special Collections, University of Nebraska-Lincoln Libraries.*

By all immediate measures, the quilts' journey to Japan was a resounding success. The director of the American Center in Kyoto reported to Holstein and van der Hoof that "the show was a smash hit everywhere it went" and that MoMAK's

---

[12] In Japan, personal names are presented as family name first, given name second, but in this publication, we follow the Western convention of given name followed by family name, in part because some of the archival documents from representatives of Japanese institutions cited here were signed in Western fashion.
[13] Kazuko Yamakawa, "Quilts from the Collection by Jonathan Holstein and Gail van der Hoof," trans. Nao Nomura, *Kurashi No Techo*, October 1972.
[14] The American Center also traveled the quilts to art galleries in the cities of Sapporo and Fukuoka in the fall of 1975.

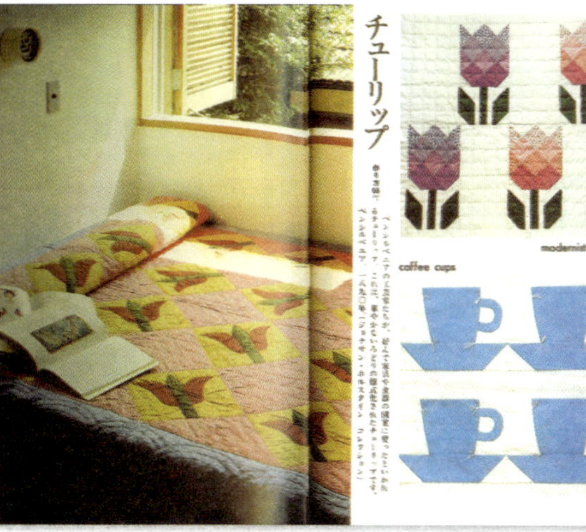


*Tezukuri no Kurashi: Patchwork Quilts*, Bunka Shuppan Kyoku, 1976, out of print. This 1976 publication featuring many of the Holstein/van der Hoof quilts that traveled to Tokyo and Kyoto was an early Japanese book focused on American quilts. *Image courtesy of Bunka Shuppan*.

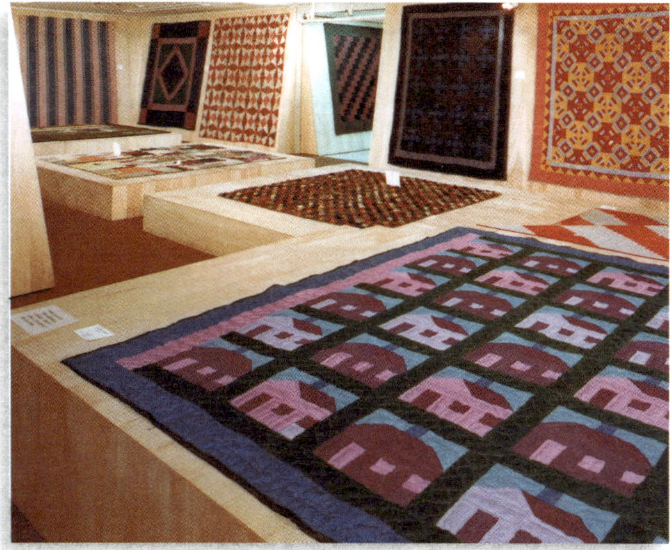

The Shiseido Gallery's *American Pieced Quilts*, curated by Jonathan Holstein and Gail van der Hoof, included *ADAQ* quilts as well as ones the collectors had more recently acquired. *Jonathan Holstein, Quilt Papers, Archives & Special Collections, University of Nebraska-Lincoln Libraries.*

attendance figure of 16,000 was 50 percent higher than normal. Additionally, the museum's two catalog printings both sold out, the exhibition was written up in major newspapers and art journals, and NHK, Japan's public broadcasting company, covered its opening event.[15] A book featuring images and patterns of over two dozen Holstein/van der Hoof quilts was published in 1976 and served as an early "how to" book for the Japanese quiltmaking market.[16]

Holstein and van der Hoof's February–March 1975 trip to Japan for the Shiseido opening was both rewarding and revealing. The two were awed at the professionalism and efficiency of the Shiseido's gallery staff, who prepared the exhibition in one evening after the store had closed for the day, including sewing hanging sleeves on the three dozen quilts, building flat and inclined platforms, installing the quilts, wall texts, and labels. They enjoyed a media blitz, participating in interviews for magazines and newspapers and appearing on the popular television show, *Oshare*

---

[15] In Japan, personal names are presented as family name first, given name second but in this publication, we follow the Western convention of given name followed by family name, in part because some of the archival documents from representatives of Japanese institutions cited here were signed in Western fashion.
[16] Kazuko Yamakawa, "Quilts from the Collection by Jonathan Holstein and Gail van Der Hoof," trans. Nao Nomura, *Kurashi No Techo*, October 1972.

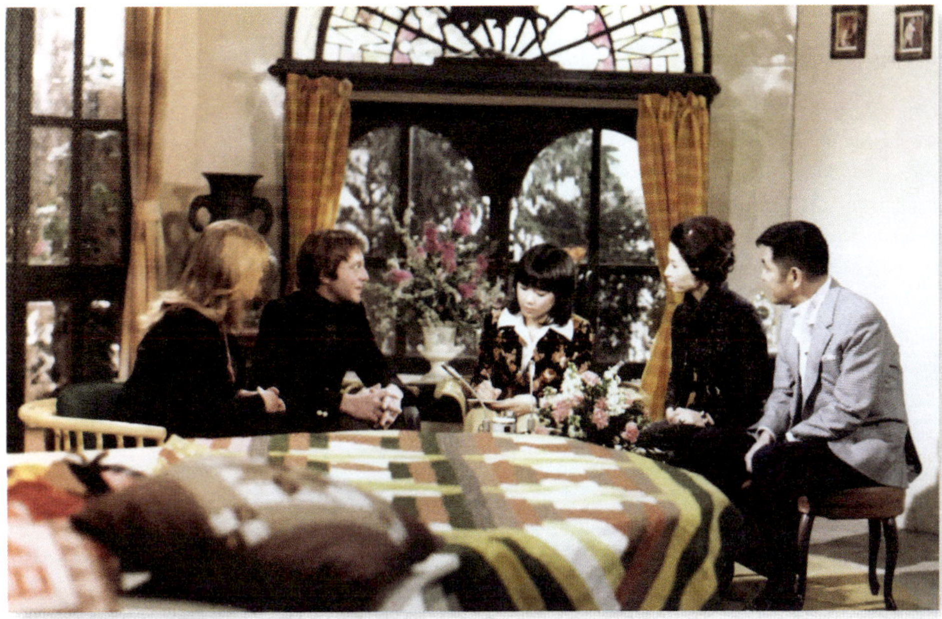

As part of their 1975 journey to Japan, Holstein and van der Hoof appeared with some of their quilts on the popular television program, *Oshare* (*Stylish*). *Jonathan Holstein, Quilt Papers, Archives & Special Collections, University of Nebraska-Lincoln Libraries.*

(*Stylish*).[17] They visited Tokyo and Kyoto museums and historic sites, during which time Holstein's ideas about the gap between American and Japanese attitudes toward folk art solidified. In an interview for Shiseido's corporate culture magazine, *Hanatsubaki*, he noted that, "Unfortunately, many good quilts, as well as other pieces of folk art, have been lost in our country, where people are less enthusiastic in preserving the past than the Japanese."[18] What he saw as Japan's veneration for historical artifacts, including textiles, is one of the things that has remained firmly in his mind over the last 45 years. In 2020, he reminisced:

> As I look back now on that first exhibition, among my fondest memories are the reactions of the Japanese women (exclusively) who came to see the quilts in the gallery on the Ginza. They got the whole thing immediately and saw absolutely no reason not to explore the quilts respectfully but thoroughly, examining how they had been pieced, tracing the quilting stitchery, turning them to inspect the backs. Many came back a number of times. When we saw their intense interest and the care approaching reverence with which they handled the quilts, we took down the "Please Do Not Touch" signs and let it happen. It was a lovely moment for us. [19]

Holstein is not surprised by the enthusiastic adoption of American-style quiltmaking in Japan around the same time that his and van der Hoof's quilts were touring the country. As in the US, people all over Japan were discovering and embracing quiltmaking as a hobby and an artistic medium, a phenomenon that can be in part attributed to *ADAQ*'s global impact.

---

[17] The American Center also traveled the quilts to art galleries in the cities of Sapporo and Fukuoka in the fall of 1975.

[18] "Interview by Miss Tetsuko Kuroyamagi," Jonathan Holstein, Quilt Papers (MS-0305) (n.d.), Archives & Special Collections, University of Nebraska-Lincoln Libraries.

[19] Jonathan Holstein to Marin Hanson, July 27, 2020.

## THE IMPACT OF THE HOLSTEIN/VAN DER HOOF QUILTS ON JAPANESE QUILTMAKING

In 1984, about a decade after the widespread adoption of American-style quiltmaking in Japan, the design magazine *Soshoku Dezain* (*Decorative Design*) featured a special issue on American quilts.[20] The issue's articles emphasized early American craft traditions and referred to them as material reminders of frugality, practicality, and creativity—values that Japanese people saw as being easily disregarded in highly consumerized, modern American society. The magazine's striking visual aesthetics coupled with its nostalgic historical narratives resonated with the contemporary Japanese audience, who also had ambivalent feelings toward their own country's unprecedented economic boom and modernization over the last several decades. The fact that a highly regarded design magazine devoted an issue to quiltmaking was a sign of its popularity in Japan, and that part of its appeal was its rootedness in history and tradition.

Several quiltmakers interviewed for *Soshoku Dezain*'s quilt-focused issue referred to the "Jonathan Holstein collection" as an inspiration for getting involved in quiltmaking—some had visited one of the Japan exhibitions and others learned about the collection through Japanese magazine articles. The American Pavilion at the 1970 World Exposition held in Osaka was also mentioned as a place where makers saw patchwork quilts for the first time. In addition, there were a few quiltmakers who learned about the practice while they lived in the United States in the 1970s.[21] These women[22] formed Japan's quilt vanguard, laying the foundation for the development of quiltmaking by institutionalizing the craft.

One key figure in the formalized spread of quiltmaking was Chuck Nohara. Nohara and her husband established one of the country's first quilt schools, Hearts & Hands Patchwork Quilt School, in 1976. She also taught at several other cultural institutions, always with an eye to nurturing future quiltmakers. More than 5,000 individuals received a certificate from her school proving that they had acquired essential skills needed to make quilts.[23] Nohara's earliest students later became leading quiltmakers themselves, contributing to the growth of this recently introduced handicraft. Takako Onoyama, who opened her Quilt House Yama store in the same year as Hearts & Hands, is another forerunner in the quilt industry. When quilts were still gaining awareness among the general public, Onoyama worked hard to disseminate quiltmaking by importing materials and inviting instructors from the United States.[24]

As the popularity of quiltmaking continued to grow, there was an increasing demand among a larger audience for opportunities to learn how to make quilts. In 1986, Japan Handicraft Instructors' Association (JHIA), a non-profit foundation accredited by the Ministry of Education, Culture, Sports, Science, and Technology, ventured into the quilt market by offering a structured certification program. In contrast to early quiltmaking schools begun in the 1970s, JHIA's certification program attracted a broader middle class audience of women who had not been previously interested in patchwork and quilting.[25] Like the Hearts & Hands school, the JHIA program was premised upon the traditional *iemoto* system, in which students closely follow a set

---

[20] The special issue also included information about early American and Native American handicrafts.
[21] *Soshoku Dezain* (*Decorative Design*), *Special Issue: American Quilts/Early American and Indian Crafts*, 1984, 68-69.
[22] In the highly gendered sphere of Japanese needlework there were relatively few male quiltmakers, a similar situation to that of the United States.
[23] "Nohara Chuck San," Quilts Japan Web, accessed September 3, 2020, tezukuritown.com/nv/c/cf1103543/.
[24] "Quilt House Yama," Quilt House Yama Archive, accessed September 3, 2020, yamakikaku.co.jp/index.html.
[25] Nao Nomura, "The Development of Quiltmaking in Japan since the 1970s," *Uncoverings* 31 (2010): 112.

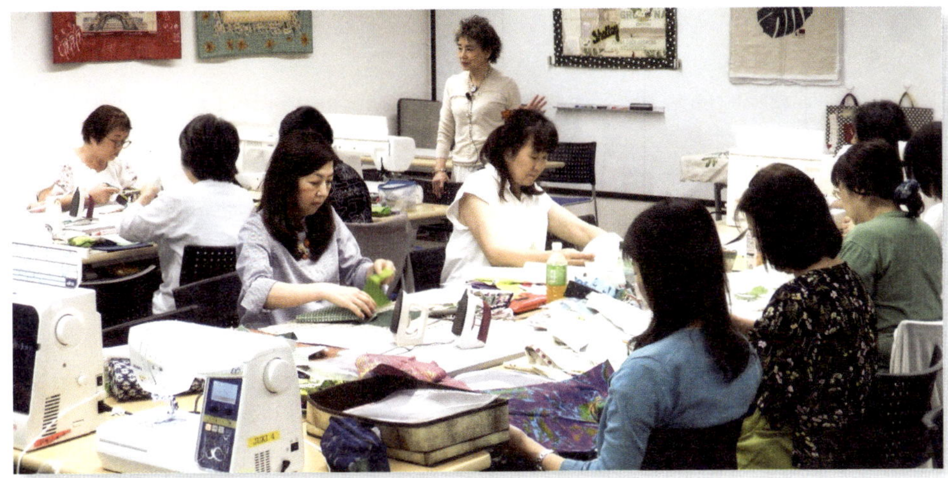

Obtaining the Japan Handicraft Instructors Association (JHIA) quiltmaking certificate requires training under well-established teachers such as Suzuko Koseki (standing), one of the *Journey to Japan* exhibition participants. *Image courtesy of the JHIA.*

curriculum that is largely based on imitation and repetition.[26] To date, nearly 18,000 instructor certificates have been issued by JHIA.[27] In this way, quiltmaking has spread widely throughout Japan.

By the late 1980s, Japanese quiltmakers had begun entering US quilt competitions and juried exhibitions and rapidly became top contenders in many categories. In 1990, the theme for Houston's International Quilt Festival, one of the most important annual quilt shows, was "The Year of Japan" and in the same year the JHIA held the first of its biennial competitions, Quilt Nihon, which has attracted top artists from Japan and abroad ever since.[28] After making big waves in the US starting in 1971 with the Holstein/van der Hoof exhibitions and in Japan with those of 1975–76, quilts had truly become a Japanese phenomenon.



## THE *JOURNEY TO JAPAN* ARTISTS

Several of the artists in the IQM's *Journey to Japan* exhibition (Plates 86–95) saw the Holstein/van der Hoof quilts either in Tokyo or Kyoto. Eiko Okano, one of Chuck Nohara's first students, visited the Tokyo Shiseido Gallery exhibition and recalls, "At that time, I felt like I saw something really special … I was overwhelmed by the energy of Americans! … That exhibition helped me discover my own style."[29] Emiko Toda Loeb, who now splits her time between Japan and the US, was newly discovering American culture when she visited the MoMAK exhibition:

> In 1976, I saw the exhibition … but did not know that it was the Holstein/van der Hoof collection. A year before that, I had traveled abroad for the first time and met my future husband, a New Yorker, and became interested in America. I remember that I went to see the exhibition because it was a great opportunity to see real American quilts. I still remember the Coffee Cup quilt. The quilt had a sense of

---

[26] Other, non-JHIA teaching programs have followed different systems, including apprenticeship, one-on-one, and general craft school models (Penny Nii and Shizuko Kuroha, "A Glimpse of the Japanese Quilting Community: The Influence of Quilting Schools," *The Quilt Journal* 2, no. 2 (1993): 1–4.).

[27] Daisuke Kojima and JHIA to Marin Hanson, September 18, 2020.

[28] Wong, *Japanese Contemporary Quilts and Quilters: The Story of an American Import*, 42.

[29] Eiko Okano to Marin Hanson and Nao Nomura, April 10, 2020. Emiko Toda Loeb to Marin Hanson and Nao Nomura, April 20, 2020.

> bygone times and I felt very warm, even nostalgic thinking about the American past that I never knew.[30]

Yoshiko Katagiri also saw the MoMAK exhibition, which opened up an exciting, new creative world to her:

> In 1976, I saw *American Quilts* in Kyoto. . . . That was the first time that I encountered "quilt." I liked appliqué when I was a student [and] I think I saw an advertisement about the exhibition in [a crafting] magazine. I was blown away to see the exhibition in person. I was familiar with sewing small pieces of fabric together, but I never imagined that the same technique could produce such beautiful designs.[31]

For those who saw the Holstein/van der Hoof quilts in Japan, it was a memorable, inspiring experience.

Even if they did not attend one of the Tokyo or Kyoto quilt exhibitions, some quiltmakers remember reading about them at the time. Keiko Goke recalls reading about the quilts and being impressed: "the[se] first real American quilts I saw were mind-blowing."[32] Likewise, Kumiko Fujita says she saw a magazine article in 1975 about an antique American quilt exhibition—likely the Shiseido or Kyoto American Center installation. Trained as a graphic designer, Fujita says discovering "early American quilts was life-changing for me, and it influenced me to make a transition from graphic design to the quilt world."[33] The widespread coverage of the exhibitions exposed the Holstein/van der Hoof collection to an audience excited and ready to begin or advance their own quiltmaking.

Despite its wide reach, however, not all Japanese quiltmakers were directly influenced by the 1975–1976 Holstein/van der Hoof exhibitions. Among the artists in the *Journey to Japan* exhibition, several were either unaware of them in the mid-1970s or didn't start making quilts until the late '70s or early '80s. Suzuko Koseki, for one, was too busy raising her three children to attend a gallery exhibition. She did, however, begin quiltmaking in the mid-1970s and discovered that it was a boon to her mental health, which had suffered due to postpartum issues and the stress of child-rearing.[34] Harue Konishi, who was also raising her children in the 1970s, did not start quiltmaking until around 1980, when she began learning from the mother of her daughter's friend.[35] Yasuko Saito came late to quiltmaking, in the early 1980s, when she was already 40 years old.[36] Indeed, Saito claims not to have been influenced by traditional American quilts like those seen in the Shiseido and MoMAK exhibitions; rather, she found inspiration in the work of worldwide contemporary quiltmakers during visits to places like the Museum of the American Quilter's Society (now the National Quilt Museum) in Paducah, Kentucky, and the International Quilt Festival in Houston, Texas.[37]

Although it is widely visible in Japan, American culture has not been uniformly influential. In fact, one characteristic of Japanese popular culture is its ability to absorb external cultural elements and transform them into something indubitably Japanese. Scholar Tim Craig notes that the abundance of creativity in Japanese popular culture springs from its hybridizing ability:

---

[30] Emiko Toda Loeb to Marin Hanson and Nao Nomura, April 20, 2020.
[31] Yoshiko Katagiri to Marin Hanson and Nao Nomura, April 29, 2020.
[32] Keiko Goke to Marin Hanson and Nao Nomura, May 8, 2020.
[33] Kumiko Fujita to Marin Hanson and Nao Nomura, May 5, 2020.
[34] Suzuko Koseki to Marin Hanson and Nao Nomura, May 3, 2020.
[35] Harue Konishi to Marin Hanson and Nao Nomura, May 2, 2020.
[36] Yasuko Saito to Marin Hanson and Nao Nomura, May 5, 2020.
[37] Wong, *Japanese Contemporary Quilts and Quilters: The Story of an American Import*, 118.

> One source of this [inventiveness] is the cross-fertilization between old and new, native and foreign, one genre and another, which is a hallmark of Japanese culture. Many observers have noted Japan's propensity to "borrow" foreign things—Chinese characters, English words, capitalism, democracy, the transistor, curry—and to tinker with them, merging them with native or other elements so that they become something new and often quite distinct from the original.[38]

Because they are a form of popular material culture, quilts are ready candidates for this melding process. As Japanese quiltmakers continued to create American-style quilts in the 1970s and '80s, some began to incorporate homegrown materials and aesthetics. For instance, *Journey to Japan* artist Shizuko Kuroha is known today for her use of antique Japanese *aizome* (indigo-dyed) fabrics. In the mid-'70s, however, she had yet to discover quilts and was not aware of the *ADAQ* exhibitions in Japan. In fact, she had swapped places with the Holstein/van der Hoof quilts, accompanying her husband to the United States in 1975 for his job. Kuroha saw her first antique quilt a mere four days into her American residency and it changed her life, as did her serendipitous introduction to Japanese antiques—with which she was ironically unfamiliar—in many American homes she visited. By the time she moved back to Japan, she was a full-fledged quiltmaker but, more distinctively, she was one of the first artists to deliberately blend cultures in her work: "When I returned to Japan, as a sponge absorbs water, I became passionate about *aizome* . . . for use in my quilts. The encounter with that [first] American quilt gave me the opportunity to get to know Japanese culture."[39] Shoko Hatano also lived in the US in the mid-1970s and, upon returning to Japan, began quiltmaking at Nohara's Hearts & Hands Patchwork Quilt School.[40] Like Kuroha, she incorporates a Japanese sensibility into her quilts—not through traditional or antique materials but through images of large, gestural brushstrokes reminiscent of calligraphy.

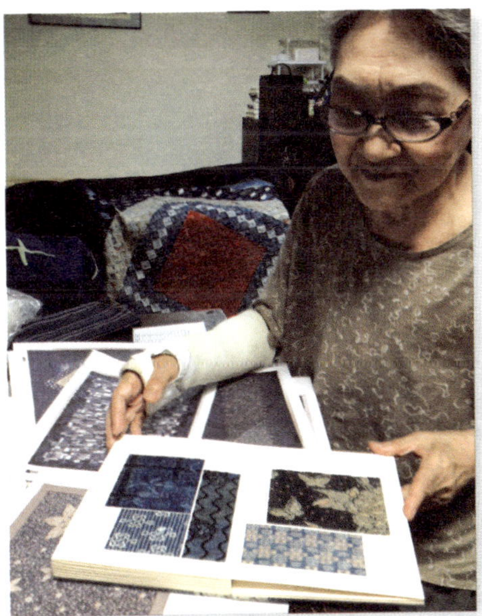

*Journey to Japan* exhibition participant Shizuko Kuroha is an avid collector of traditional Japanese indigo-dyed fabrics (including antique swatchbooks), which she incorporates into her complex patchwork quilts. *Photograph by: Marin F. Hanson.*

Japanese quiltmaking today is rich and varied. It has roots in numerous homegrown and imported sources, including the country's own long history of patchwork and quilting, post-WWII economic growth and leisure-time expansion, ongoing American cultural influence, and longstanding teaching systems that facilitated the spread of handicraft practices. But also important were the 1975–1976 Japanese exhibitions of the Holstein/van der Hoof collection. As with the original installation of *Abstract Design in American Quilts* in New York, the Tokyo and Kyoto exhibitions functioned as triggers that helped set off rapid and enthusiastic growth of quilt-related activity, forever changing the Japanese quilt and handicraft landscape.



---

38 T. J. Craig, "Introduction," in *Japan Pop: Inside the World of Japanese Popular Culture*, ed. Timothy J. Craig (New York: Routledge, 2015), 8.

39 Shizuko Kuroha, *Indigo & Sarasa: Les Quilts de Shizuko Kuroha = the Quilts of Shizuko Kuroha* (Saint-Étienne-de-Montluc (La Castillerie, 44360): Quiltmania, 2011), 64.

40 Wong, *Japanese Contemporary Quilts and Quilters: The Story of an American Import*, 47.

# EXHIBITION PLATES

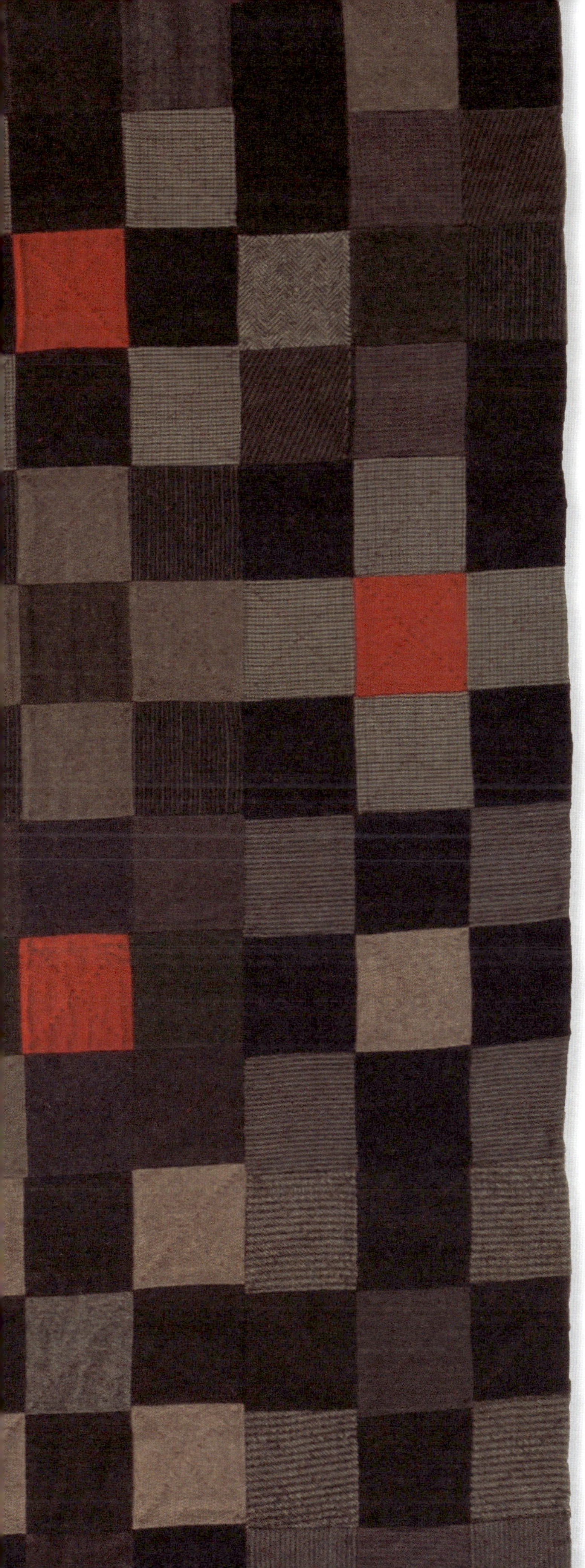

# ABSTRACT DESIGN IN AMERICAN QUILTS AT 50

In *Abstract Design in American Quilts at 50*, the International Quilt Museum (IQM) presents 59 of the 61 quilts shown at the Whitney Museum of American Art in 1971 (two of the exhibition's quilts did not enter the IQM collections). All quilts are part of the IQM's Jonathan Holstein and Gail van der Hoof Collection, except for Plate 59.

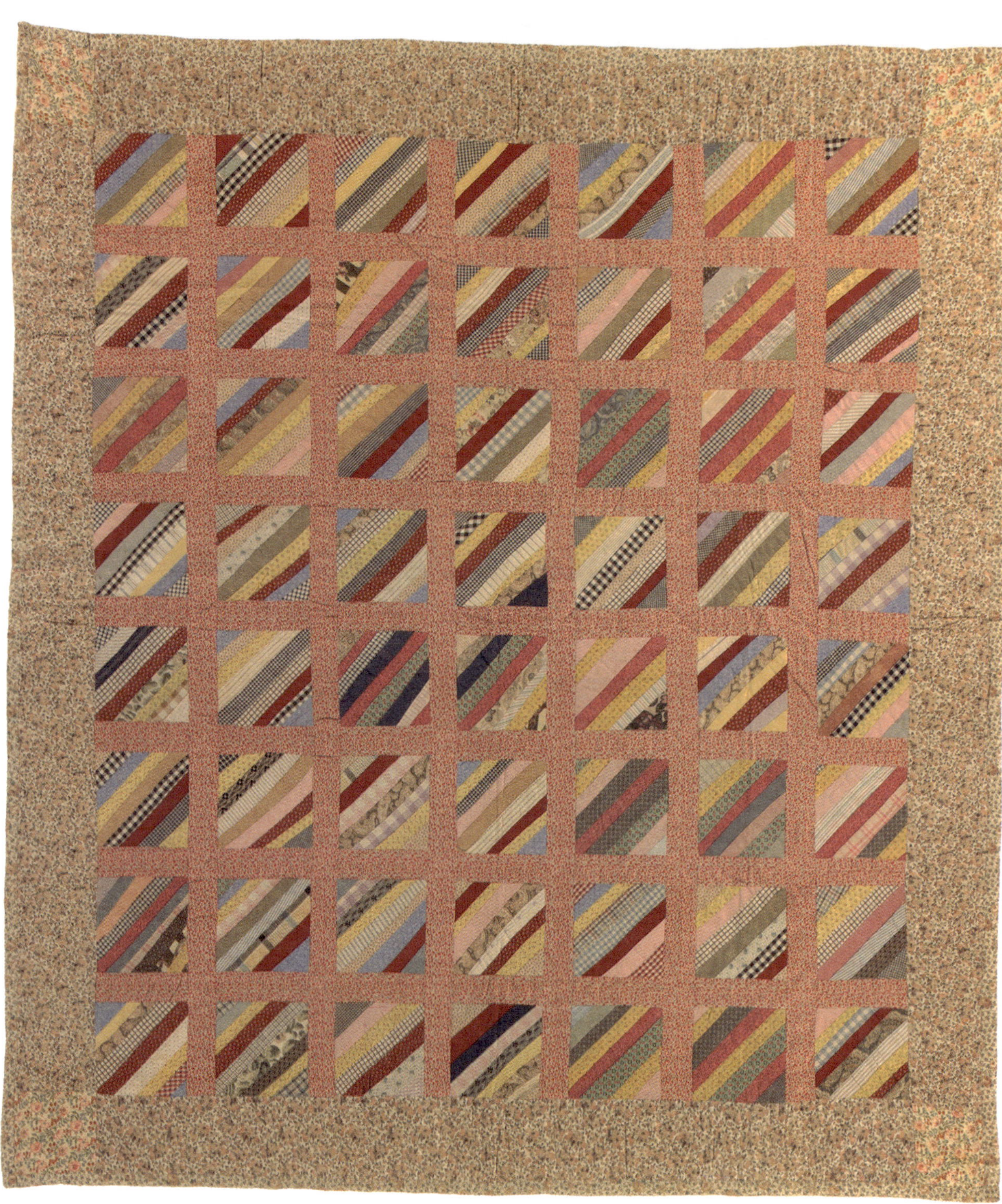

1. **String Squares**
   Maker unidentified
   Probably made in Pennsylvania, 1920–1940
   Cotton; hand pieced and quilted; 82.5 x 72.5 in.
   Jonathan Holstein and Gail van der Hoof Collection, IQM 2003.003.0001

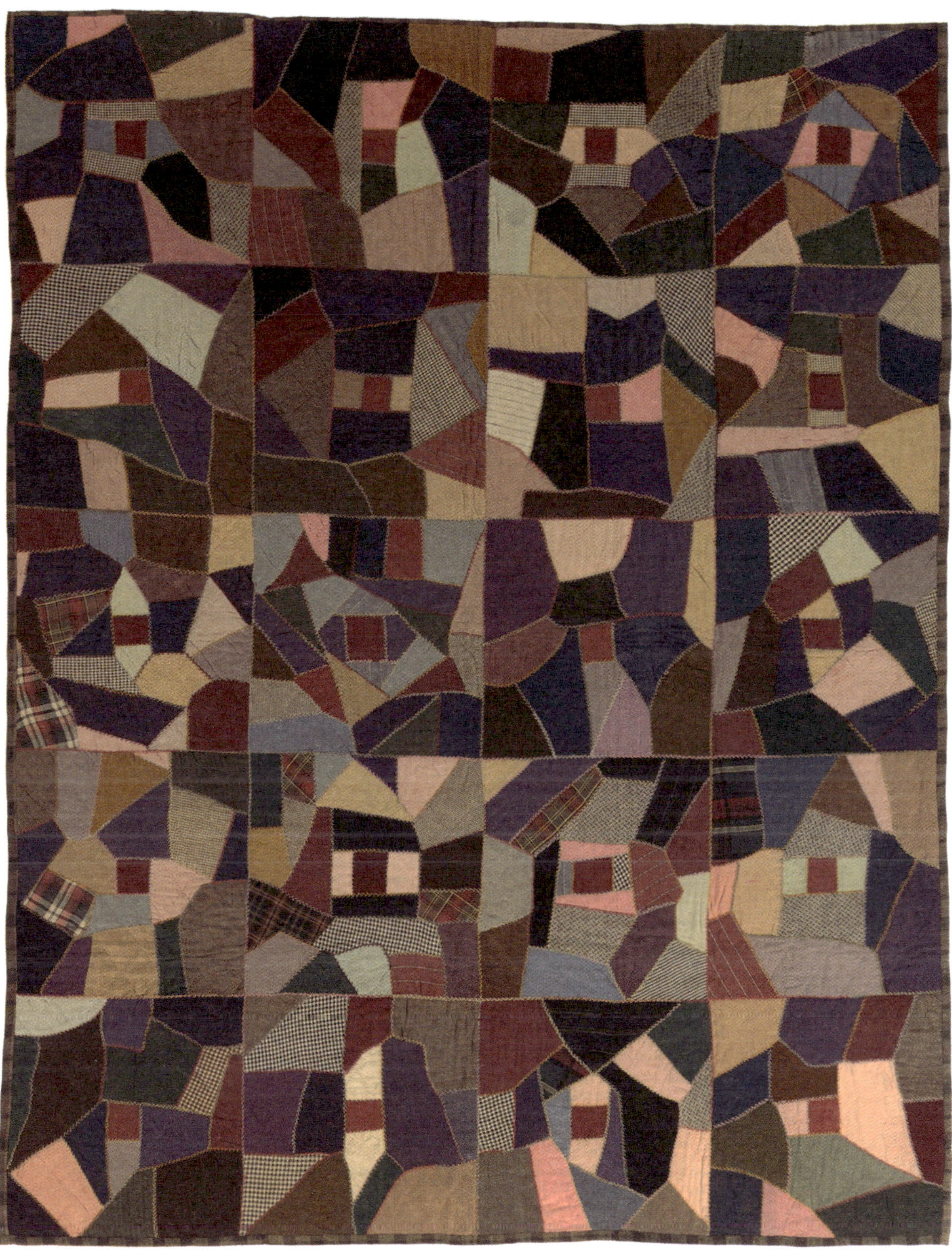

2. **Crazy quilt**
Maker unidentified
Possibly made in Pennsylvania or New England, 1900–1920
Wool; hand pieced, embroidered, and quilted; 88 x 70.5 in.
Jonathan Holstein and Gail van der Hoof Collection, IQM 2003.003.0002

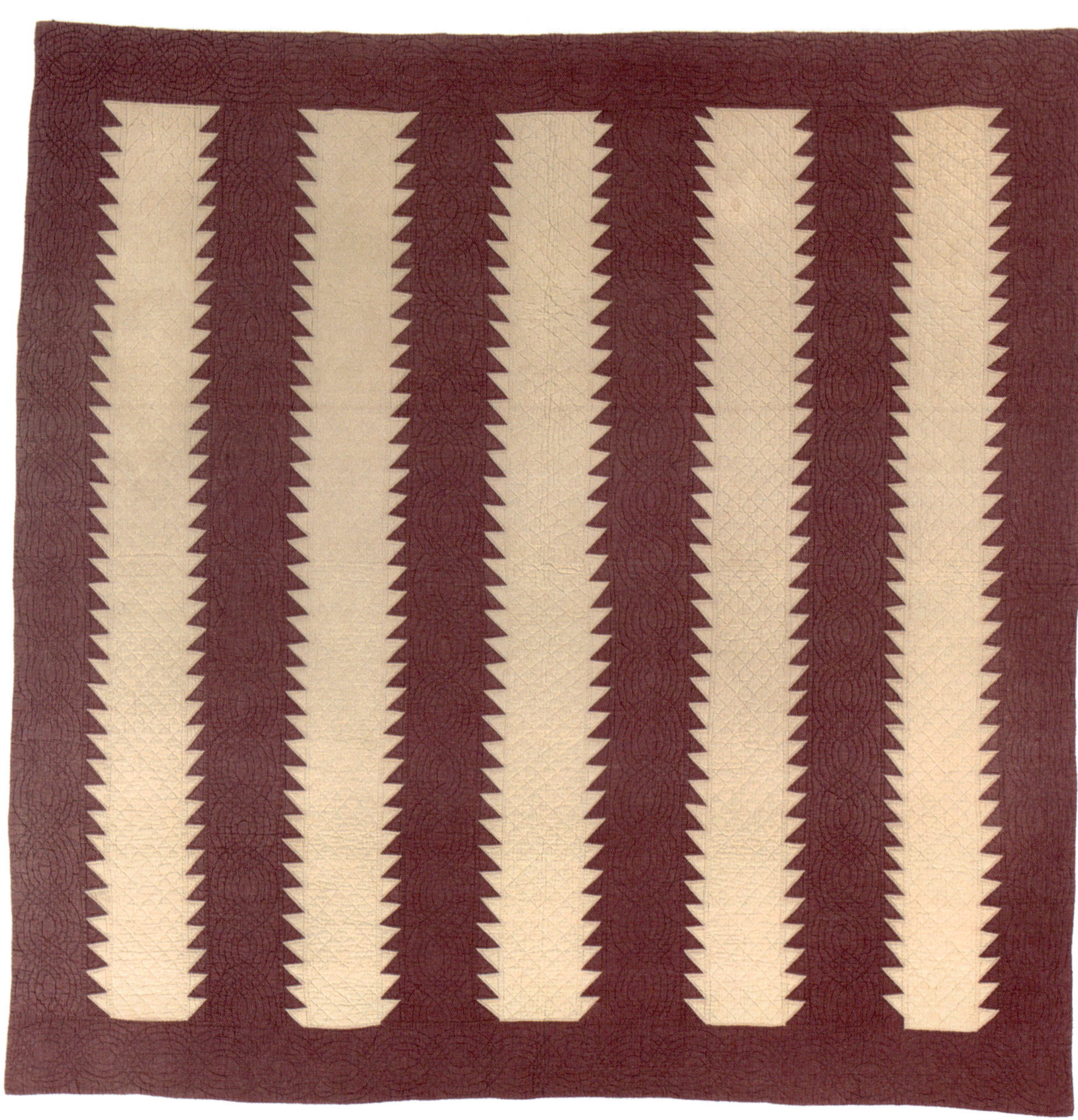

3. **Tree Everlasting**
Maker unidentified
Probably made in Pennsylvania, 1880–1900
Cotton; machine pieced and hand quilted; 72 x 75 in.
Jonathan Holstein and Gail van der Hoof Collection, IQM 2003.003.0003

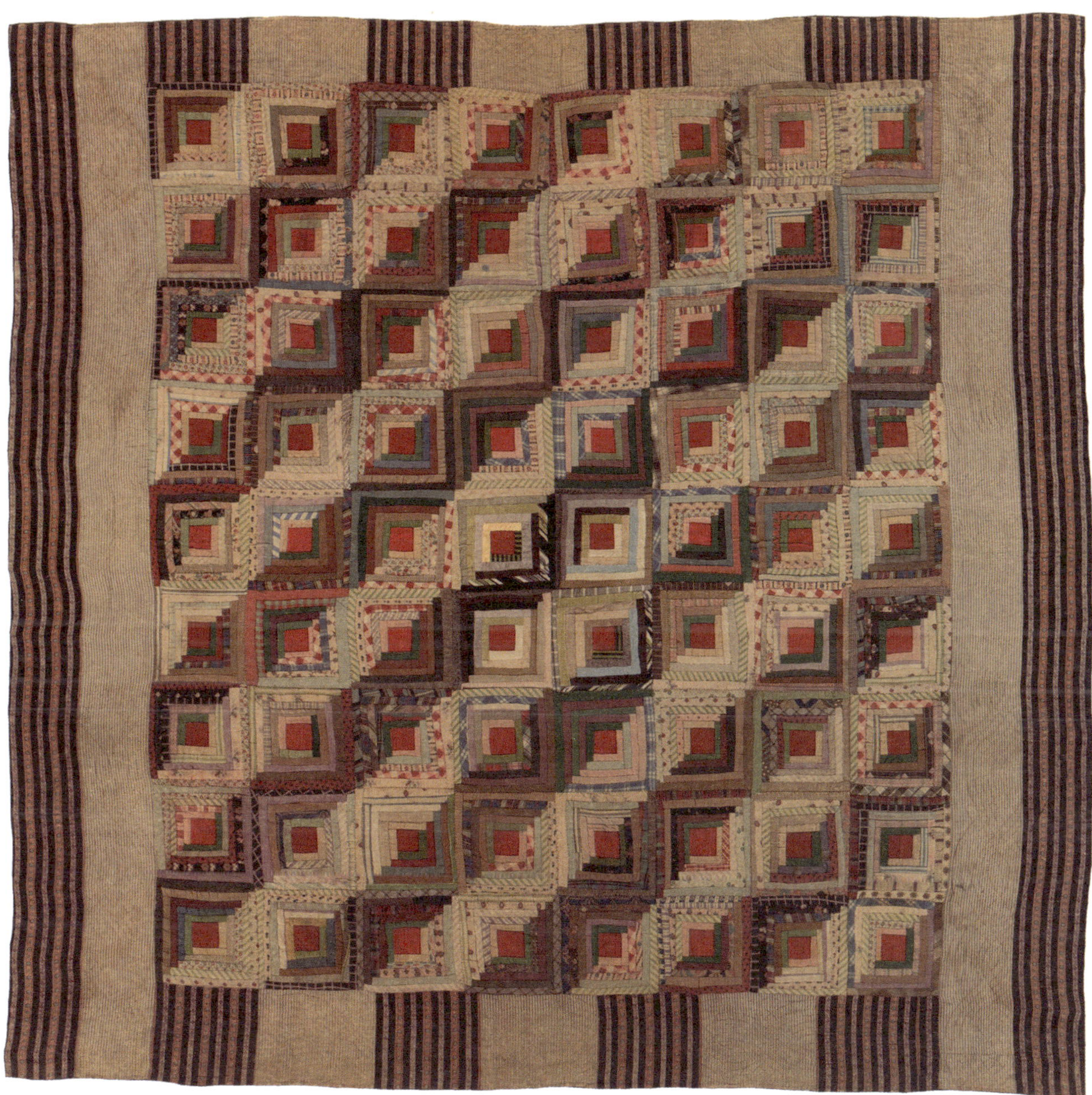

4. **Log Cabin, Straight Furrows setting**
Maker unidentified
Probably made in New Jersey, 1870–1890
Wool; hand pieced and quilted; 86.5 x 88.5 in.
Jonathan Holstein and Gail van der Hoof Collection, IQM 2003.003.0004

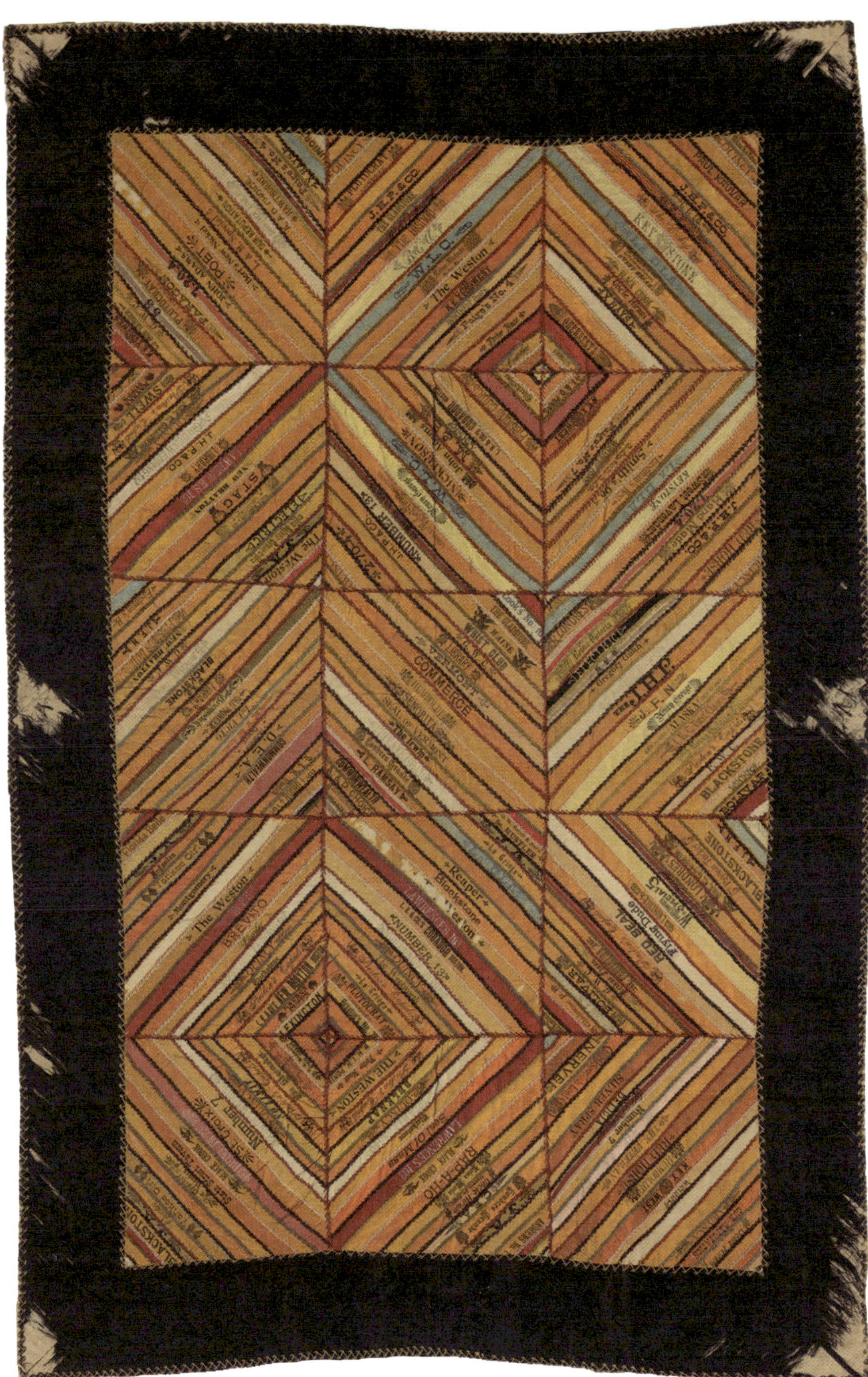

5. **Stripes (Cigar Ribbons)**
Maker unidentified
Possibly made in Maine or Vermont, 1890–1910
Silk; hand pieced and embroidered; 63 x 41 in.
Jonathan Holstein and Gail van der Hoof Collection, IQM 2003.003.0005

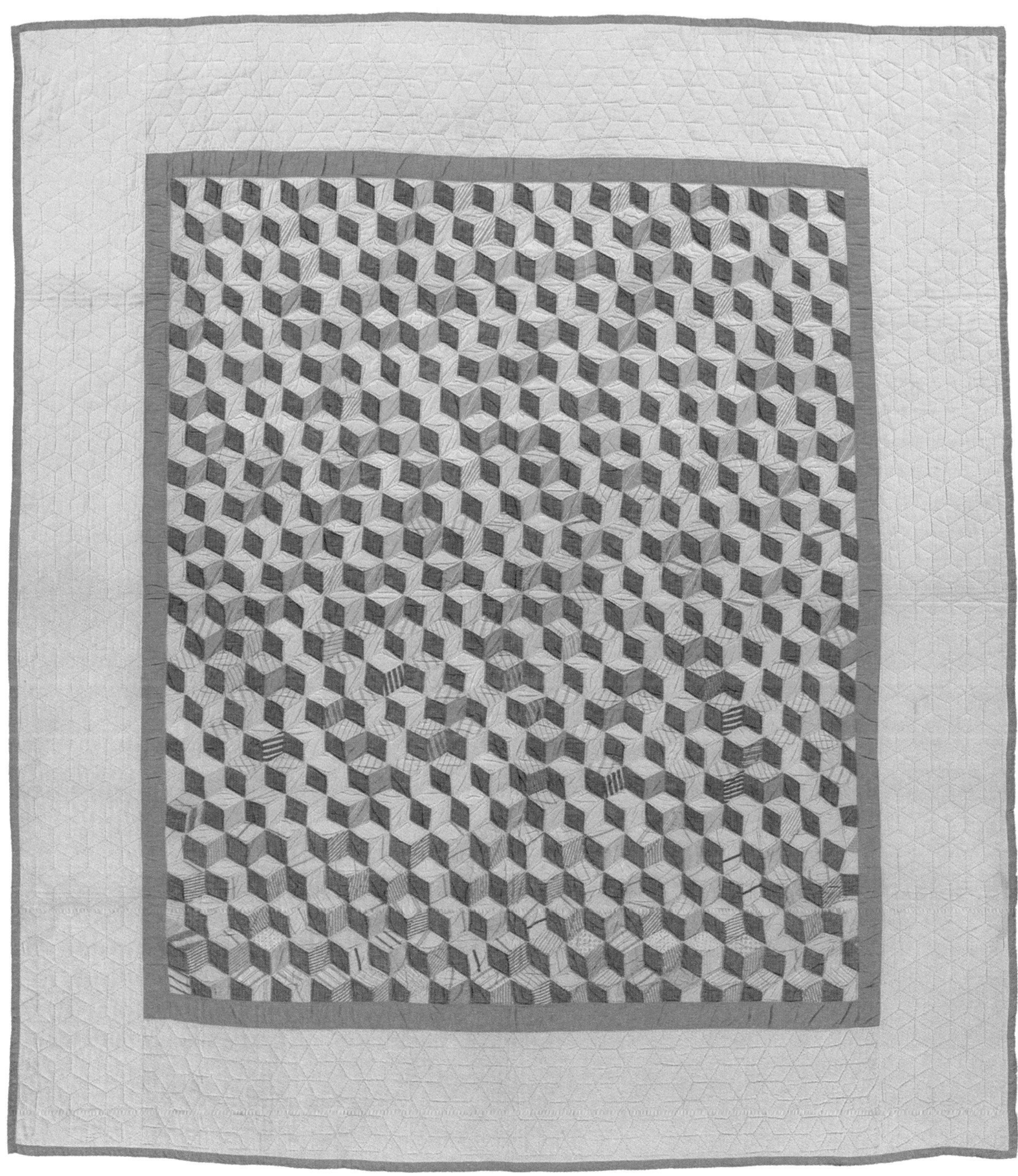

6. **Baby's Blocks**
Maker unidentified
Probably made in Pennsylvania, 1900–1920
Cotton; machine and hand pieced, hand quilted; 78.5 x 72 in.
Jonathan Holstein and Gail van der Hoof Collection, IQM 2003.003.0006

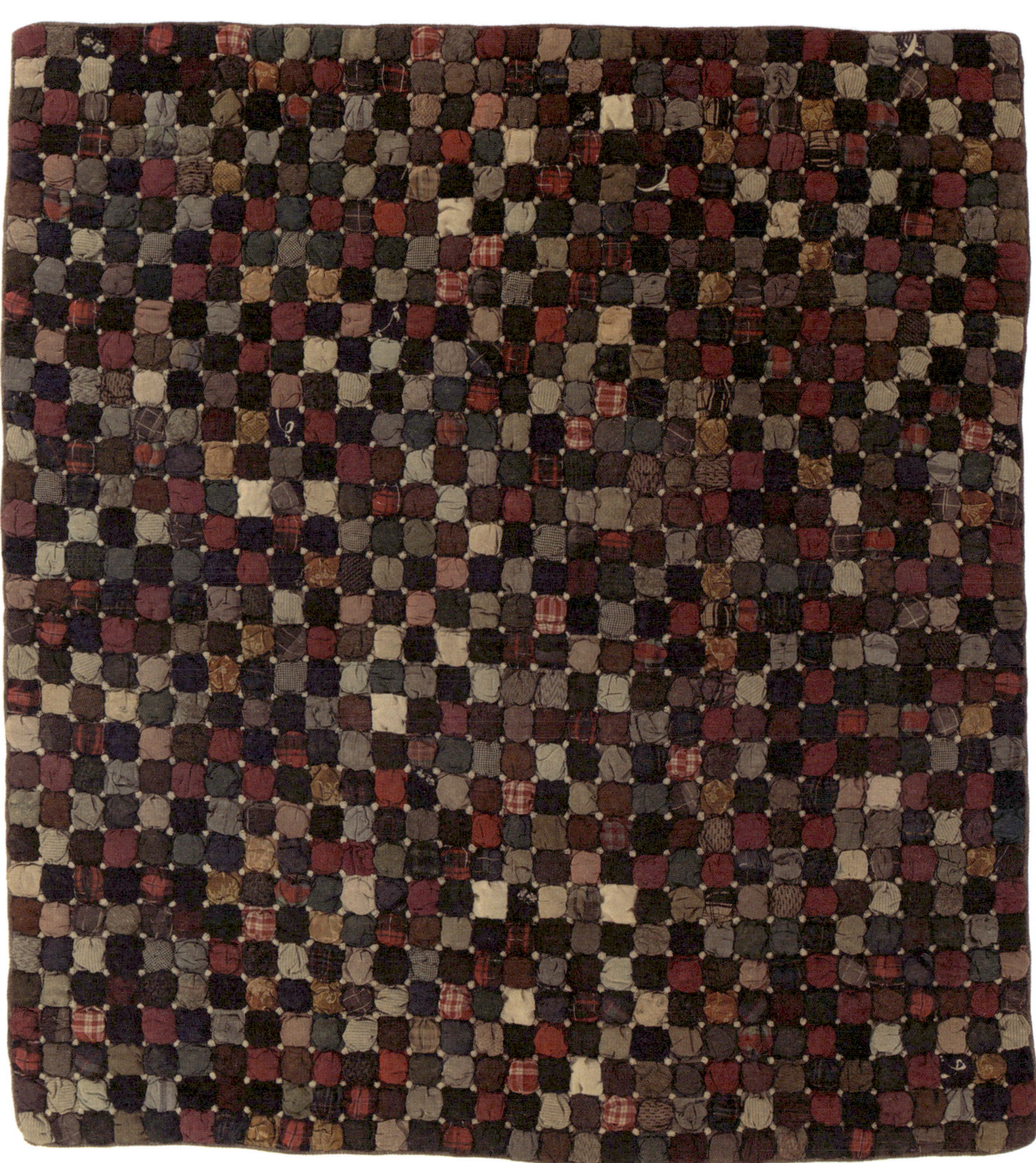

7. **Puffs**
Maker unidentified
Probably made in Maine, 1900–1920
Wool; hand pieced, tied; 76 x 71 in.
Jonathan Holstein and Gail van der Hoof Collection, IQM 2003.003.0007

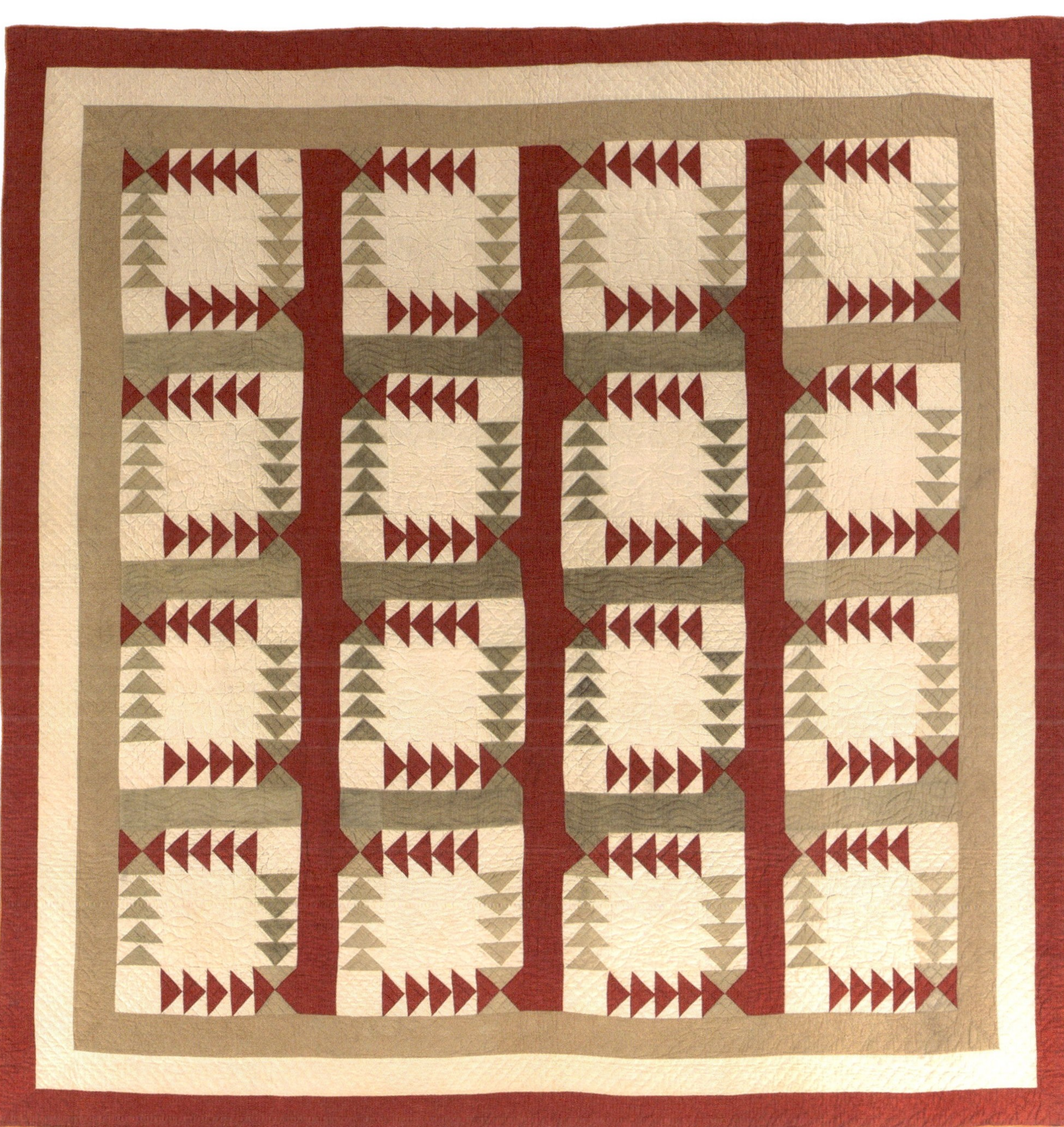

8. **Wild Goose Chase variation**
Maker unidentified
Probably made in Pennsylvania, 1880–1900
Cotton; machine pieced, hand quilted; 81.5 x 81.5 in.
Jonathan Holstein and Gail van der Hoof Collection, IQM 2003.003.0008

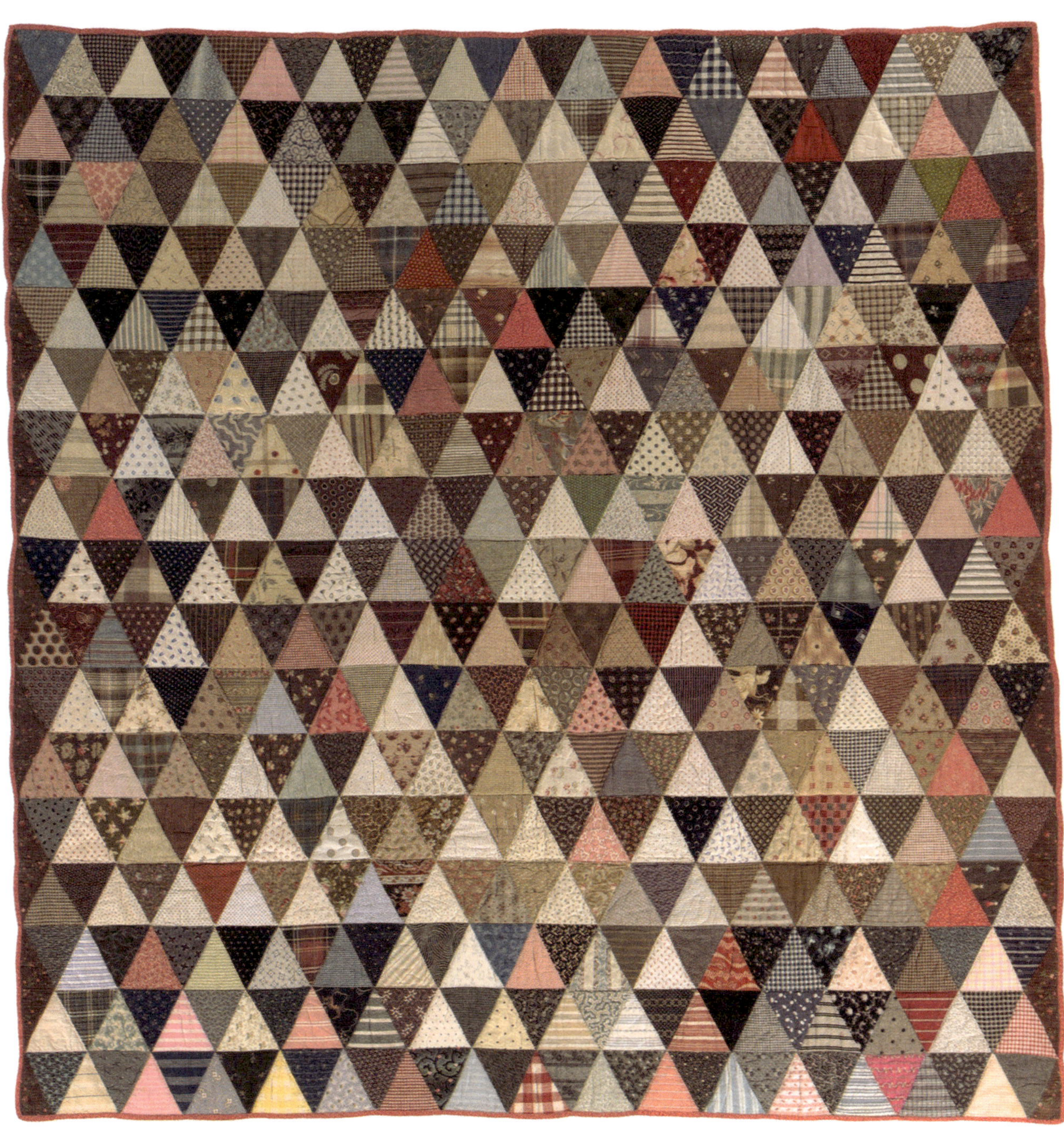

9. **Thousand Pyramids**
Maker unidentified
Probably made in Pennsylvania, 1880–1900
Cotton; hand pieced and quilted; 77.5 x 78 in.
Jonathan Holstein and Gail van der Hoof Collection, IQM 2003.003.0009

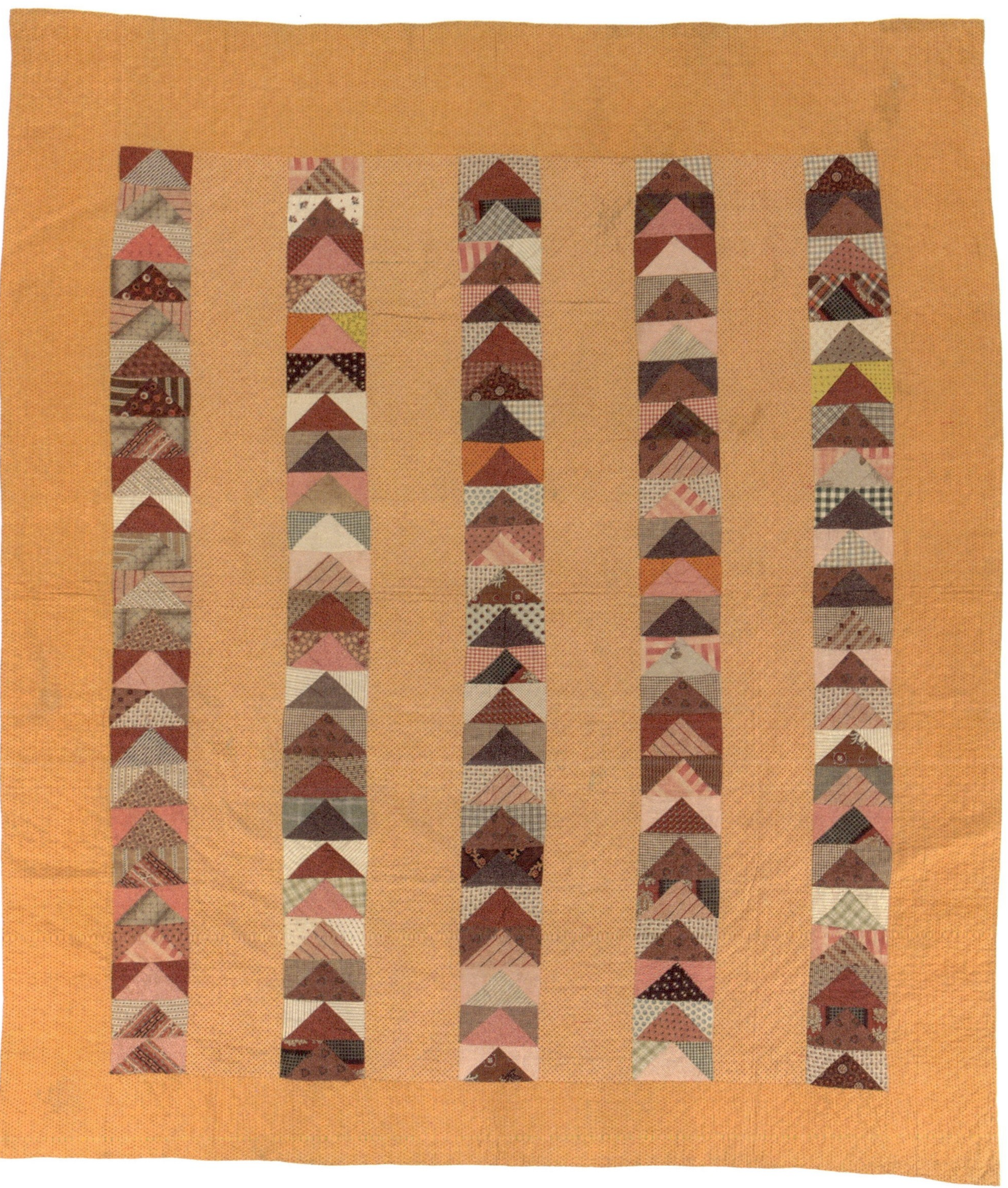

10. **Wild Goose Chase**
Maker unidentified
Probably made in Pennsylvania, 1870–1890
Cotton; hand and machine pieced, hand quilted; 85 x 76.5 in.
Jonathan Holstein and Gail van der Hoof Collection, IQM 2003.003.0010

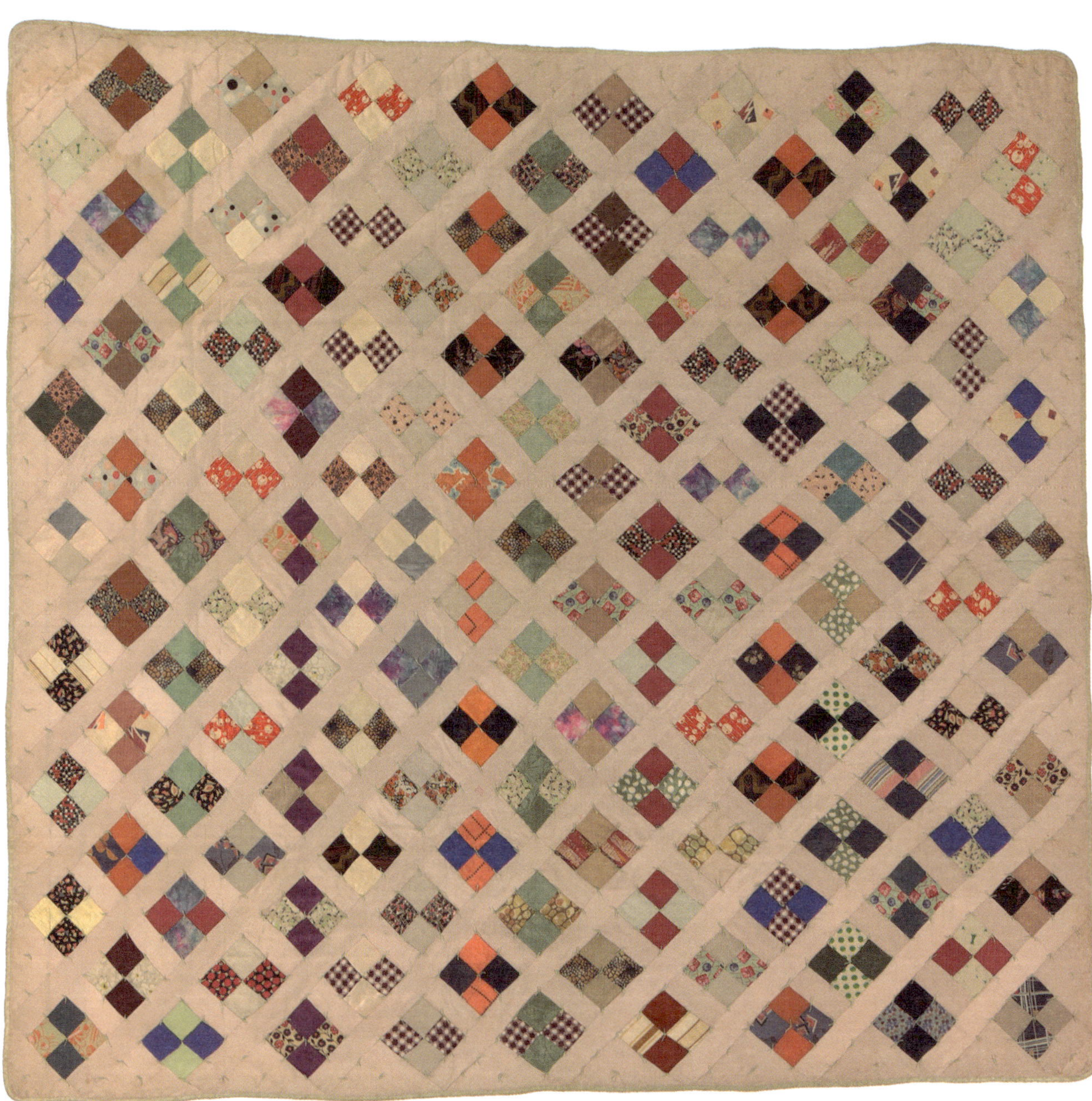

11. **Four Patch**
Maker unidentified
Possibly made in Pennsylvania, 1930–1950
Rayon and silk; machine pieced, tied; 81 x 83 in.
Jonathan Holstein and Gail van der Hoof Collection, IQM 2003.003.0011

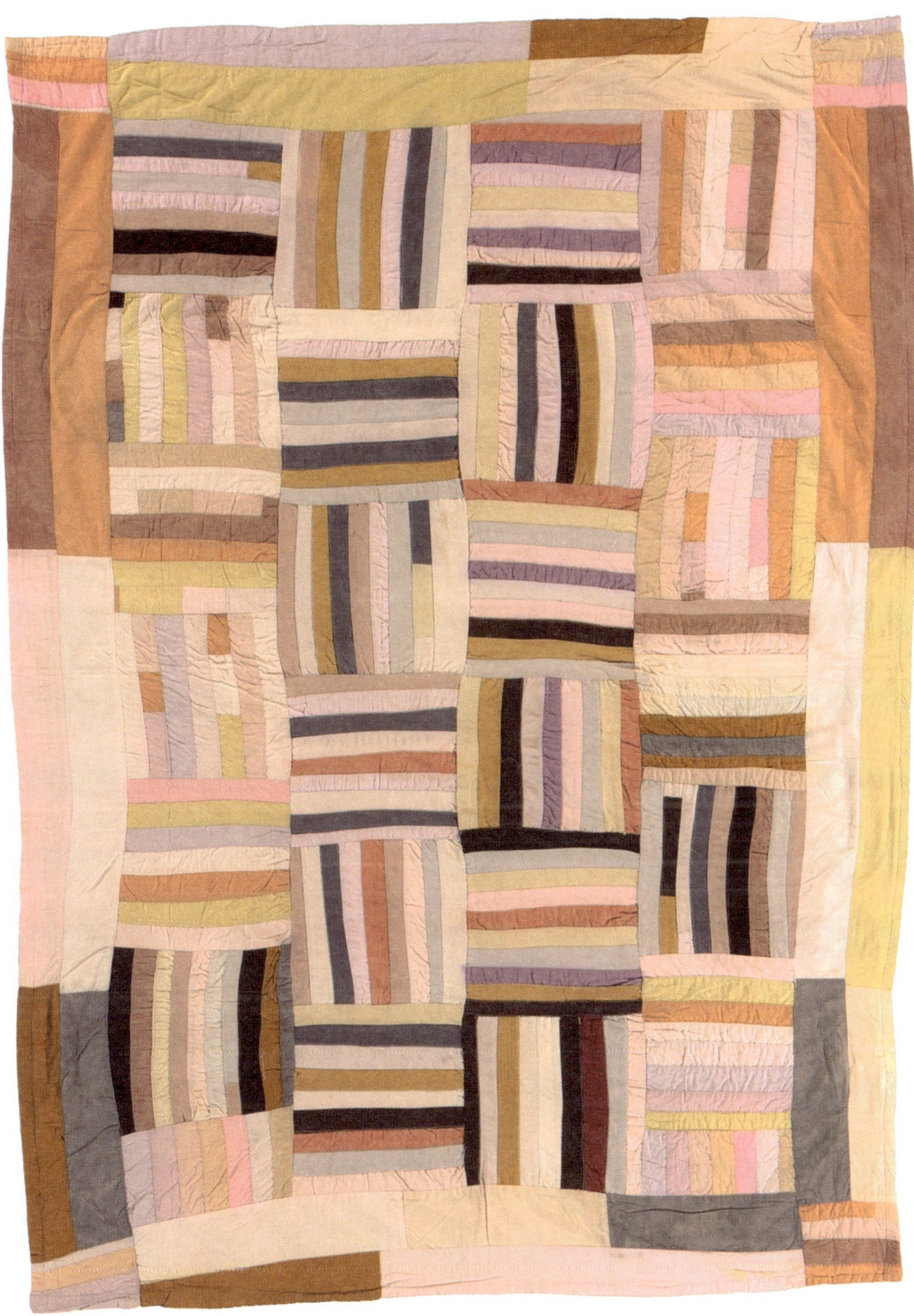

12. **Roman Stripe variation**
    Maker unidentified
    Possibly made in Vermont, 1930–1950
    Cotton and rayon; machine pieced; 86 x 63 in.
    Jonathan Holstein and Gail van der Hoof Collection, IQM 2003.003.0012

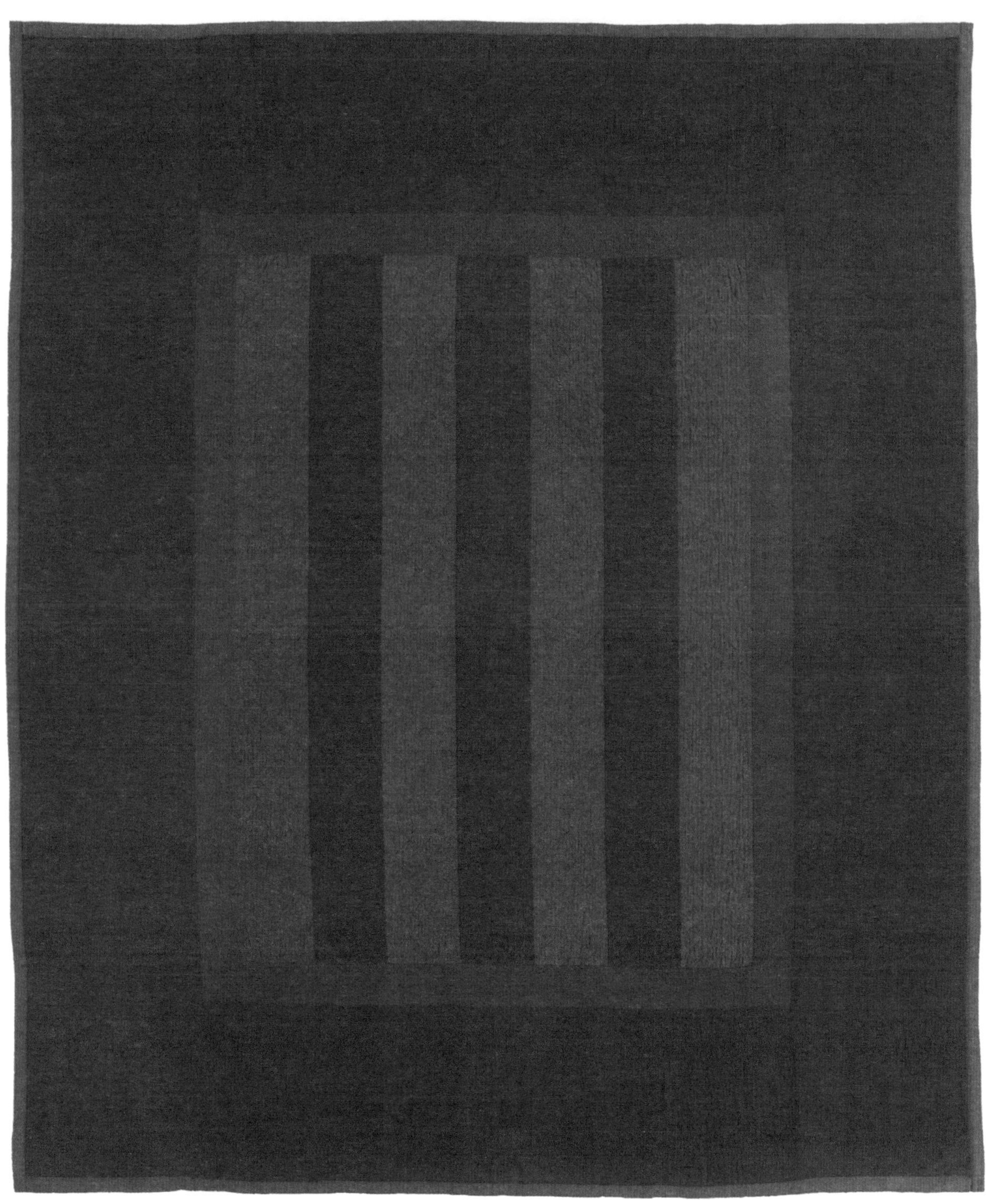

13. **Bars**
Amish maker unidentified
Made in Lancaster County, Pennsylvania, 1890–1910
Wool; machine pieced, hand quilted; 84 x 71 in.
Jonathan Holstein and Gail van der Hoof Collection, IQM 2003.003.0013

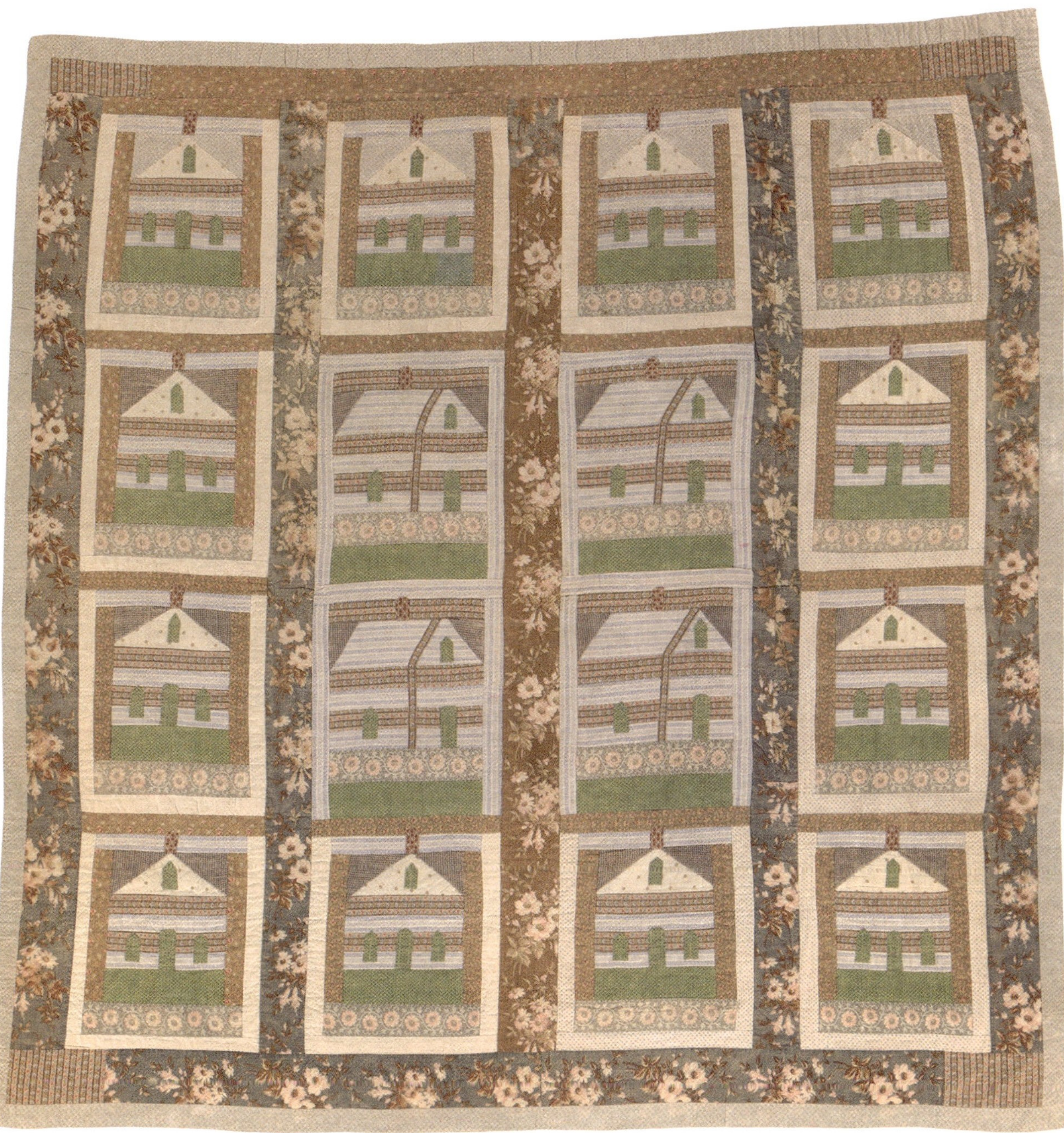

14. **Schoolhouse**
Maker unidentified
Probably made in New Hampshire, 1880–1900
Cotton; hand pieced and quilted; 75 x 76 in.
Jonathan Holstein and Gail van der Hoof Collection, IQM 2003.003.0014

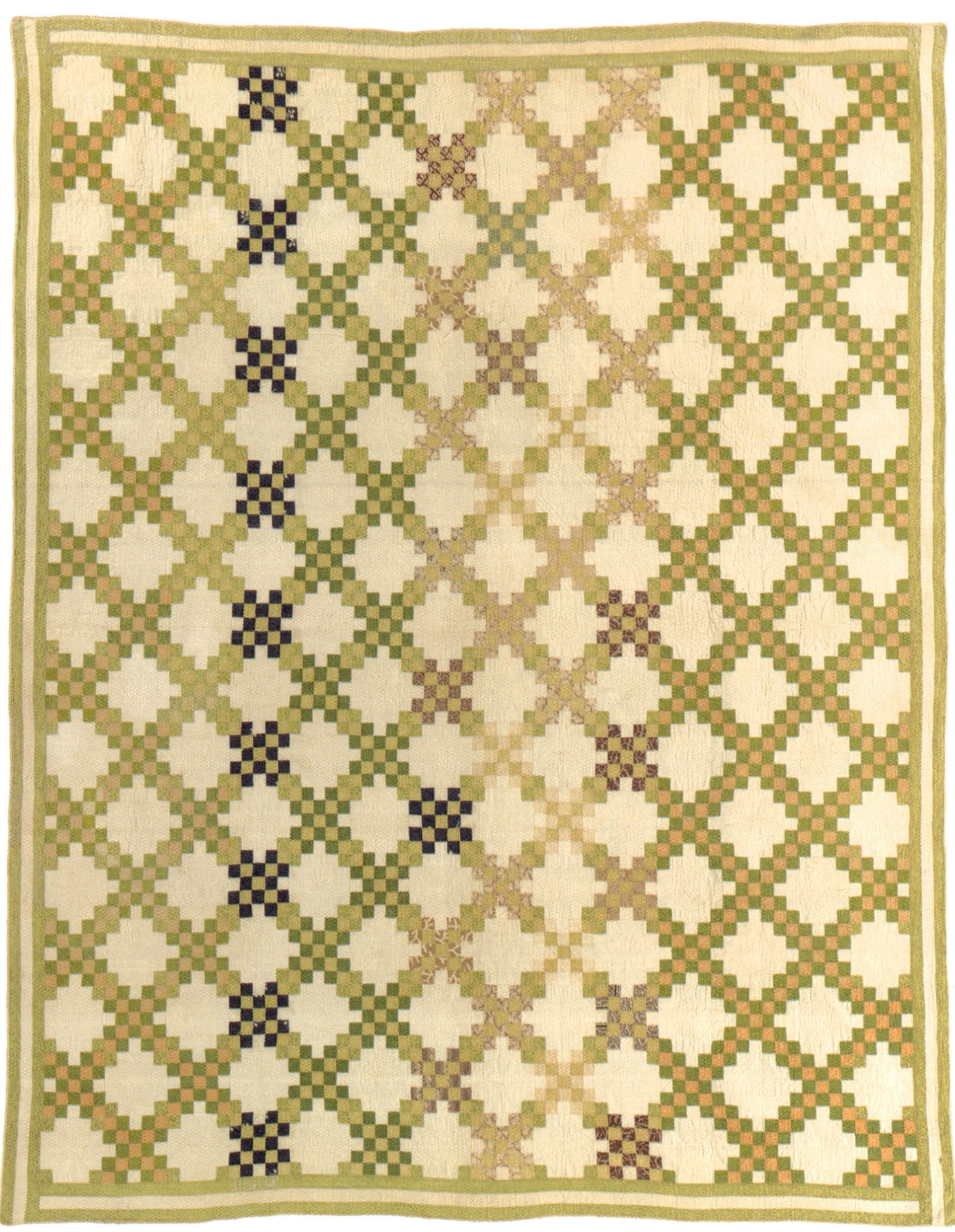

15. **Double Irish Chain**
Maker unidentified
Probably made in Pennsylvania, 1850–1870
Cotton; hand pieced and quilted; 95 x 76 in.
Jonathan Holstein and Gail van der Hoof Collection, IQM 2003.003.0015

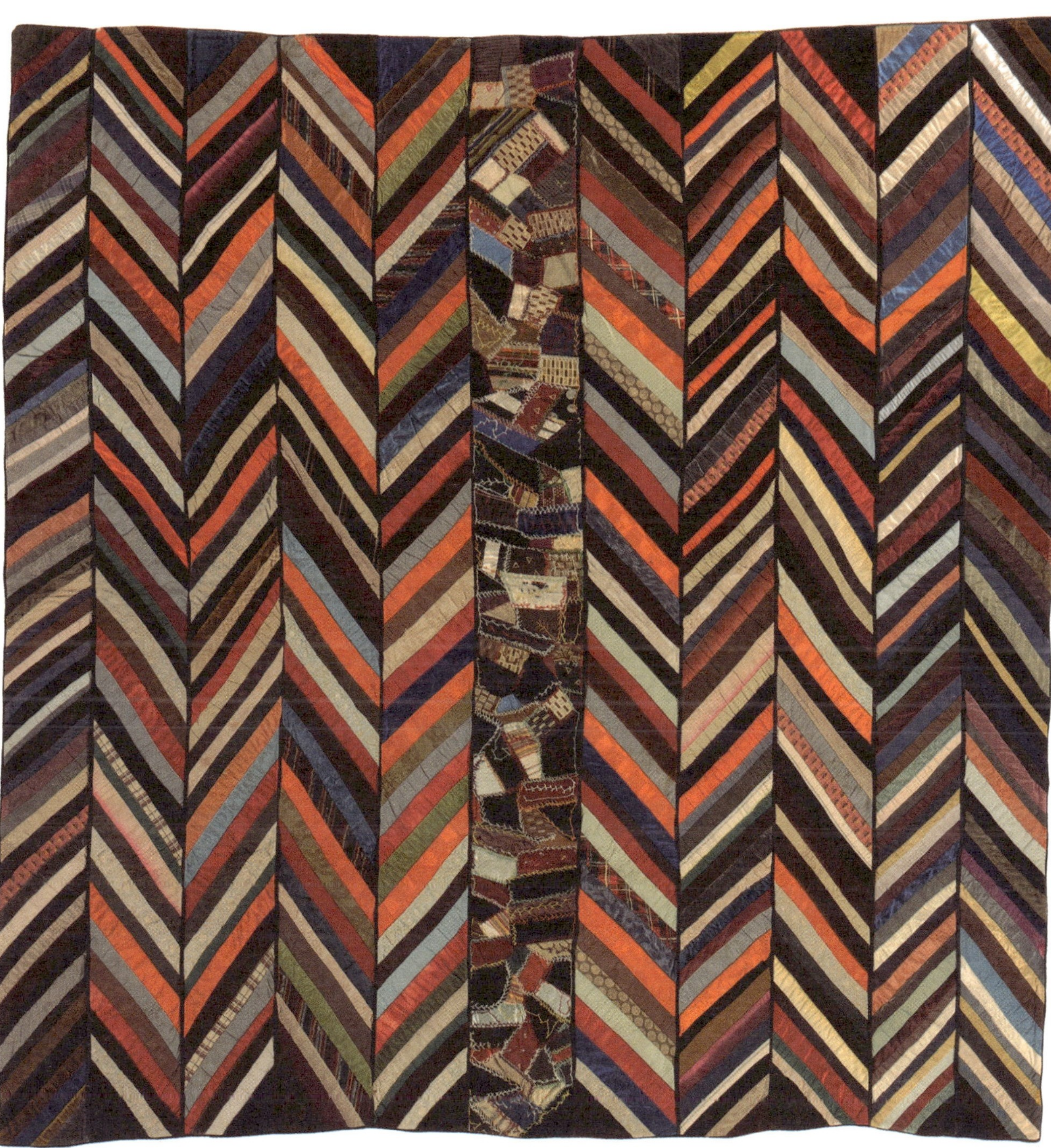

16. **Zig Zag**
Maker unidentified
Probably made in Pennsylvania, 1880–1900
Silk; hand pieced and embroidered, tied; 77 x 76 in.
Jonathan Holstein and Gail van der Hoof Collection, IQM 2003.003.0016

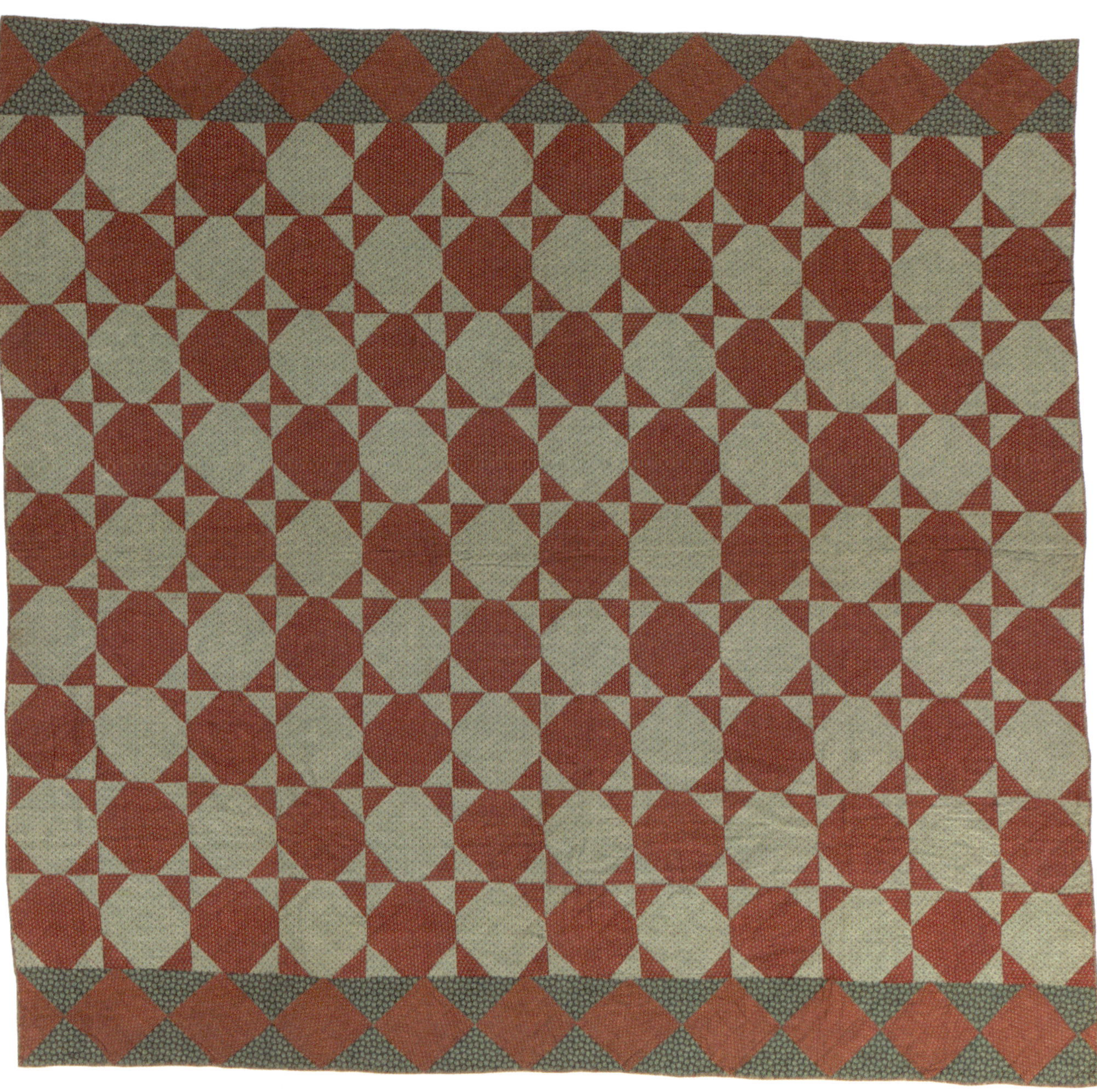

17. **Rob Peter to Pay Paul**
Maker unidentified
Probably made in Pennsylvania, 1880–1900
Cotton; hand pieced and quilted; 83 x 77.5 in.
Jonathan Holstein and Gail van der Hoof Collection, IQM 2003.003.0017

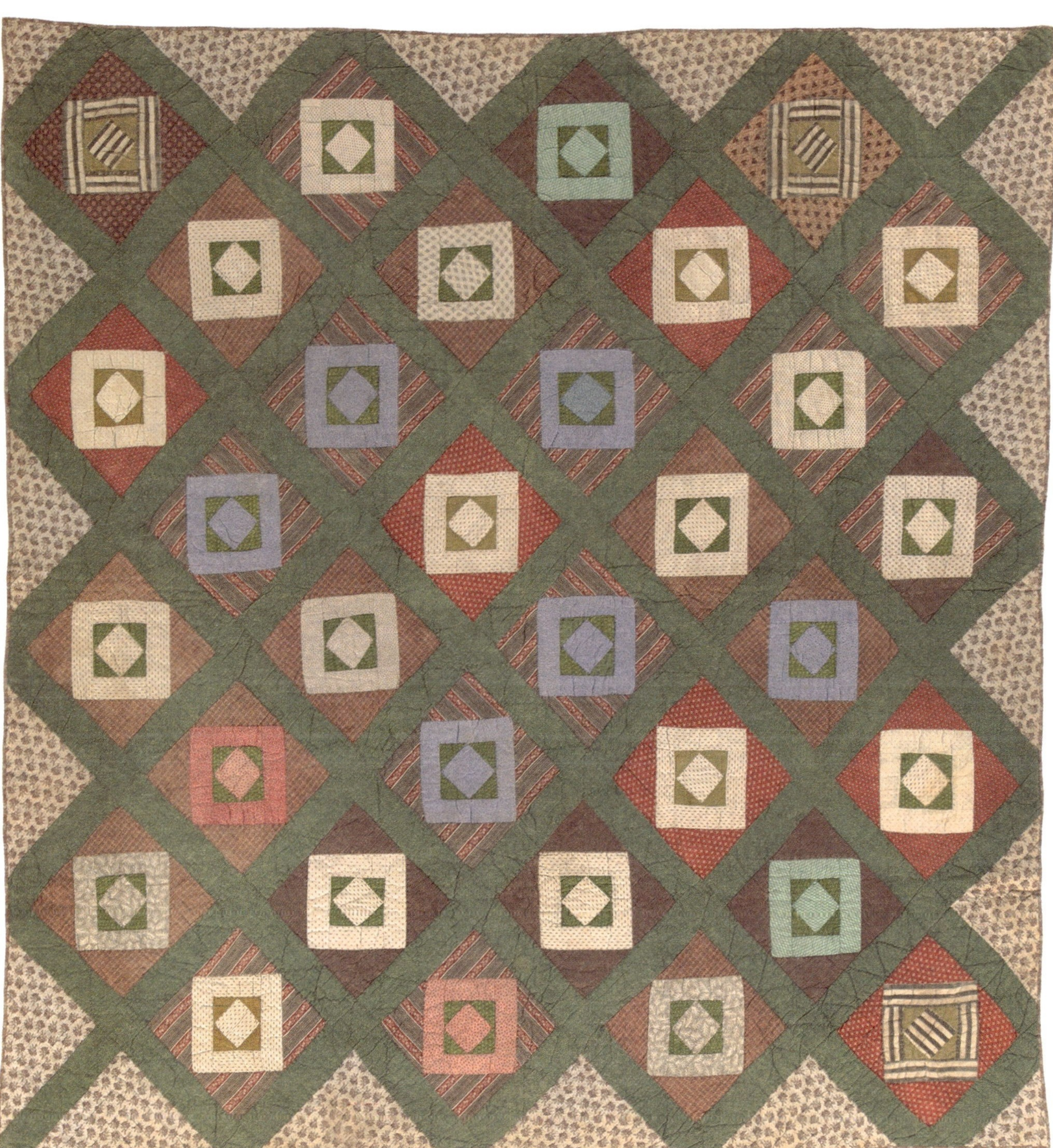

18. **King's Crown**
Maker unidentified
Probably made in Pennsylvania, 1880–1900
Cotton; machine pieced, hand quilted; 82 x 79 in.
Jonathan Holstein and Gail van der Hoof Collection, IQM 2003.003.0018

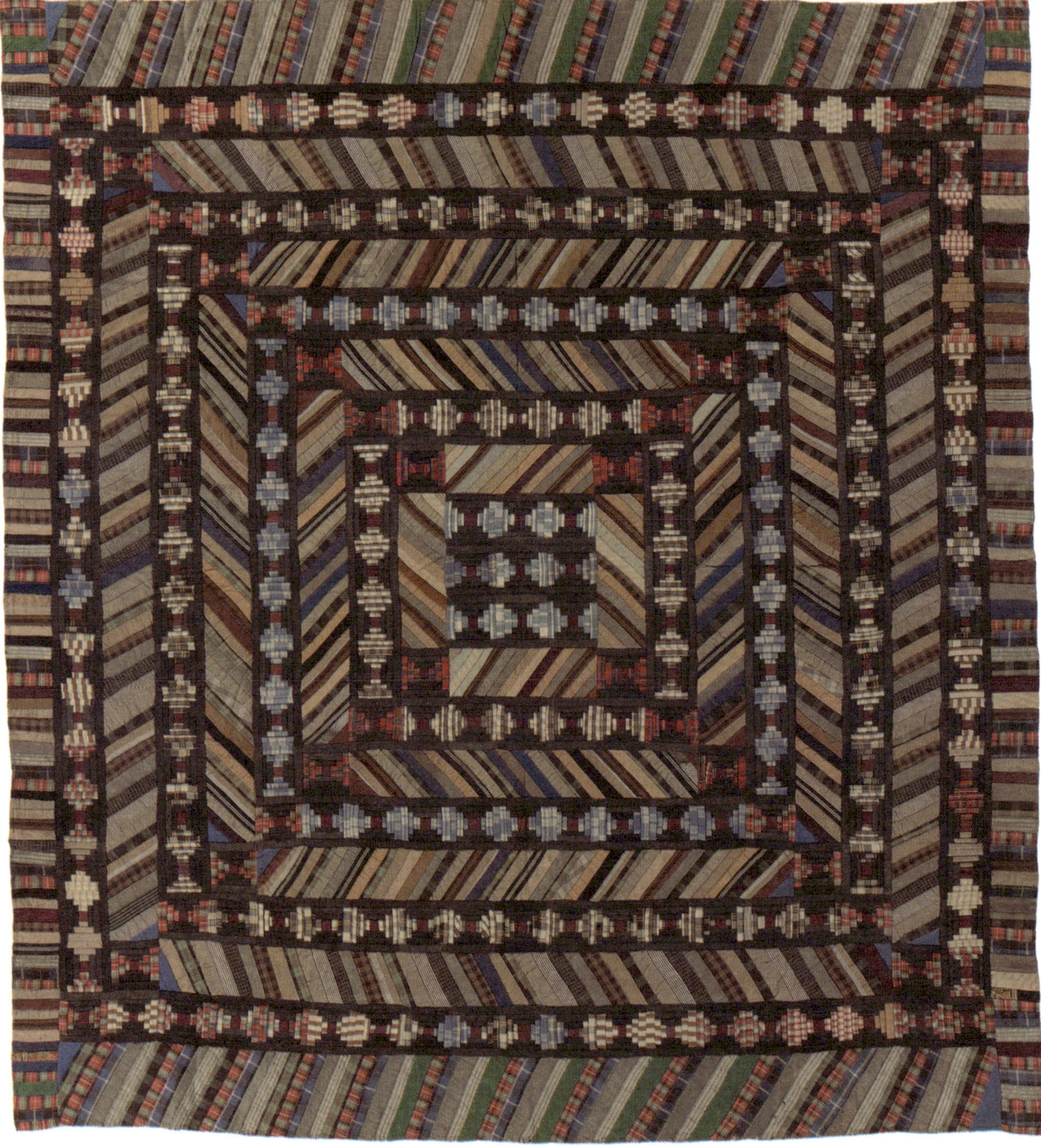

19. **Log Cabin, Courthouse Steps variation**
Maker unidentified
Probably made in Pennsylvania, 1880–1900
Wool; hand pieced, unquilted; 88.5 x 84 in.
Jonathan Holstein and Gail van der Hoof Collection, IQM 2003.003.0019

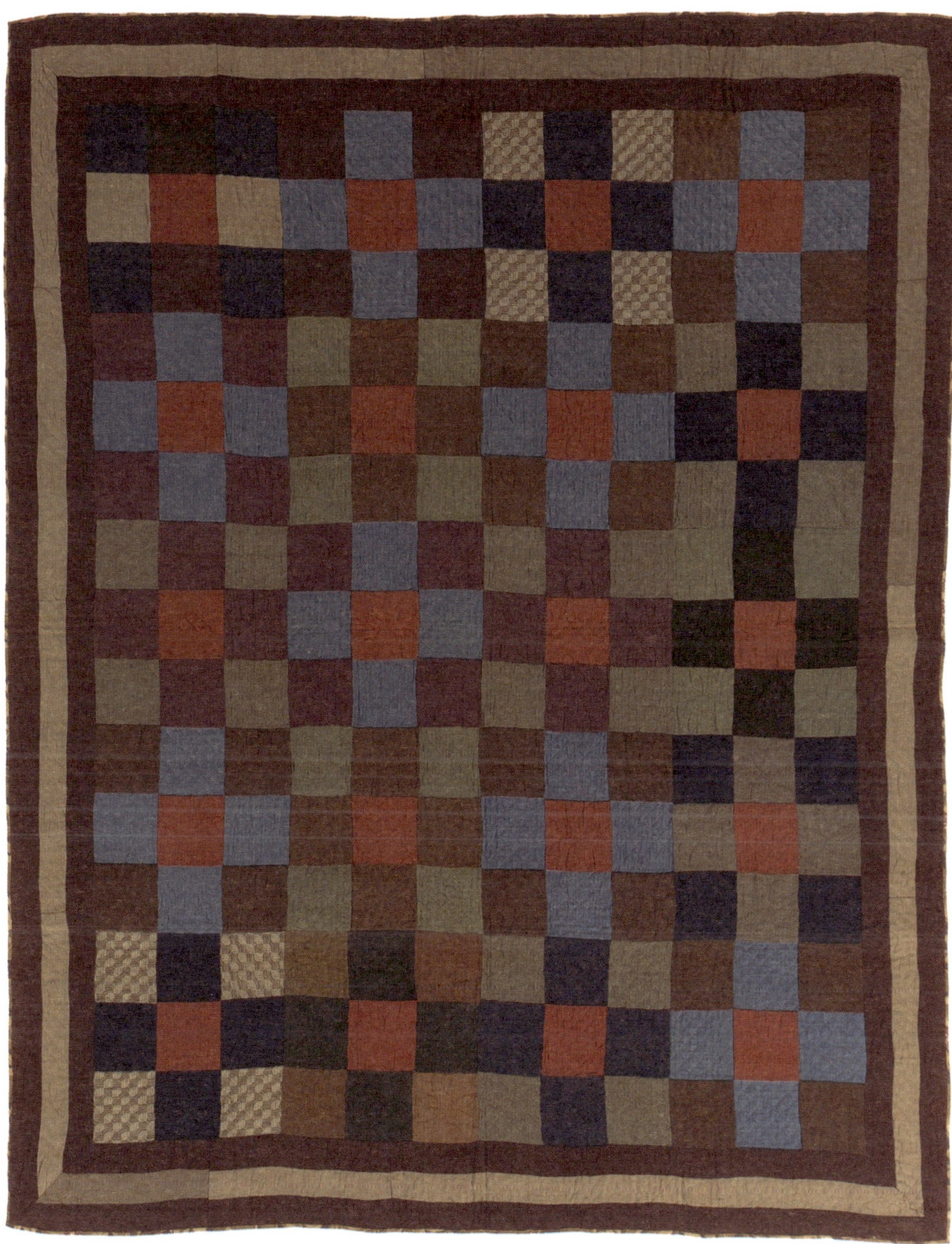

20. **Nine Patch**
Maker unidentified
Probably made in Pennsylvania, 1880–1900
Wool; machine pieced, hand quilted; 85 x 68 in.
Jonathan Holstein and Gail van der Hoof Collection, IQM 2003.003.0020

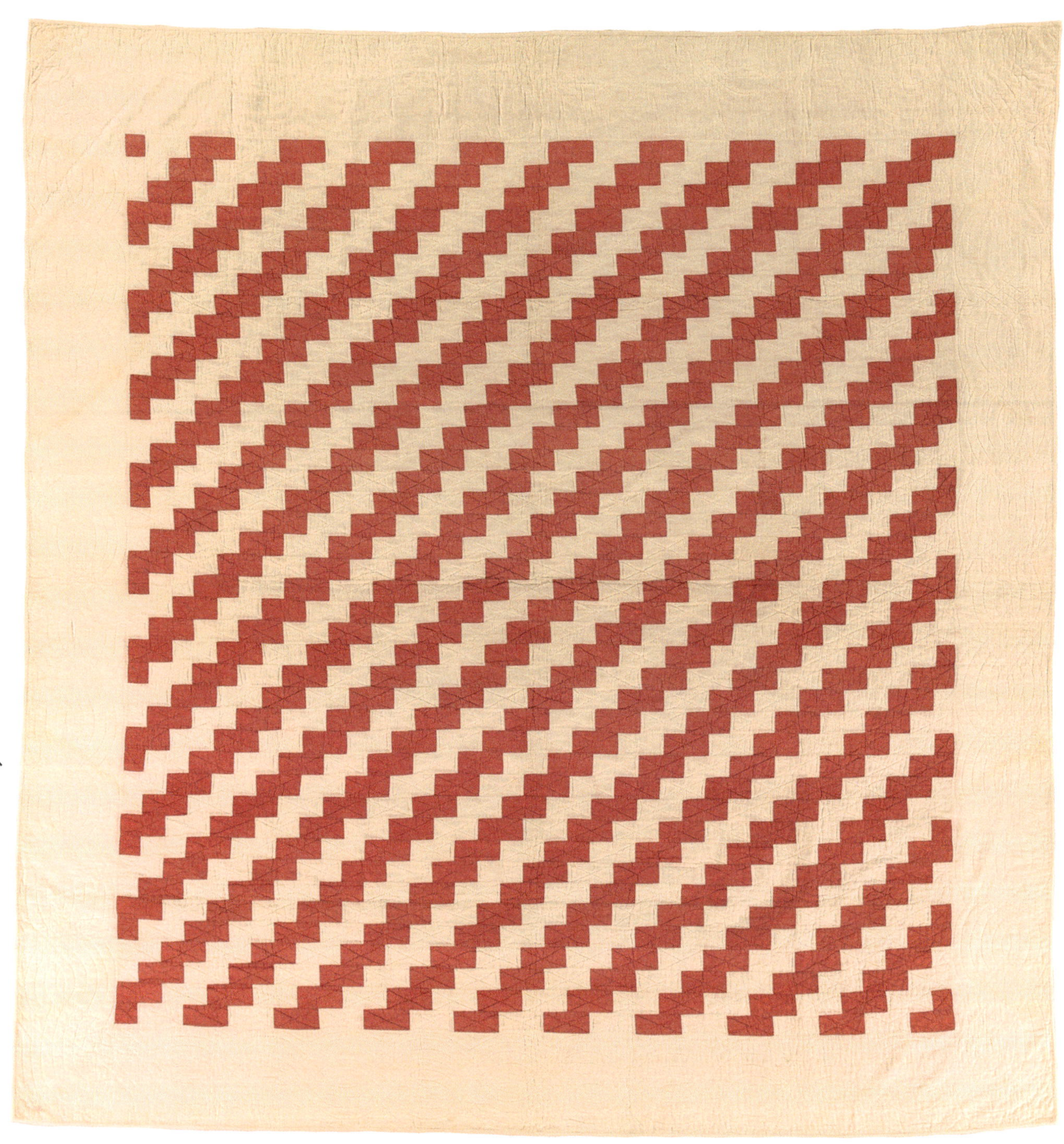

21. **Streak of Lightning**
Maker unidentified
Probably made in Pennsylvania, 1890–1910
Cotton; machine pieced, hand quilted; 79.5 x 77 in.
Jonathan Holstein and Gail van der Hoof Collection, IQM 2003.003.0021

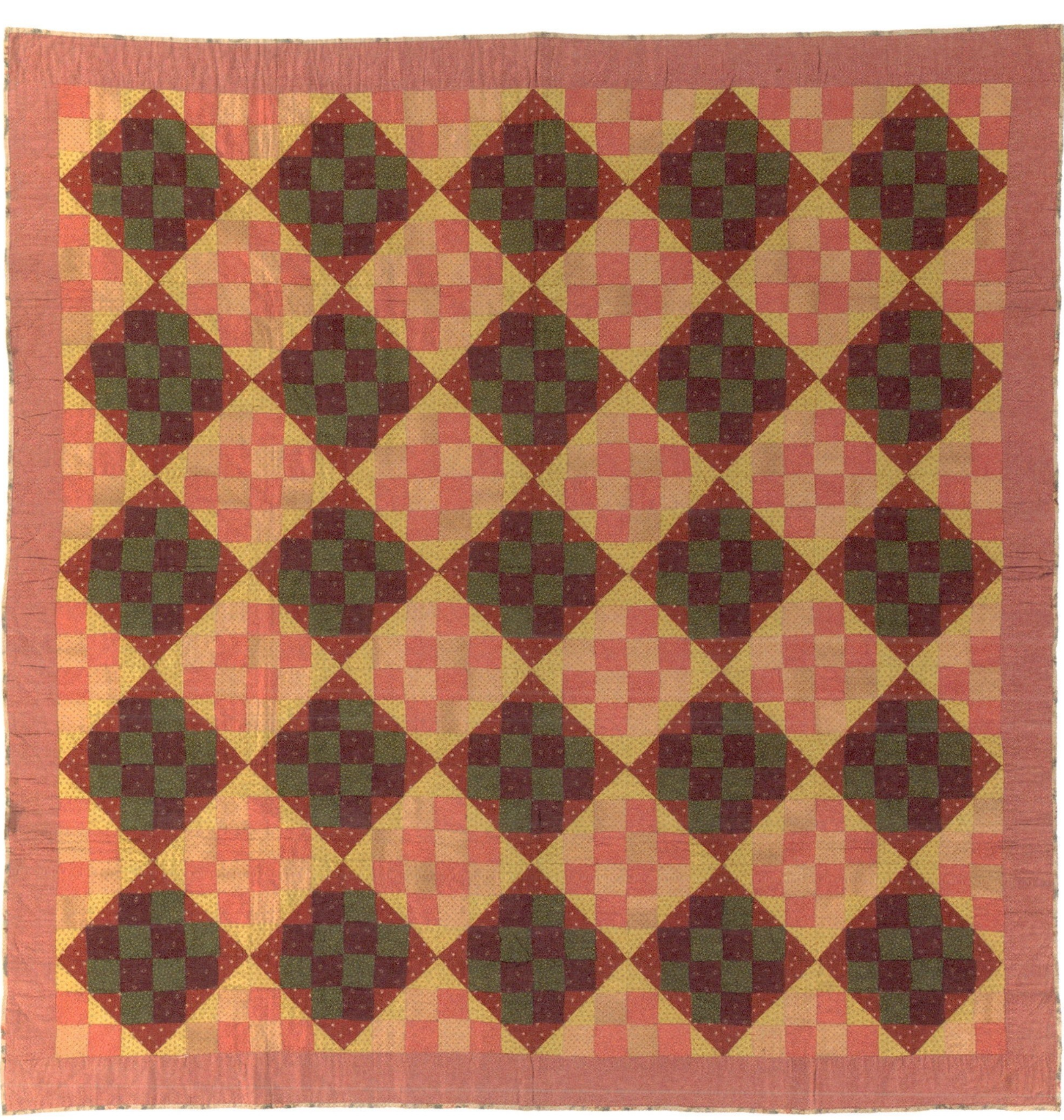

22. **Checkerboard**
Maker unidentified
Probably made in New Jersey, 1880–1900
Cotton; machine pieced, hand quilted; 87 x 88 in.
Jonathan Holstein and Gail van der Hoof Collection, IQM 2003.003.0022

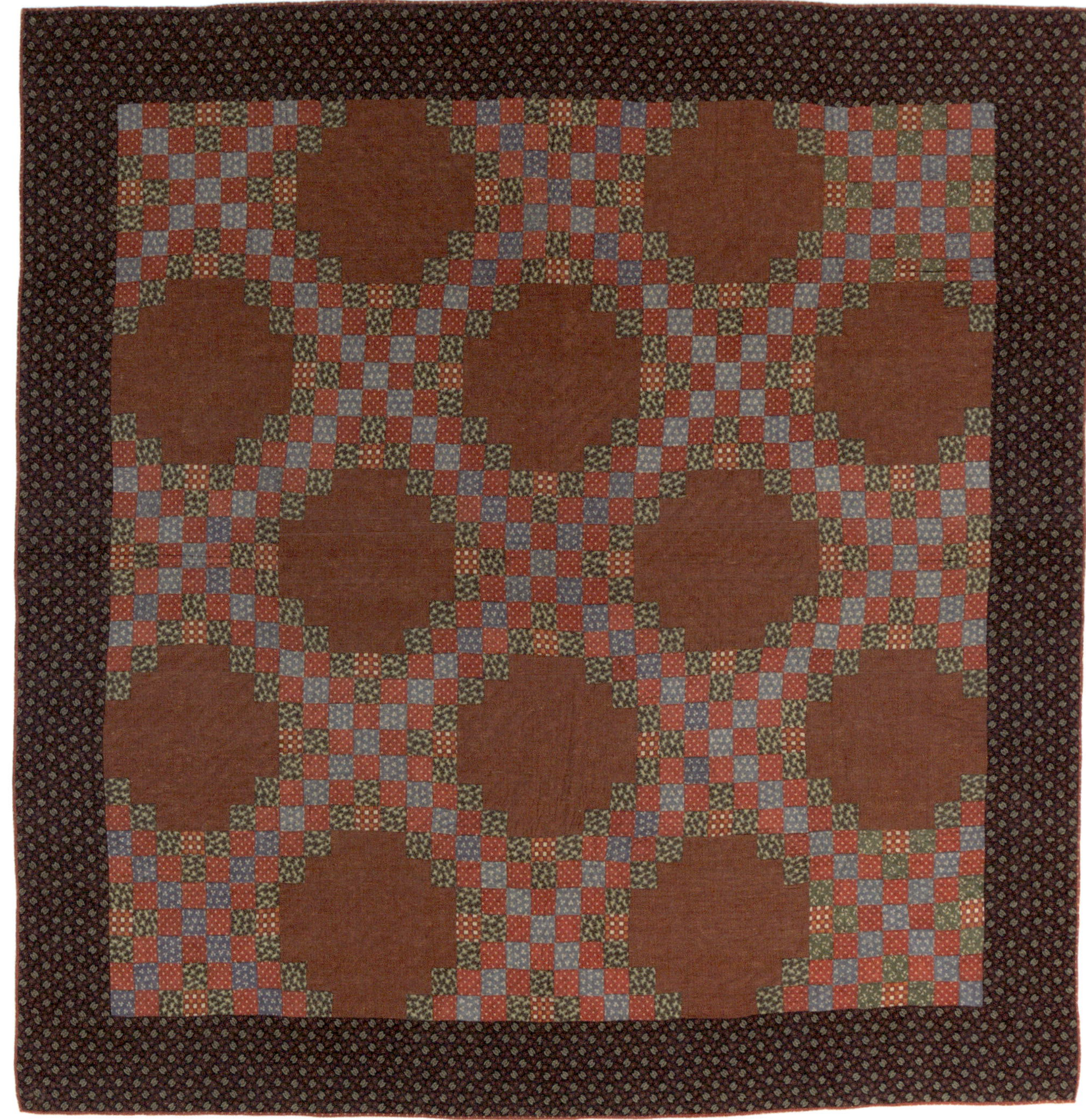

23. **Triple Irish Chain**
Maker unidentified
Probably made in Pennsylvania, 1880–1900
Wool; hand pieced and quilted; 84 x 83 in.
Jonathan Holstein and Gail van der Hoof Collection, IQM 2003.003.0023

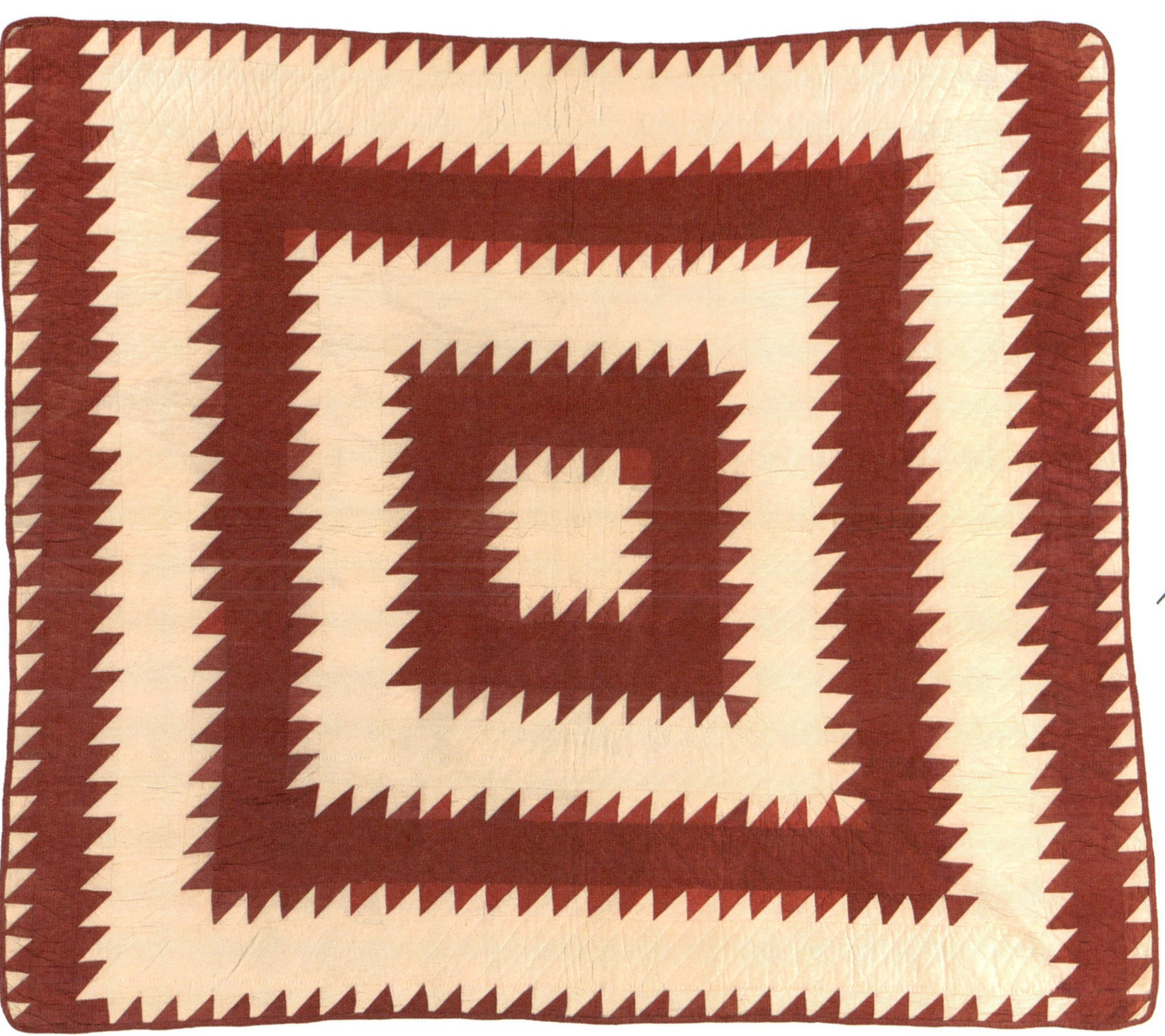

24. **Sawtooth**
Maker unidentified
Probably made in Massachusetts, 1890–1910
Cotton; hand pieced and quilted; 89.5 x 76 in.
Jonathan Holstein and Gail van der Hoof Collection, IQM 2003.003.0024

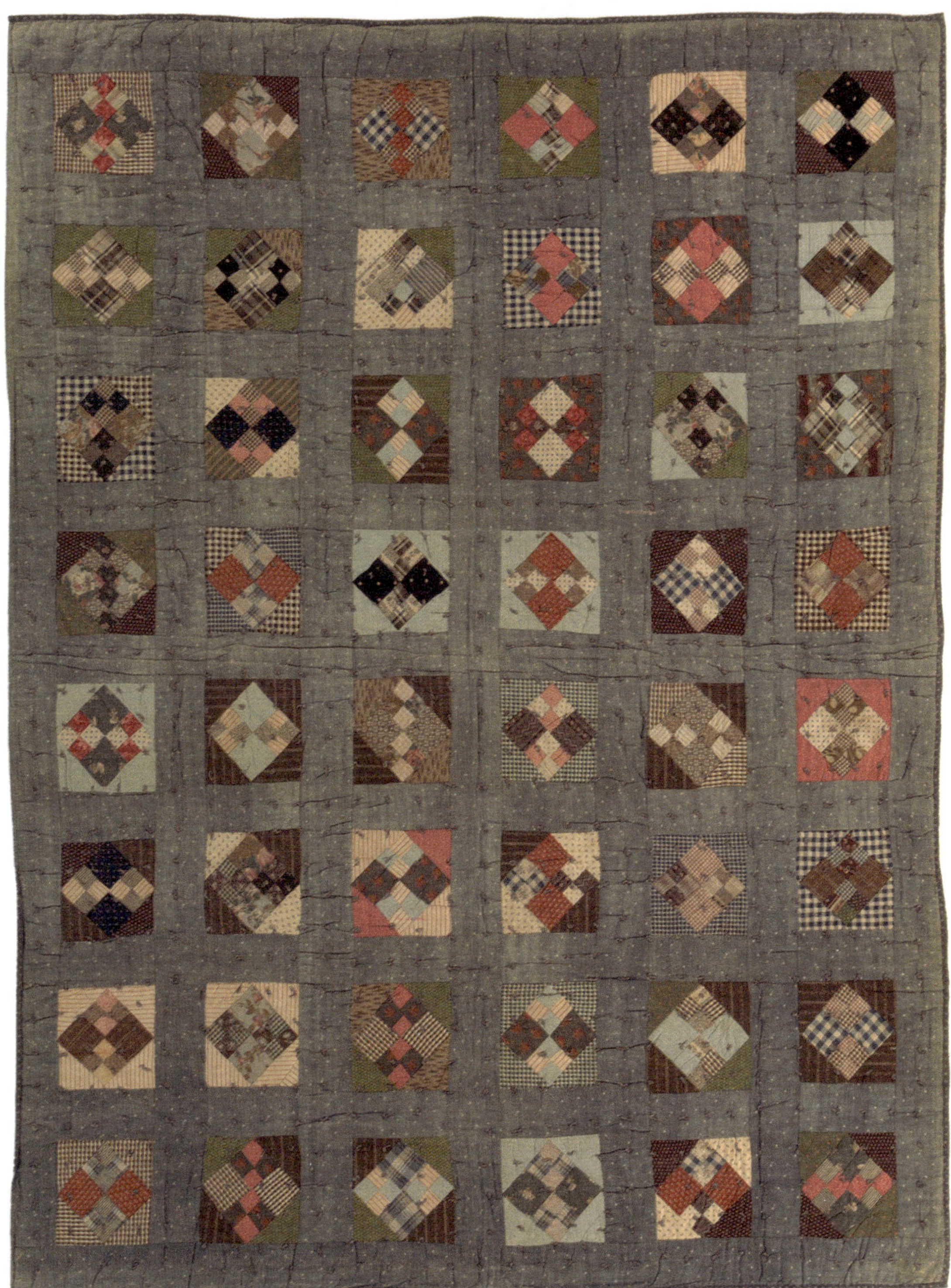

25. **Four Patch**
Maker unidentified
Probably made in Pennsylvania, 1890–1910
Cotton; hand pieced, tied; 87 x 66 in.
Jonathan Holstein and Gail van der Hoof Collection, IQM 2003.003.0025

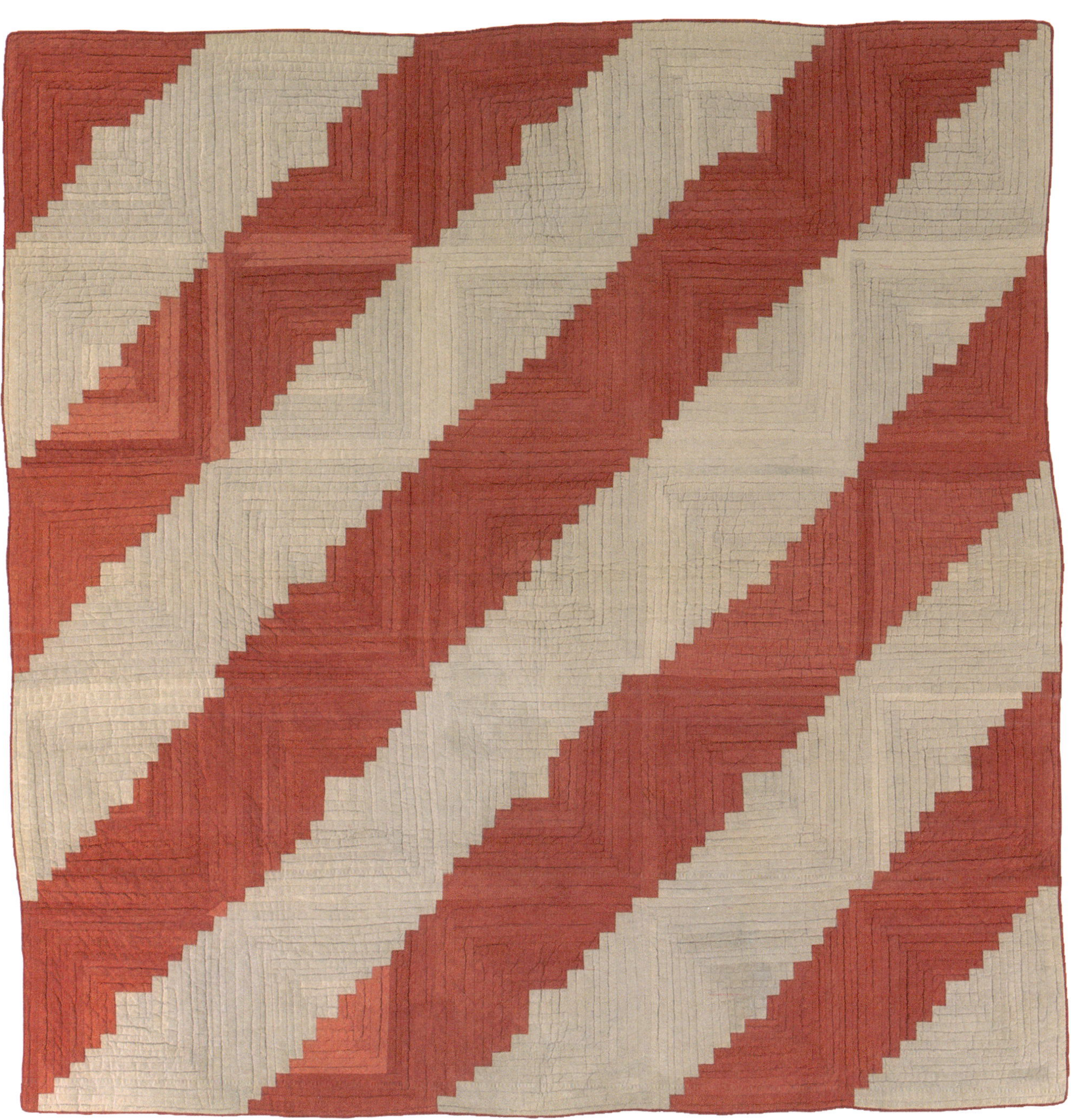

26. **Log Cabin, Straight Furrows setting**
Maker unidentified
Probably made in Pennsylvania, 1890–1910
Cotton; machine pieced, hand quilted; 74 x 74.5 in.
Jonathan Holstein and Gail van der Hoof Collection, IQM 2003.003.0026

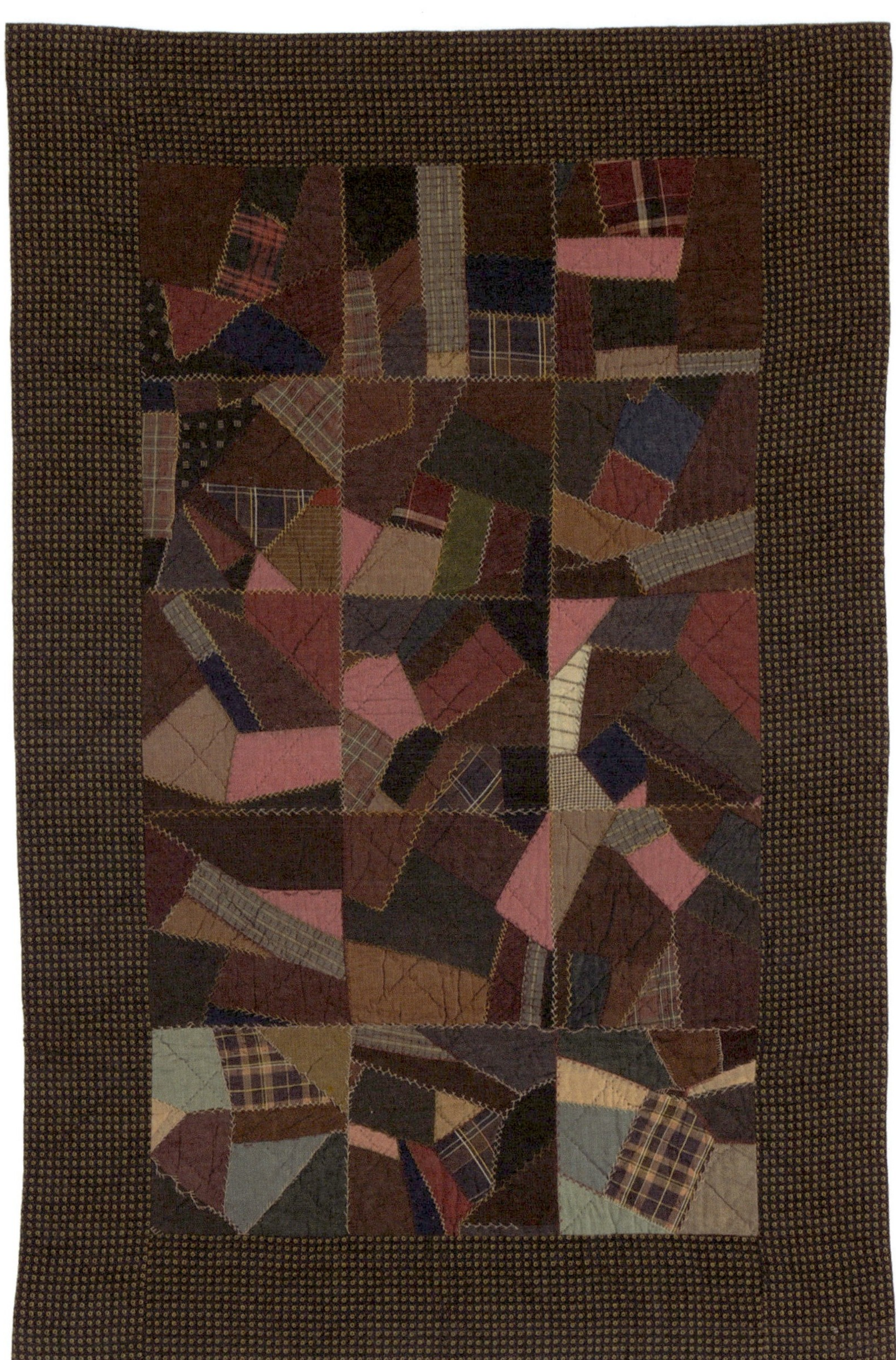

27. **Crazy quilt**
Maker unidentified
Probably made in Pennsylvania, 1920–1940
Wool; hand and machine pieced, hand embroidered and quilted; 79.5 x 54 in.
Jonathan Holstein and Gail van der Hoof Collection, IQM 2003.003.0027

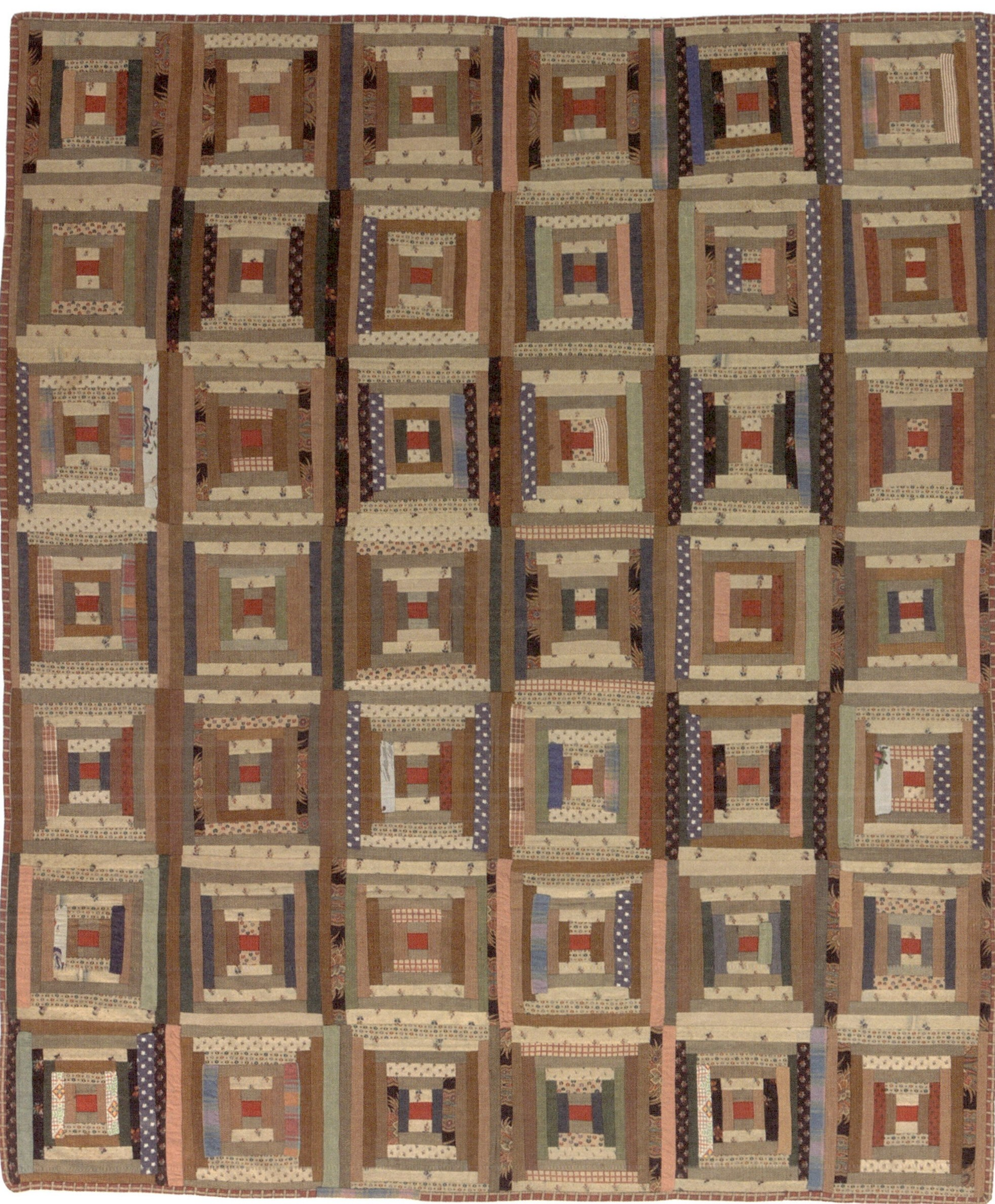

28. **Log Cabin, Courthouse Steps variation**
Maker unidentified
Probably made in Pennsylvania, 1880–1900
Wool; hand pieced, unquilted; 84 x 73.5 in.
Jonathan Holstein and Gail van der Hoof Collection, IQM 2003.003.0028

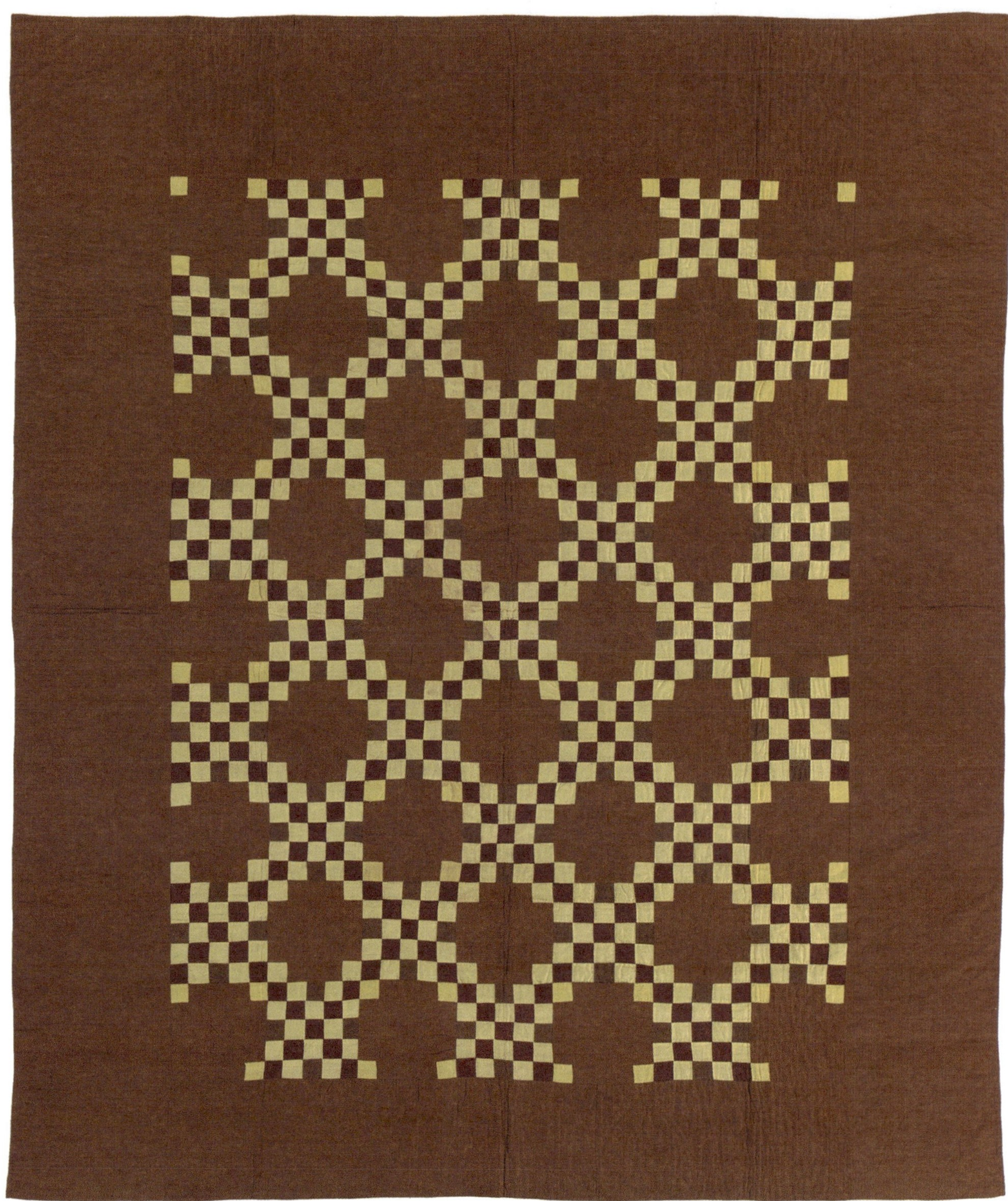

29. **Double Irish Chain**
Maker unidentified
Probably made in Maine, 1900–1920
Cotton; machine pieced, hand quilted; 85.5 x 74.5 in.
Jonathan Holstein and Gail van der Hoof Collection, IQM 2003.003.0029

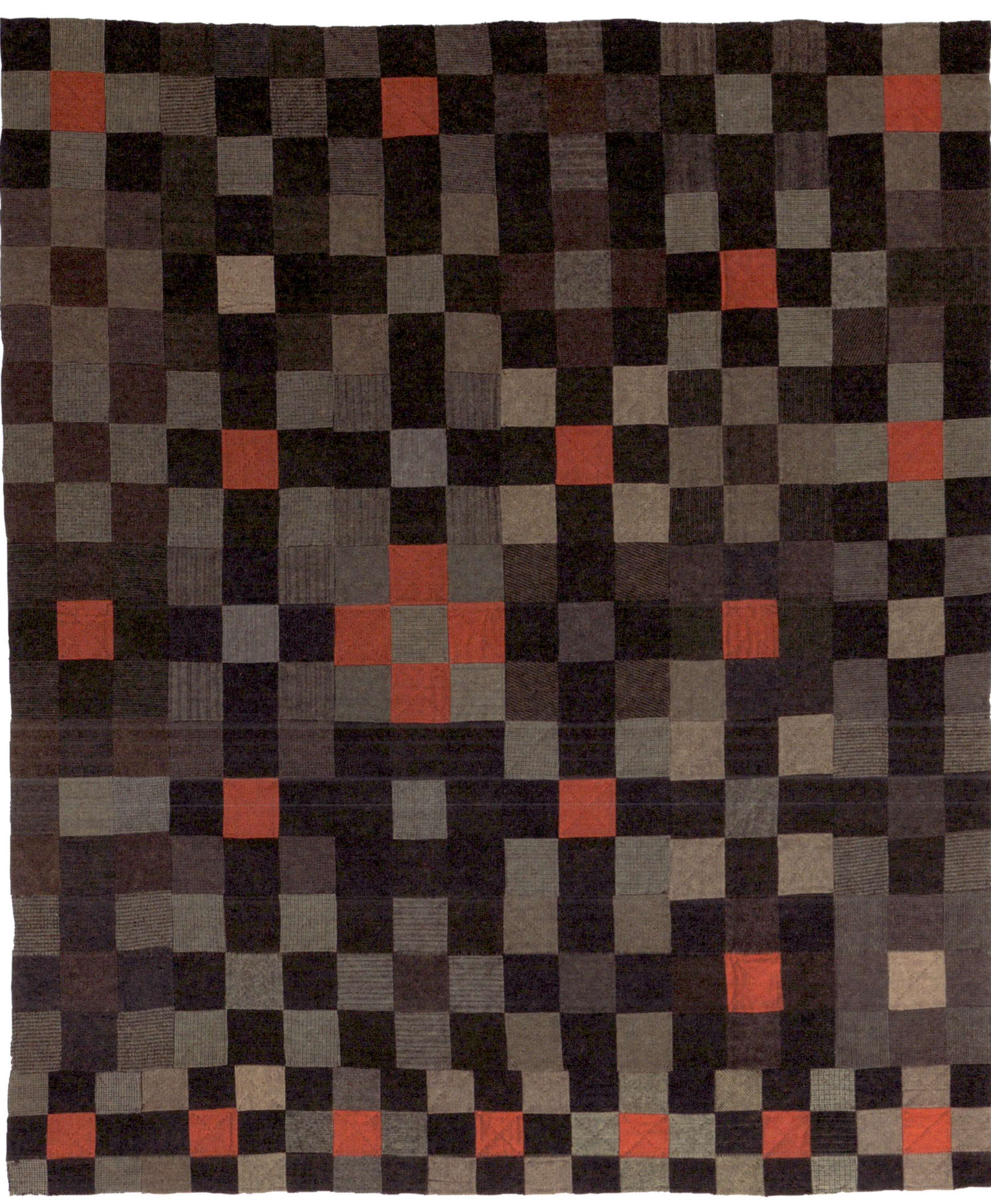

30. **Nine Patch**
Maker unidentified
Probably made in New Jersey, 1900–1920
Wool; hand pieced and quilted; 72 x 64 in.
Jonathan Holstein and Gail van der Hoof Collection, IQM 2003.003.0030

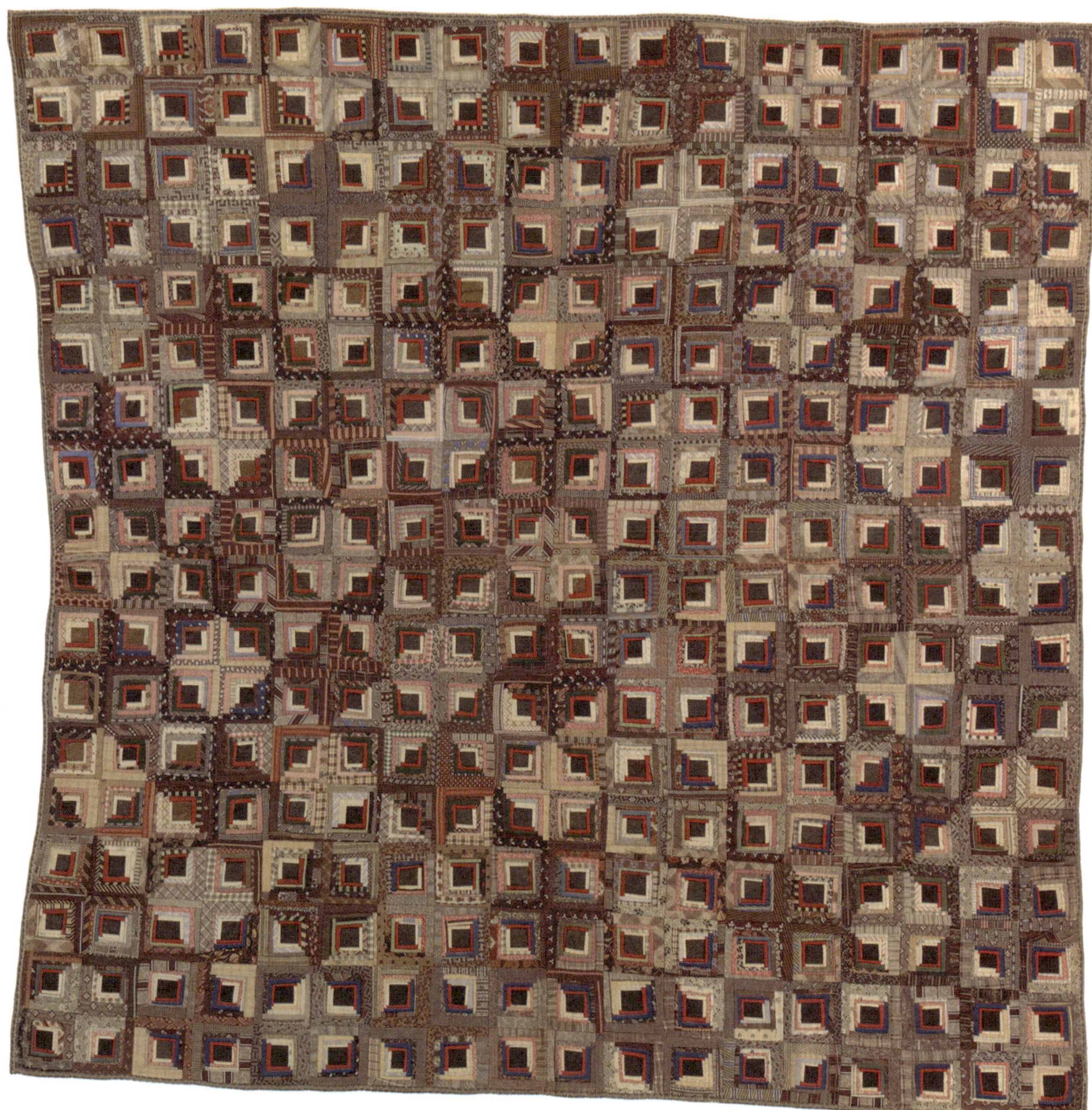

31. **Log Cabin, Light and Dark setting**
Maker unidentified
Probably made in Pennsylvania, 1870–1890
Cotton; hand pieced, unquilted; 72 x 74 in.
Jonathan Holstein and Gail van der Hoof Collection, IQM 2003.003.0031

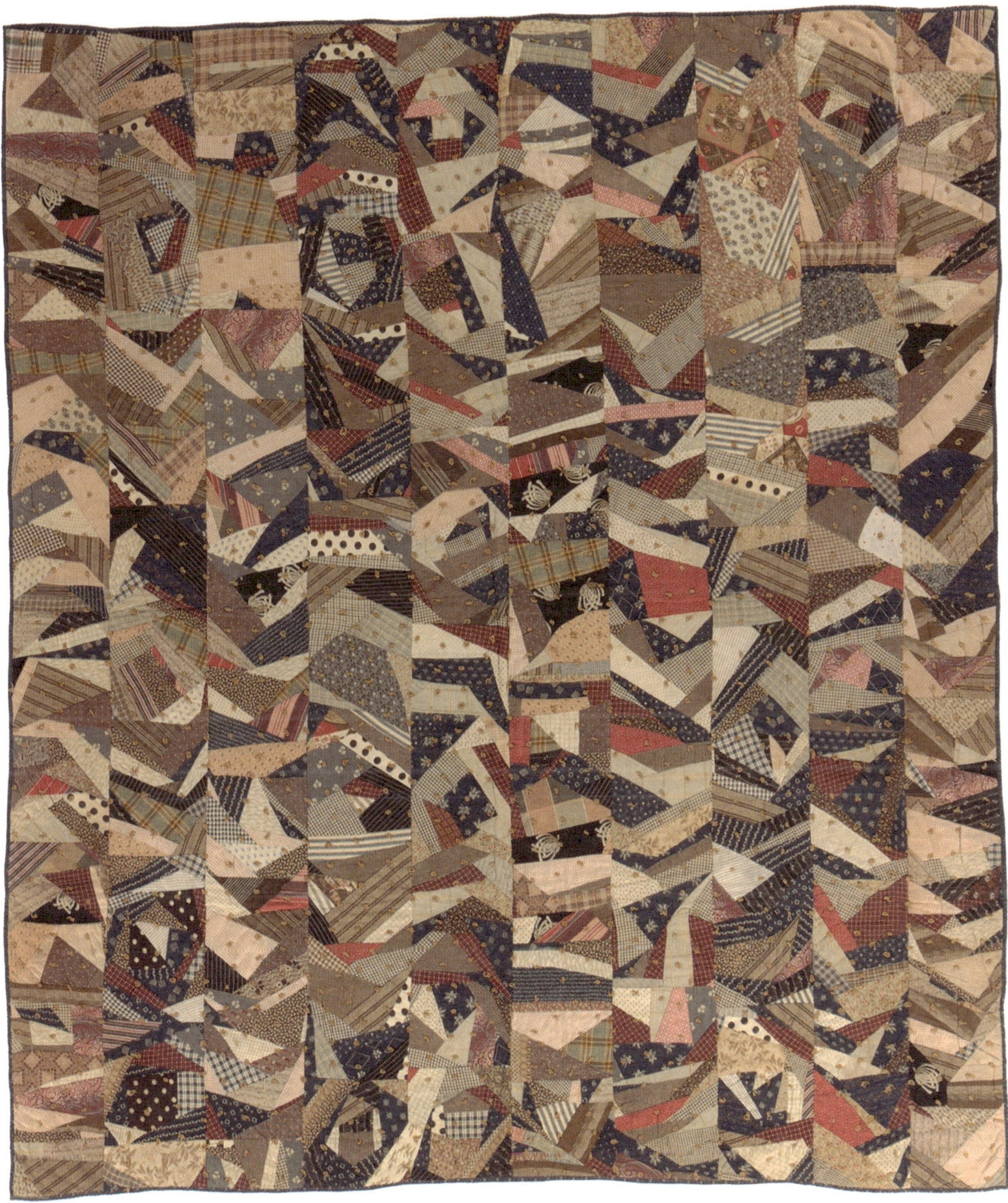

32. **Crazy quilt**
Maker unidentified
Probably made in Vermont, 1890–1900
Cotton; hand and machine pieced, tied; 86.5 x 76.5 in.
Jonathan Holstein and Gail van der Hoof Collection, IQM 2003.003.0032

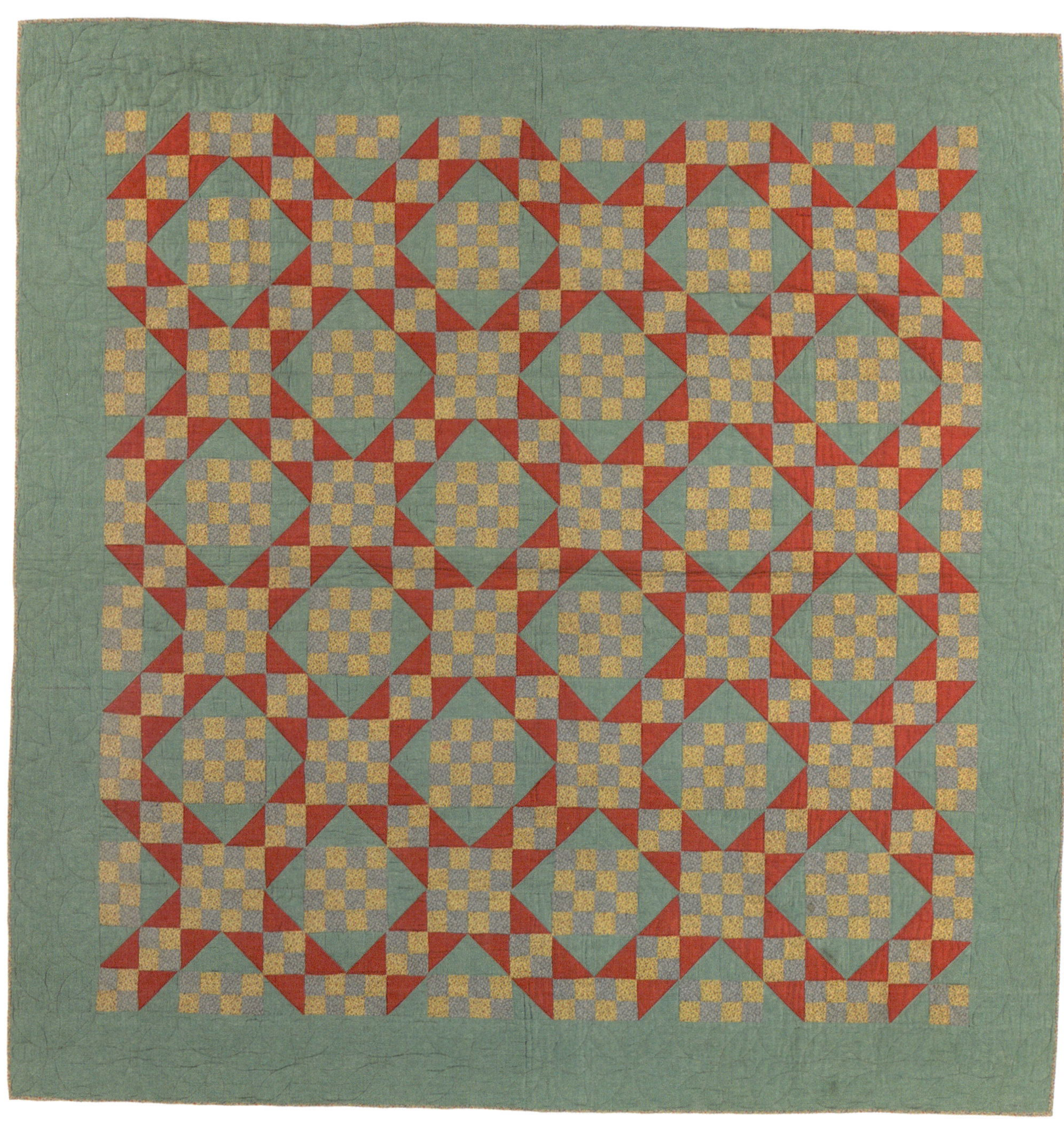

33. **Rocky Road to California**
Maker unidentified
Probably made in Pennsylvania, 1930–1940
Cotton; machine pieced, hand quilted; 77 x 77.5 in.
Jonathan Holstein and Gail van der Hoof Collection, IQM 2003.003.0033

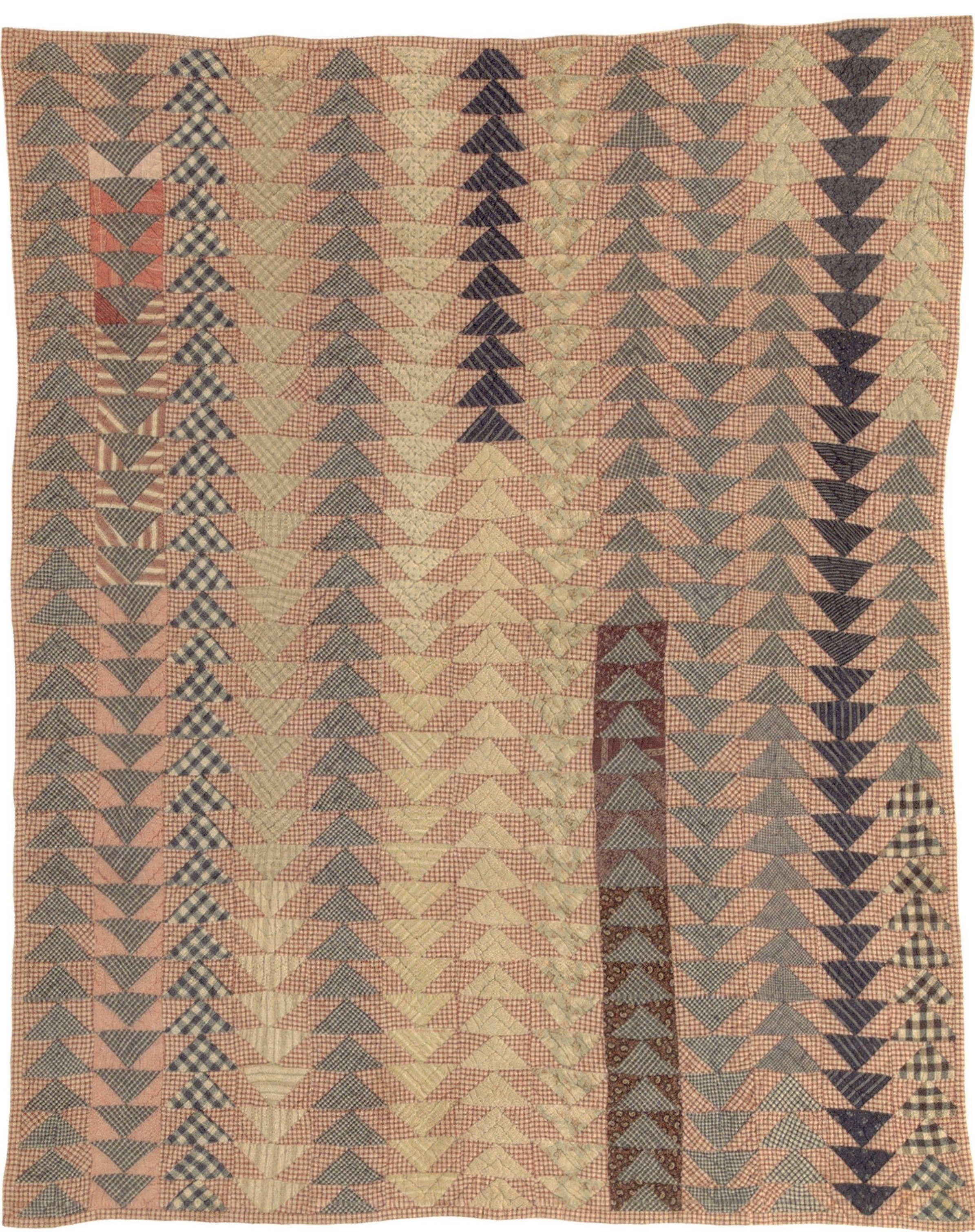

34. **Wild Goose Chase**
Maker unidentified
Probably made in Pennsylvania, 1900–1920
Cotton; hand pieced and quilted; 66 x 55.5 in.
Jonathan Holstein and Gail van der Hoof Collection, IQM 2003.003.0034

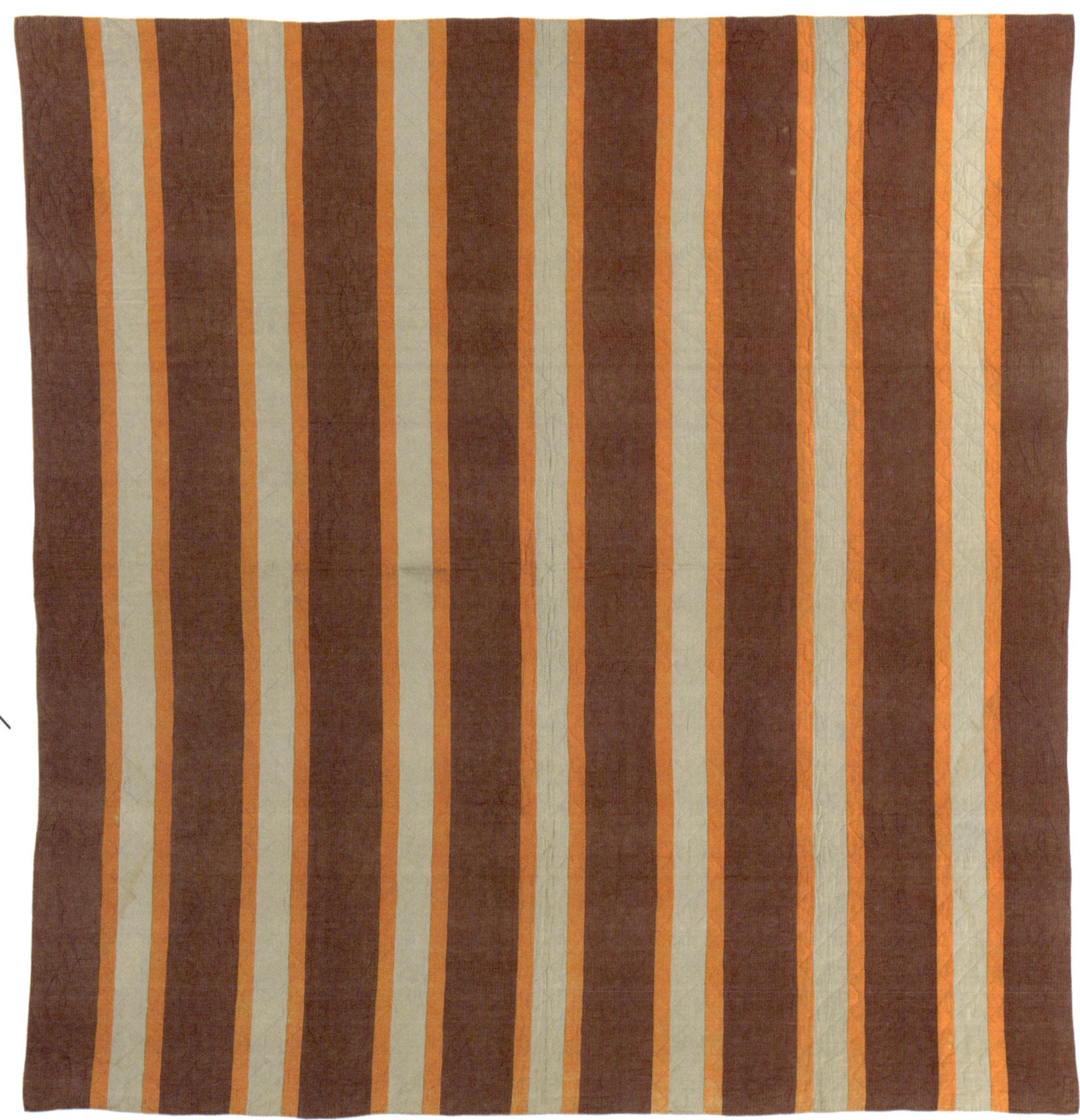

35. **Stripes**
Maker unidentified
Probably made in Pennsylvania, 1880–1900
Cotton; machine pieced, hand quilted; 85 x 84 in.
Jonathan Holstein and Gail van der Hoof Collection, IQM 2003.003.0035

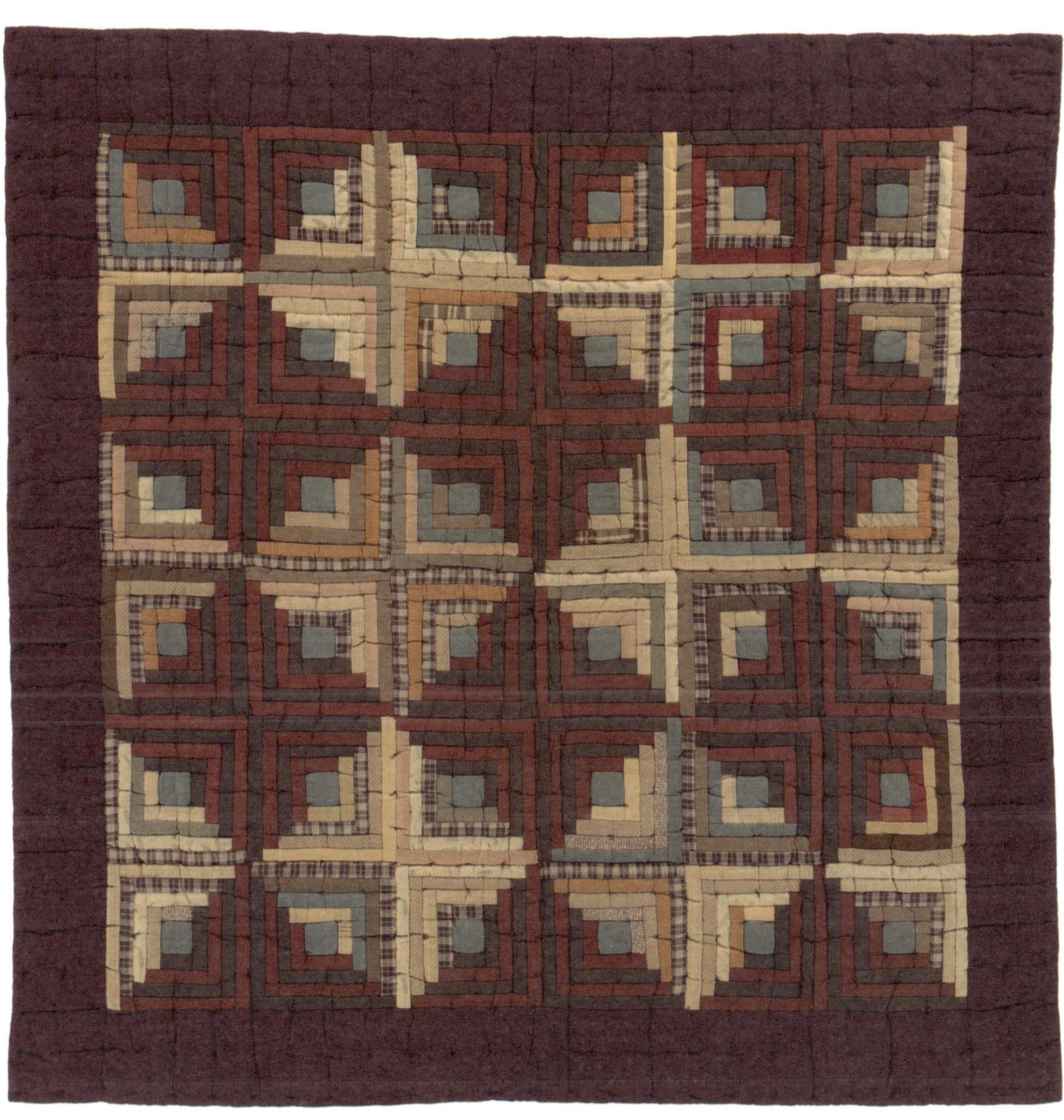

36. **Log Cabin, Light and Dark setting**
Maker unidentified
Probably made in Pennsylvania, 1900–1920
Wool; hand pieced, tied; 69 x 67.5 in.
Jonathan Holstein and Gail van der Hoof Collection, IQM 2003.003.0036

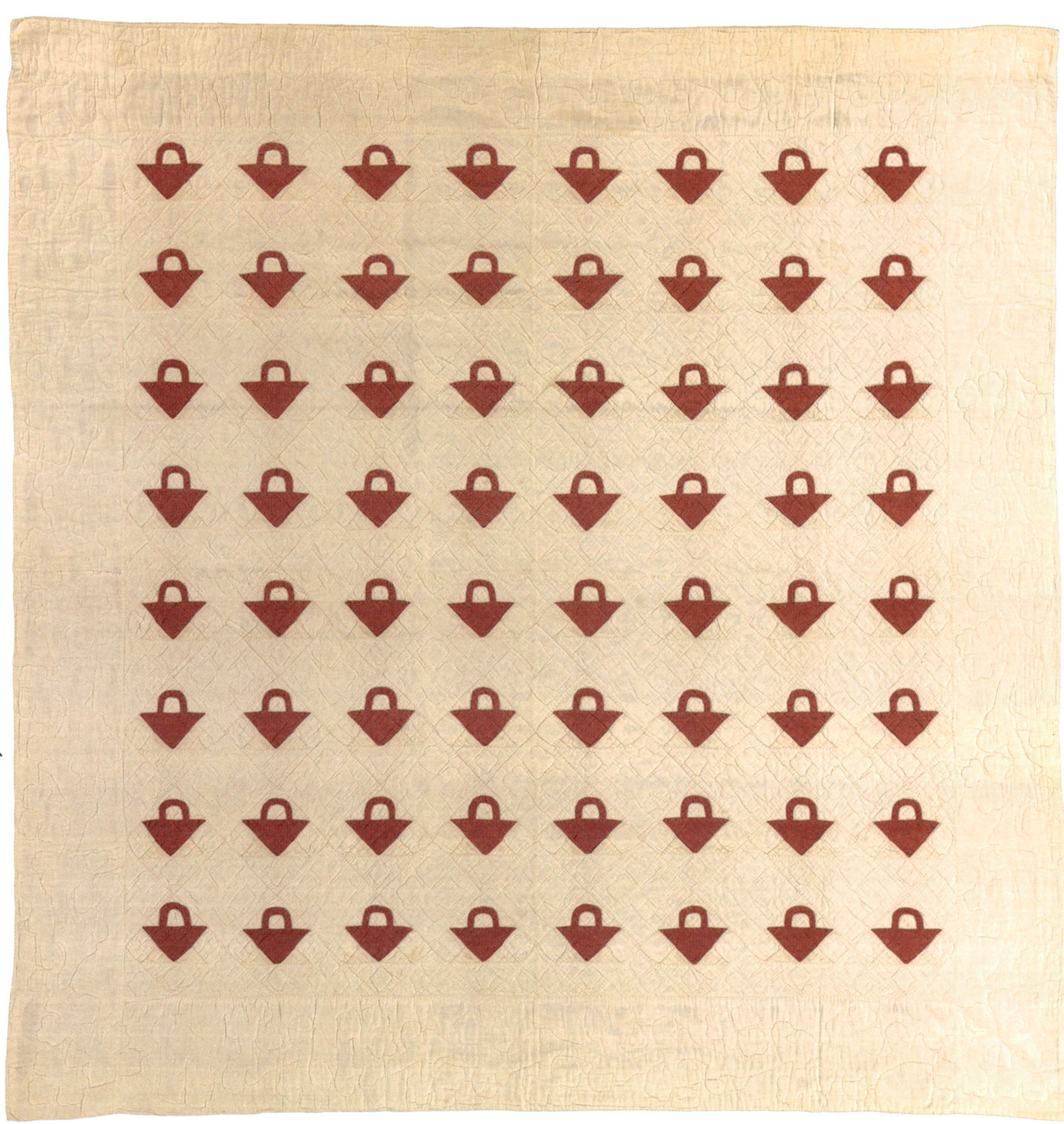

37. **Basket**
Maker unidentified
Probably made in New Jersey, 1900–1920
Cotton; machine pieced, hand appliquéd and quilted; 68 x 67 in.
Jonathan Holstein and Gail van der Hoof Collection, IQM 2003.003.0037

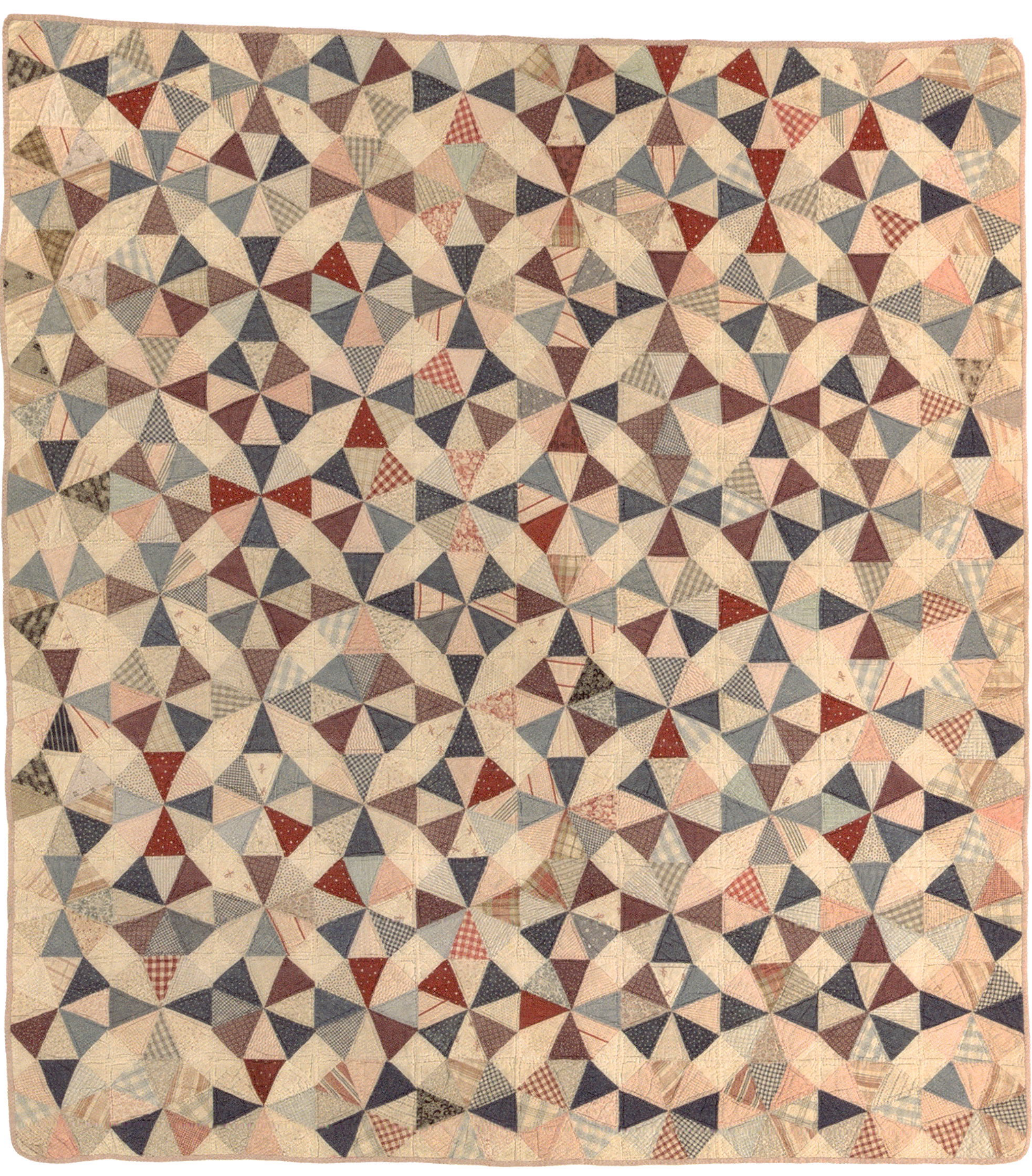

38. **Kaleidoscope**
Maker unidentified
Probably made in Pennsylvania, 1900–1920
Cotton; hand pieced and quilted; 72.5 x 67 in.
Jonathan Holstein and Gail van der Hoof Collection, IQM 2003.003.0038

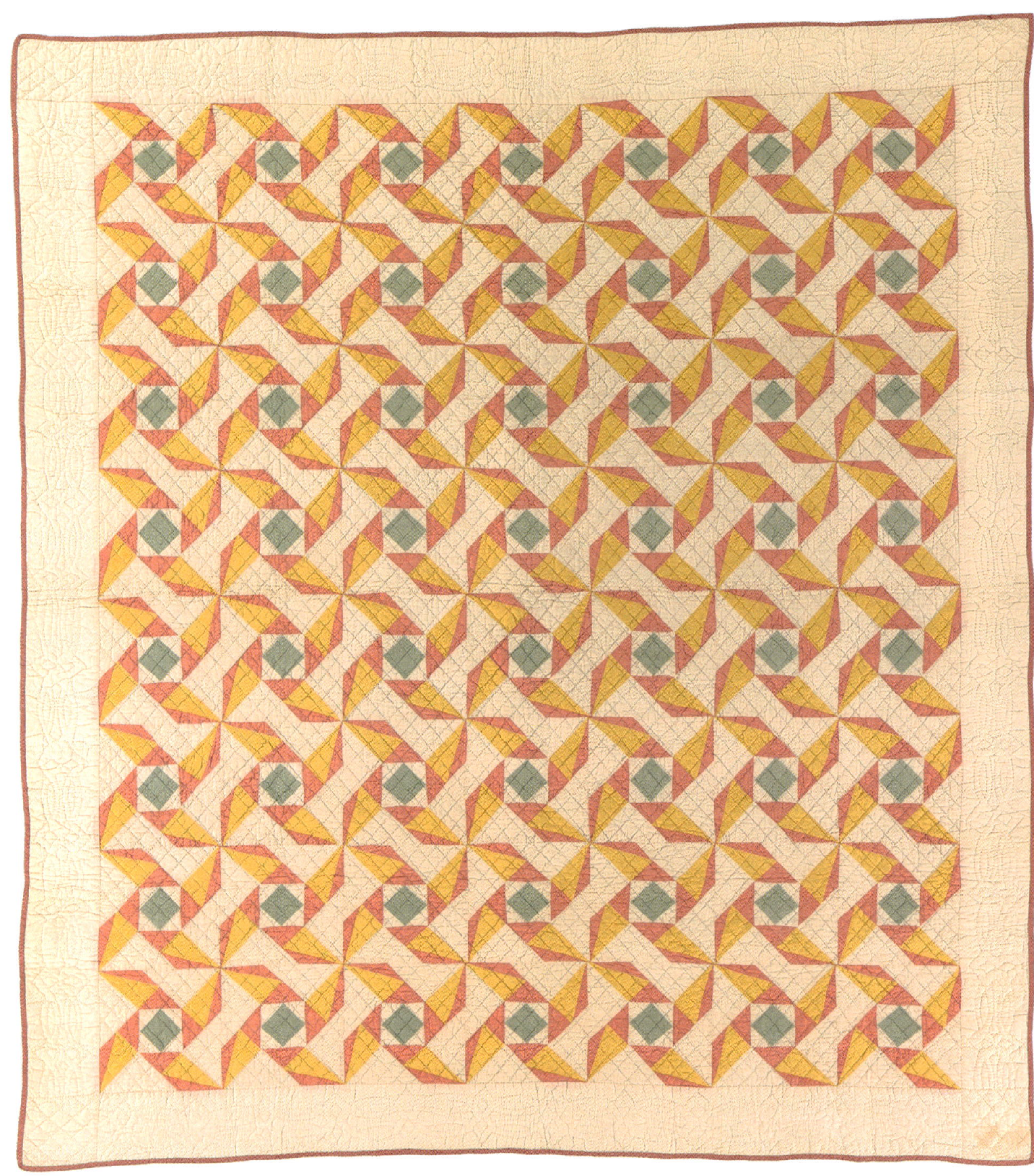

39. **Eccentric Star**
Maker unidentified
Probably made in Pennsylvania, 1930–1940
Cotton; machine pieced, hand quilted; 83.5 x 77 in.
Jonathan Holstein and Gail van der Hoof Collection, IQM 2003.003.0039

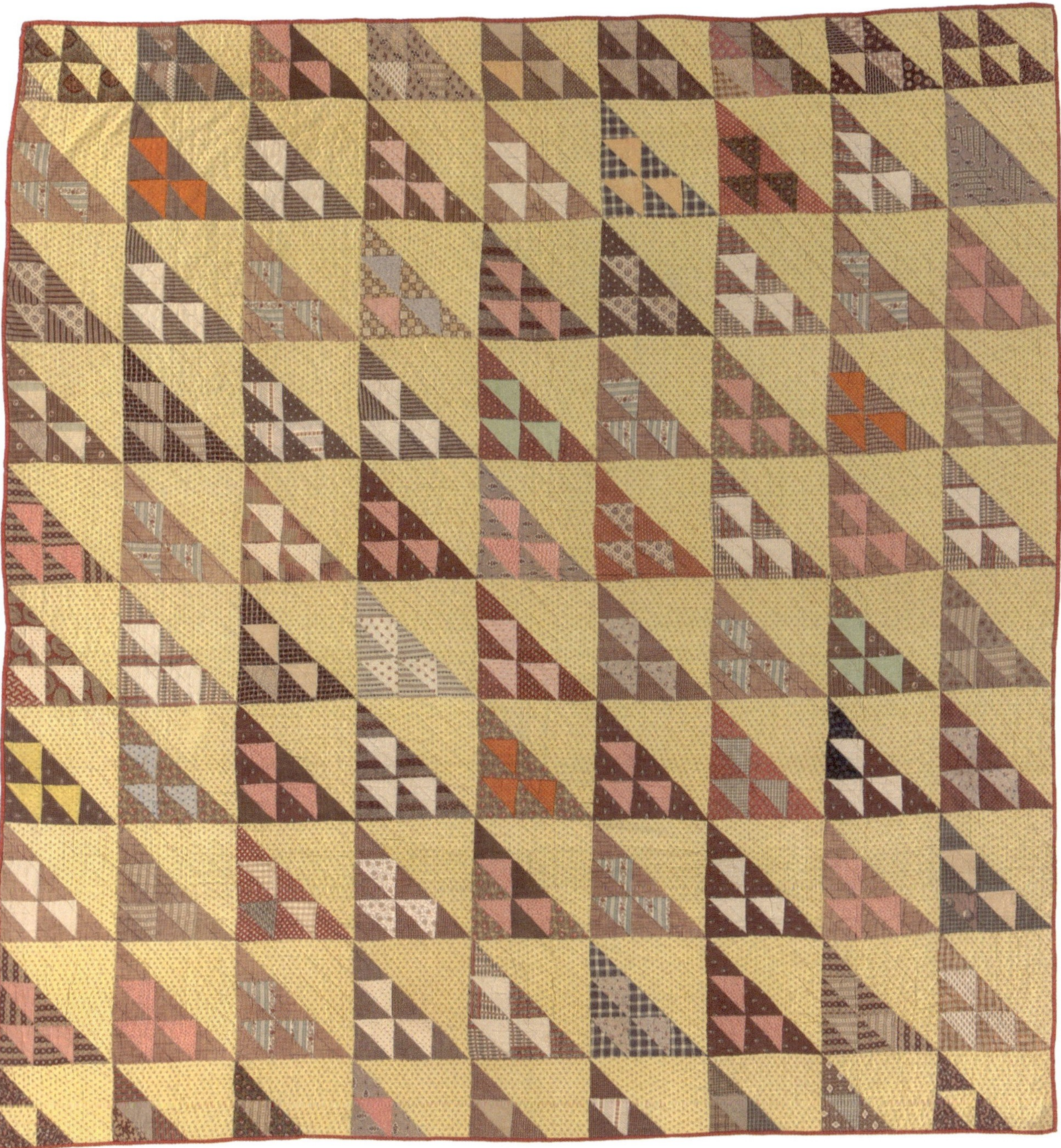

40. **Birds in Air**
Maker unidentified
Probably made in Pennsylvania, 1870–1890
Cotton; hand pieced and quilted; 83 x 80.5 in.
Jonathan Holstein and Gail van der Hoof Collection, IQM 2003.003.0040

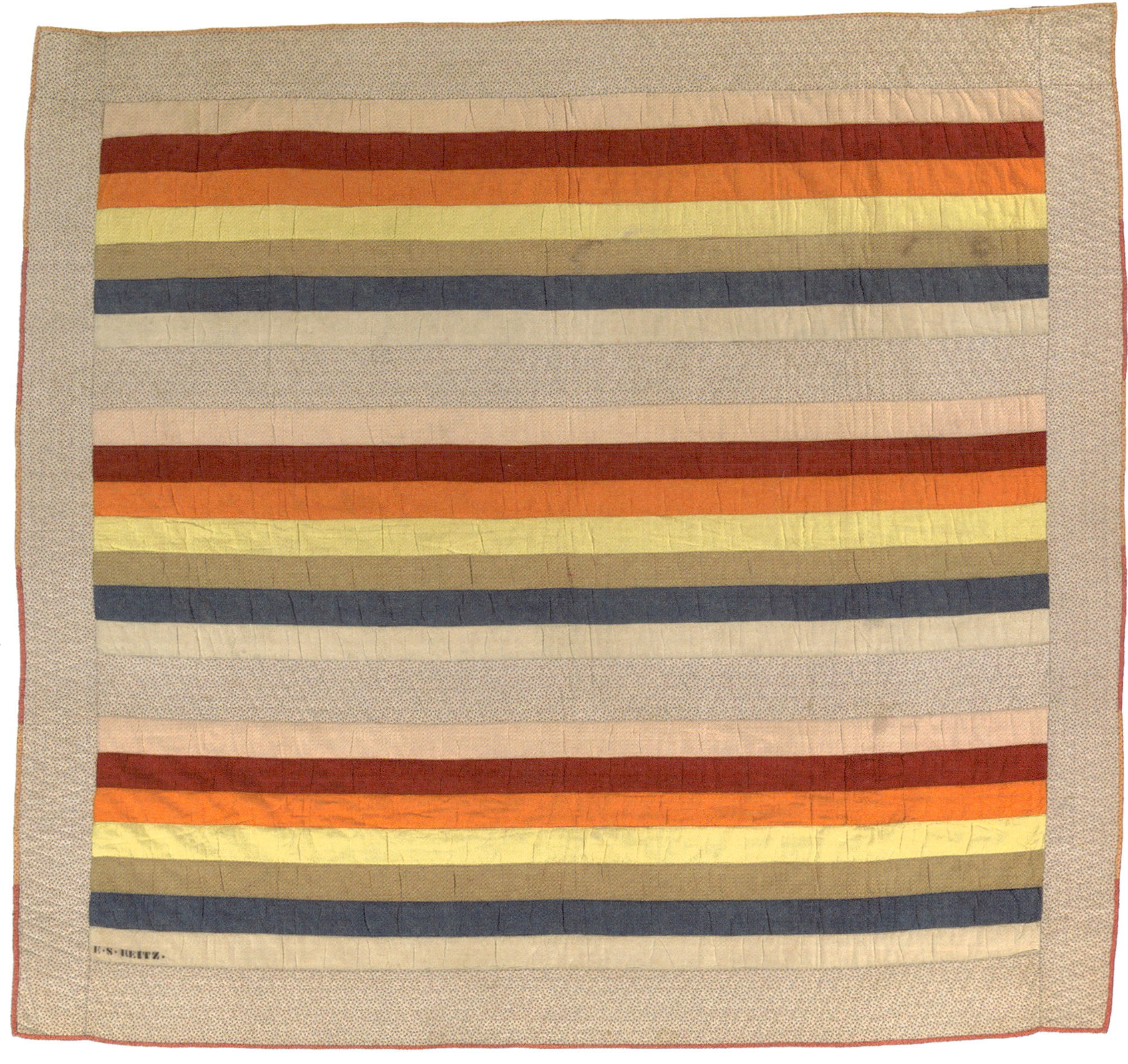


41. **Rainbow Stripes**
Inscribed E.S. Reitz
Probably made in Pennsylvania, 1890–1910
Cotton; machine pieced, hand quilted; 73 x 80 in.
Jonathan Holstein and Gail van der Hoof Collection, IQM 2003.003.0041

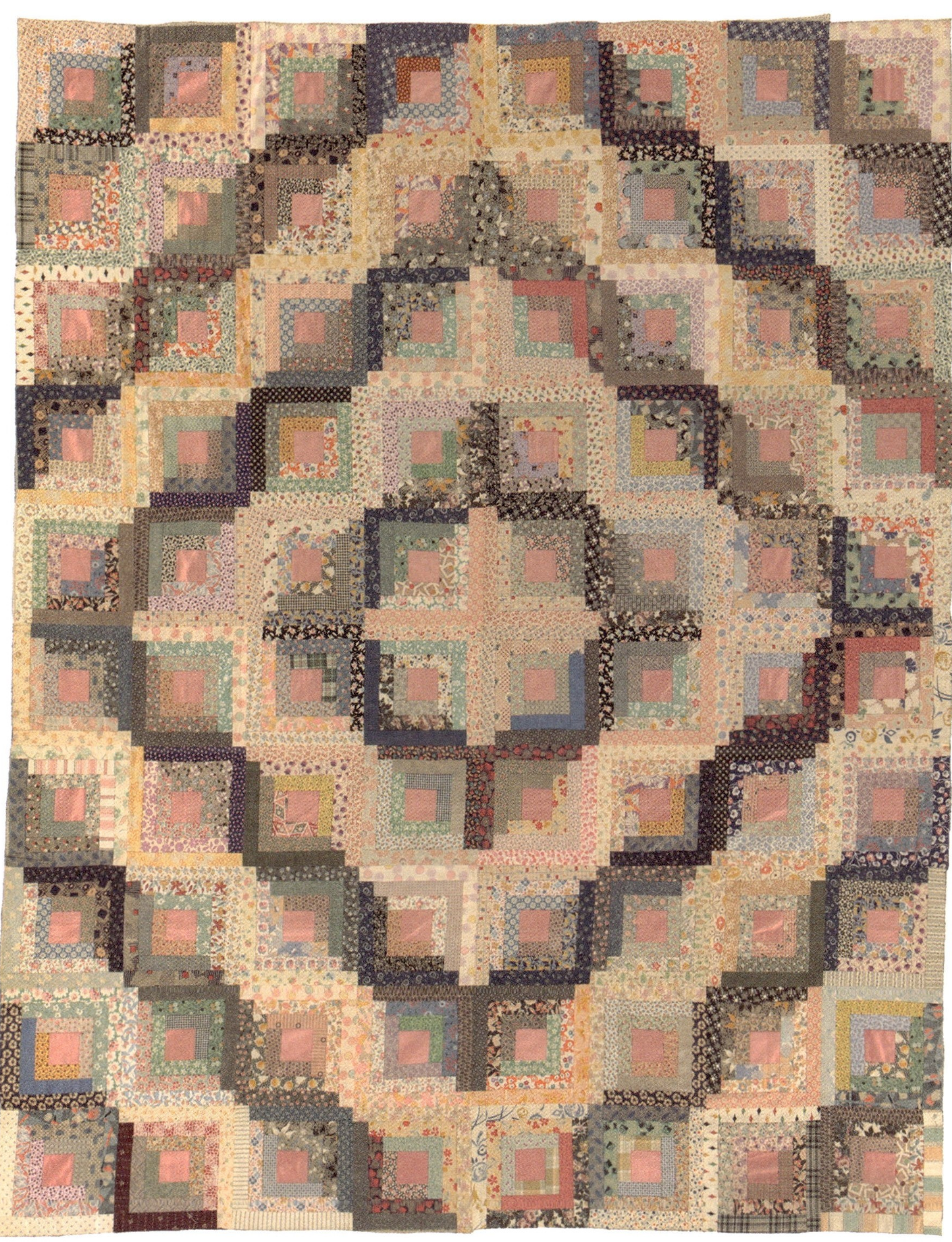

42. **Log Cabin, Barn Raising setting**
Maker unidentified
Probably made in New Jersey, 1930–1950
Cotton; hand and machine pieced, unquilted; 88 x 70.5 in.
Jonathan Holstein and Gail van der Hoof Collection, IQM 2003.003.0042

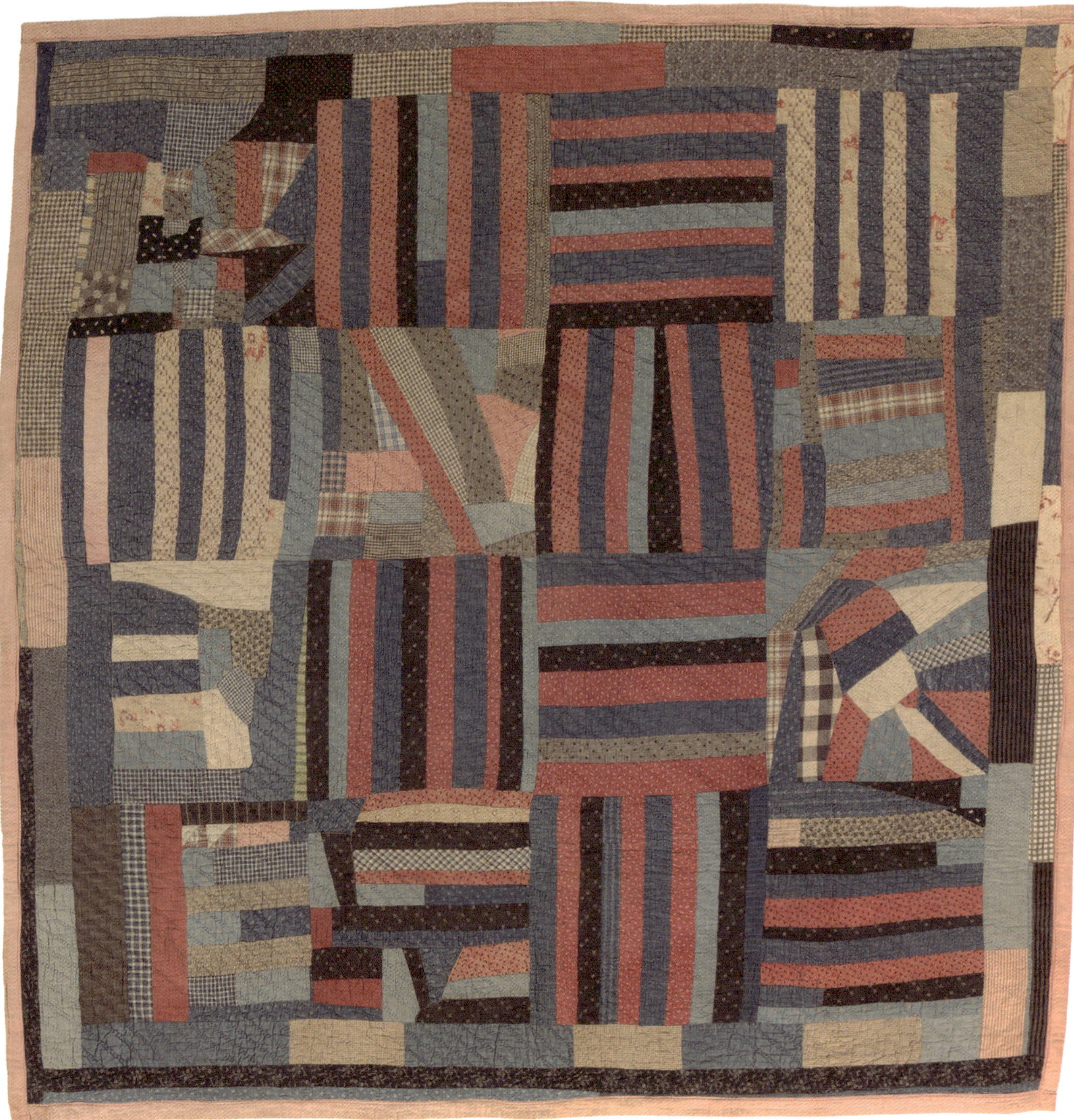

43. **Crazy quilt**
Maker unidentified
Probably made in Pennsylvania, 1900–1920
Cotton; hand and machine pieced, hand quilted; 73 x 73.5 in.
Jonathan Holstein and Gail van der Hoof Collection, IQM 2003.003.0043

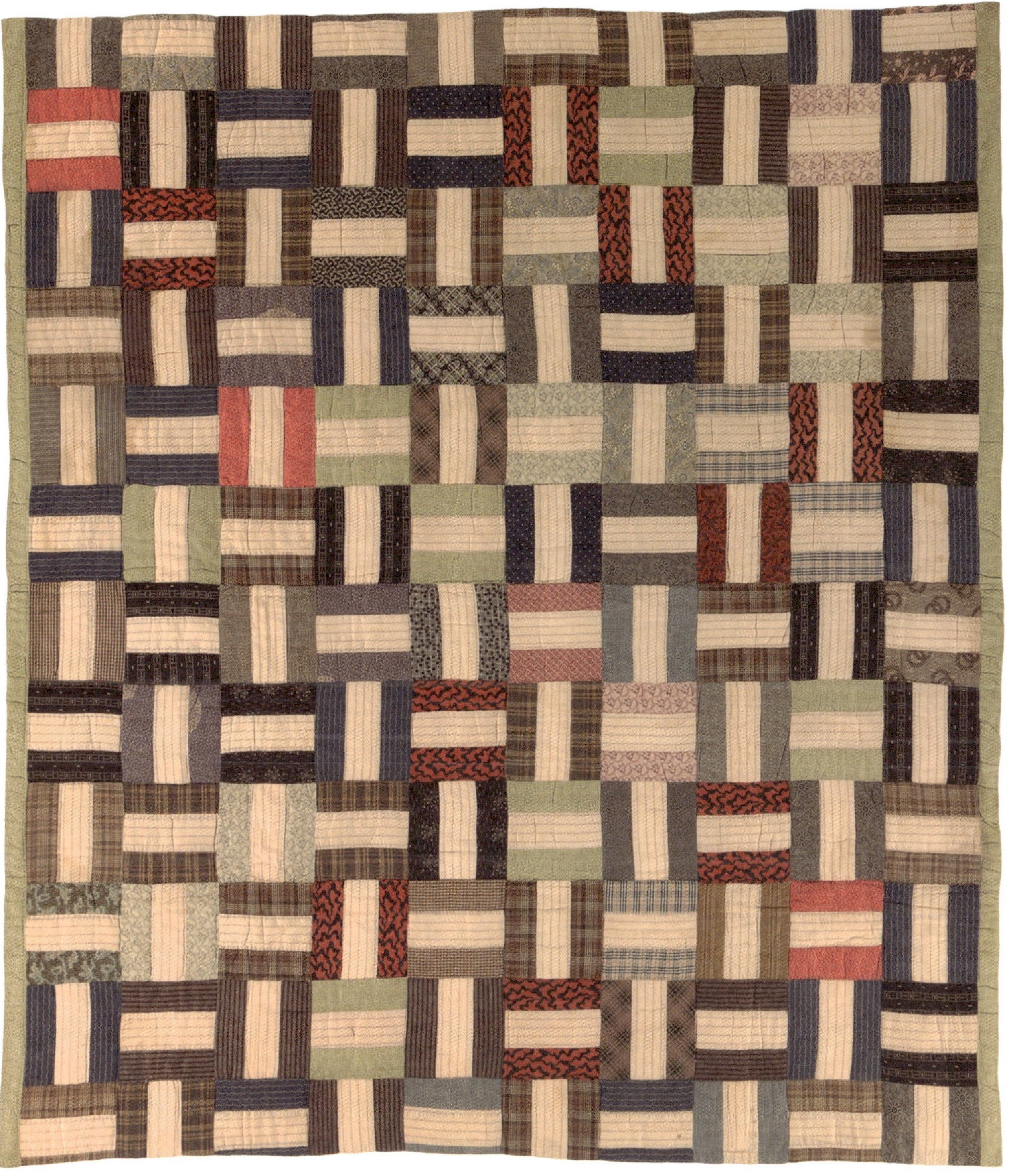

44. **Roman Square**
Maker unidentified
Probably made in New Jersey, 1890–1910
Cotton; hand pieced and quilted; 80 x 71 in.
Jonathan Holstein and Gail van der Hoof Collection, IQM 2003.003.0044

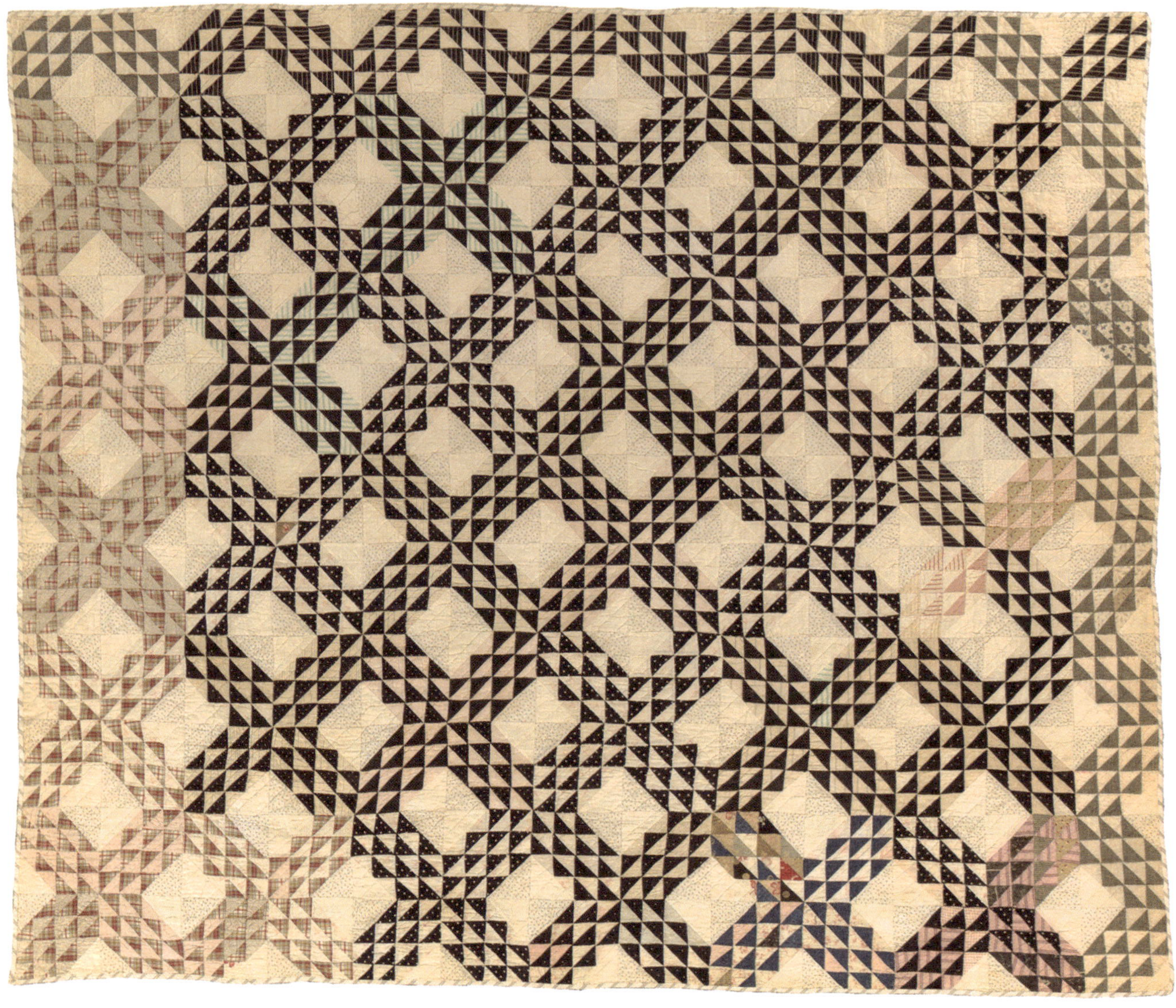

45. **Ocean Waves**
Maker unidentified
Probably made in Sandgate, Vermont, 1890–1910
Cotton; hand pieced and quilted; 78 x 94 in.
Jonathan Holstein and Gail van der Hoof Collection, IQM 2003.003.0045

46. **Crazy quilt**
Maker unidentified
Possibly made in Maine, 1900–1920
Cotton; hand and machine pieced, hand embroidered, tied; 66.5 x 35 in.
Jonathan Holstein and Gail van der Hoof Collection, IQM 2003.003.0046

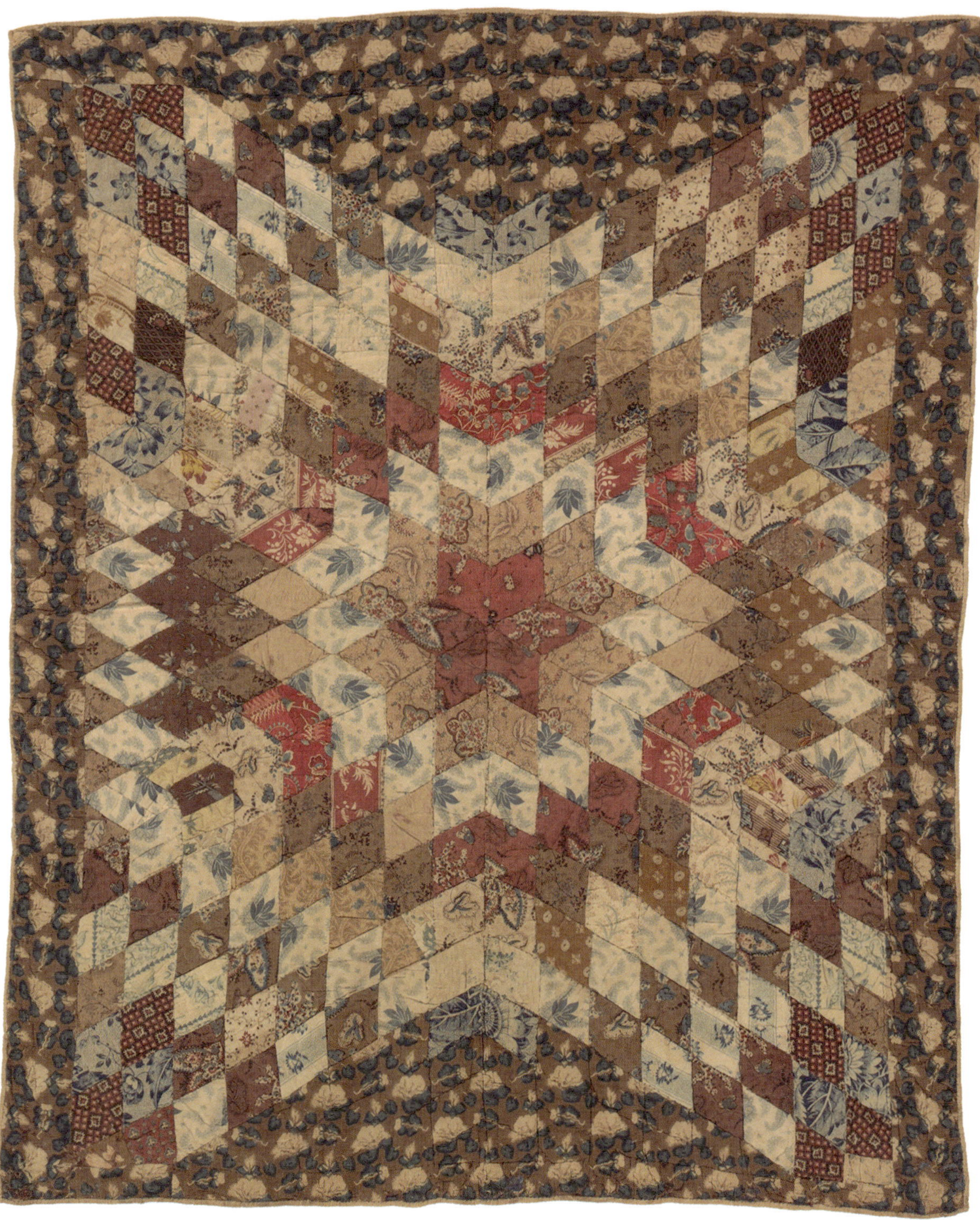

47. **Eastern Star**
Maker unidentified
Probably made in Pennsylvania, 1830–1850
Cotton; hand pieced and quilted; 40 x 33.5 in.
Jonathan Holstein and Gail van der Hoof Collection, IQM 2003.003.0047

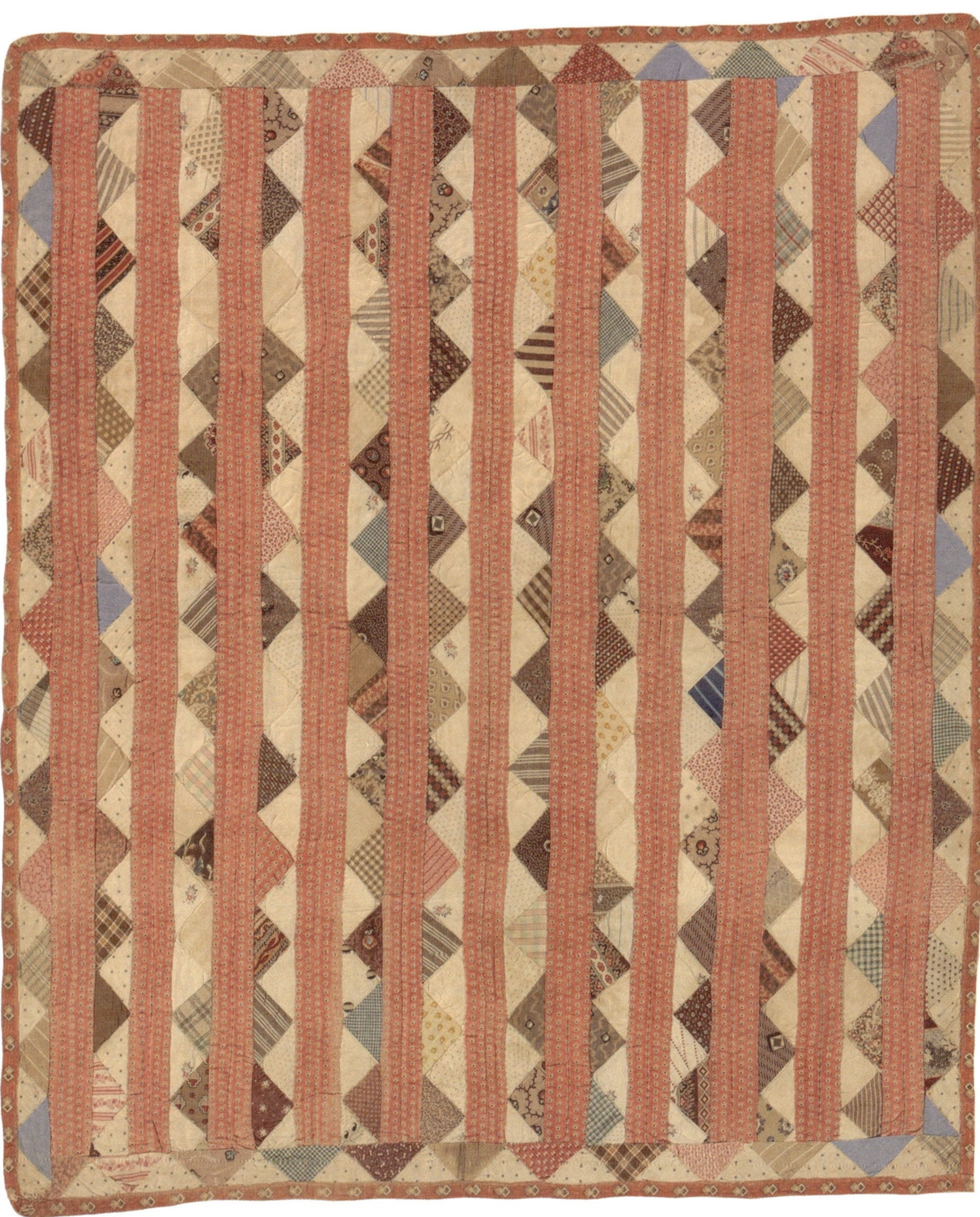

48. **Bars variation**
Maker unidentified
Possibly made in Massachusetts, 1860–1880
Cotton; hand pieced, machine quilted; 36 x 31.5 in.
Jonathan Holstein and Gail van der Hoof Collection, IQM 2003.003.0048

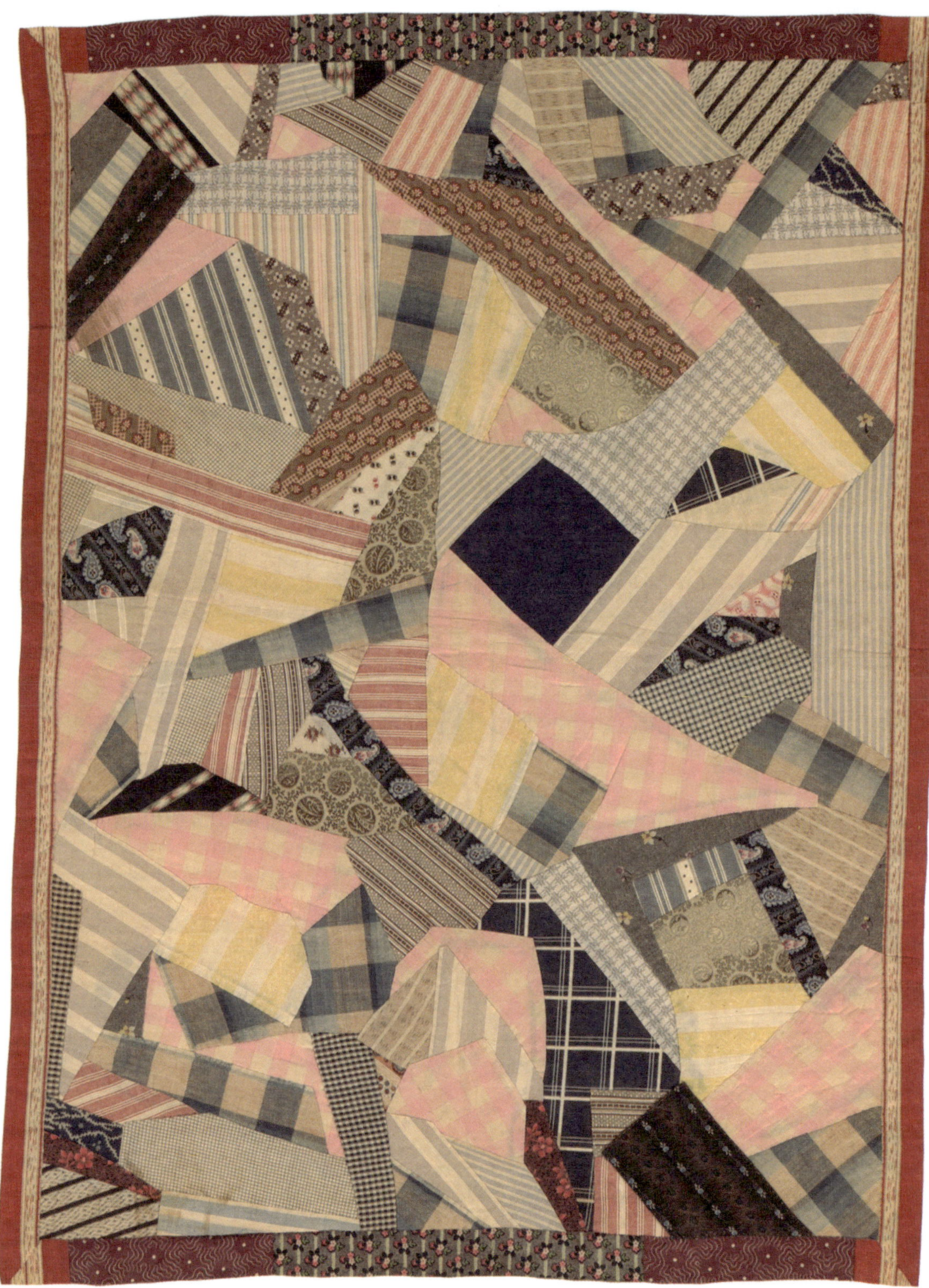

49. **Crazy quilt**
Maker unidentified
Possibly made in Pennsylvania, 1900–1920
Cotton; hand pieced, unquilted; 37.5 x 28 in.
Jonathan Holstein and Gail van der Hoof Collection, IQM 2003.003.0049

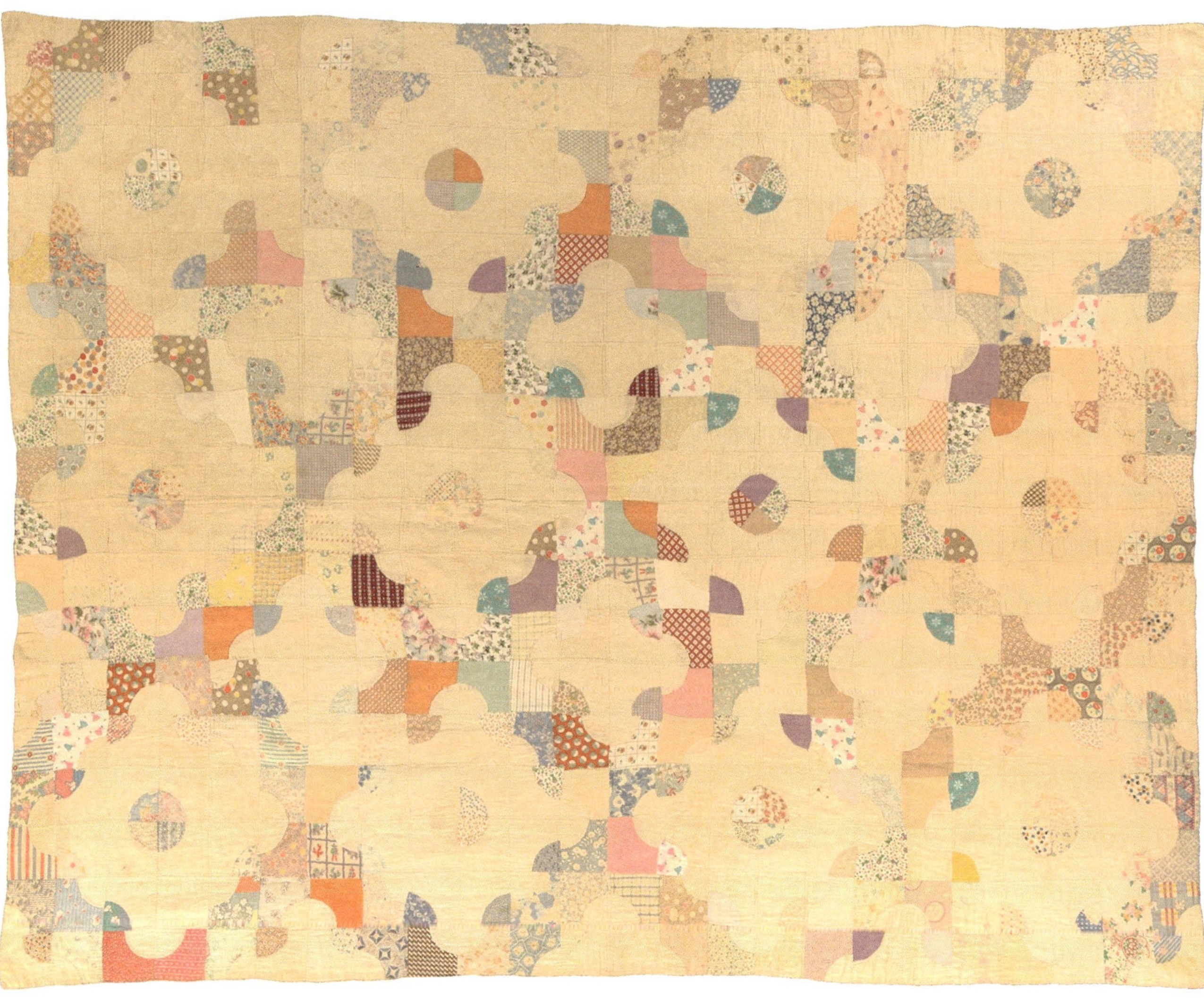

50. **Around the World**
Maker unidentified
Probably made in New Hampshire, 1930–1950
Cotton; hand pieced and quilted; 80 x 101 in.
Jonathan Holstein and Gail van der Hoof Collection, IQM 2003.003.0050

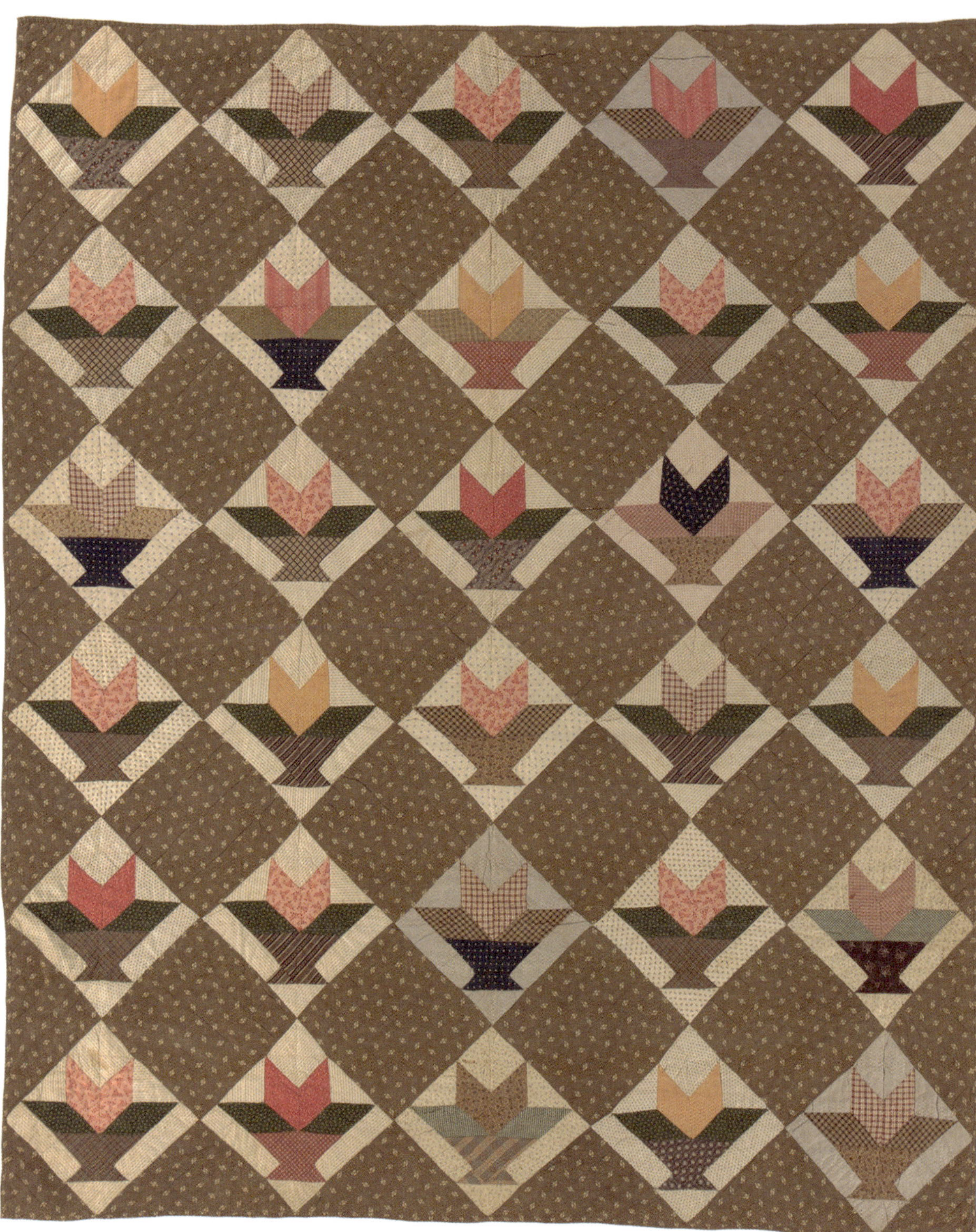

51. **Basket**
Maker unidentified
Probably made in Pennsylvania, 1870–1890
Cotton; hand pieced and quilted; 91.5 x 75 in.
Jonathan Holstein and Gail van der Hoof Collection, IQM 2003.003.0051

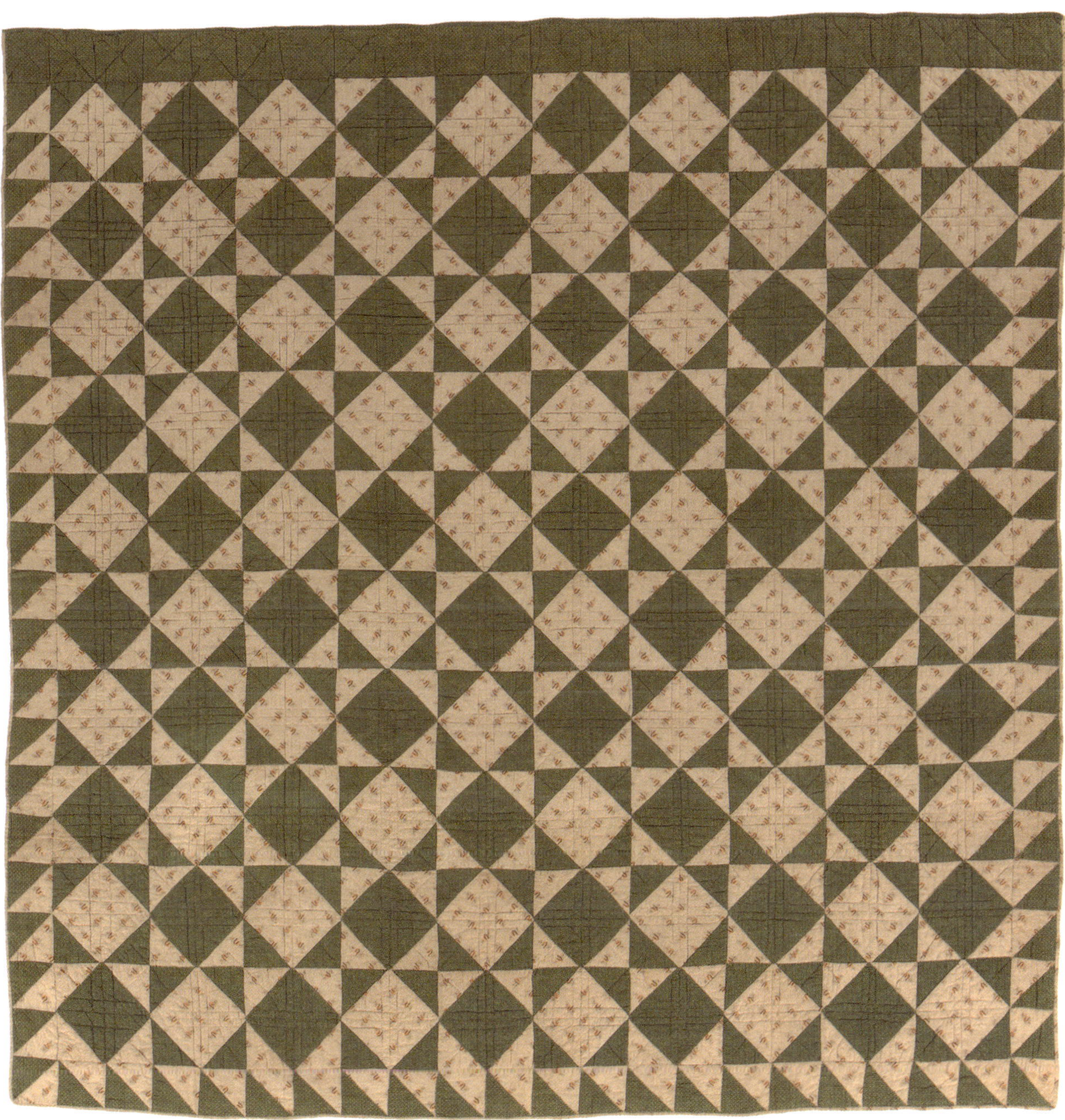

52. **Shoo Fly**
Maker unidentified
Probably made in Vermont, 1880–1900
Cotton; hand pieced and quilted; 75 x 76 in.
Jonathan Holstein and Gail van der Hoof Collection, IQM 2003.003.0052

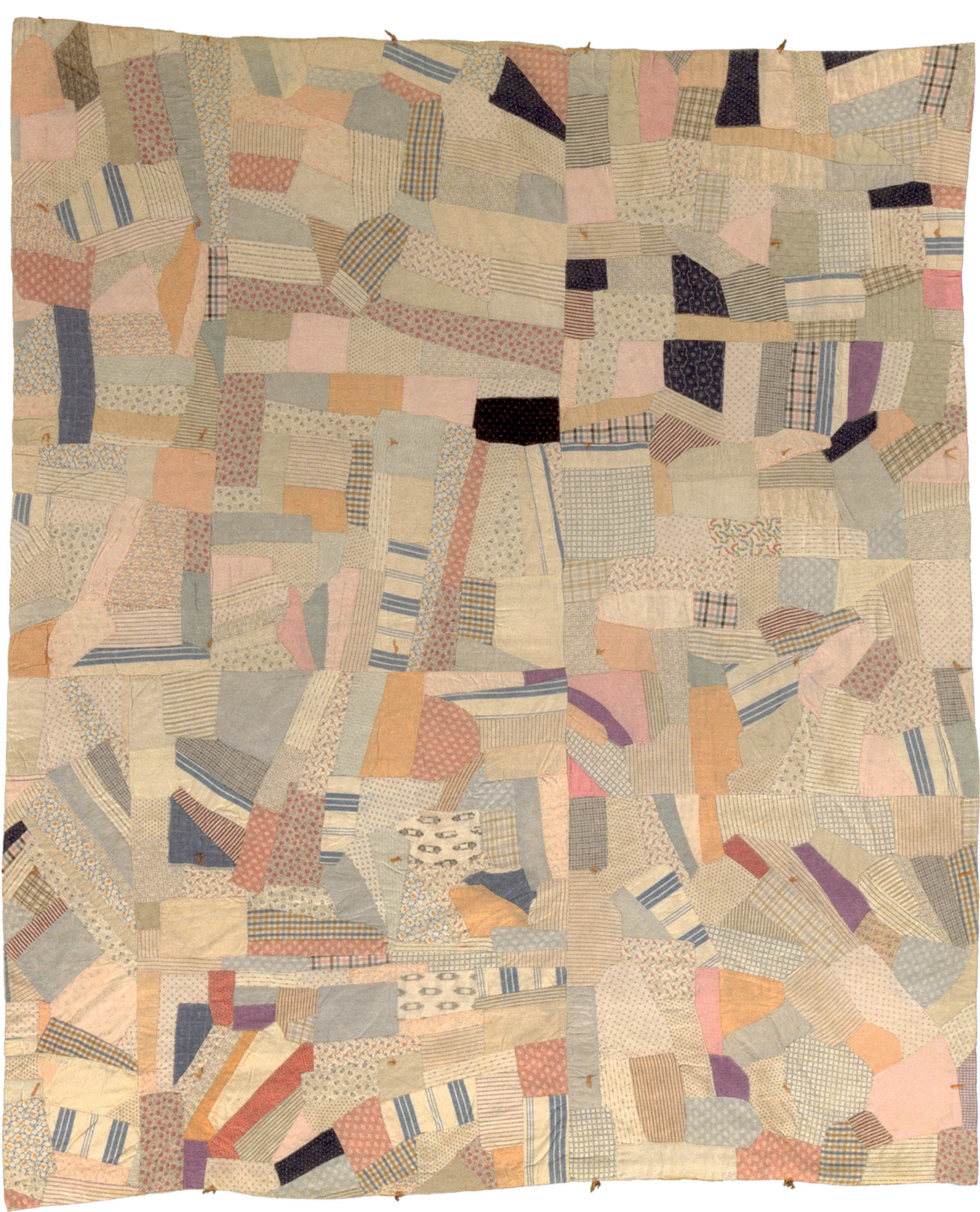

53. **Crazy quilt**
Maker unidentified
Possibly made in Vermont, 1910–1930
Cotton; hand and machine pieced, tied; 72.5 x 63.5 in.
Jonathan Holstein and Gail van der Hoof Collection, IQM 2003.003.0053

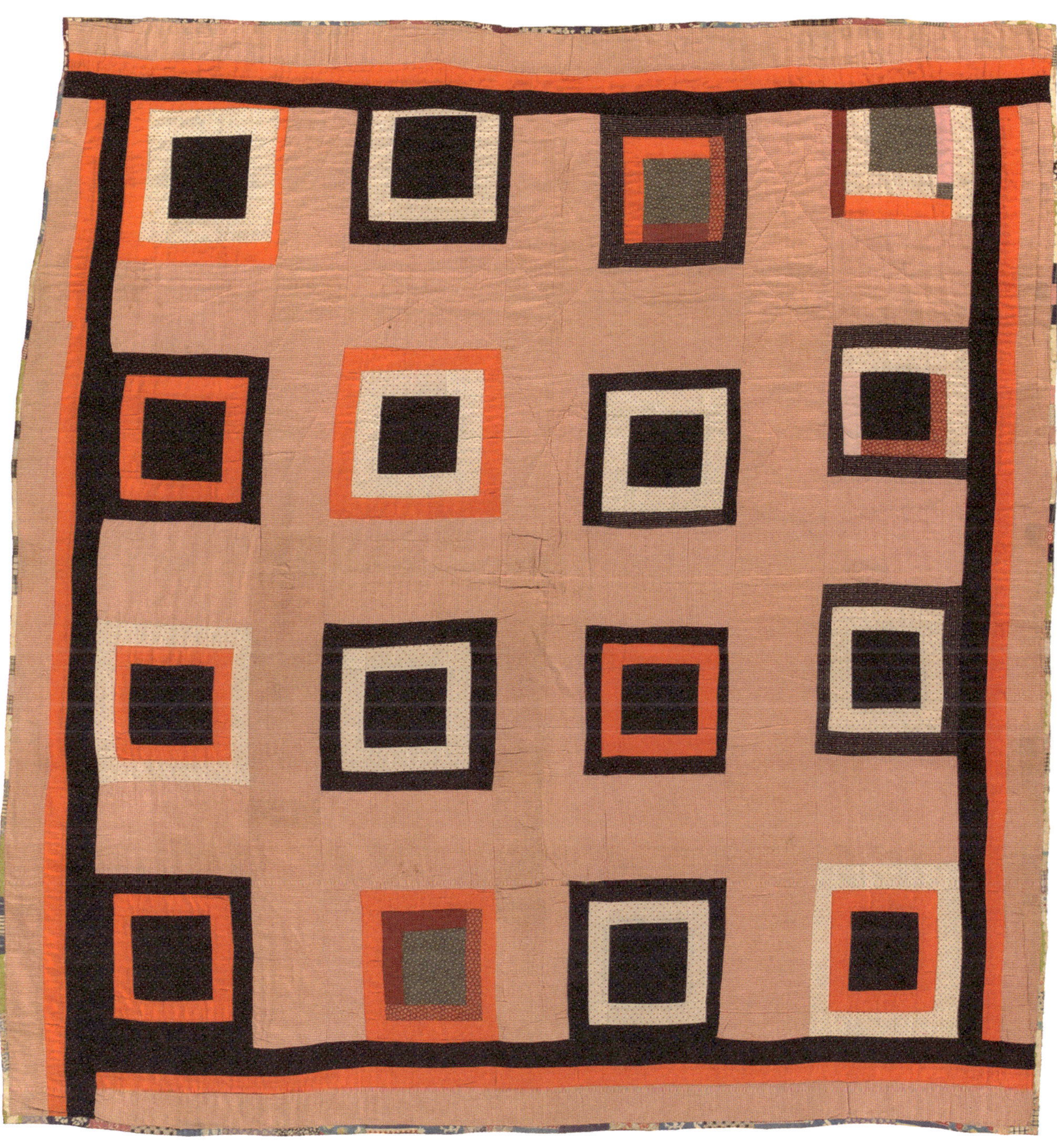

54. **Square in a Square**
Maker unidentified
Possibly made in Pennsylvania, 1930–1950
Cotton; machine pieced, hand quilted; 78 x 72 in.
Jonathan Holstein and Gail van der Hoof Collection, IQM 2003.003.0054

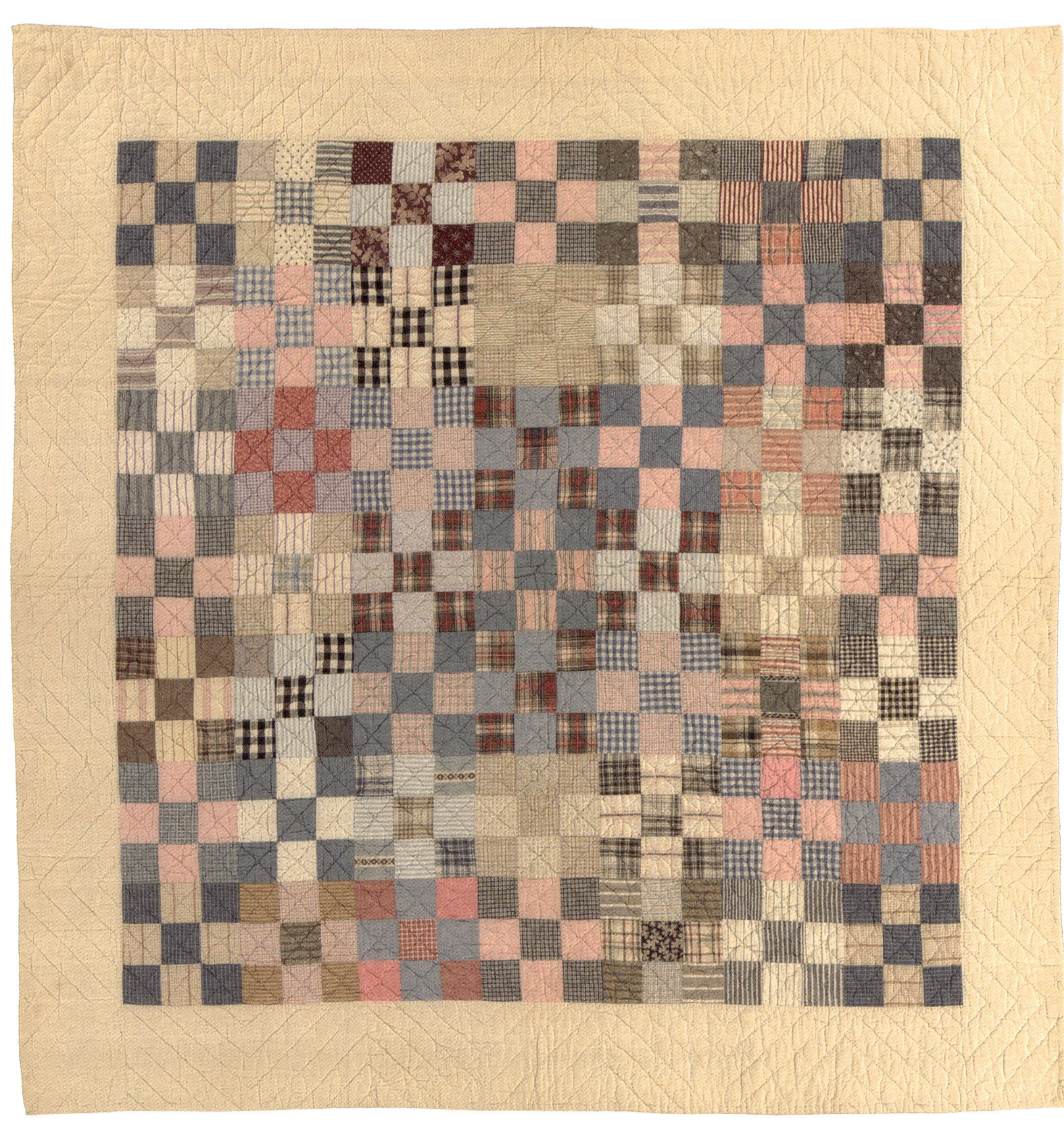

55. **Nine Patch**
Maker unidentified
Probably made in Pennsylvania, 1910–1930
Cotton; machine pieced, hand quilted; 69.5 x 69 in.
Jonathan Holstein and Gail van der Hoof Collection, IQM 2003.003.0055

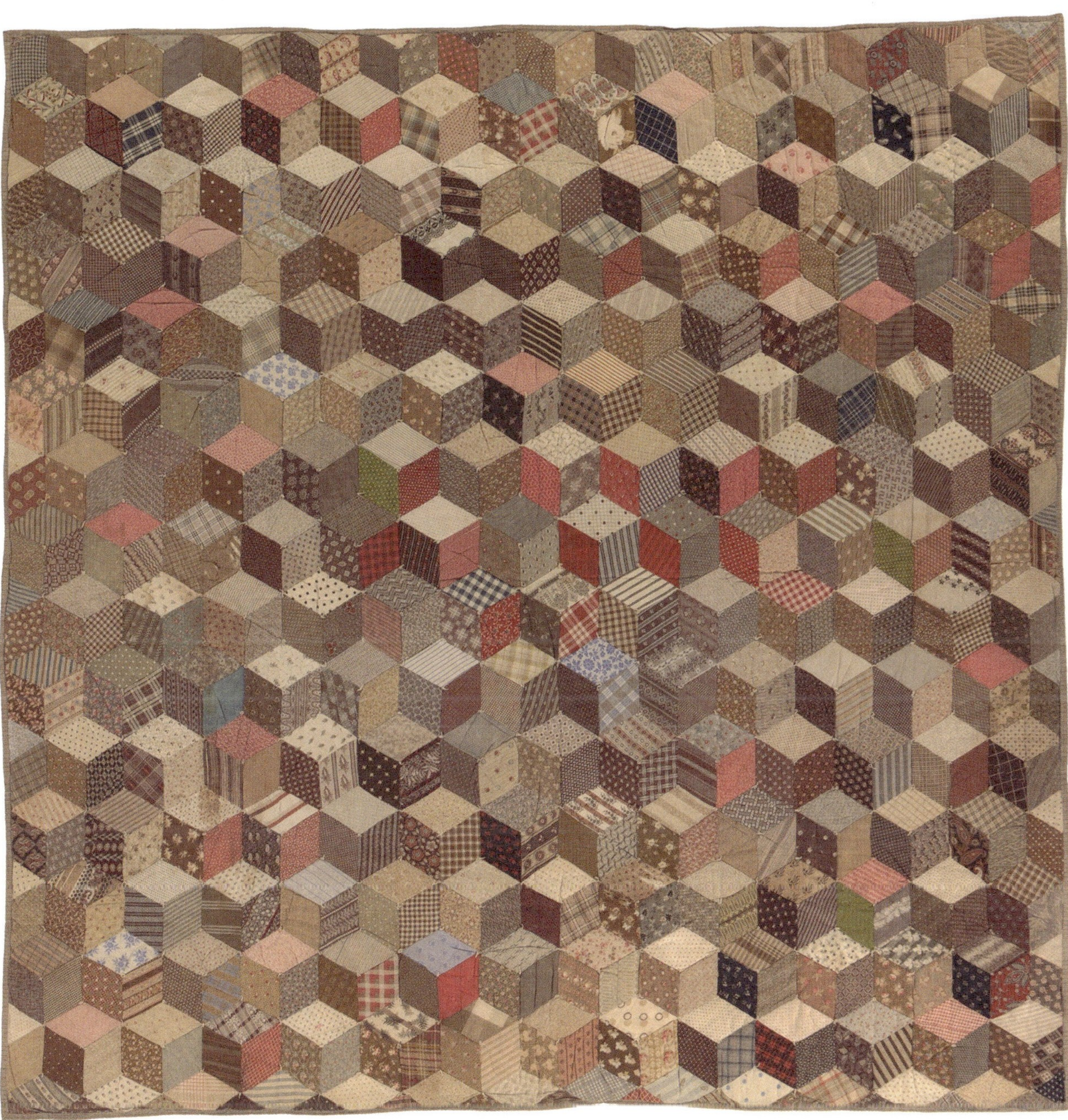

56. **Baby's Blocks**
Maker unidentified
Possibly made in Massachusetts, 1880–1900
Cotton; hand and machine pieced, tied; 80.5 x 79 in.
Jonathan Holstein and Gail van der Hoof Collection, IQM 2003.003.0056

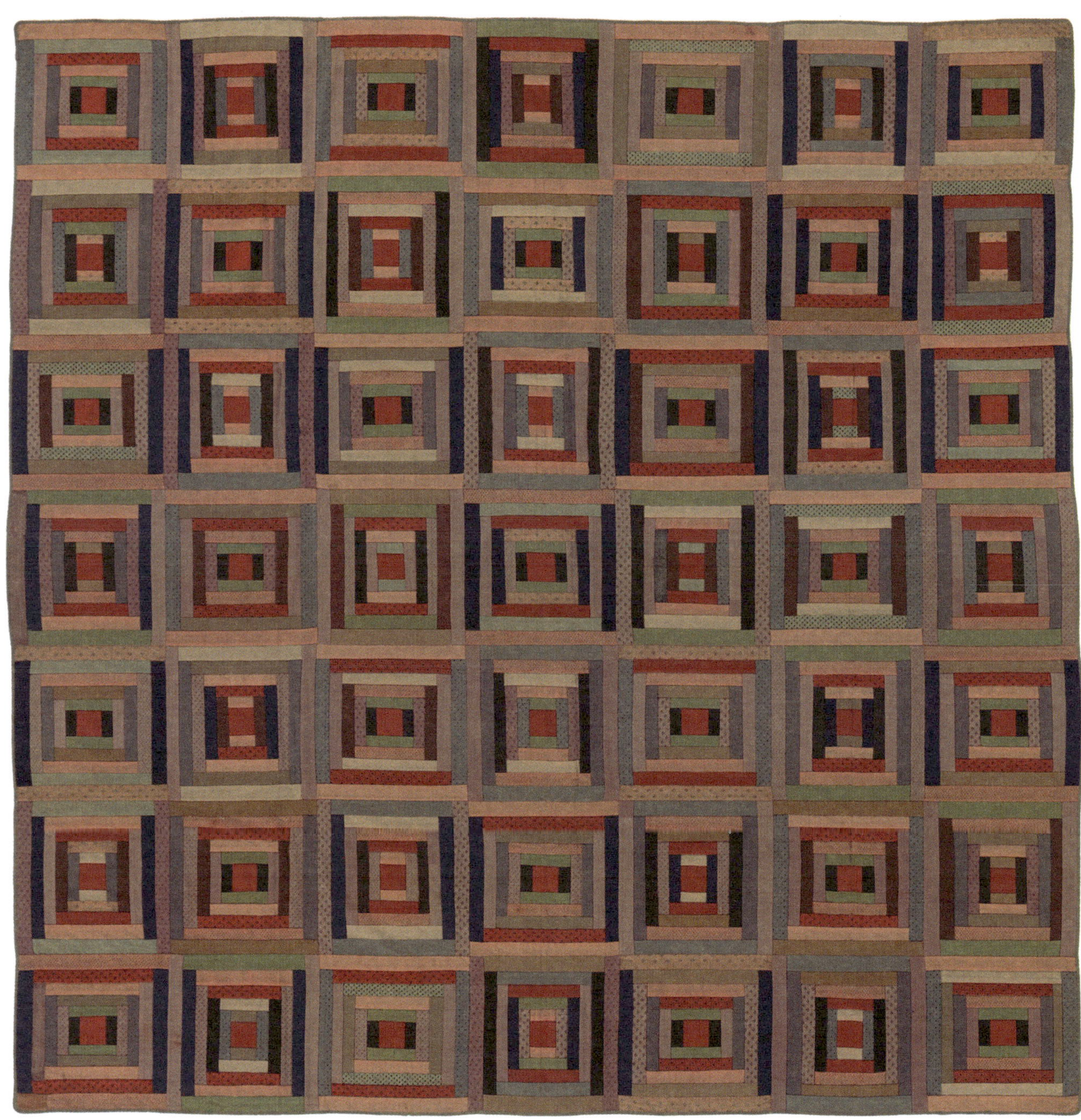

57. **Log Cabin, Courthouse Steps variation**
Maker unidentified
Probably made in Pennsylvania, 1870–1890
Wool; hand pieced, unquilted; 86.5 x 86 in.
Jonathan Holstein and Gail van der Hoof Collection, IQM 2003.003.0057

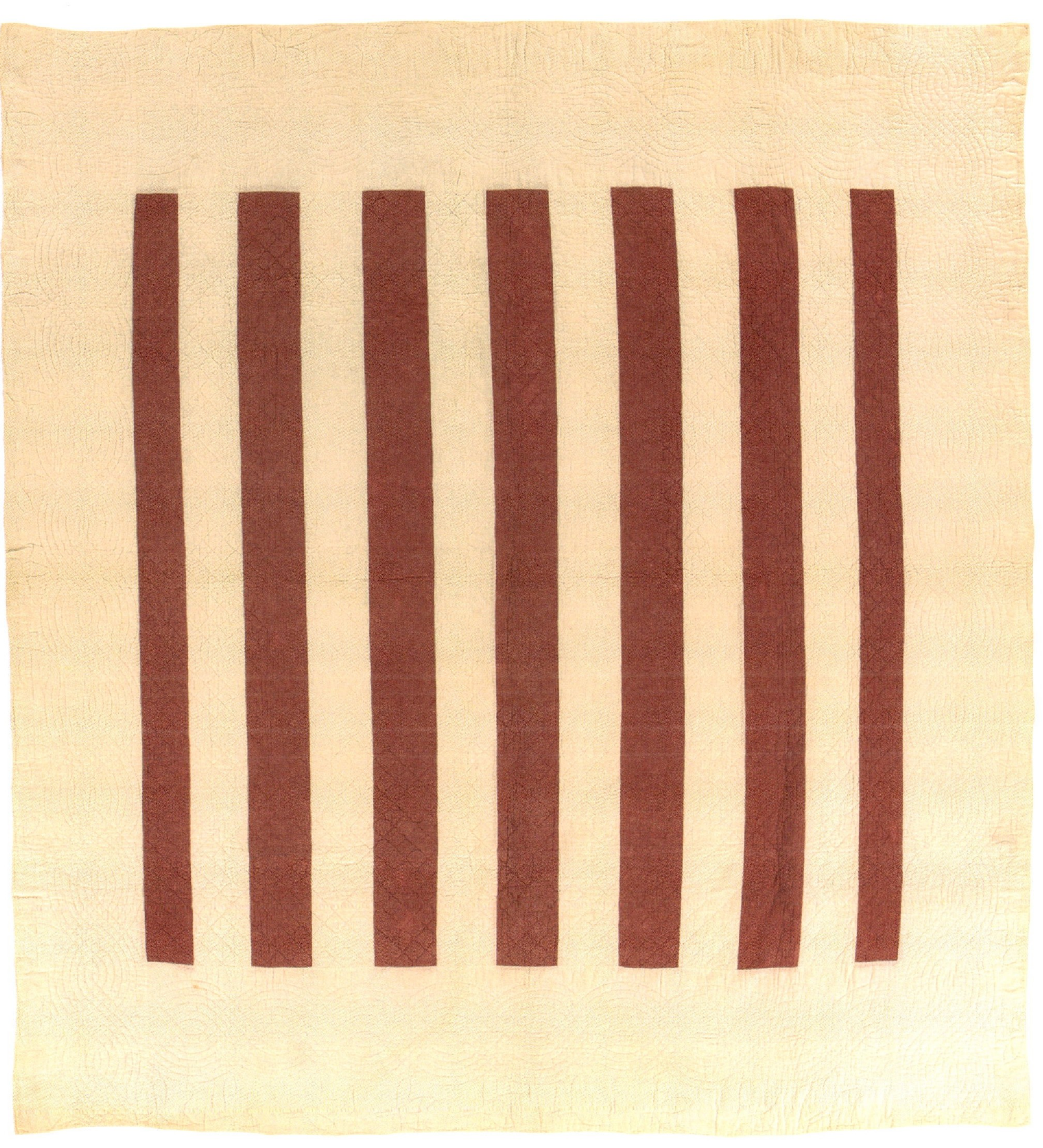

58. **Bars**
Maker unidentified
Probably made in Pennsylvania, 1890–1910
Cotton; machine pieced, hand quilted; 79 x 75 in.
Jonathan Holstein and Gail van der Hoof Collection, IQM 2003.003.0058

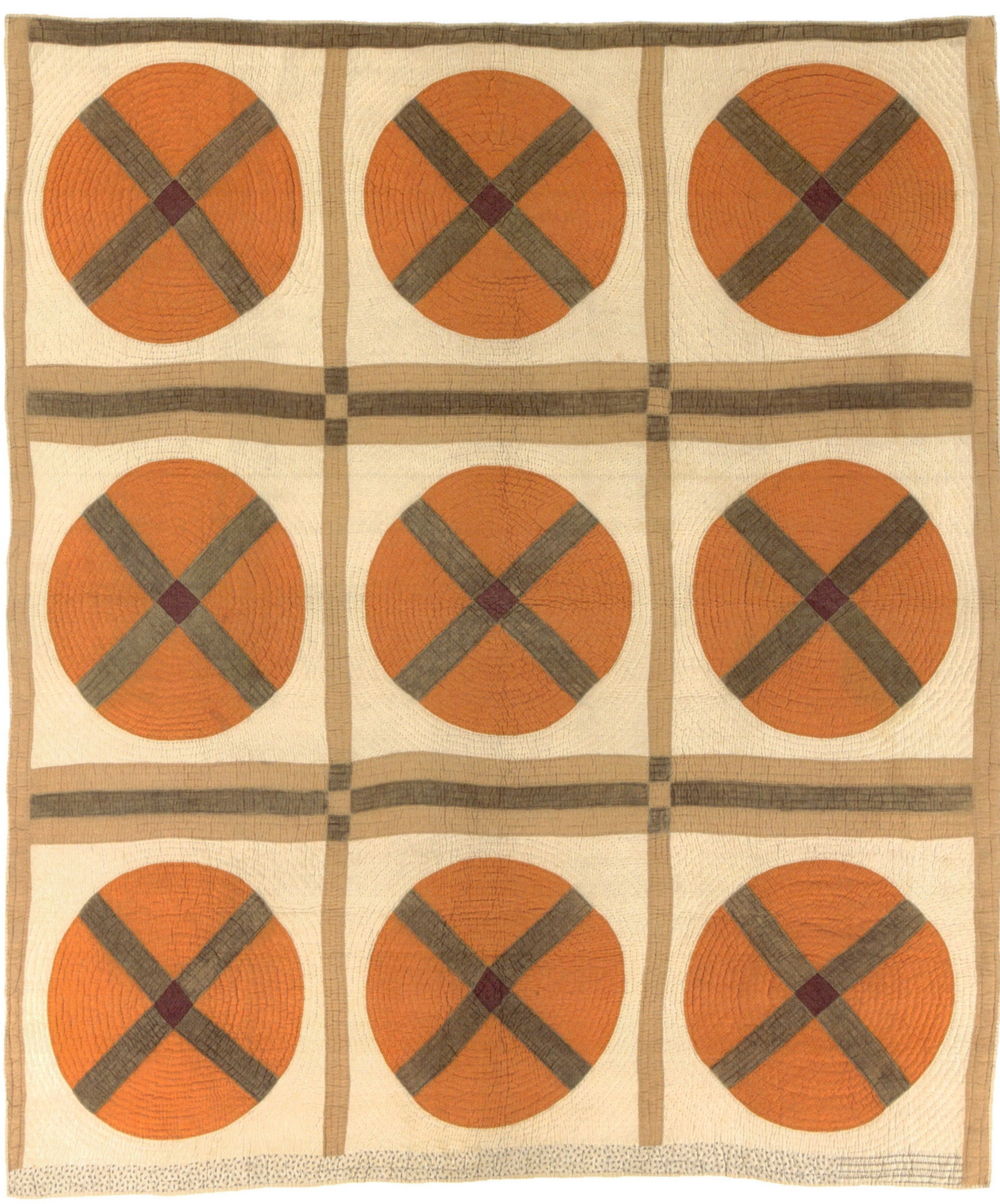

59. **Circles with Crosses**
Maker unidentified
Probably made in Colorado, 1890–1900
Cotton; hand pieced and quilted; 83.25 x 72.5 in.
Gift of Philip Holstein, IQM 2019.134.0001

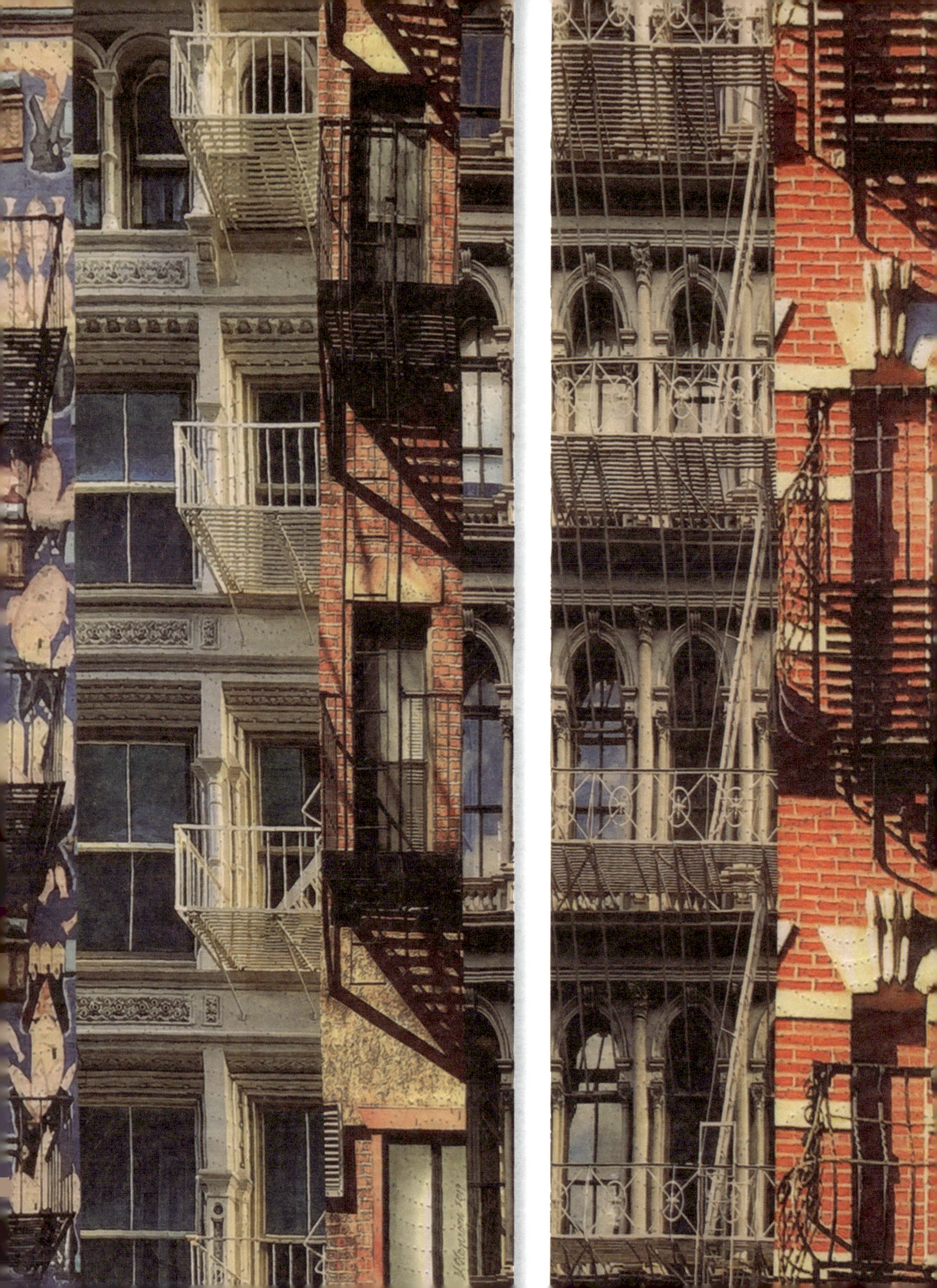

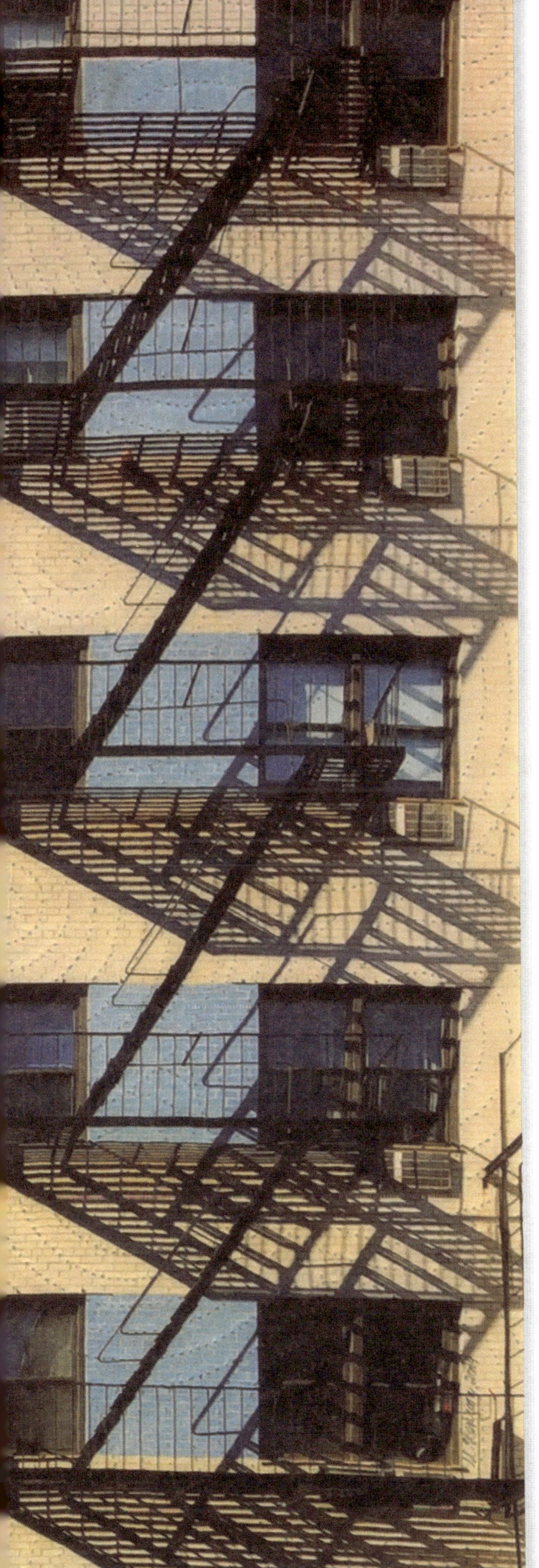

# NEW YORK NEXUS



The artists in the *New York Nexus* exhibition were key figures in the development of the genre that came to be known as "art quilts" or "studio quilts." Working in New York in the 1970s and beyond, the artists were both influenced by and instrumental in the city's atmosphere of innovation in fiber art. These new ways of thinking about textiles—antique and contemporary—were affected in part by the popular success of the Whitney's *Abstract Design in American Quilts* exhibition.

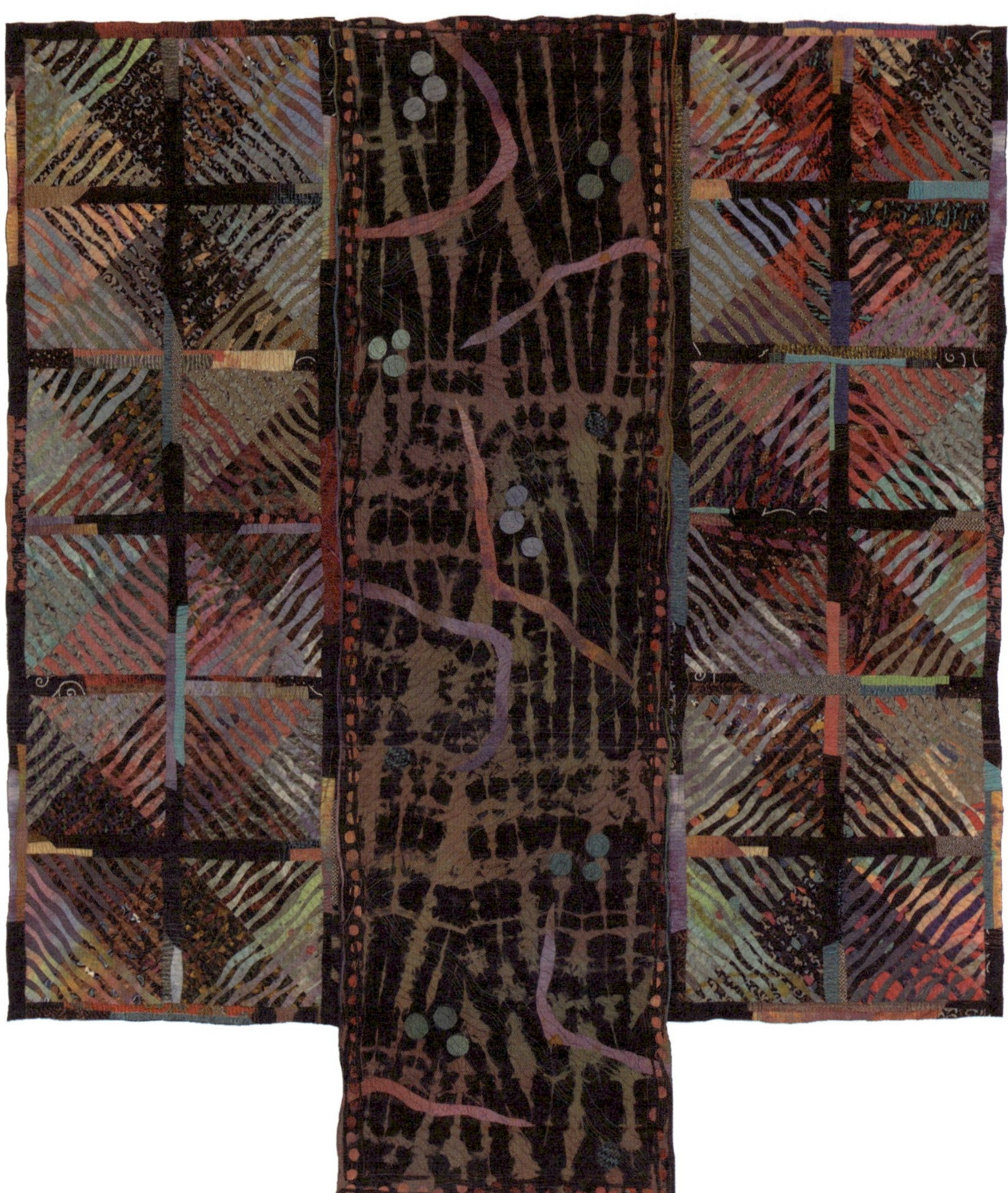

60. **Watchful Eye X: Deep Ogalu and Uli**
Sue Benner
Dallas, Texas, 1997
Dye and paint on silk and cotton, found fabrics, discharged and overdyed *shibori* (shaped-resist dyeing) fabrics; fused collage, machine quilted, composed of three panels sewn together, hand stitched; 68 x 59 in.
Collection of the artist

The concentric diamond pattern in the outer panels has several sources, the first being a traditional pieced pattern, Roman Stripe. The diamonds also reference the God's Eye ritual object from the Huichol peoples of Mexico. This quilt also indicates the artist's fascination with patterns that the Igbo women of Nigeria paint on their houses, *Ogalu*, derived from a skin scarification pattern. The Igbo motif over the quilt's central panel is known as *Uli*. Sue Benner sees all these motifs as a sort of universal visual language.

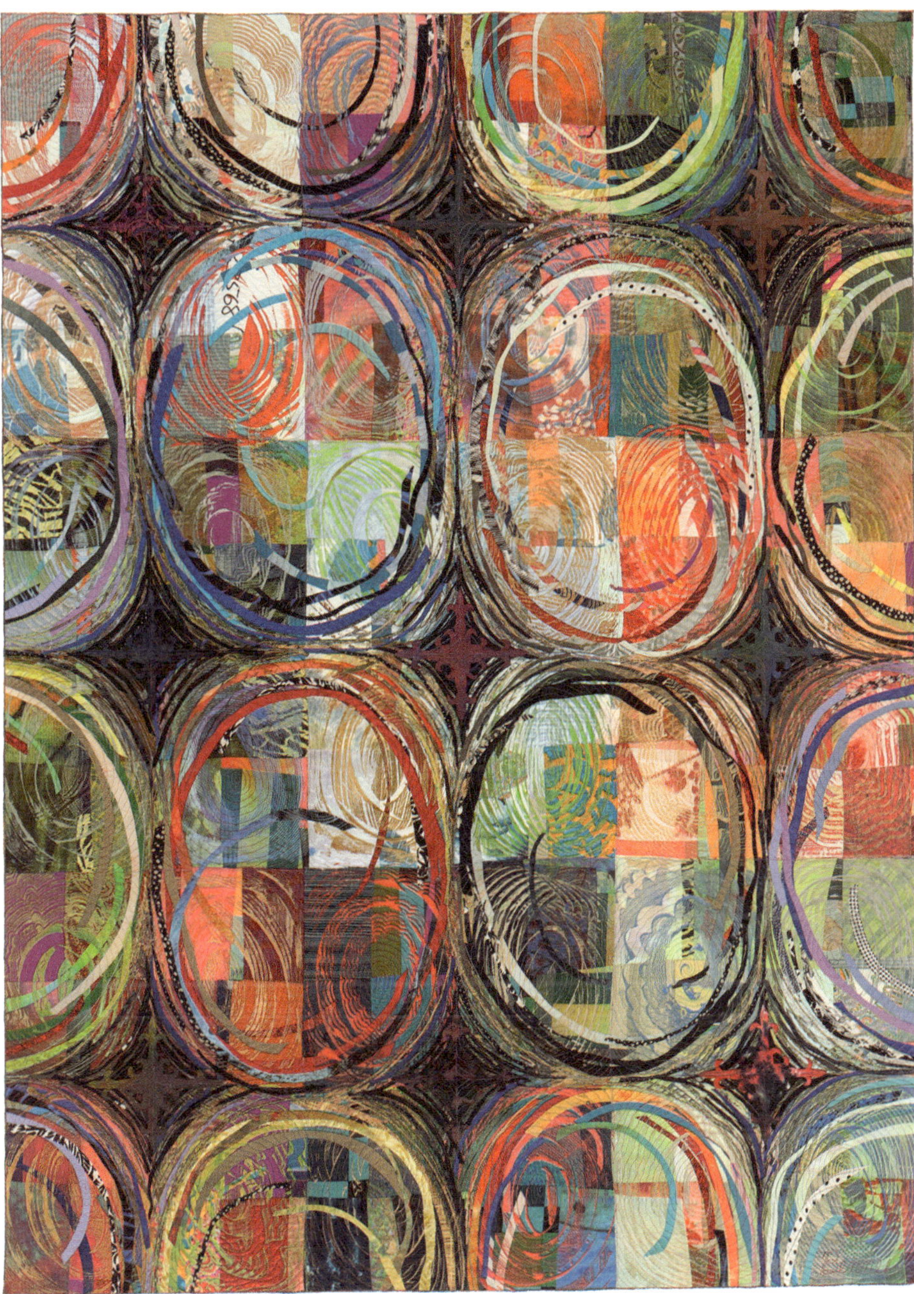

61. **Cellular Structure VIII: Oval Shift**
Sue Benner
Dallas, Texas, 2007
Dye and paint on silk and cotton, found fabrics, fused collage, monoprinted, machine quilted; 70 x 52 in.
Gift of IQM Friends and Volunteers, and the Robert and Ardis James Foundation, IQM 2013.047.0001

In her Cellular Structure series, Sue Benner thinks about the layering of structure and looking deeply to see what is beyond the surface. Her education in biomedical science inspires artwork concerned with the human body and the microscopic universe. Benner sees a direct connection between the concept of quilt and the assembly of units, whether in cells or fabric. These shapes inhabit her mind and are the building blocks of her world and art.

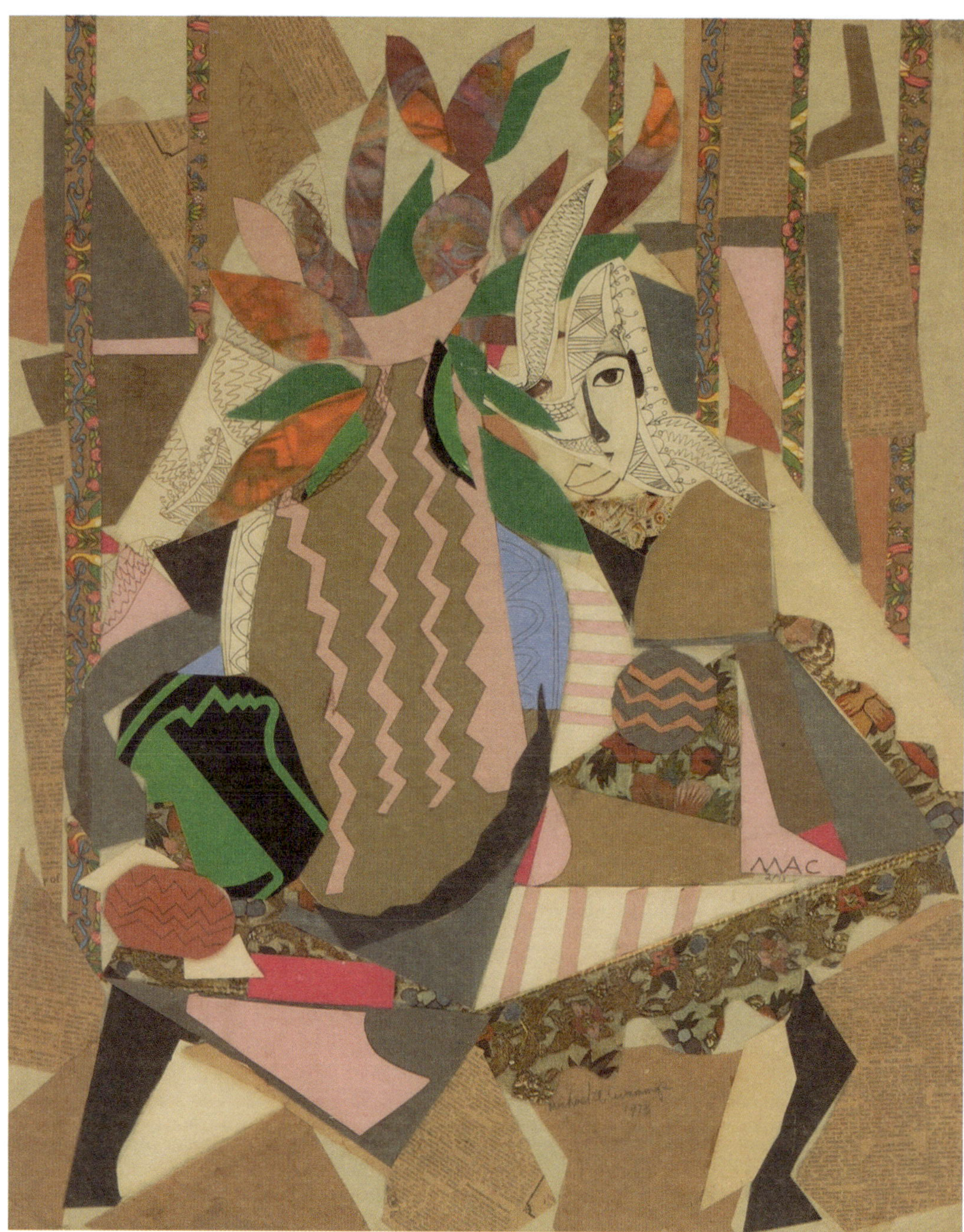


62. **Reflections**
Michael A. Cummings
New York, New York, 1973
Paper, newspaper; glued and framed; 36 x 26 in.
Gift of the Robert and Ardis James Foundation, IQM 2021.002.0001

American artist Romare Bearden influenced Michael Cummings in New York during his early career as an artist, when the future quilt artist was painting and making collages. *Reflections* exemplifies his work around the time he viewed *Abstract Design in American Quilts* at the Whitney Museum. While the collage aesthetic has continued throughout his career, including his fascination with the Cubist style of Braque and Picasso, Cummings transitioned from paper to fabric not long after he completed this collage.

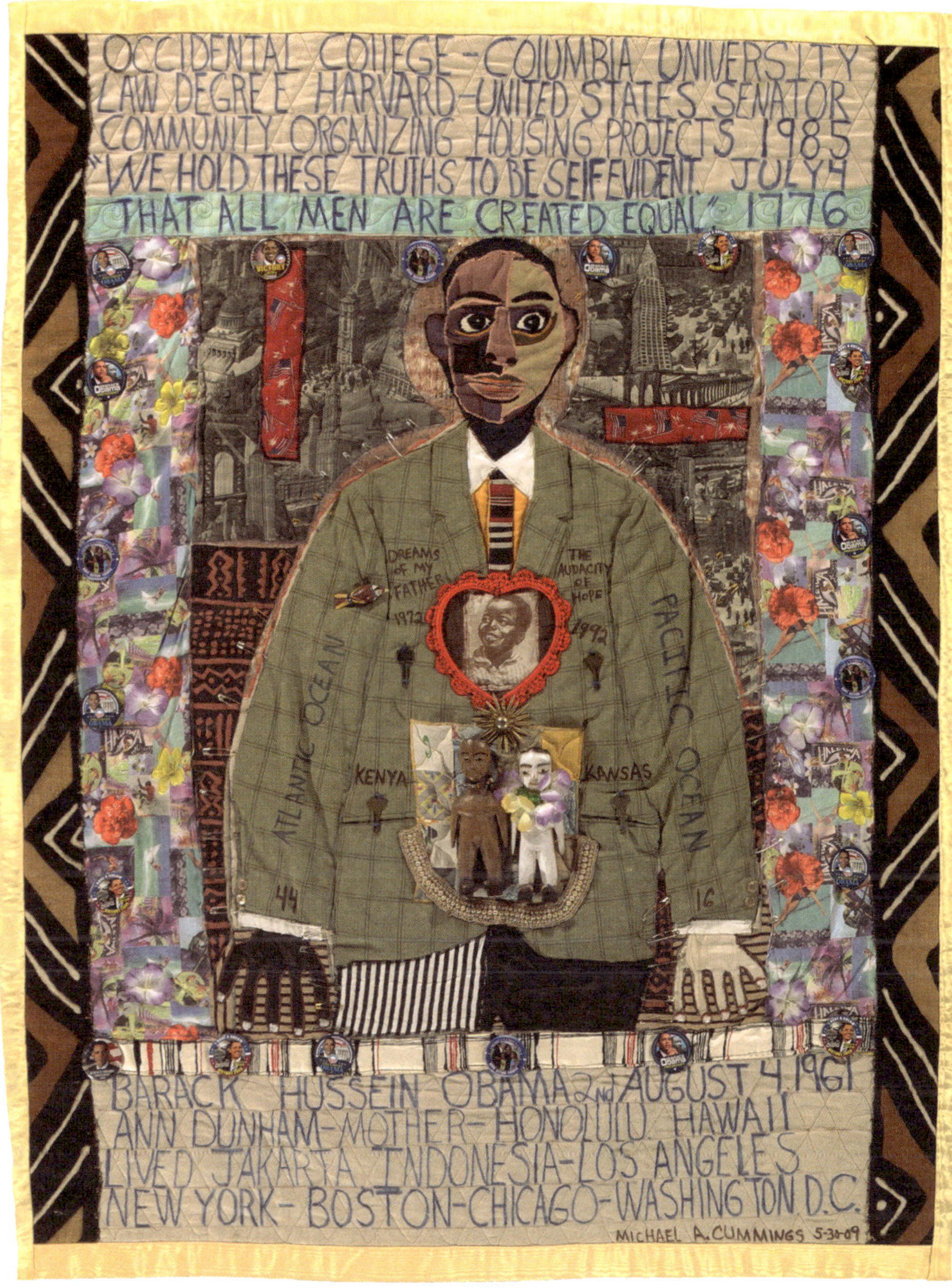


63. **Young Obama**
Michael A. Cummings
New York, New York, 2009
African wooden dolls and fabrics, man's jacket and tie, safety pins, keys, fabric paint; machine appliquéd and quilted, machine and hand pieced; 66 x 51 in.
Gift of the Robert & Ardis James Foundation, IQM 2018.077.0002

Referencing the highly decorative nature of many African textiles, Michael Cummings celebrated several aspects of Afrocentric culture in his early quilts, including Egungun costume from Nigeria and Haitian folklore. His most recent work features heroic interpretations of political and literary icons, such as Shirley Chisholm, Barack Obama, and James Baldwin. Throughout his career as a quilt artist, Cummings has remained true to his roots, exploring various aspects of what it means to be a Black artist in this country.

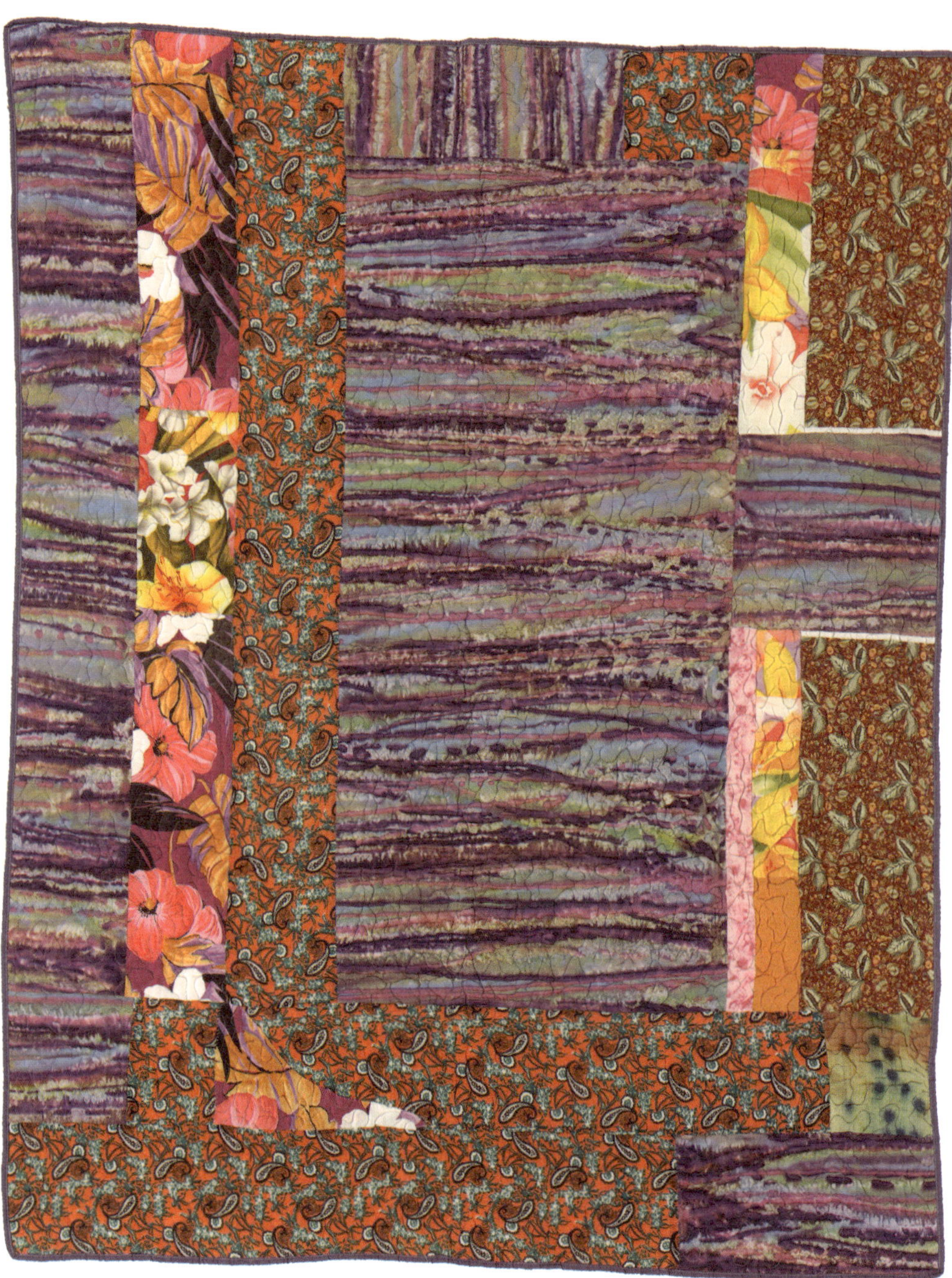

64. **Eva's Garden from the Paradise Dozen**
Radka Donnell
Cambridge, Massachusetts, 2006
Cotton; machine pieced and quilted; 69.5 x 55.5 in.
Private collection

Trained as a painter, Radka Donnell (1928–2018) began using fabrics in her quilt art by the mid-1960s. Her wide swaths of energetic prints reveal her painterly aesthetic. An ardent feminist, she became even more politicized through creating quilts, associating that process with women's lives and bodies. Although Donnell viewed quilts as art forms, the sizes and proportions of most of her work suggest the bed as a human nexus.

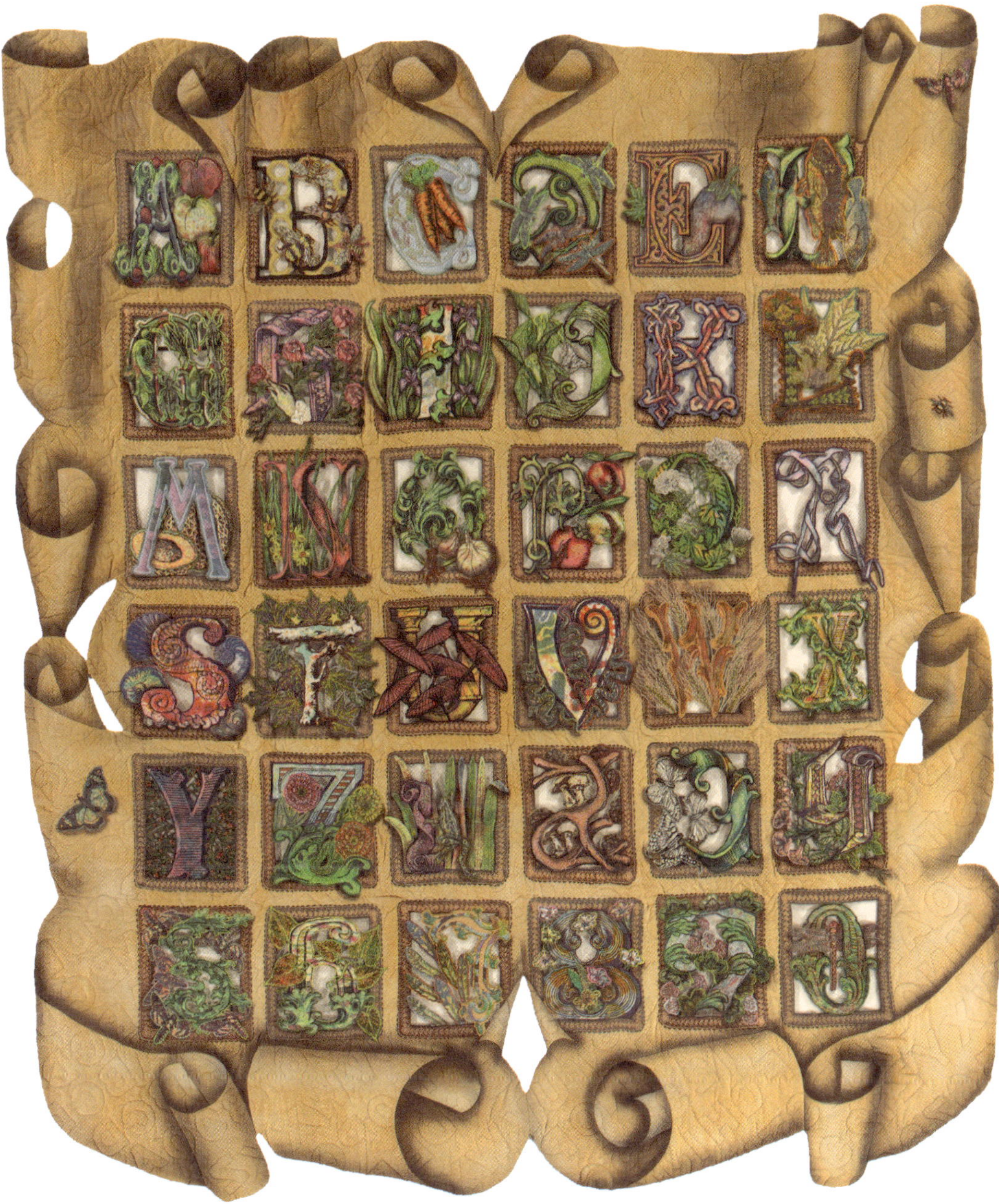

65. **A Riddling Tale**
M. Joan Lintault
Carbondale, Illinois, 1998
Hand-dyed fabrics, *katazome* (stenciled paste-resist dyeing) fabrics; machine sewn;
97 x 86 in.
Illinois State Museum, Illinois Legacy Collection

In 1984, Joan Lintault (1938–2020) received a Fulbright Research Grant to study textile processes and techniques in Japan, which influenced her lifelong career as a quilt artist. *A Riddling Tale* features letters of the alphabet, along with images representing letters, as in a children's nursery story. The title suggests an old-time fairy tale involving a riddle, thus the trompe l'oeil reference to antique manuscripts.

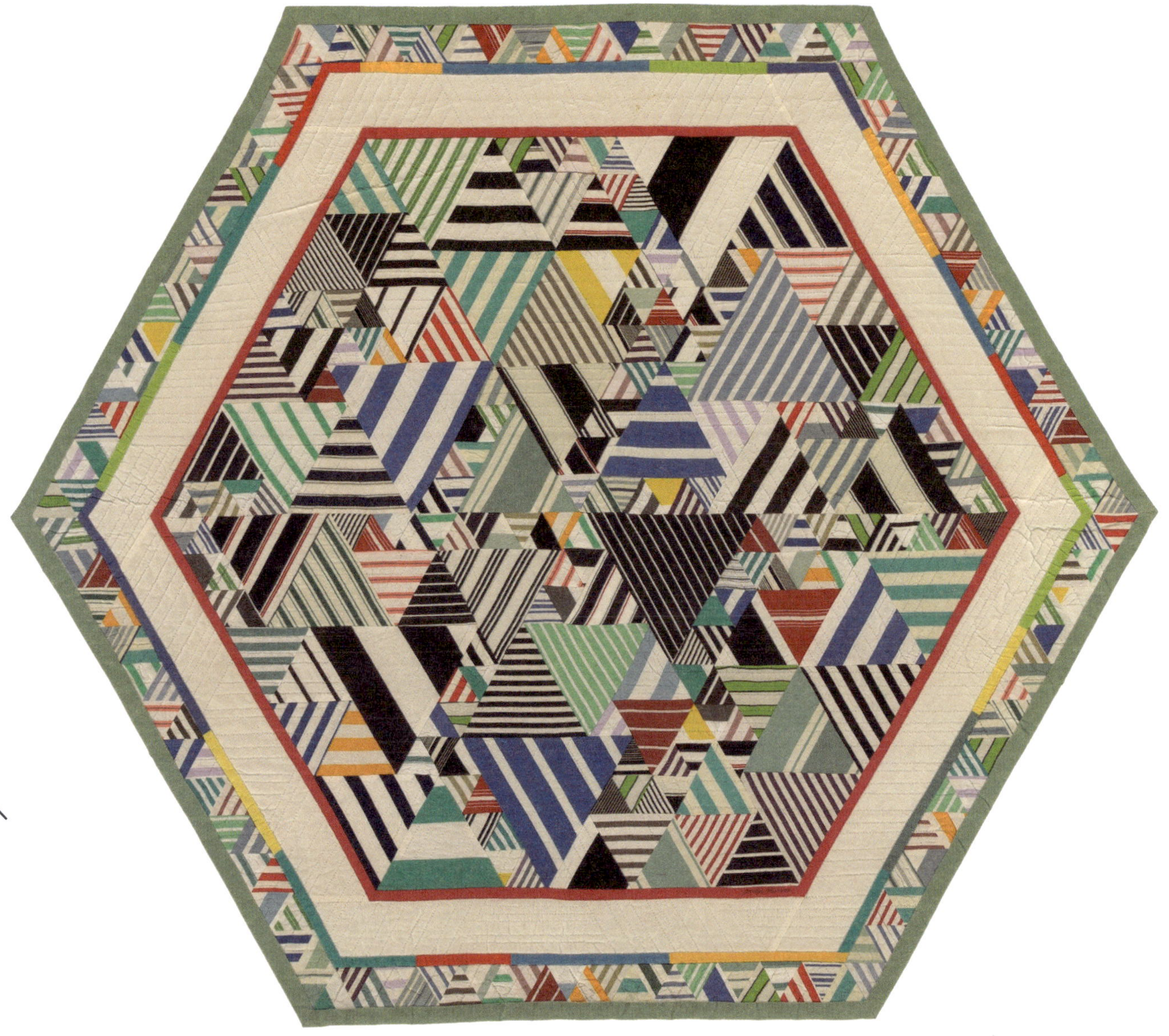

66. **Brighton Beach Memories**
Marilyn Henrion
New York, New York, 1995
Cotton; machine pieced and hand quilted; 45 x 52 in.
Collection of the artist

Marilyn Henrion's aesthetic vision has always been deeply rooted in the geometry of her surroundings. Having grown up in the Brooklyn neighborhood of Brighton Beach, she spent much of her childhood at that beach. The indelible memory of striped umbrellas was imprinted in her mind at an early age. Echoes of this fascination with linear geometry can be seen throughout Henrion's extensive body of work, in both her patterning and hand quilting that often functions as "drawing."

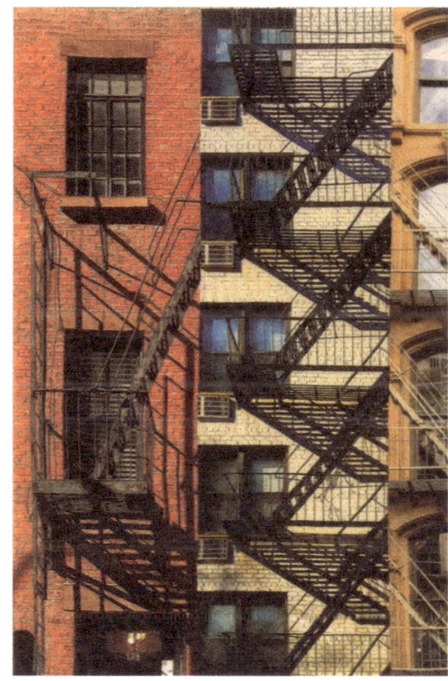
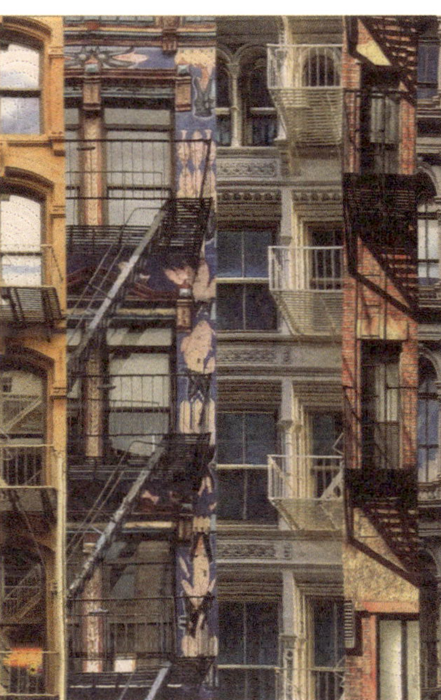
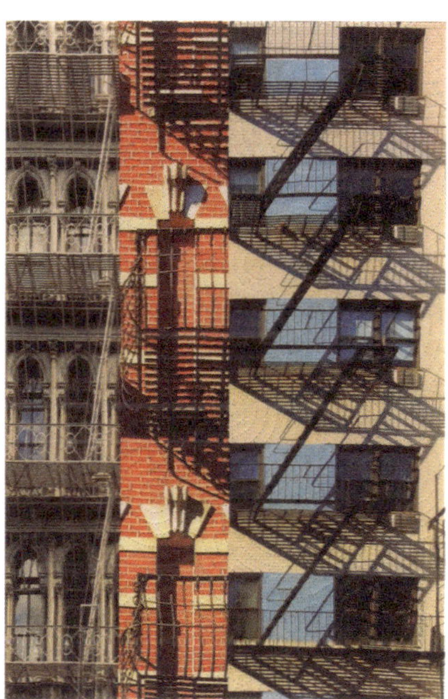

67. **Great Escapes**
Marilyn Henrion
New York, New York, 2019
Digitally manipulated photography, pigment printed on cotton; hand quilted, gallery-wrapped on stretched canvas; 30 x 60 in.
Collection of the artist

Marilyn Henrion is a native New Yorker, and the urban geometry of the city in which she has lived for almost 90 years has been the source of much of her inspiration. The verticals, horizontals, and diagonals of the ubiquitous fire escapes provide endless delight as she walks the streets of her SoHo neighborhood. The overlapping concentric circles of her quilting symbolize the ephemeral nature of our existence on this landscape.

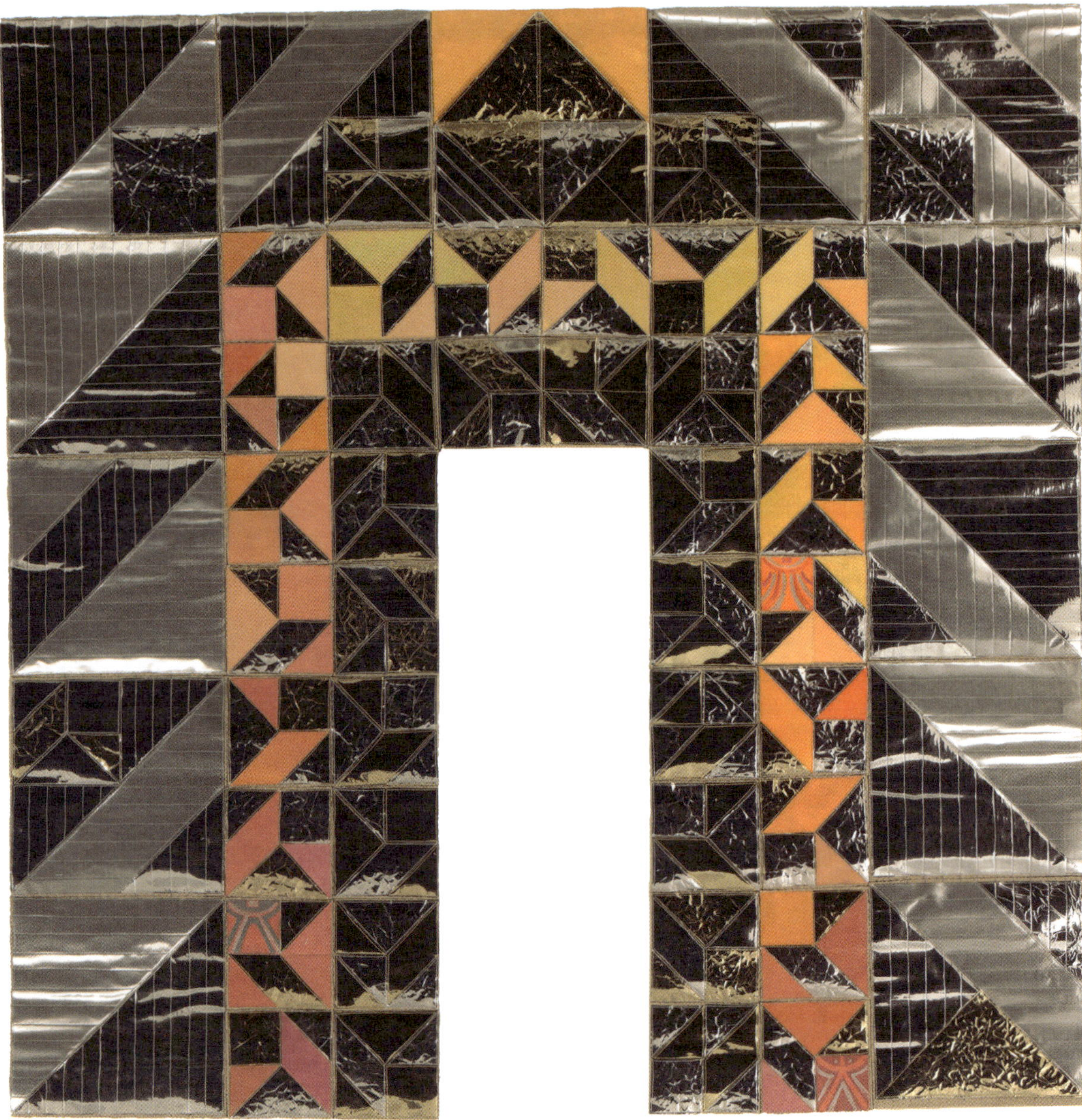

68. **Sundoor**
Patricia Malarcher
Englewood, New Jersey, 1988
Mylar, fabric, acrylic paint; machine and hand sewn; 60 x 60 in.
Collection of the artist

*Sundoor* is part of a series with central "doorways." The title initially alluded to the progression of pinks through yellows that suggested the course of the sun through the day. Later, in a book by comparative religion/myth expert Joseph Campbell titled *The Hero with a Thousand Faces*, Patricia Malarcher found a reference to a sun door as "a guide through which one passes from infantile illusion to revelation of being." That thought resonated with her experience of creating the piece.

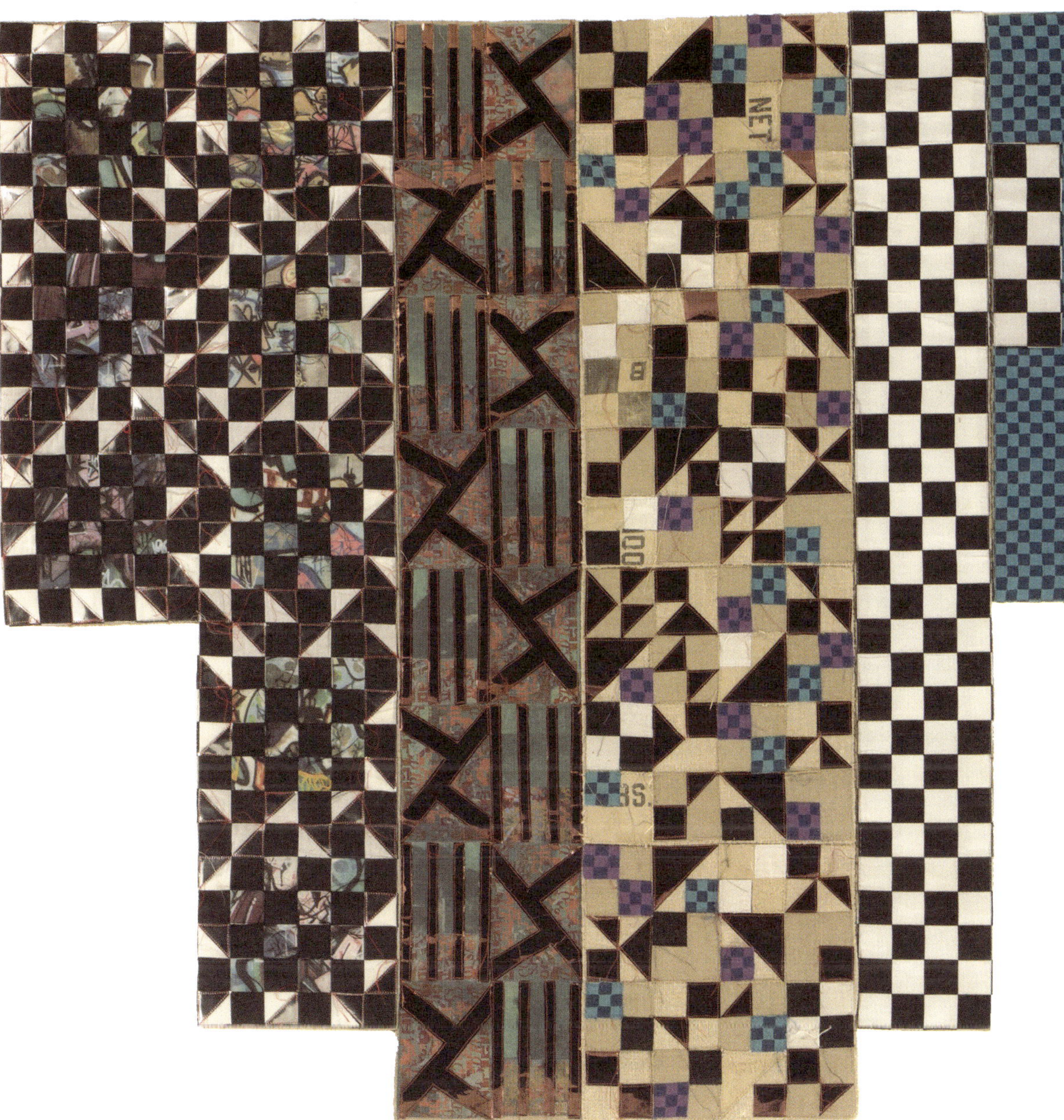


69. **Interrupted Continuum**
Patricia Malarcher
Englewood, New Jersey, 2003
Mylar, fabric, acrylic paint; machine and hand sewn; 48 x 48.5 in.
Collection of the artist

Incorporating transfer-printed images of New York graffiti and the Twin Towers burning, *Interrupted Continuum* is an abstract meditation on the period immediately following the horrific events of September 11, 2001. Viewed from left to right, this quilt represents a transition from rhythmic vitality through abrupt discontinuance and chaos to cessation of activity.

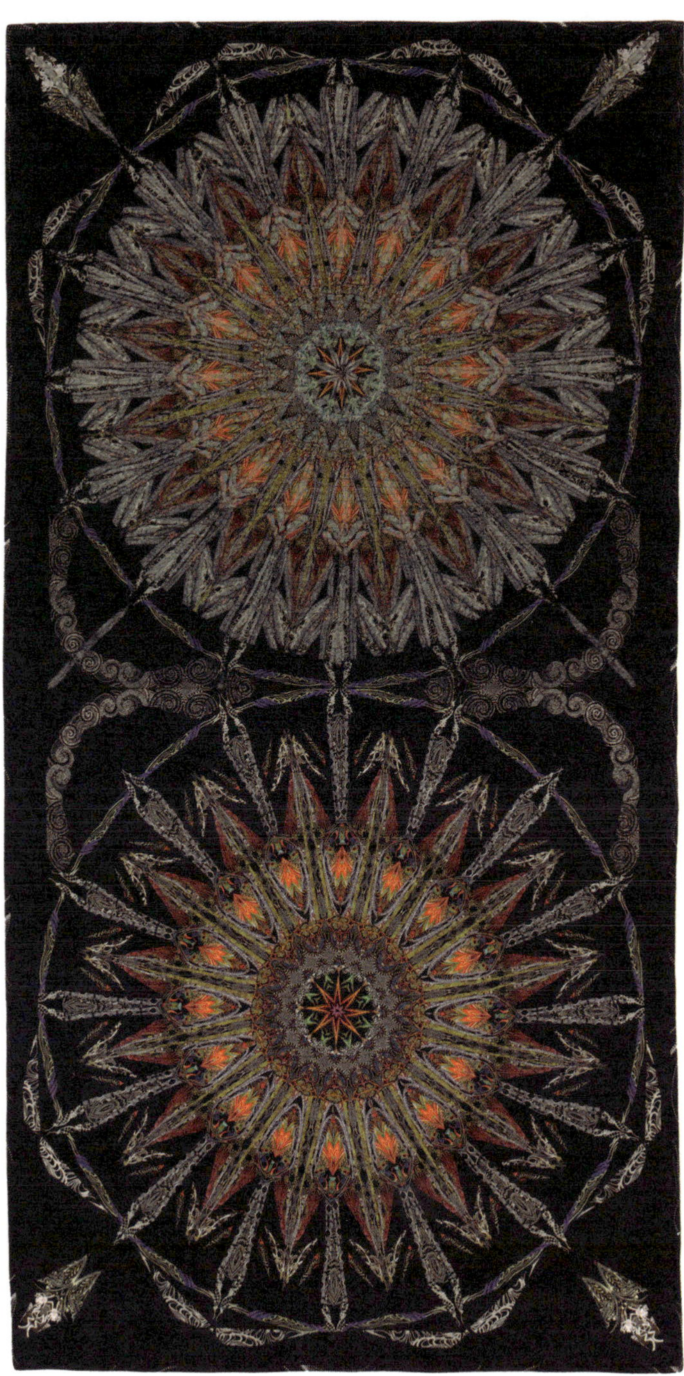

70. **Kaleidoscopic XXXIX: Right and Wrong Sides Together**
Paula Nadelstern
Bronx, New York, 2015
Cotton fabrics designed by the artist except for batiks and netting; machine pieced and quilted; 86 x 45 in.
Collection of the artist

The top kaleidoscope was pieced traditionally by sewing the right sides of the fabric together. The patches of the bottom kaleidoscope were pieced by sewing the wrong sides together. Paula Nadelstern's usual design strategy is to camouflage the piece's construction units, encouraging an uninterrupted flow from one section to the next. Instead of sharp, straight edges defining shapes, the result is a smooth transition creating the illusion that there are no seams at all. But this quilt reveals the complex construction for which Nadelstern is known.

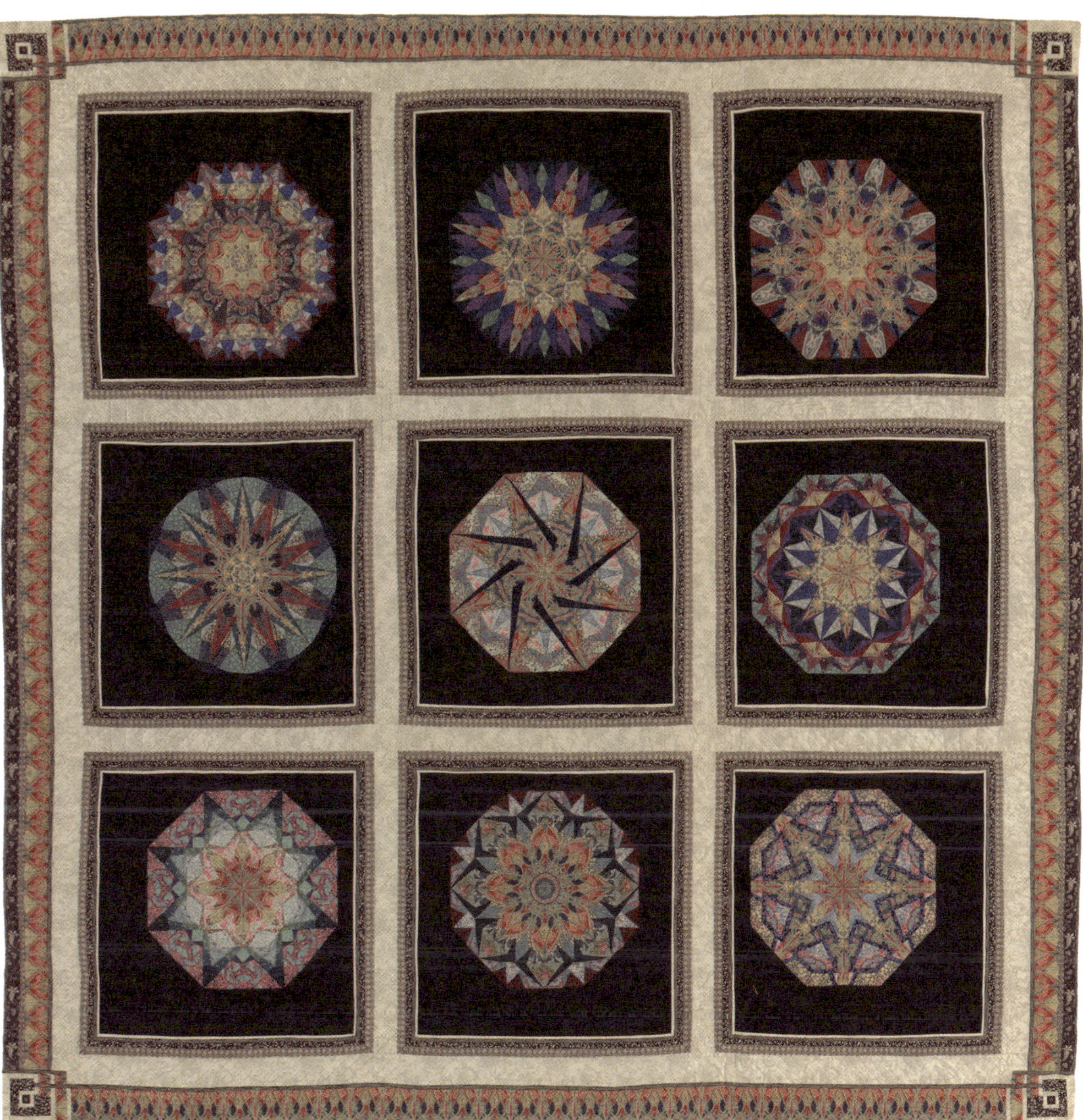

71. **Kaleidoscopic III: Stained Glass Anthology**
Paula Nadelstern
Bronx, New York, 1989
Cotton and cotton blend; machine pieced, hand quilted; 66 x 67 in.
Collection of the artist

In 1987, Paula Nadelstern was struck by a bolt of fabric. She contemplated the $36-per-yard Liberty of London fabric for more than an hour before purchasing a quarter yard. Somehow, she intuited that the print's bilateral symmetry would reconnect into graceful kaleidoscopic designs, which became her hallmark. The results were fascinating, prompting "what if" questions that propelled Nadelstern along a new creative path. She was encouraged to make more kaleidoscope quilts, exploring the world of actual kaleidoscopes for further inspiration.

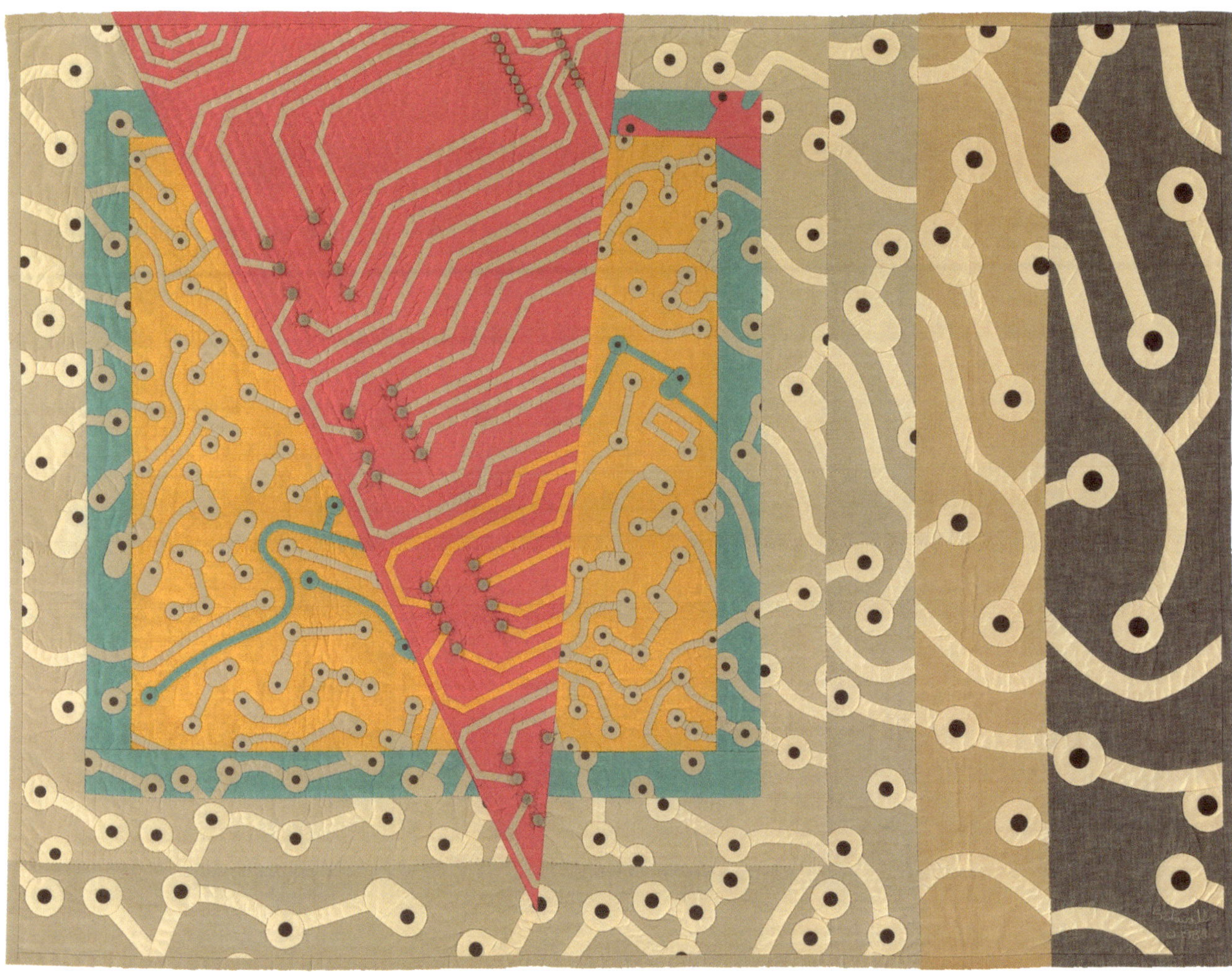

72. **PCB Bop**
Robin Schwalb
New York, New York, 1988
Cotton fabrics, some stenciled, metal studs; machine pieced, hand appliquéd and quilted; 41 x 55 in.
Collection of the artist

The initial inspiration for this piece was both sublime and ridiculous: a combination of a print by premier twentieth-century photographer Edward Weston and the sweat stains on singer Joe Cocker's brocade shirt during a rousing 1987 performance. The design evolved into the patterns of printed circuit boards (PCBs). While Robin Schwalb hesitates to hang ideological baggage onto what is essentially a lyrical, happy piece, the viewer is encouraged to maintain a thoughtful attitude towards technological innovation.

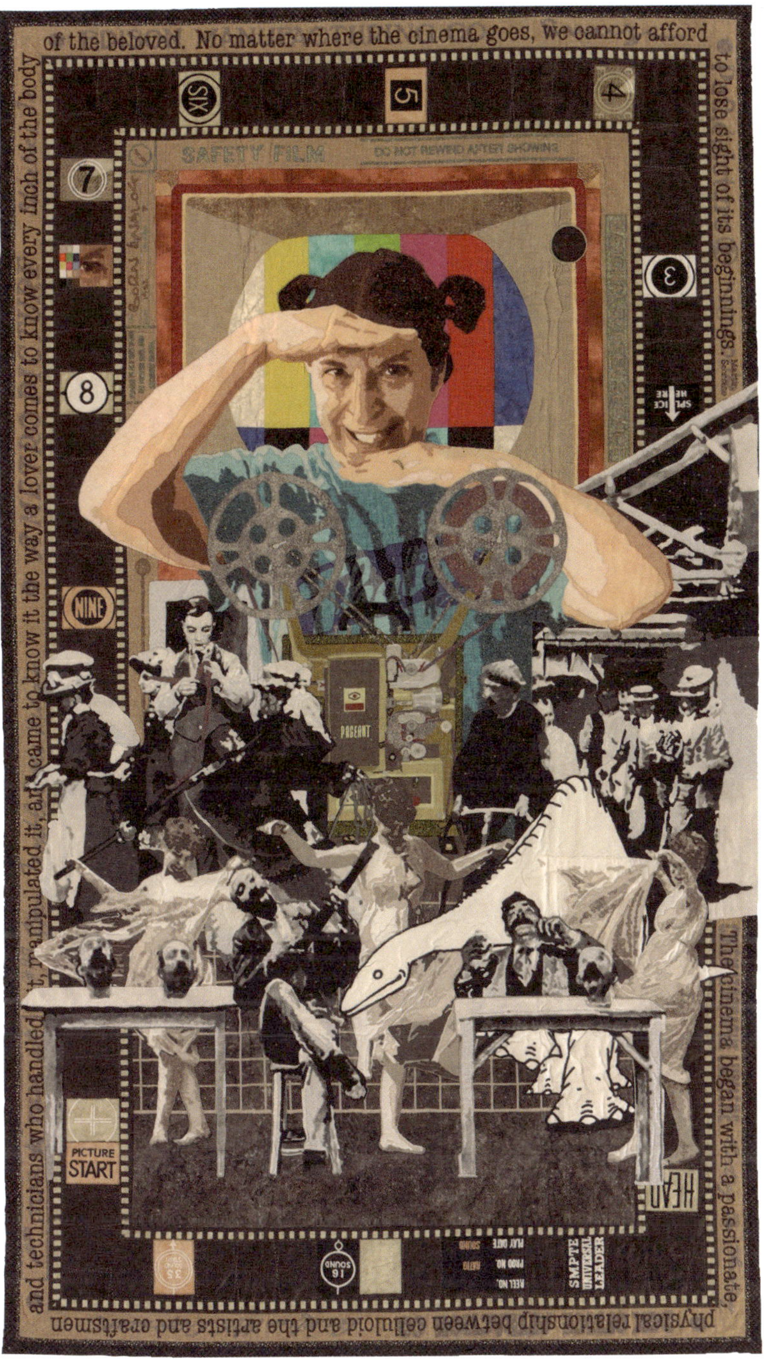


73. **Born Analog**
Robin Schwalb
New York, New York, 2016
Silk-screened and commercial cotton fabrics; fused, machine and hand appliquéd, machine pieced, hand quilted; 80 x 47 in.
Collection of the artist

Robin Schwalb identifies as a "dinosaur" because, in this increasingly digital and digitized age, from 1976 through 2018 she was licensed by the City of New York to run 35mm motion picture film. Here she celebrates classic works of proto and early cinema by Eadweard Muybridge, the Lumière brothers, Georges Méliès, Thomas Edison, Buster Keaton, and Robert Flaherty, as well as Schwalb's own history as a film projectionist.

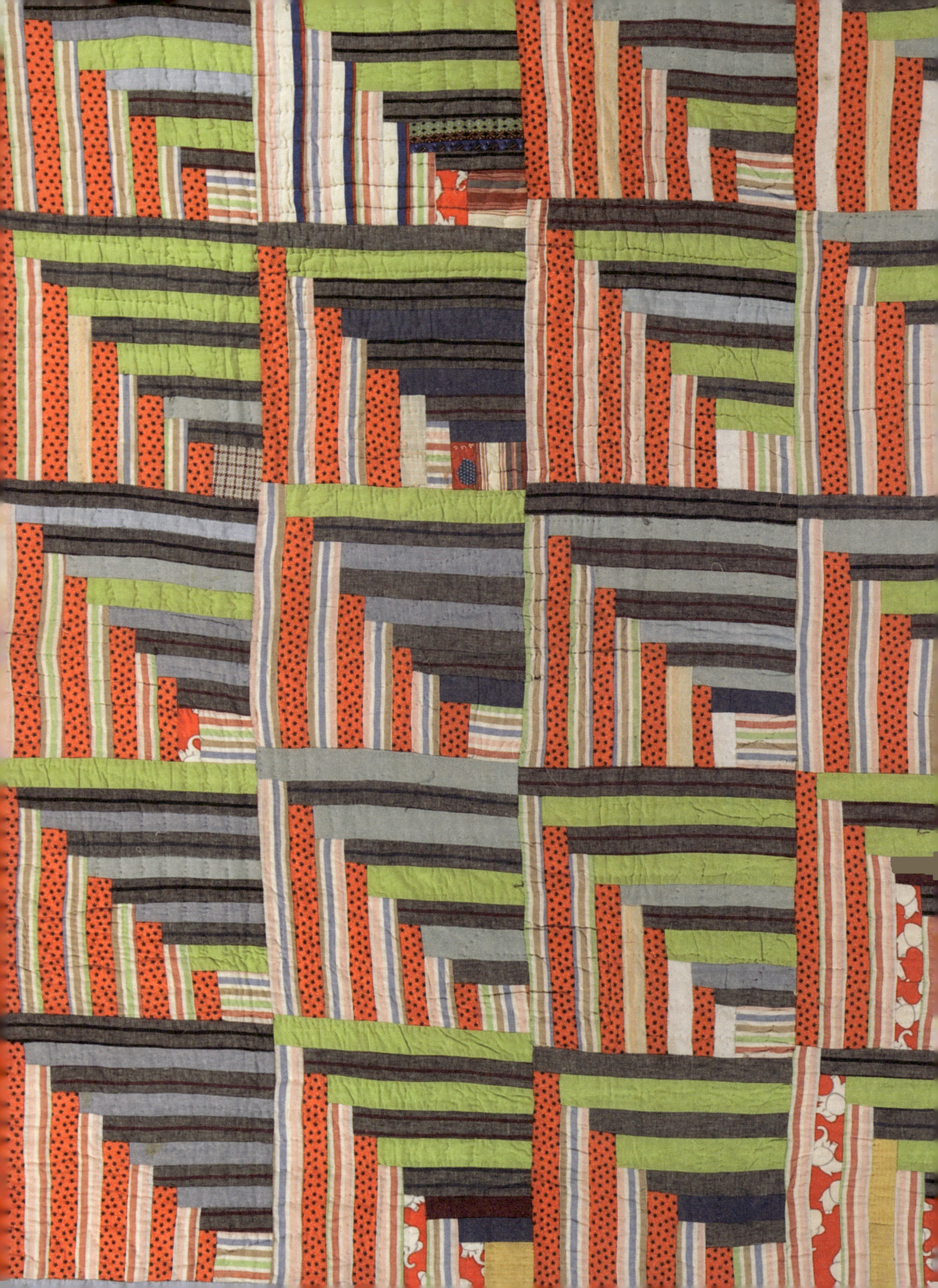

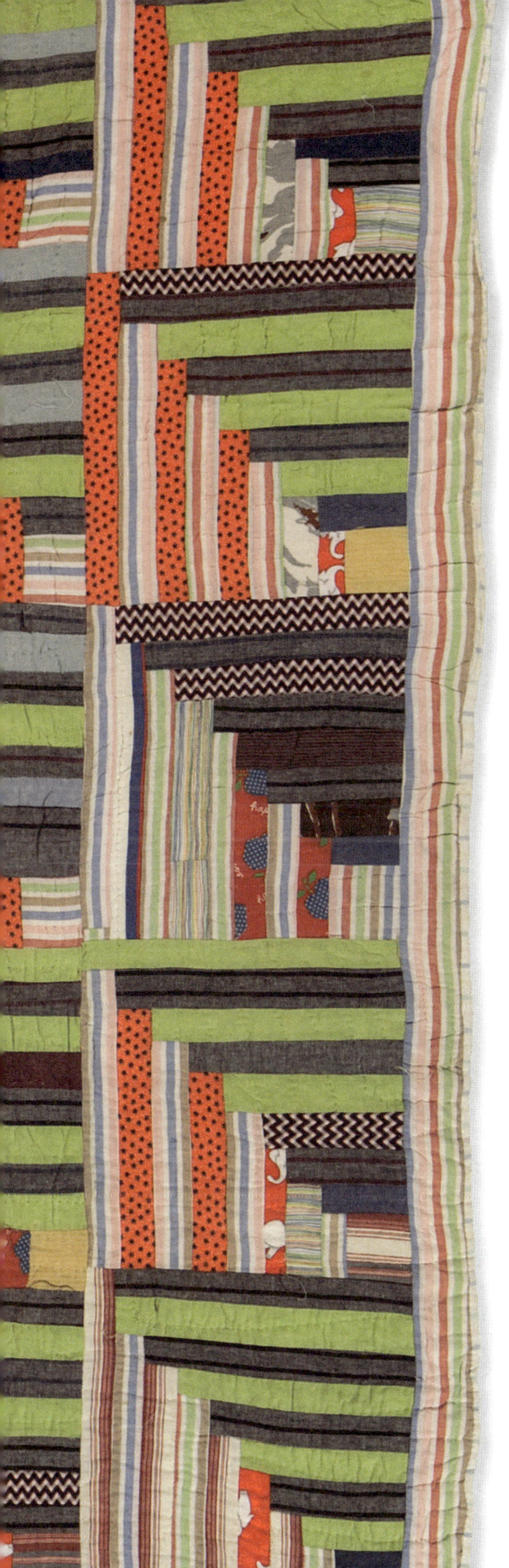

# RAISING THE PROFILE



The exhibition *Abstract Design in American Quilts* and other cultural factors kindled a renewed and more serious interest in quilts from artists and art critics; collectors of art, folk art, and Americana; and from new and long-time quiltmakers. As a result, quilts began appearing in art venues more frequently, and quilt collectors emerged along with the market framework to serve them. Also, the journey of American quilts—objects intimately connected with women's lives for more than 150 years—from their ancestral homes to antique shops and collectors' walls fueled grassroots-to-academic documentation and in-depth study. The quilts and quiltmakers in the *Raising the Profile* exhibition reveal personal and granular details of these phenomena.

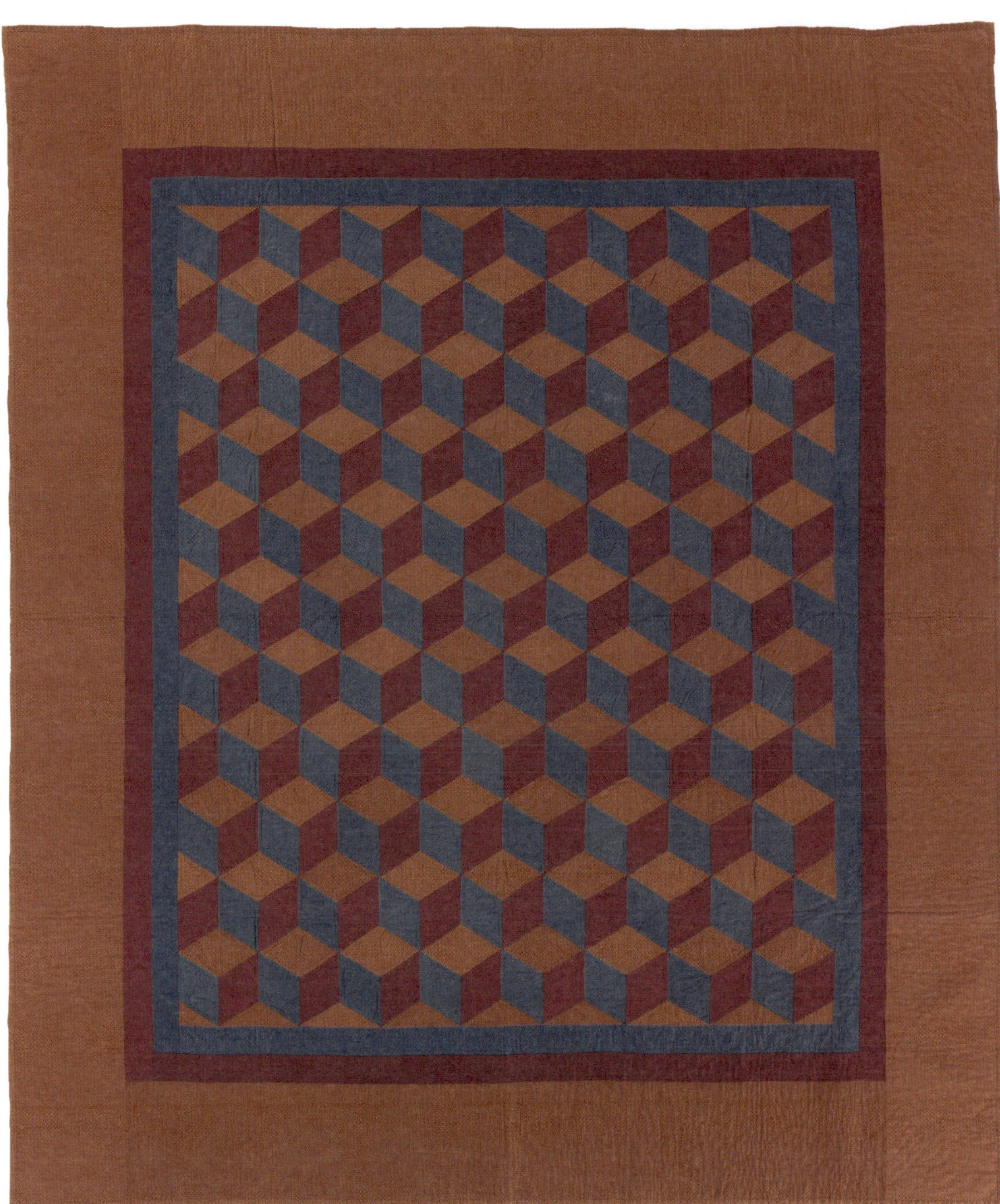

74. **Tumbling Blocks**
L. Miller
Wayne County, Ohio, circa 1975
Cotton; machine pieced, hand quilted; 81.5 x 70 in.
Ardis and Robert James Collection, IQM 1997.007.0512

Classic-style Amish quilts, made with fine woolens in deeply saturated colors, were the quintessential quilt analog to mid-century modernist abstract paintings. Because of the similarity, demand for these antique quilts drove prices quickly upwards. Ohio dealers Susan and George Delagrange offered an alternative: Susan designed quilts inspired by classic Amish quilts and the Delagrange's company, Amish Design, hired Amish women to make them. Amish Design sold the pieces as new quilts; nevertheless, they were easily mistaken for classic Amish quilts.

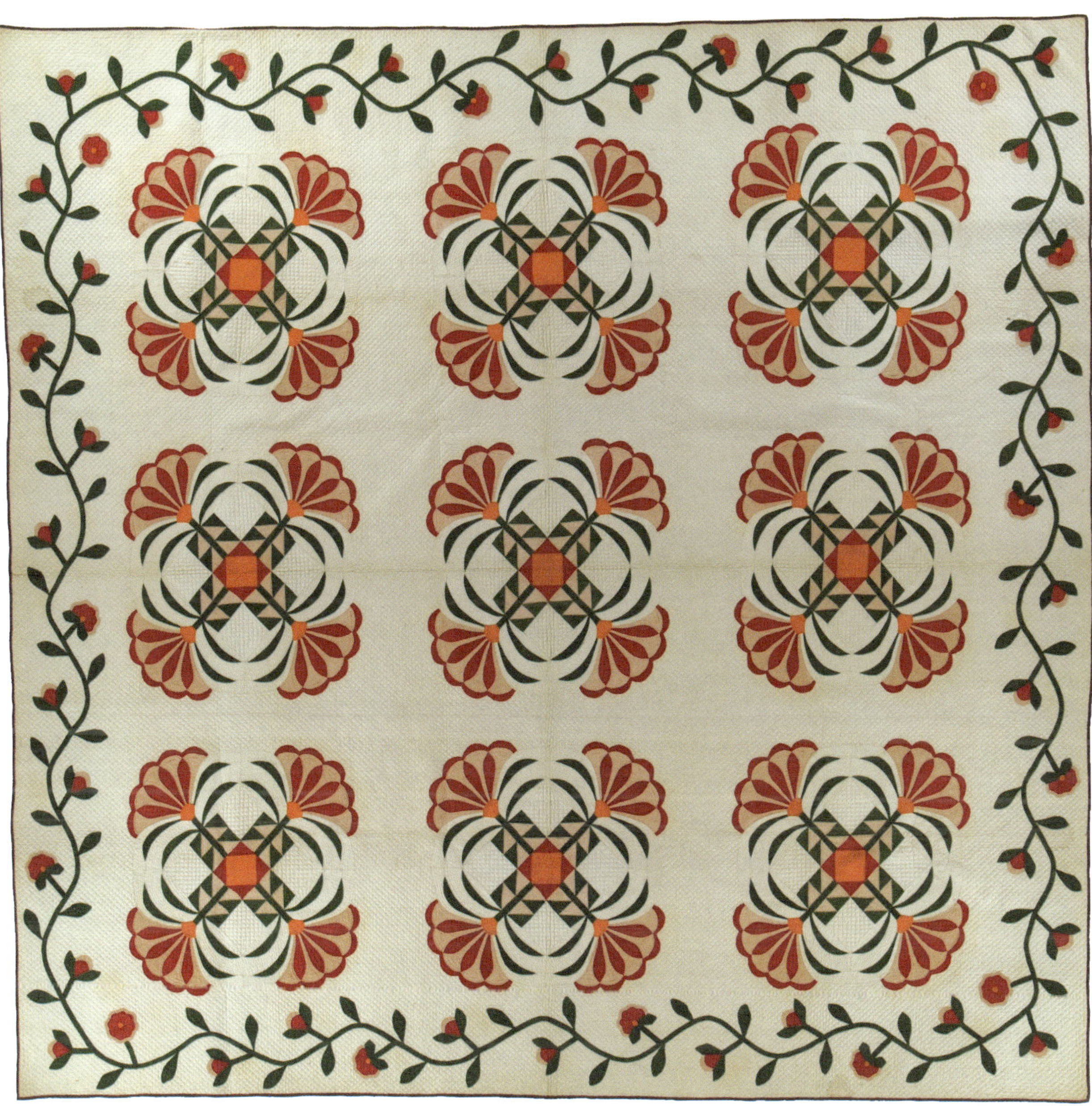

75. **Coxcomb**
Sarah Margaret Franklin Hart
Probably made in Clark County, Kentucky, dated 1858
Cotton; hand appliquéd and quilted; 97.5 x 101.5 in.
Ardis and Robert James Collection, IQM 1997.007.0720

"S. M. Hart, Oct. 1858," is quilted in the white background of this quilt. The Ohio quilt dealer from whom it was purchased had no information on the quilt's history other than the Kentucky Quilt Project had documented a nearly identical quilt made by a member of the Hart family of Clark County, Kentucky. With this lead, IQM genealogists identified Sarah Margaret Hart as the maker. Documentation efforts by individuals, state documentation projects, and collecting institutions have enabled connections between quilts now dispersed from their origins to be re-established.

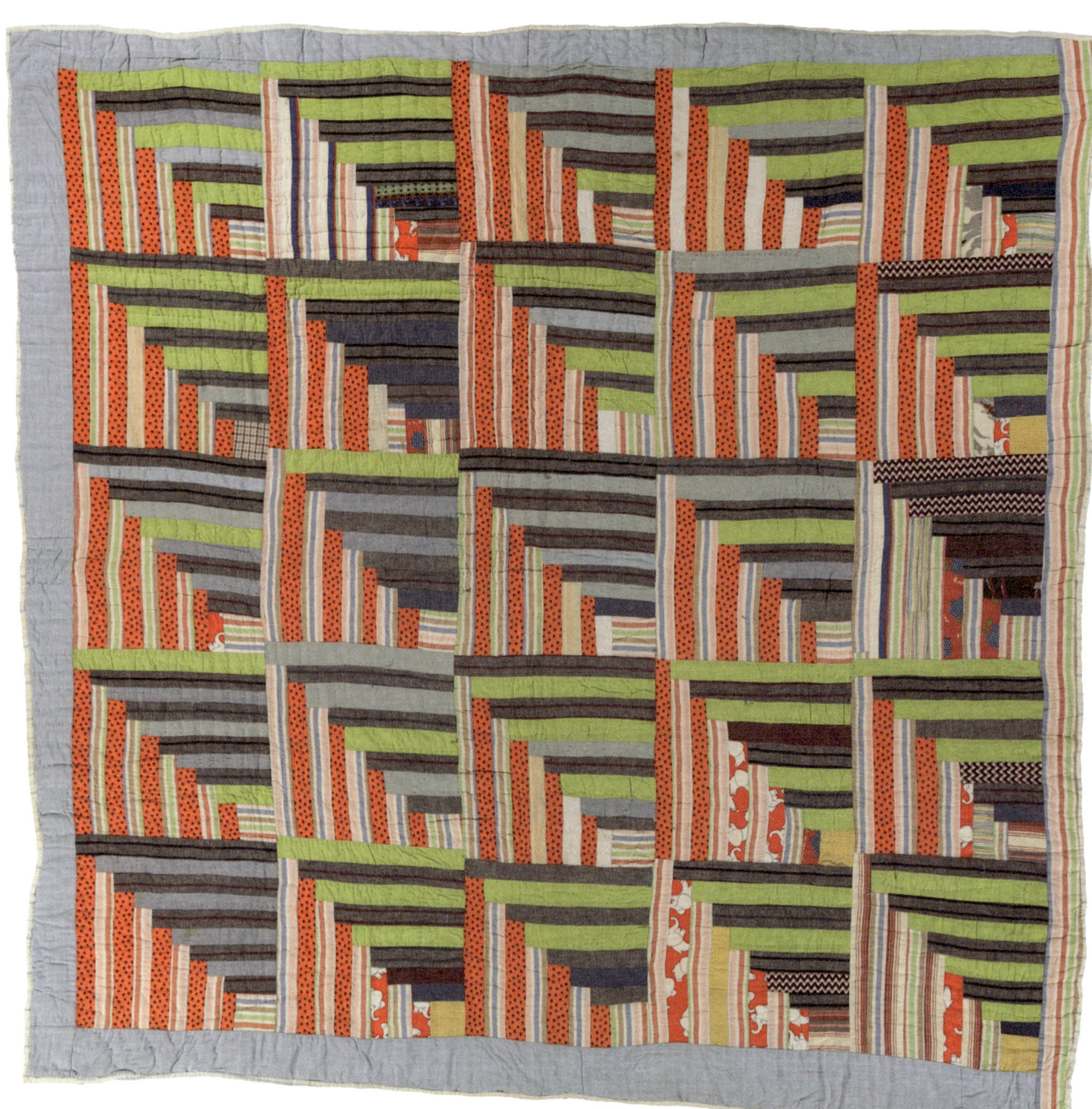

76. **Log Cabin variation**
RSVP Club
Greene County, Alabama, circa 1987
Cotton blend; hand pieced and quilted; 76.5 x 76 in.
Robert and Helen Cargo Collection, IQM 2000.004.0112

Members of the Greene County, Alabama, Retired Senior Volunteer Corps (RSVP) chapter sold this quilt to Alabama folk art dealer Robert Cargo. Collectors' interest in folk art allowed these RSVP members to leverage an art form with a long history in their predominantly Black community to benefit their neighbors. Similarly, the Freedom Quilting Bee, a cooperative founded in 1966 in nearby Wilcox County, sold quilts by mail order to benefit impoverished Black residents who were being evicted and harassed because they participated in the Civil Rights Movement and registered to vote under the Voting Rights Act of 1965.

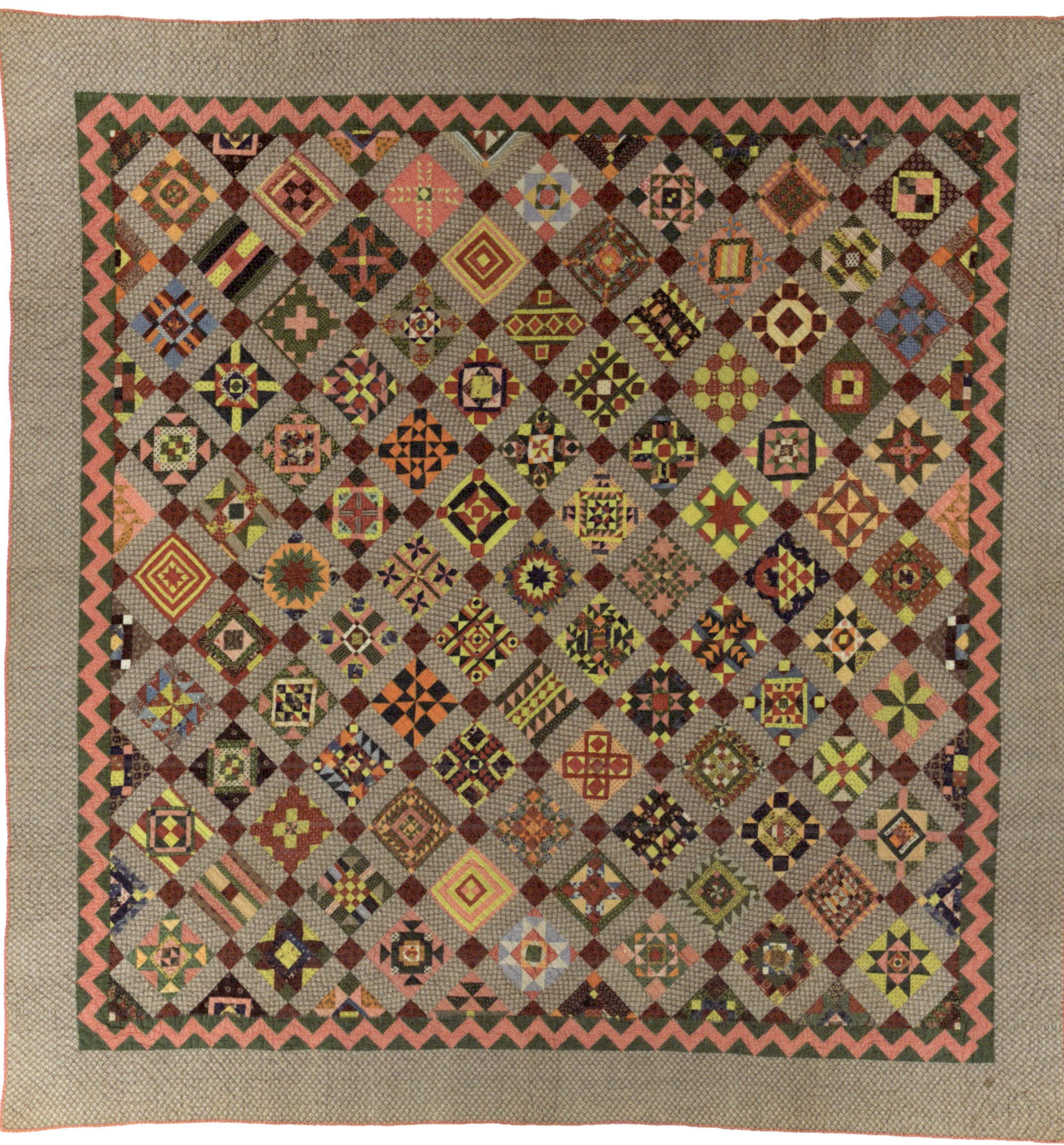

77. **Album**
Salinda W. Rupp
Lancaster County, Pennsylvania, 1870 1890
Cotton; hand pieced and quilted; 88 x 88 in.
Robert and Ardis James Collection, IQM 2006.043.0226

Had it not been for the inscription on this quilt, "Salinda W. Rupp," its history might have been lost forever. As the antique quilt market developed during the 1970s and '80s, it was not typical for pickers to gather an object's history prior to offering it for sale to retail dealers. As a result, when Kate and Joel Kopp, the leading New York City retail quilt dealers, sold it to collectors Ardis and Robert James they had no provenance to share. Recent genealogical research has established this quilt's relationship to another in the IQM collection (1997.007.0862) and another made by Rupp in a private collection.

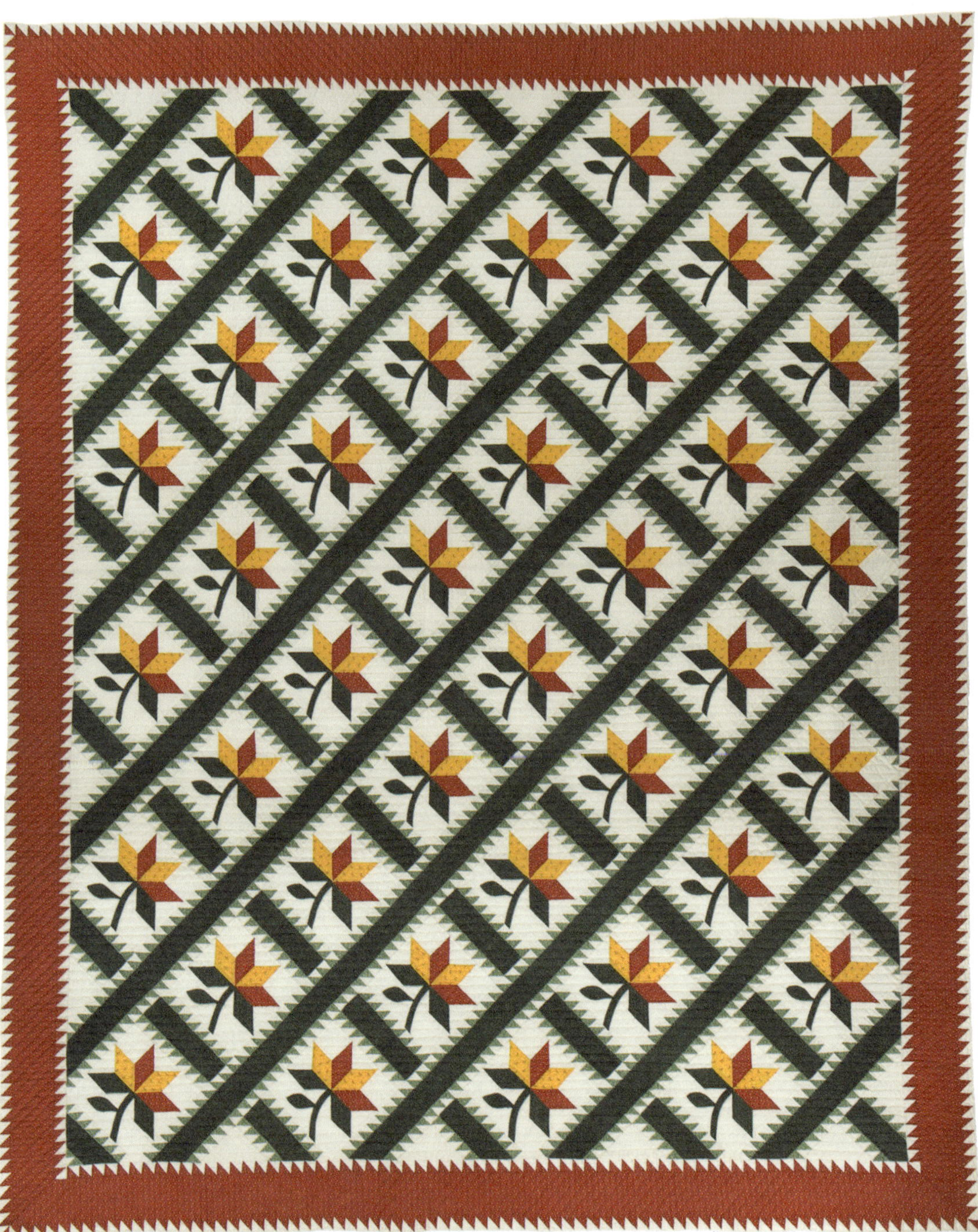

78. **Peony Variation**
Mary Campbell Ghormley
Lincoln, Nebraska, dated 1992
Cotton; hand pieced, appliquéd, quilted; 97.5 x 81 in.
Mary and Roger Ghormley Collection, IQM 2007.031.0002

Mary Ghormley (1919–2015) entered *Peony Variation* in the 1992 Nebraska State Fair, earning a first prize. In the early 1970s, Ghormley taught women to quilt and co-founded the Lincoln Quilters Guild (LQG) in 1973. After seeing the Holstein and van der Hoof Collection at the University of Iowa's art museum, she initiated a guild-sponsored project for an exhibition of Nebraska quilts at the University of Nebraska's Sheldon Art Gallery in 1974. Ghormley was instrumental in the LQG organizing a national quilt symposium in 1977 and the Nebraska Quilt Documentation Project a decade later.

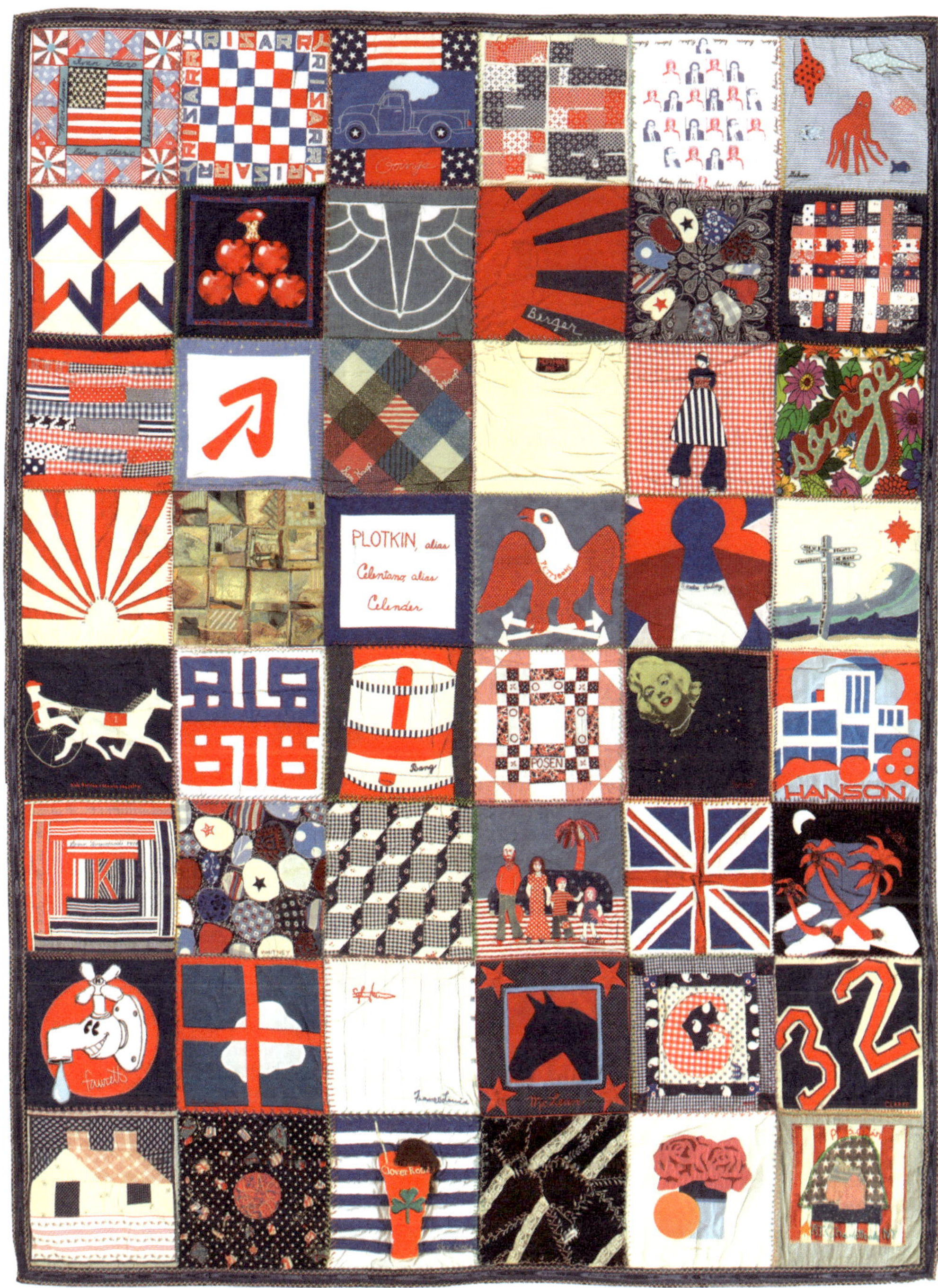


79. **Album, The Great Quilt**
Marilynn Gelfman Karp and friends
New York, New York, dated 1974
Cotton; hand appliquéd, tied; 75.5 x 72.25 in.
Gift of Marilynn and Ivan Karp, IQM 2008.005.0001

In 1973, Marilynn Gelfman Karp, an artist and designer, planned a personal way to commemorate the United States 1976 Bicentennial. Drawing from quilts' higher profile in the art world and their historical place in women's lives, she organized a "contemporary art friendship quilt." Karp invited her and her husband Ivan Karp's friends in the New York art scene to make fabric blocks that included their names and something symbolic of themselves. Many contributors were friends known through Ivan Karp's OK Harris Gallery, Works of Art, in SoHo. Among them are Richard Artschwager, Ralph Goings, James Wines, and Alison Sky.

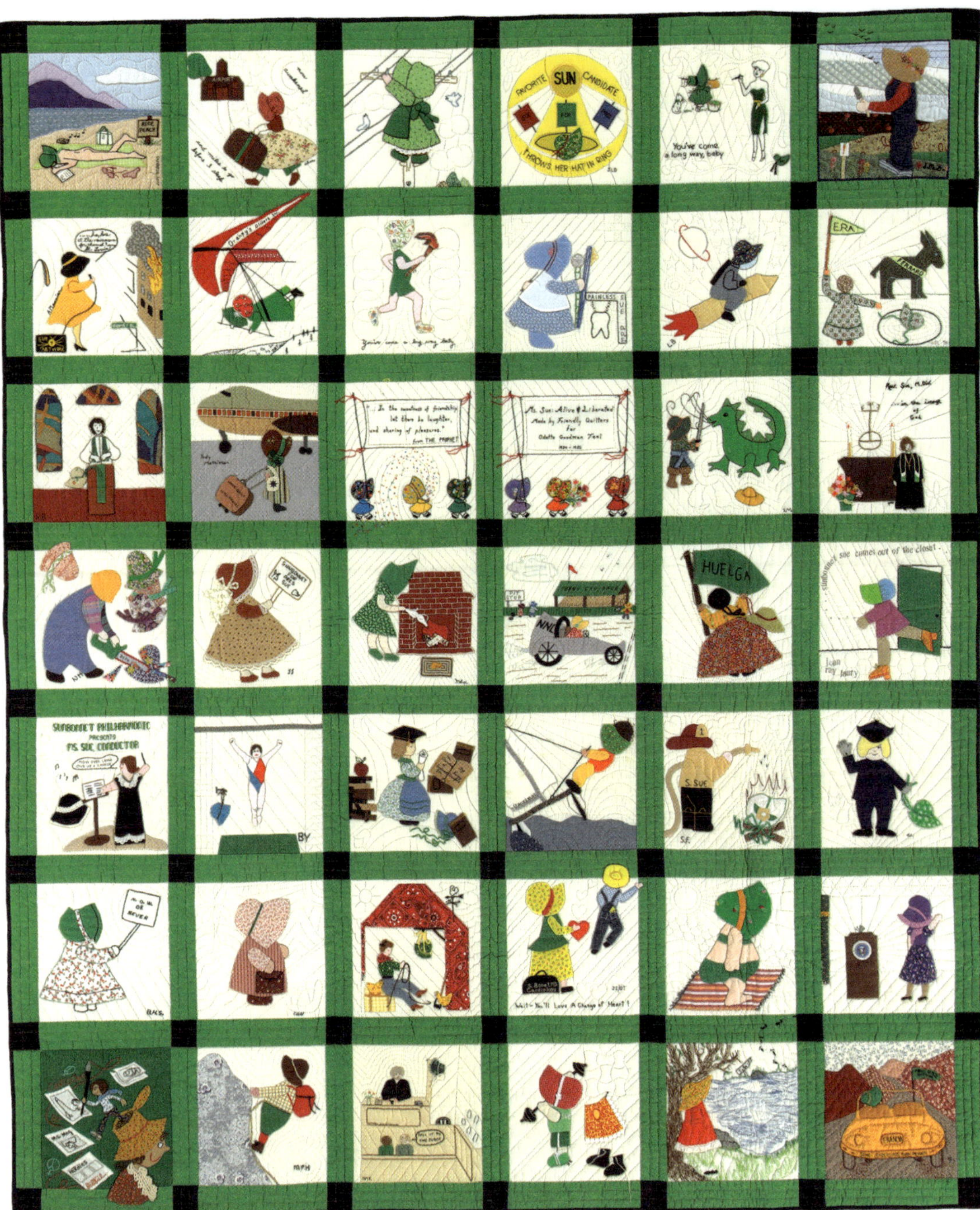


80. **Ms. Sue: Alive & Liberated**
Odette Goodman Teel and the Friendly Quilters
California, dated 1984–1986
Cotton; hand appliquéd and quilted; 83 x 70 in.
Gift of Odette Goodman Teel, IQM 2008.010.0001

Coinciding with the growth of the Women's Movement in the United States, the proposed Equal Rights Amendment (ERA) to the US Constitution was sent by Congress in 1972 to the states for ratification. Opposition from conservative women's and labor groups undermined support and not enough states ratified it. What the ERA did not accomplish constitutionally, Odette Teel and friends asserted through the oft-quilted Sunbonnet Sue pattern. More than 40 women from Walnut Creek, California, to Leicester, England, depicted many poses of Sue as a woman free of the restrictions society had placed on women for centuries.

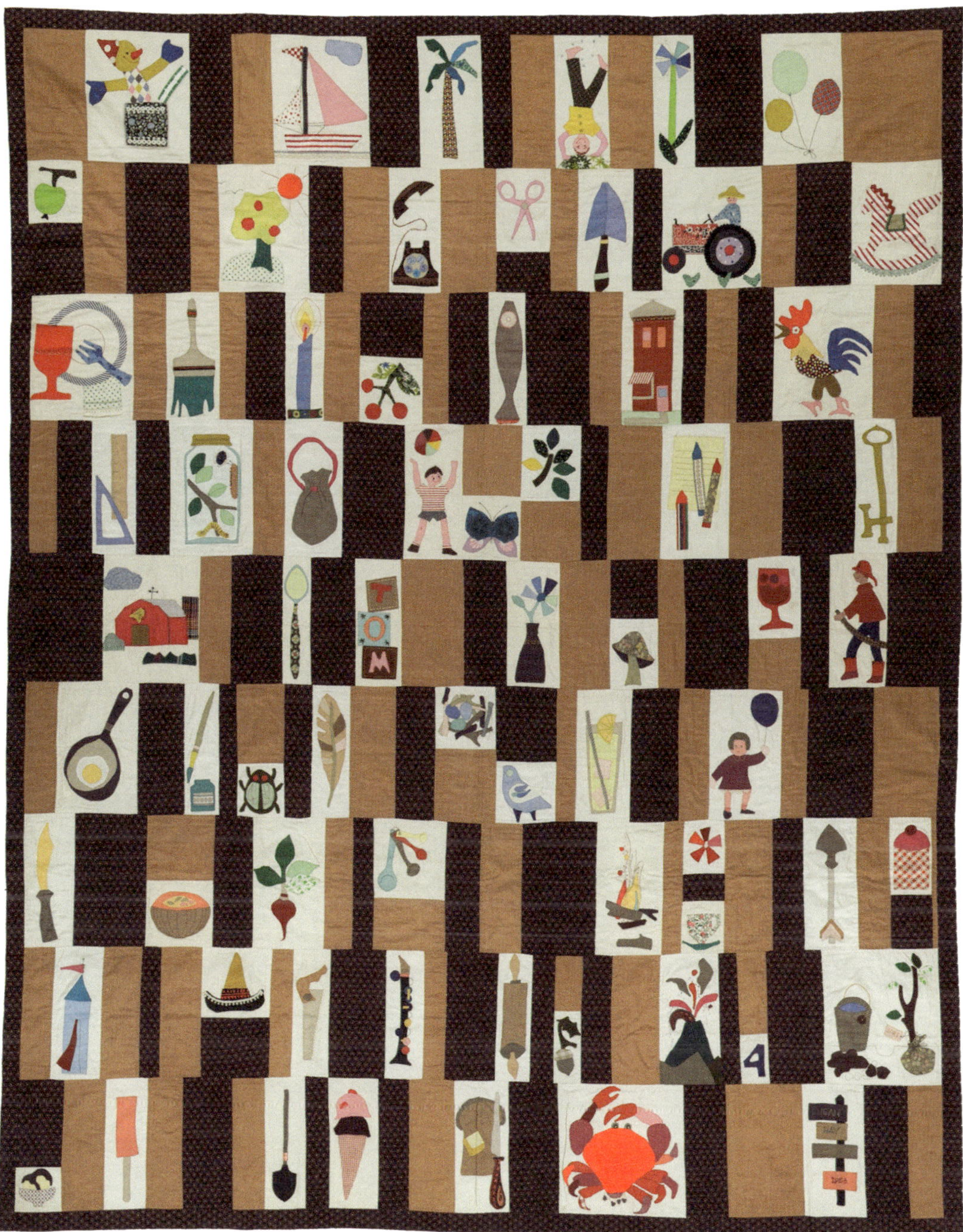

81. **Child's Quilt**
Jean Ray Laury
Redwood City, California, dated 1958
Cotton; hand appliquéd and quilted; 84 x 69.5 in.
Gift of Jean Ray Laury, IQM 2010.014.0025

*Child's Quilt* is notably similar to the first quilt Jean Ray Laury (1928–2011) made in 1956 for her Master of Arts degree in design at Stanford University. In both, she used a women's art form and common materials to make everyday objects the subjects of art. In this way, she brought art and life together and encouraged quiltmakers to see themselves as artists. Her designing, writing, speaking, and teaching, which forged a way for quilts to reflect women's contemporary experiences, paralleled the social progress in women's roles in the 1960s and '70s, including those who were wives, mothers, and homemakers, as Laury was.

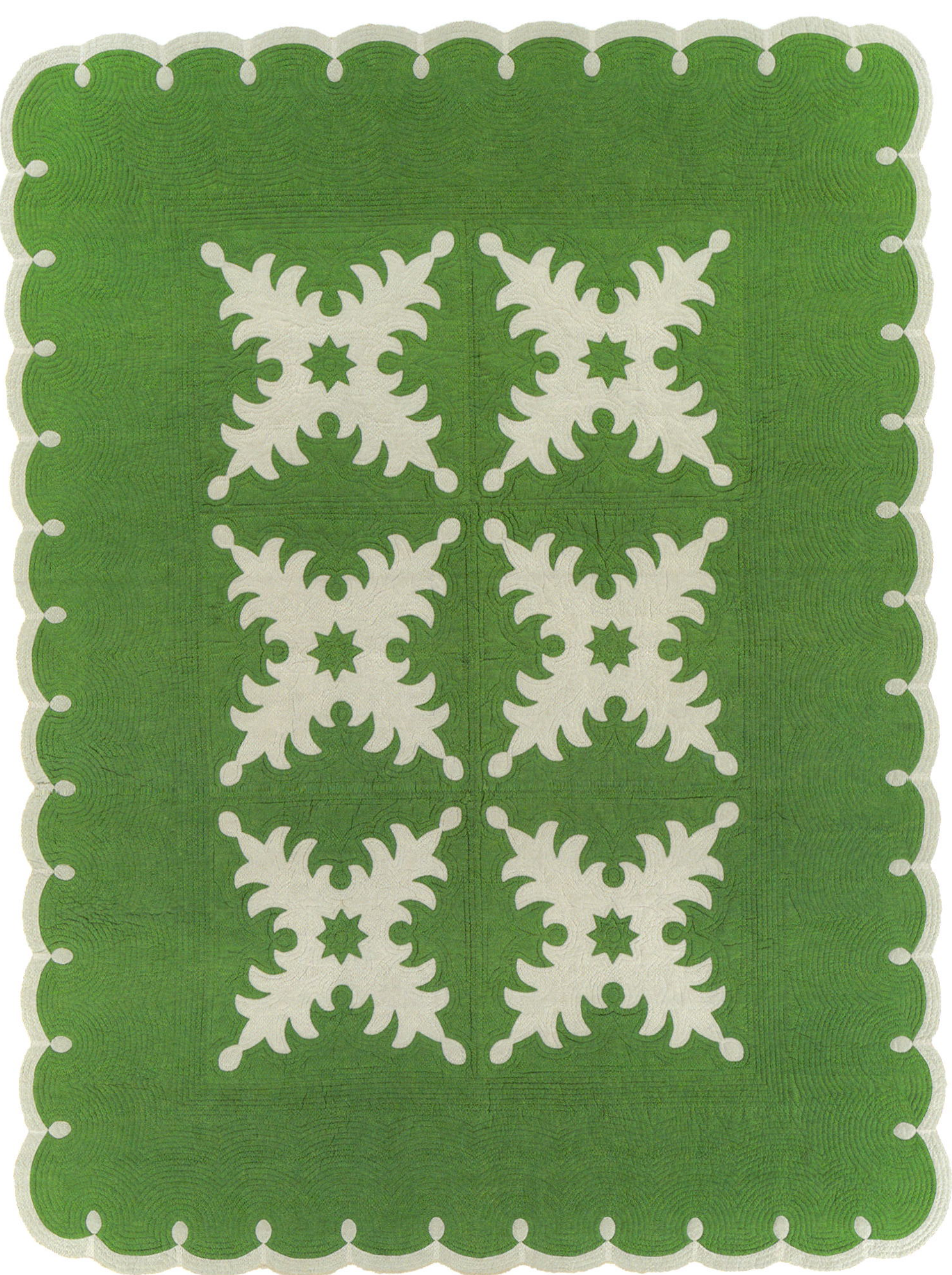

82. **Friendship Plume**
Marie Hart Mattison
Minneapolis, Minnesota, dated 1976
Cotton blend; hand appliquéd and quilted; 106.75 x 84.5 in.
Gift of Marie Hart Mattison, IQM 2013.015.0001.01

In 1973, when Marie Mattison was in her mid-30s, her mother suggested they make a quilt together. They had often cooperated on sewing home-decor projects, so this, according to Mattison, "... was just the next project to work on." After this, Mattison saw *Friendship Plume*, a Mountain Mist design, in a magazine and ordered the pattern. The quilt became the centerpiece of her redecorated master bedroom, complete with coordinating curtains, green plaid wallpaper, and green shag carpeting. Mattison and her mother reflect the do-it-yourself decorating trend that paralleled shelter magazines whose editors featured quilts in professional interior designs.

83. **Cup of Gold**
Marion Ekstrom Wright
Naval Air Station, Barbers Point, Hawaii, dated 1972
Cotton; hand appliquéd and quilted; 95.5 x 85.5 in.
Gift of quiltmaker Marion Ekstrom Wright, IQM 2015.055.0001

*Cup of Gold* is one of nearly 5,000 quilts documented by the Nebraska Quilt Project between 1987 and 1989, but its origins are far from the Cornhusker state. Marion Wright made the quilt near Ewa Beach, Oahu, Hawaii, where her husband was stationed as an officer at Barber's Point Naval Air Station. As did many women at this time without quilting experience, she found a teacher. Mealii Kalama, a native of the island, taught Wright to make a traditional Hawaiian-style appliqué quilt with echo quilting. Wright made two quilts in this style.

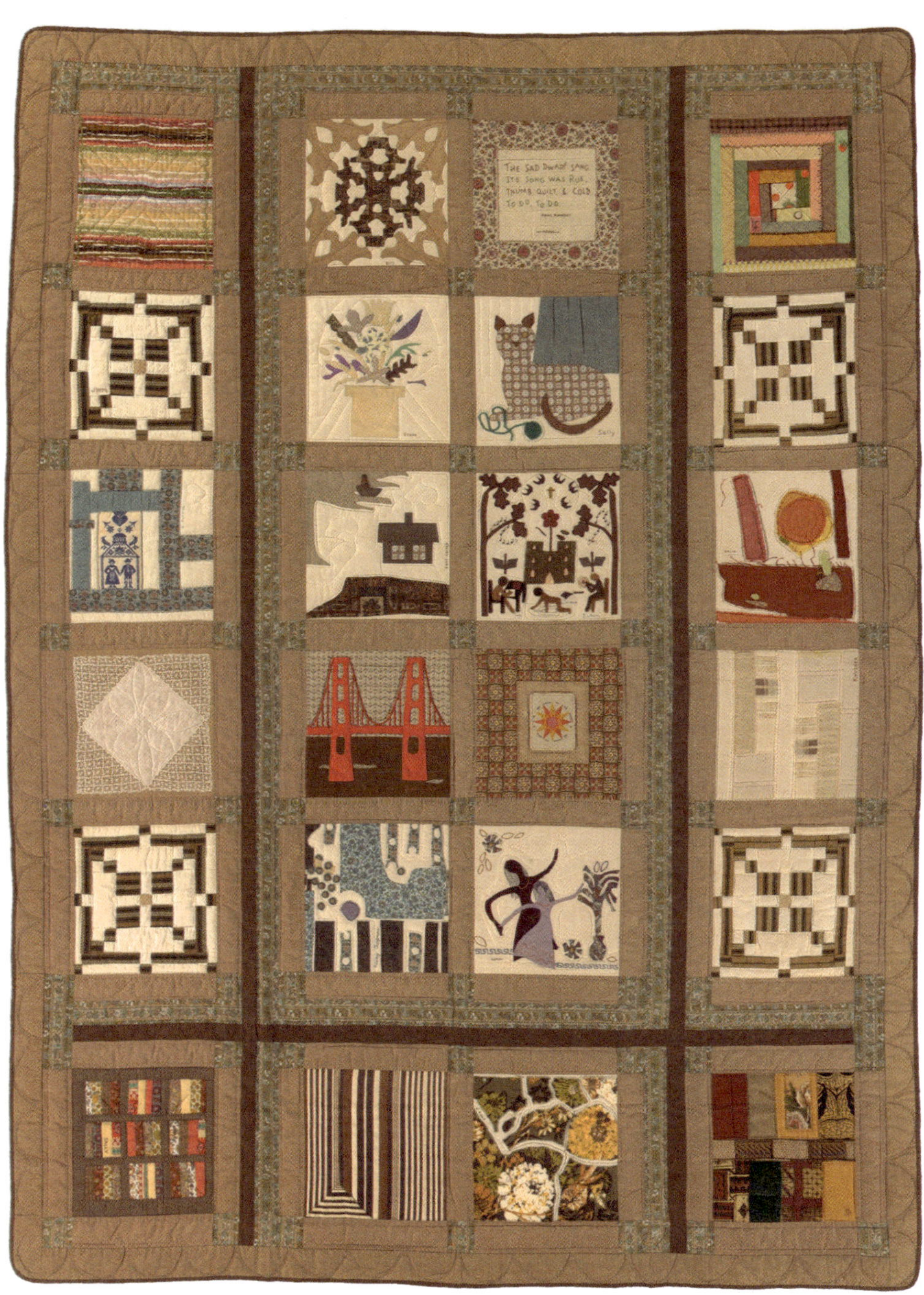

84. **Friendship Block**
Betty June "Bets" Ramsey and friends
Chattanooga, Tennessee, dated 1973
Cotton; hand pieced, appliquéd, and quilted; 100.25 x 75.25 in.
Gift of Bets Ramsey, IQM 2018.004.0001

About 1970, while reading extensively on quilt history for her master's degree in craft, Bets Ramsey asked family, friends, and fellow artists in Chattanooga to contribute blocks for a Friendship quilt. While she taught fiber arts at the Hunter Museum, the organization hosted Jonathan Holstein and Gail van der Hoof's *The Pieced Quilt* in 1974. Holstein declined to speak during the exhibition and Ramsey spoke in his place. She also organized the Southern Quilt Symposium for the museum, the first public seminar devoted to quilts, which became an annual event through 1991. Years later, Ramsey told Holstein that his decision not to speak launched her lifelong career in quilts.

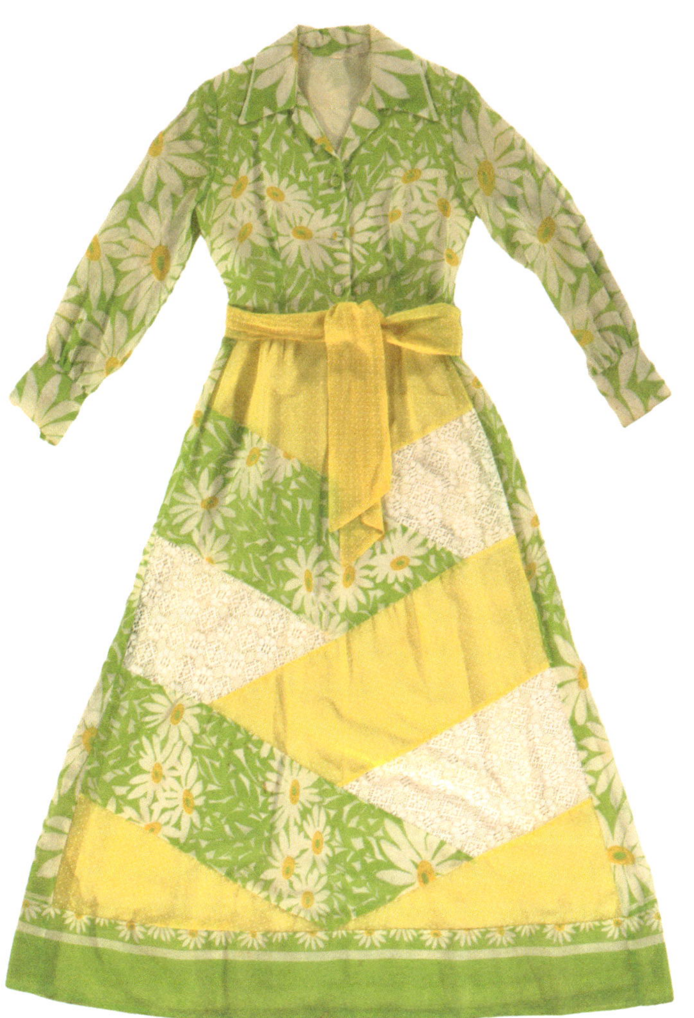

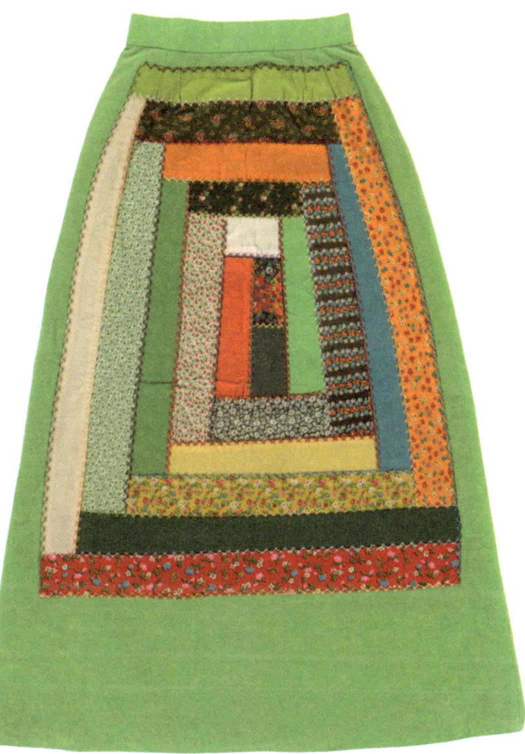





85. **Patchwork Dress**
Designer unidentified
Circa 1970–1975
Polyester or cotton-polyester; lined; 59 x 40 in.
Gift of Mary Louise Babst estate, Historic Textile and Costume Collection, University of Nebraska-Lincoln, Acc. 1999.009.015

**Skirt**
Made by "Mole"
Cotton-polyester; hand appliquéd and embroidered, lined; 40 x 31 in
Lake Havasu, Arizona, circa 1965–80
Private collection

Quilts gained the attention of the fashion design industry in the 1960s and 1970s. Elements of quilt design, such as the chevron patchwork construction of this dress, appeared in couture and ready-to-wear lines. Similarly, this skirt's designer included a pieced quilt block, tapered to match the garment's shape and appliquéd to the skirt with embroidery stitches typical of late-1800s crazy quilts.

Periodically, since the 1970s, fashion houses have "discovered" quilts as a fresh design element. Ralph Lauren, for example, was (in)famous for cutting apart antique quilts and quilt tops and transforming them into clothing and fashion accessories.

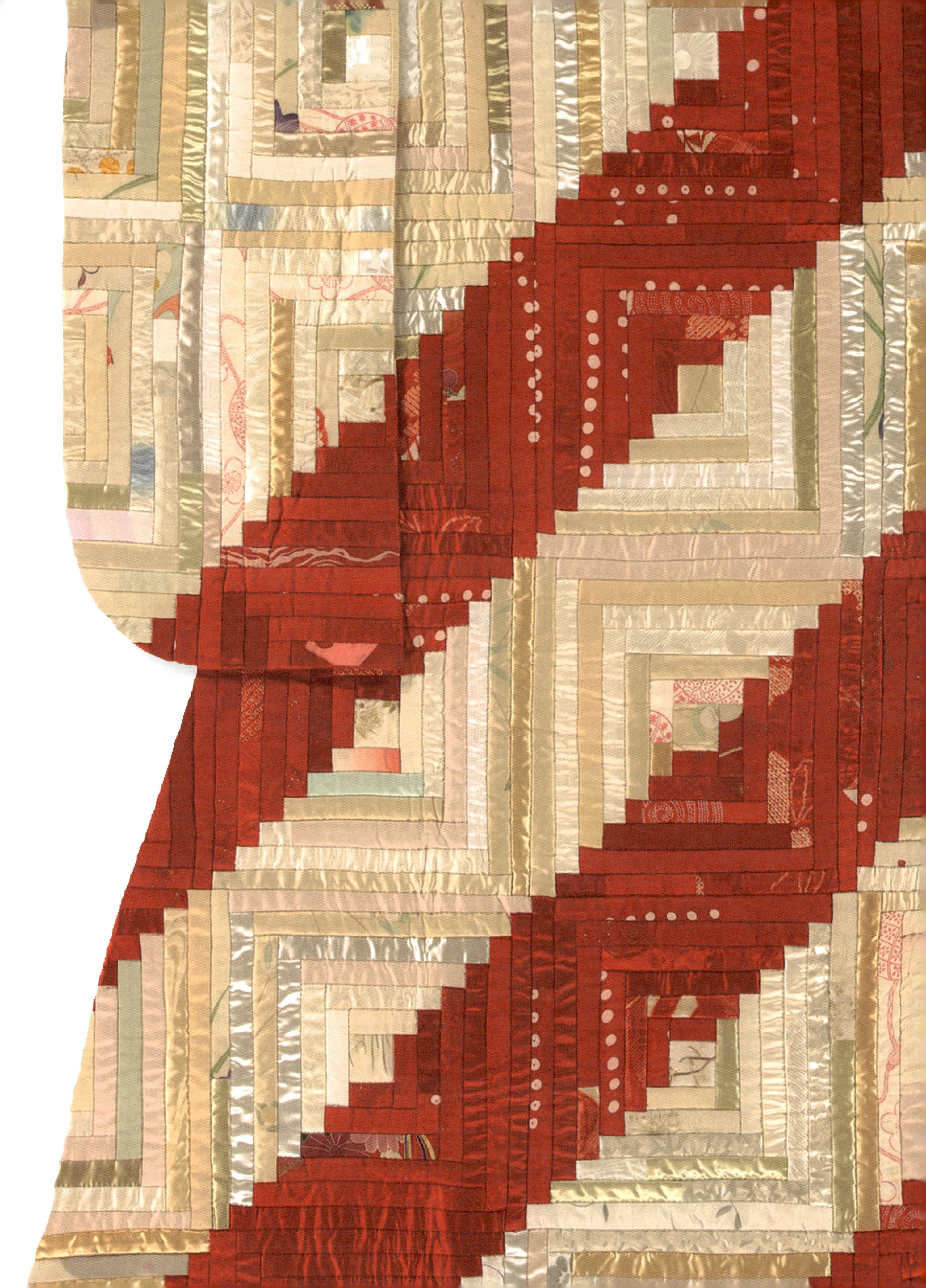

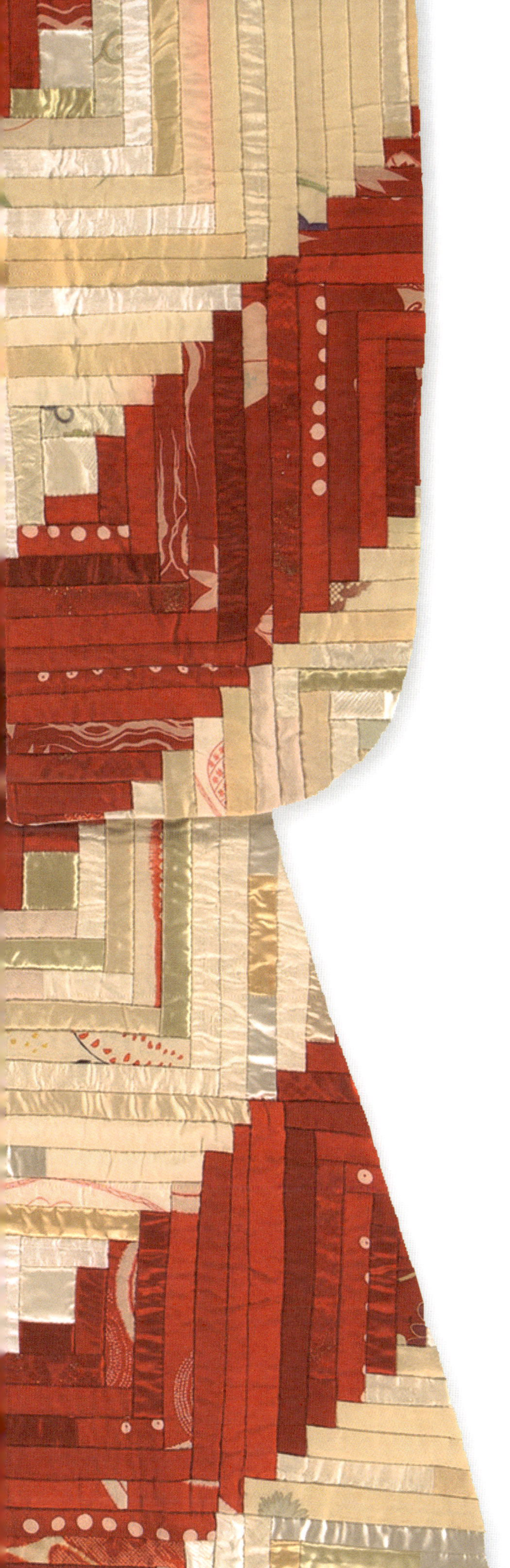

# JOURNEY TO JAPAN

The International Quilt Museum (IQM) commissioned the *Journey to Japan* exhibition quilts from 10 of today's top Japanese quilt artists and teachers. The IQM asked each artist to select a piece from the Whitney Museum of American Art's original *Abstract Design in American Quilts* exhibition and respond to it using her own techniques, materials, and aesthetic sensibility. Beside each quilt title is a reference to the Whitney exhibition quilt to which the artist responded.

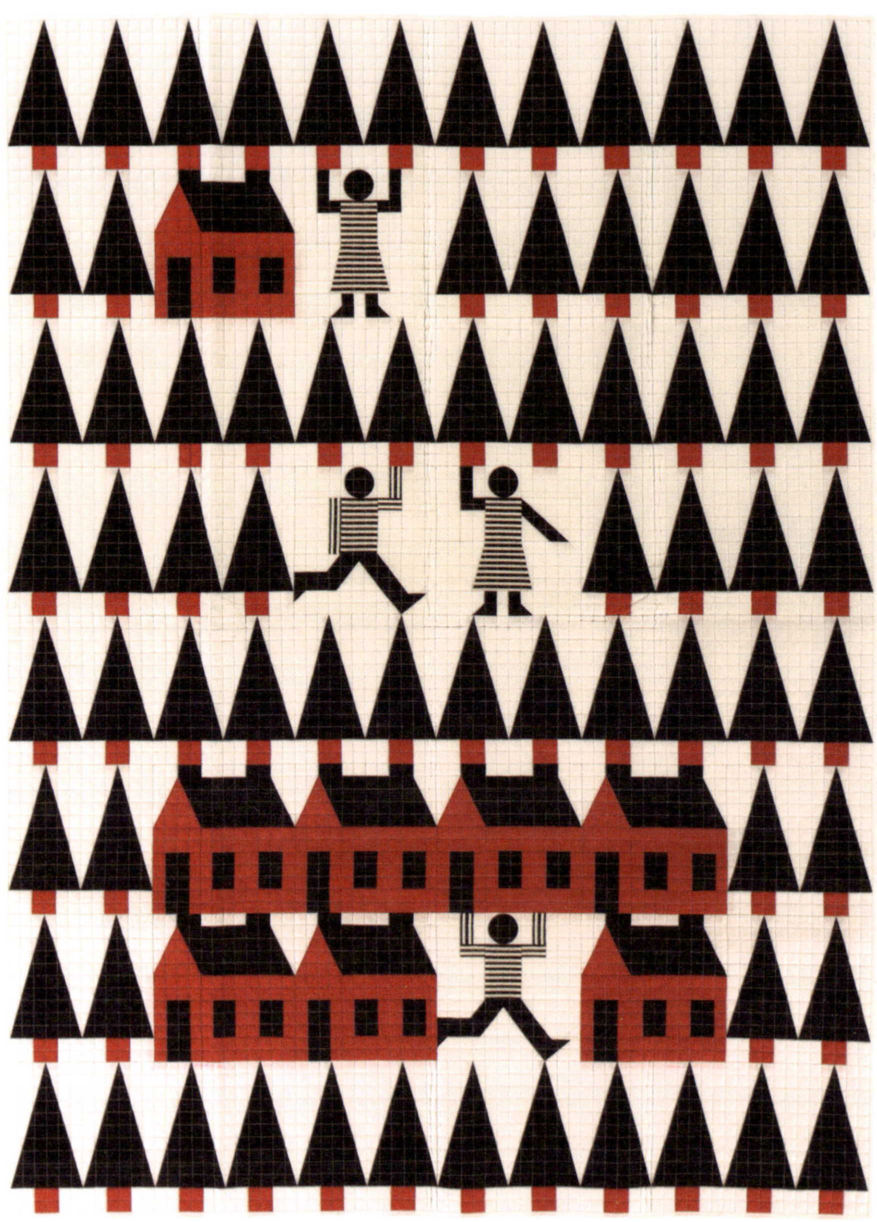

86. **Untitled**
Kumiko Fujita
Tokyo, Japan, 2020
Cotton; machine pieced and quilted, hand appliquéd;
75.5 x 56.5 in.
Gift of the Robert and Ardis James Foundation,
IQM 2020.058.0001

Kumiko Fujita's training as a graphic designer is evident in her bold, crisply executed shapes and simple color palette. Fujita usually prefers to work with abstract designs but for *Journey to Japan*, she says, "I intentionally chose the House pattern, which is representational, because I like the combination of red, black, and white, inspired by the black roof and red walls of the classic American schoolhouse." She sees the schoolhouse as a world of imagination, with children studying and playing in and around the building.

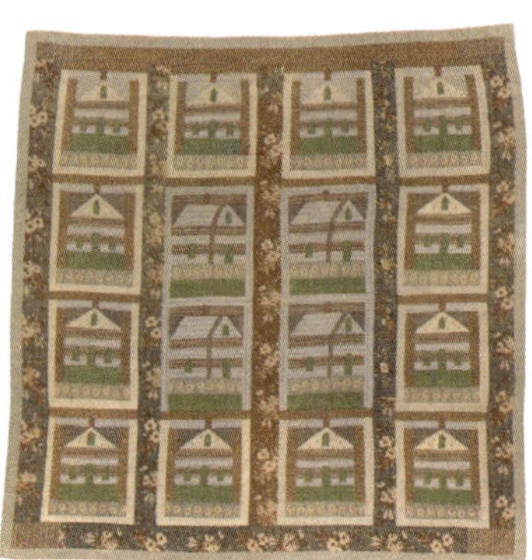

**Schoolhouse**
Plate 14

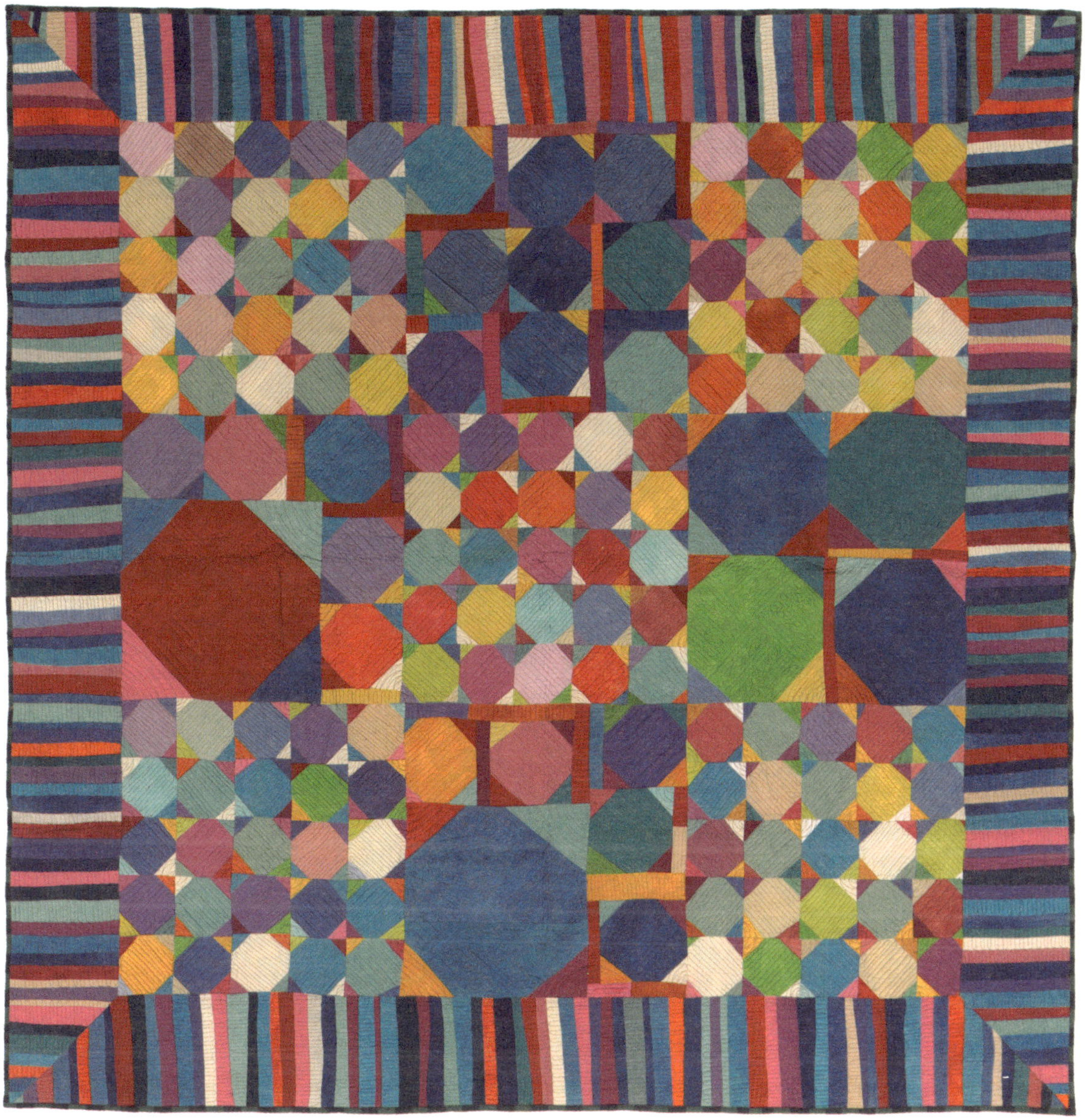

87. **My Rob Peter to Pay Paul II**
Keiko Goke
Sendai, Japan, 2020
Cotton; machine pieced and quilted; 74.5 x 74 in.
Gift of the Robert and Ardis James Foundation,
IQM 2020.052.0002

Keiko Goke's meditation on the original Rob Peter to Pay Paul quilt creates an updated, richly colored and spontaneous version of the traditional pattern. When Goke first began quiltmaking 50 years ago, she focused on what she calls "picture quilts" made with figurative appliqué because, she says, "I didn't want my quilts to look similar to other quiltmakers' work." Later, she embraced traditional pieced patterns, but only by approaching them extemporaneously, without templates and by cutting and placing hand-dyed fabrics directly as she worked.

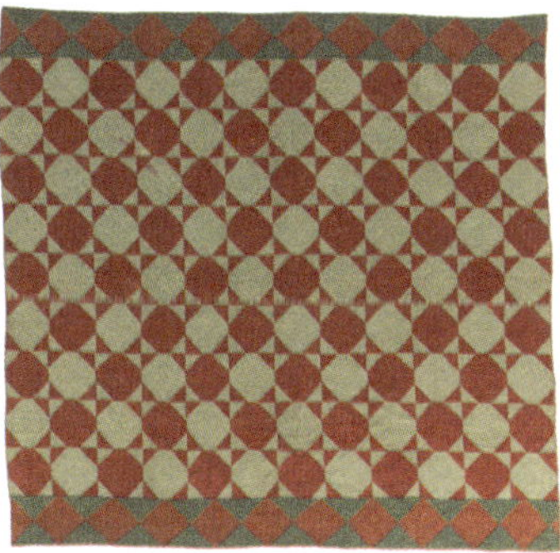

**Rob Peter to Pay Paul**
Plate 17

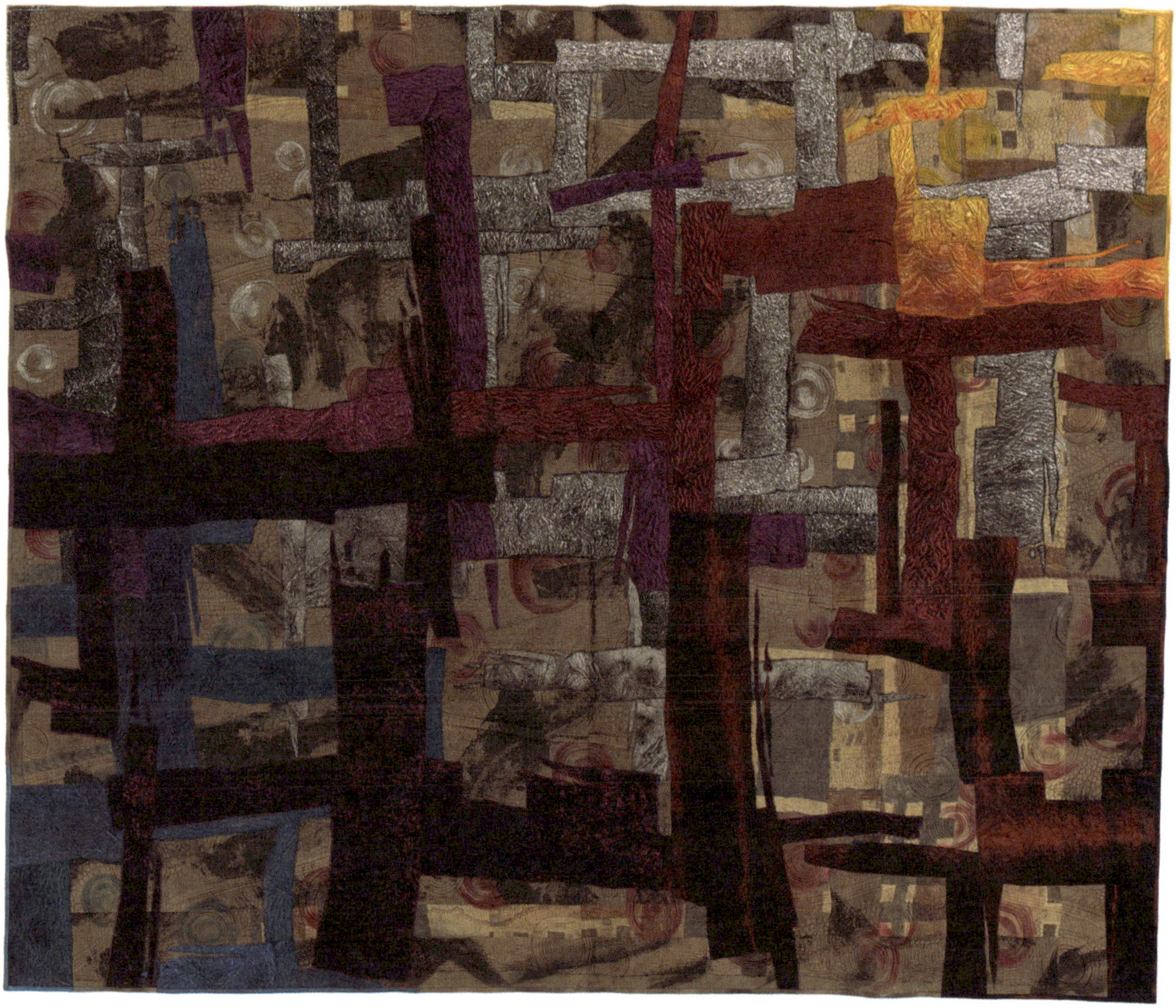

88. **Untitled**
Shoko Hatano
Tokyo, Japan, 2020
Cotton, silk, cotton/polyester; machine appliquéd, pieced, and quilted; 65 x 78.75 in.
Gift of the Robert and Ardis James Foundation, IQM 2020.057.0001

Without simply imitating her chosen inspiration piece, Shoko Hatano captures the spirit of the crazy quilt and adds her distinctly personal stamp to the composition. Just like the block-style original, Hatano's piece is haphazard yet structured, both following and breaking free from a grid. She adds further complexity through the use of overprinted fabrics and abundant, textural quilting. Hatano's abstract imagery often includes a gestural quality reminiscent of calligraphic brushstrokes.

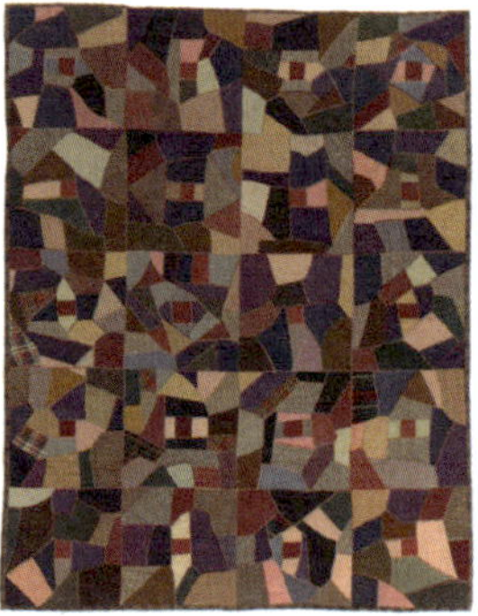

**Crazy quilt**
Plate 2

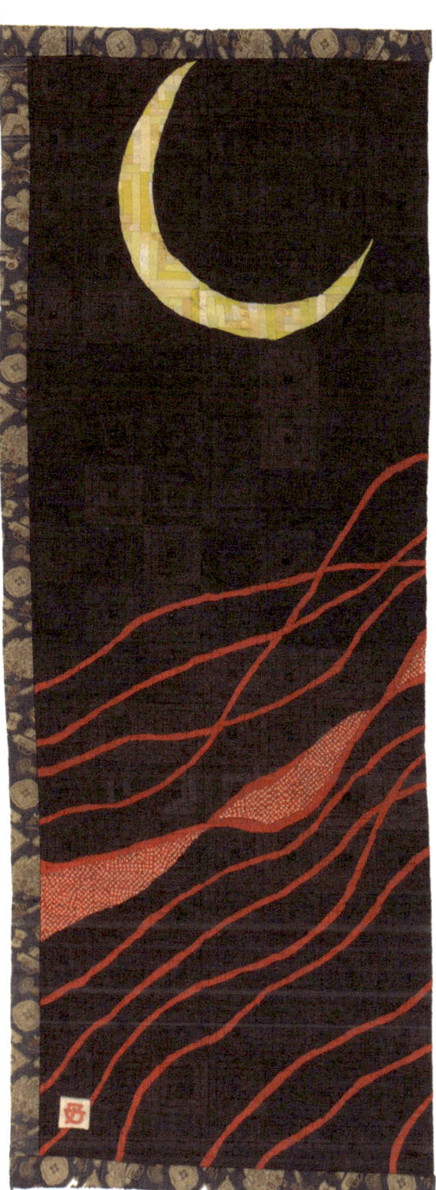
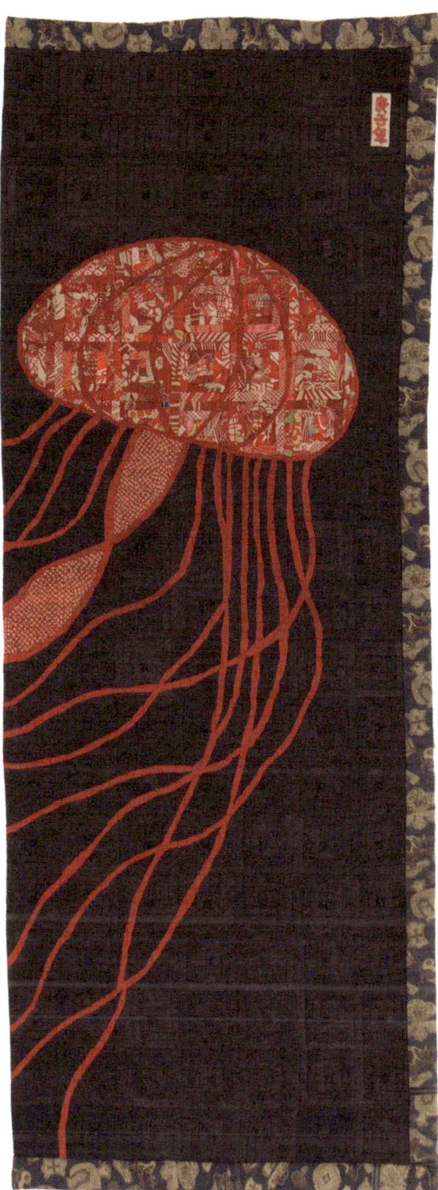

89. **Mother – La Mer**
Yoshiko Katagiri
Nara, Japan, 2020
Cotton, silk; hand pieced, appliquéd, and quilted;
78.75 x 29.5 in. (each panel)
Gift of the Robert and Ardis James Foundation,
IQM 2020.051.0001

In this diptych, Yoshiko Katagiri combines her fondness for Log Cabin blocks with her love of appliqué and intricate handwork. She said, "It was challenging to blend together the linear, geometric pattern with the curved, organic shapes of the jellyfish motif." She titled the piece *Mother – La Mer (the Sea)* in reference to the fact that the Japanese kanji for "sea" (海) contains the kanji for "mother" (母) and also to how the Holstein/van der Hoof Collection can be seen as the "mother" of Japanese quilt culture.

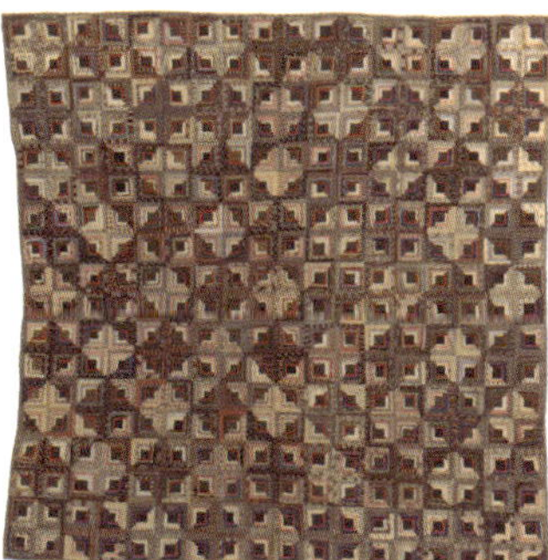

**Log Cabin, Light and Dark setting**
Plate 31

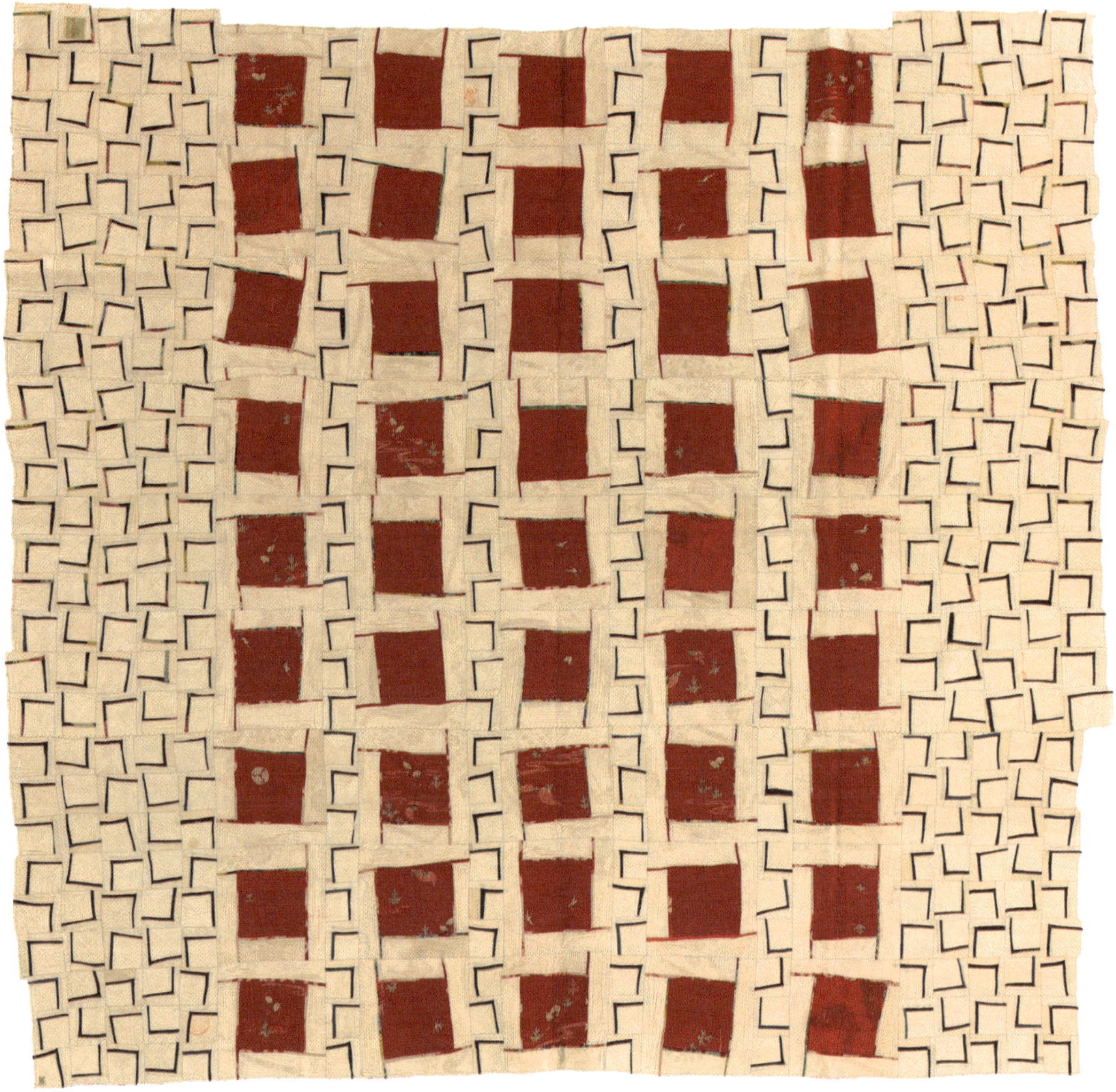

90. **Halu #5**
Harue Konishi
Tokyo, Japan, 2020
Silk; machine pieced and quilted; 72 x 68 in.
Gift of the Robert and Ardis James Foundation,
IQM 2020.059.0001

In *Halu #5*, Harue Konishi visually references the original red and white Bars quilt with columns of red squares separated and surrounded by quirky, off-kilter black and white infill patterns. The quilt's fabrics are largely recycled from pre-WWII garments: an embroidered red wedding kimono and the artist's mother-in-law's white kimono. About the quilt's metaphorical theme, she says, "I created this piece hoping an unknown world—a special dimension—would unfold by rearranging a single, repetitive pattern."

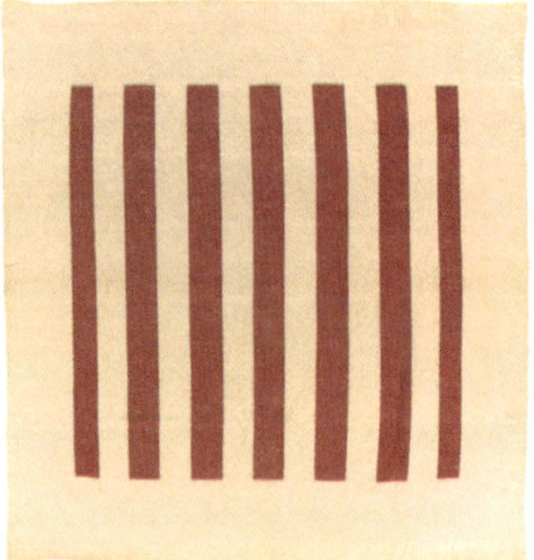

**Bars**
Plate 58

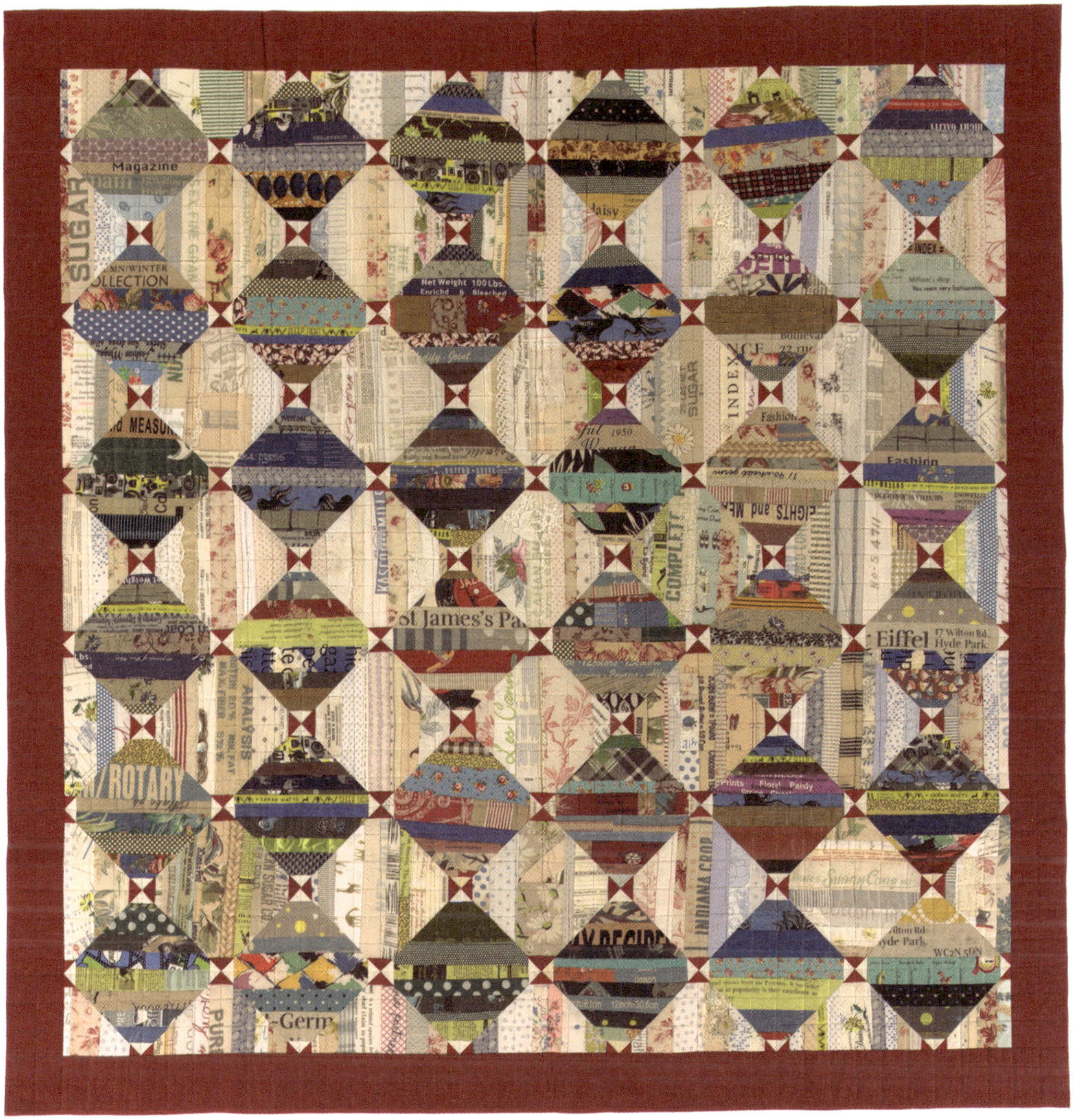

91. **Untitled**
Suzuko Koseki
Tokyo, Japan, 2020
Cotton, polyester; machine pieced and quilted; 74 x 74 in.
Gift of the Robert and Ardis James Foundation,
IQM 2020.054.0001

Suzuko Koseki is known for using fabrics with printed words. Although she primarily sees them as simply another pattern to work with, sometimes the words appear in interesting combinations. About her process, she says, "I end up with a lot of small scrap fabrics as I make quilts. I find it most pleasing to use the scraps to come up with unexpectedly beautiful and fun color matches. This time, I approached the project playfully by freely composing the quilt on paper foundation blocks and not using a template."

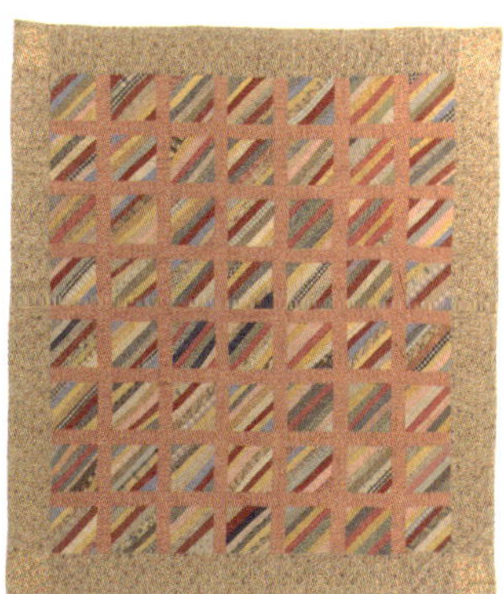

**String Squares**
Plate 1

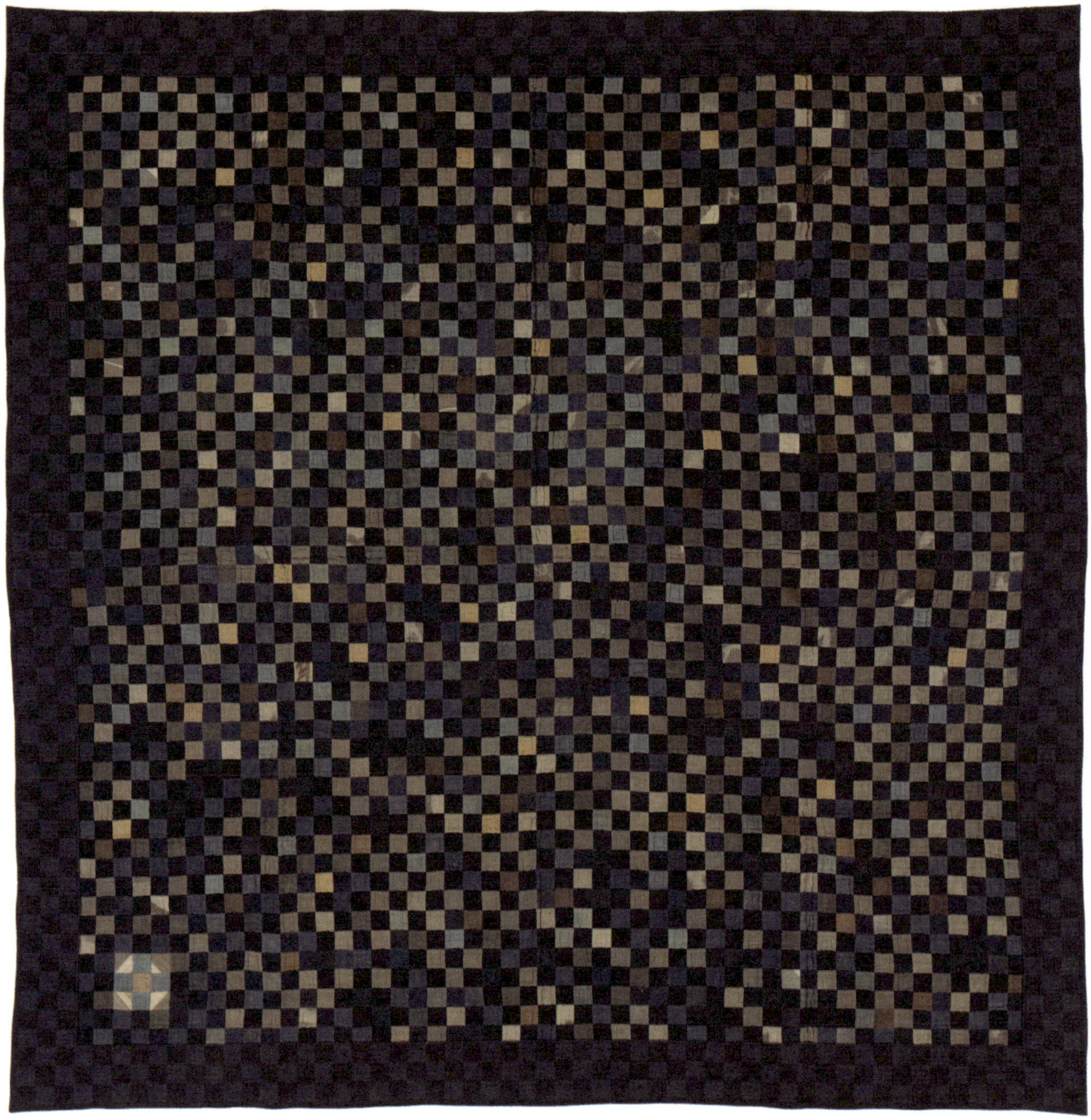

92. **Chic**
Shizuko Kuroha
Tokyo, Japan, 2020
Cotton; machine pieced, hand quilted; 75 x 75 in.
Gift of the Robert and Ardis James Foundation,
IQM 2020.060.0001

Shizuko Kuroha cleverly references the original Nine Patch quilt's varying degrees of value contrast (lights vs. darks) by emphasizing one light Shoo Fly block in the lower left. Kuroha is well known for her use of antique Japanese indigo-dyed fabrics, though in this piece they are mostly plain rather than decorated with resist-dyed designs, as is more usual for her work. Traces of sumi ink calligraphy are still visible on some of the lighter fabrics.

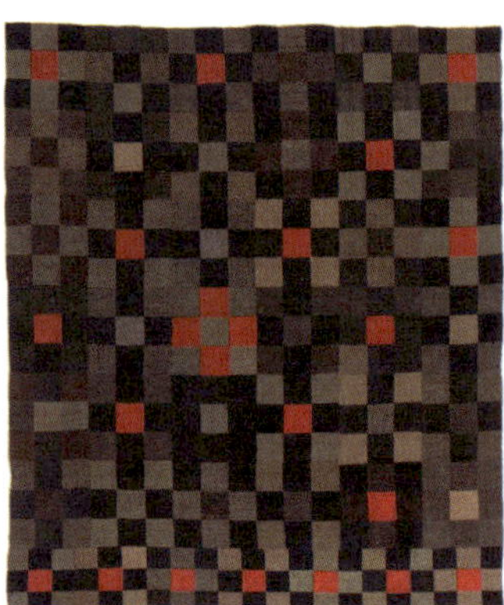

**Nine Patch**
Plate 30

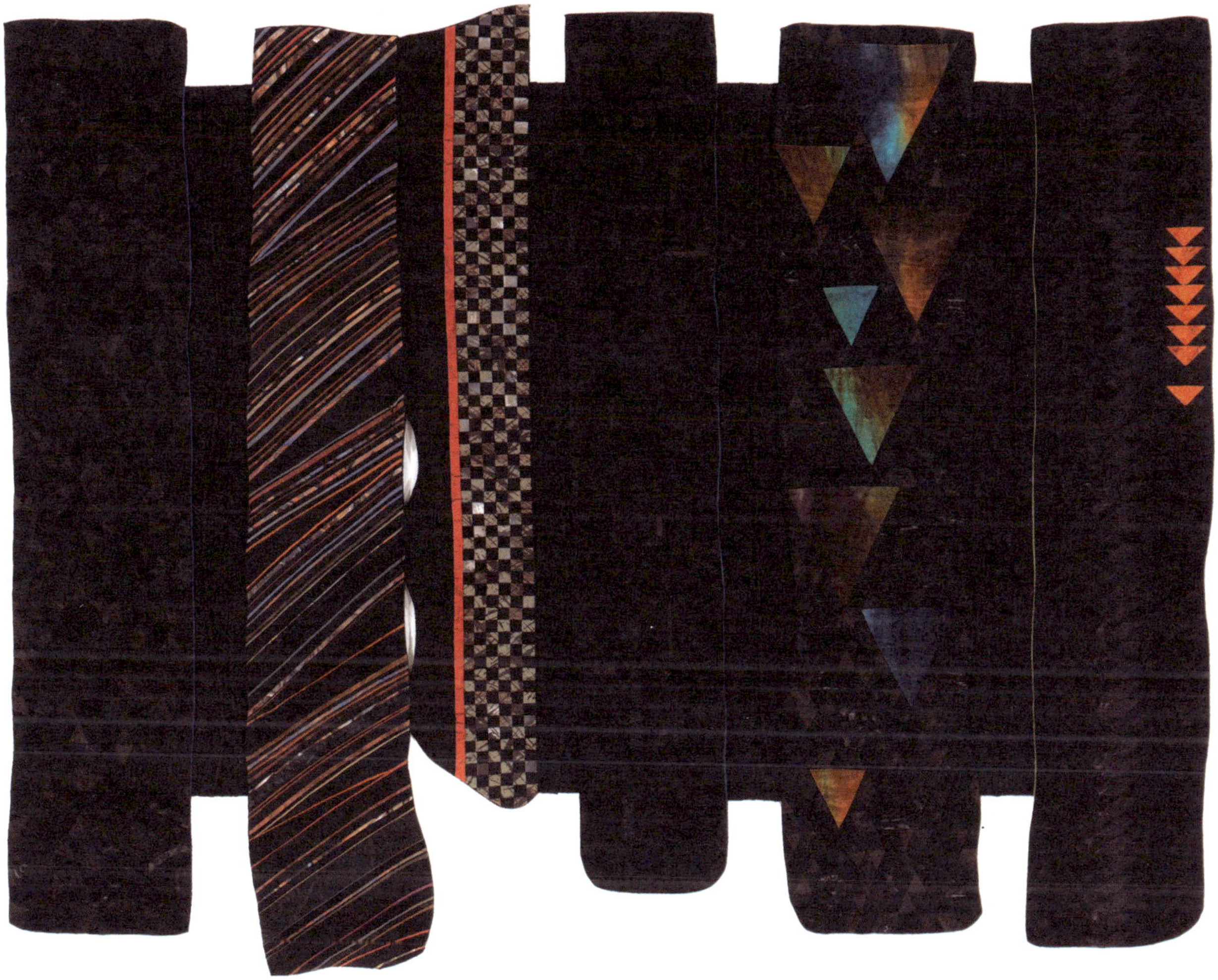

93. **Depart Again**
Emiko Toda Loeb
Kyoto, Japan, 2020
Silk, cotton; machine and hand pieced, hand quilted;
61.5 x 77.5 in.
Gift of the Robert and Ardis James Foundation,
IQM 2020.056.0001

Although Emiko Toda Loeb's inspiration quilt was *Kaleidoscope*, which you can see referenced in the far-left strip of *Depart Again*, Toda Loeb drew ideas from many of the other Holstein/van der Hoof quilts as well. Starting from the next strip to the right, these references include: Plate 1 (String Squares), Plate 30 (Nine Patch), Plates 26, 31, 42, and 57 (Log Cabins), Plate 9 (Thousand Pyramids), and Plate 34 (Wild Goose Chase).

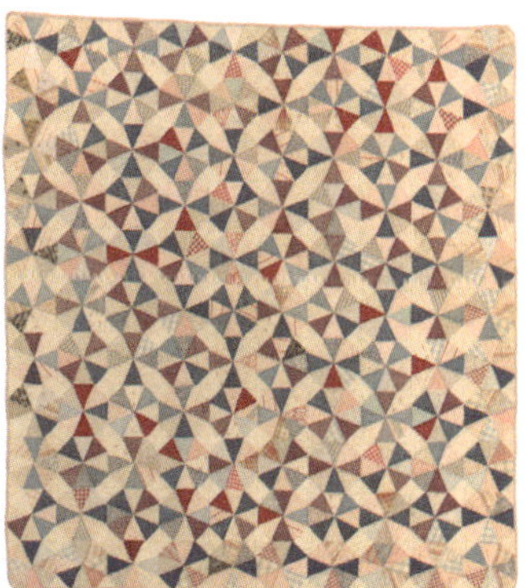

**Kaleidoscope**
Plate 38

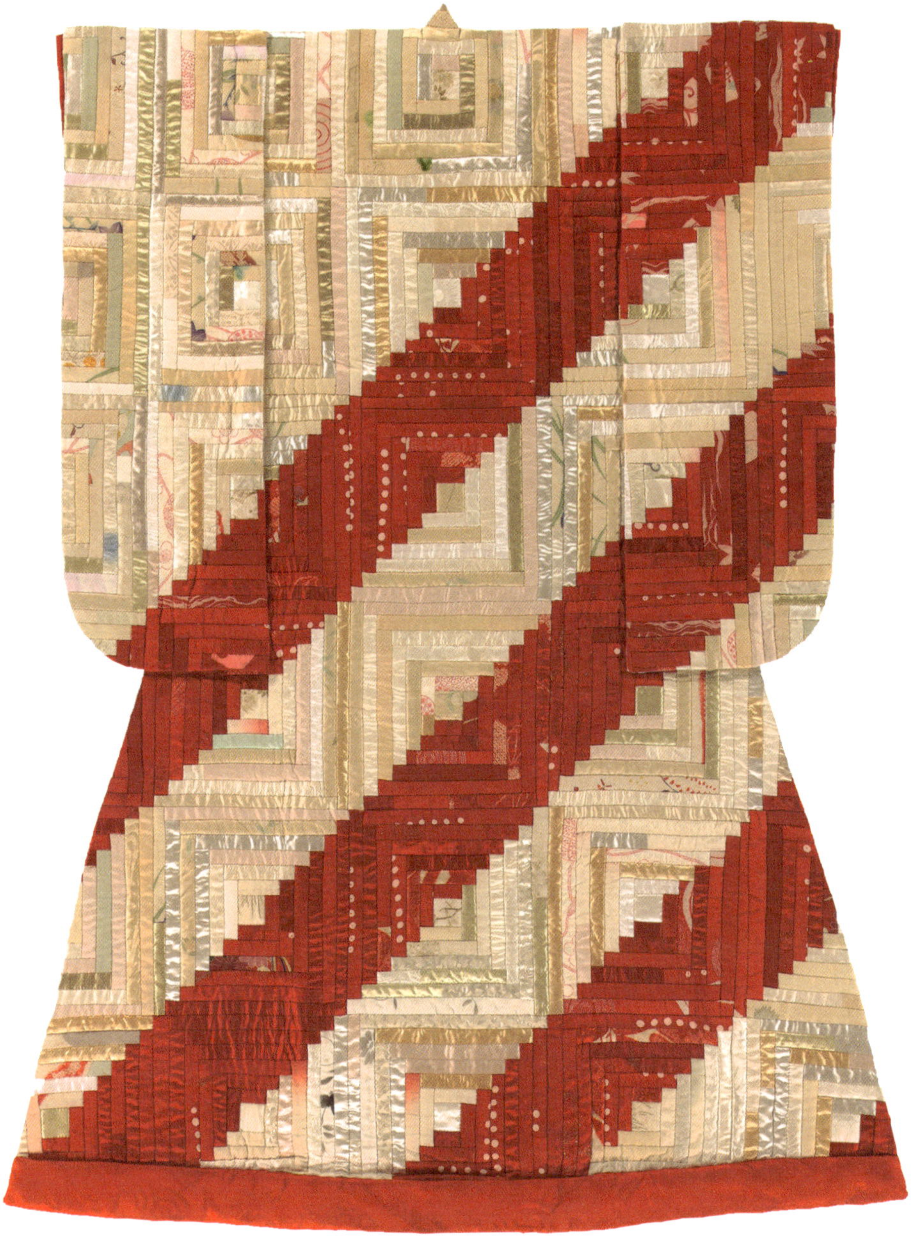

95. **It's a Beautiful Day, Vol. 16**
Eiko Okano
Tokyo, Japan, 2020
Silk, polyester; machine pieced, hand quilted; 78.75 x 59 in.
Gift of the Robert and Ardis James Foundation,
IQM 2020.053.0001

This *uchikake* (wedding kimono)-shaped quilt is the latest in Eiko Okano's *It's a Beautiful Day* series, three others of which are part of the IQM collection. Echoing the diagonal stripes in the original Log Cabin quilt, Okano leaves out the upper left shoulder stripe in order to emphasize the subtle beauty of the white fabrics. Okano felt like her quilt selection was foreordained, noting while she was constructing it: "Making my own quilt inspired by a Holstein/van der Hoof quilt that I admired like the Bible—this seems like my fate. I am working on my quilt as if it was decided a long time ago."

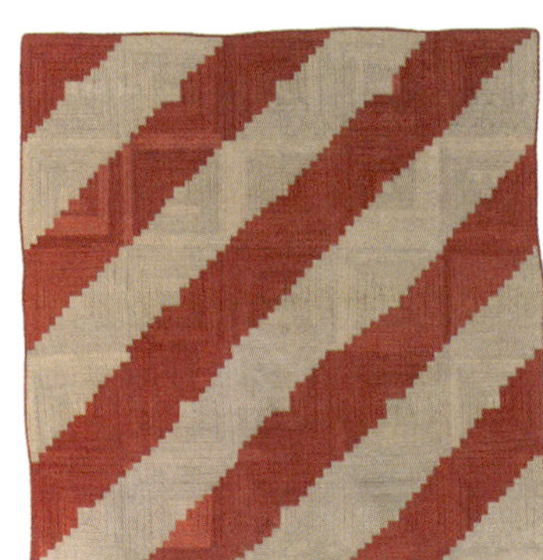

**Log Cabin**
Plate 26

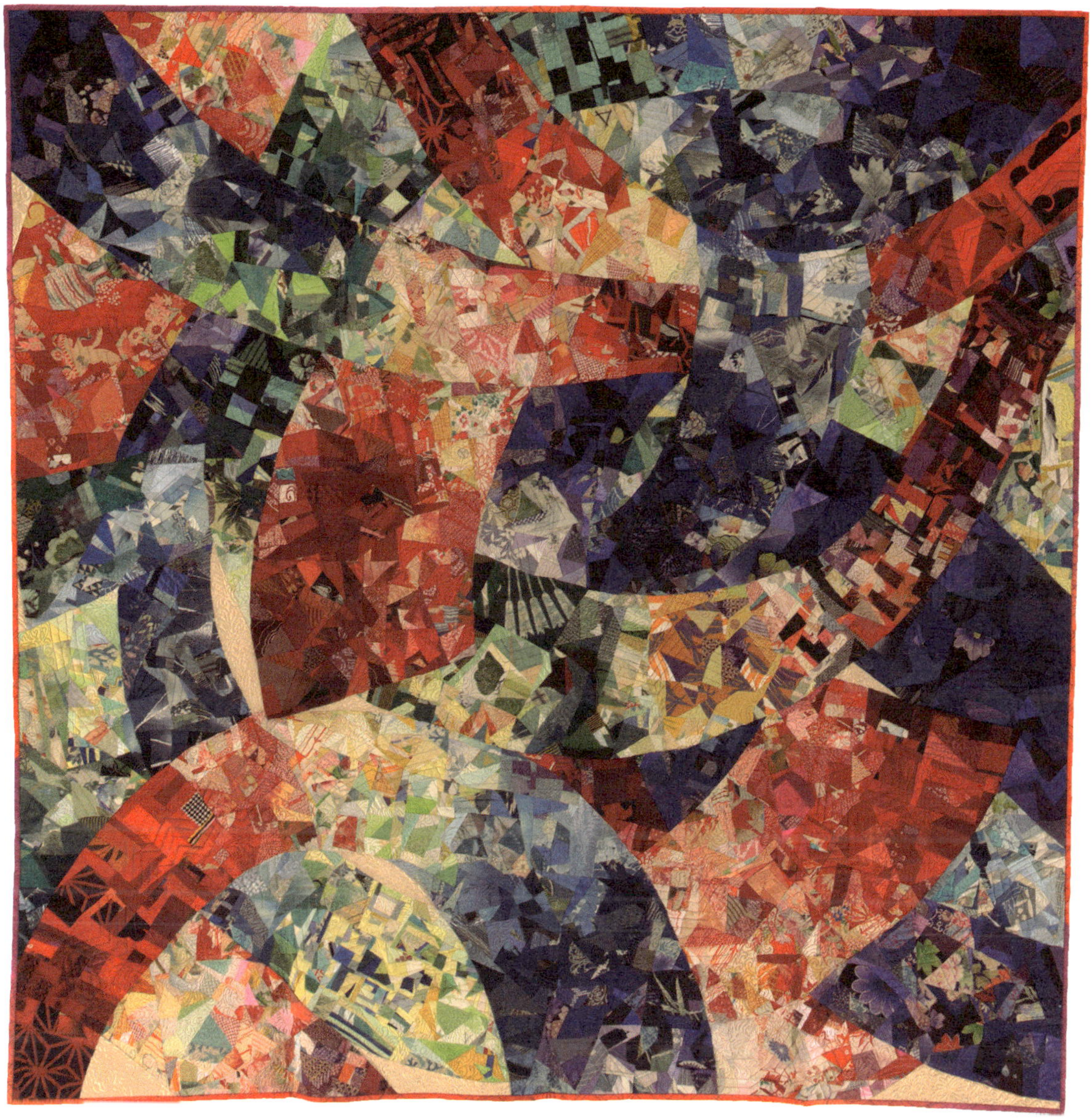

95. **Movement #89**
Yasuko Saito
Tokyo, Japan, 2020
Silk, cotton, linen, Japanese handmade paper (washi); machine pieced and quilted; 76.5 x 78.5 in.
Gift of the Robert and Ardis James Foundation, IQM 2020.055.0001

Yasuko Saito's quilts are often characterized by intricate patchwork contained within wide, sweeping arcs of color. Another unique quality of her work is her use of washi, handmade paper, along with hand- and custom-dyed fabrics. About this quilt Saito says, "The year 2020 is in a state of emergency because of the coronavirus disease . . . With what's going on right now, I worked with the theme of 'rainbow' in order to express my hope for [the return of] dreams, happy and fulfilling life, and fun."

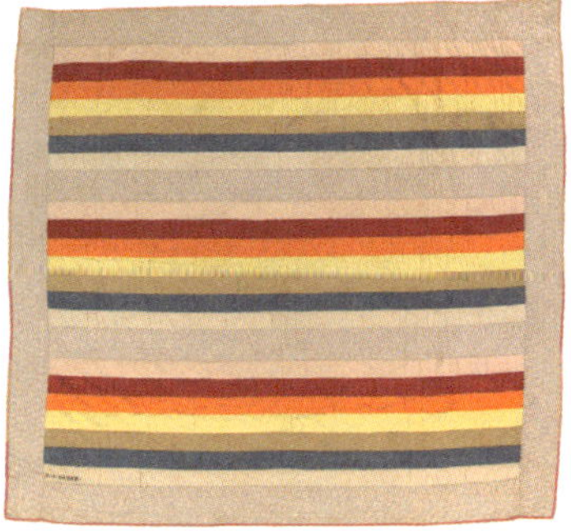

**Rainbow Stripes**
Plate 41

# CONTRIBUTORS

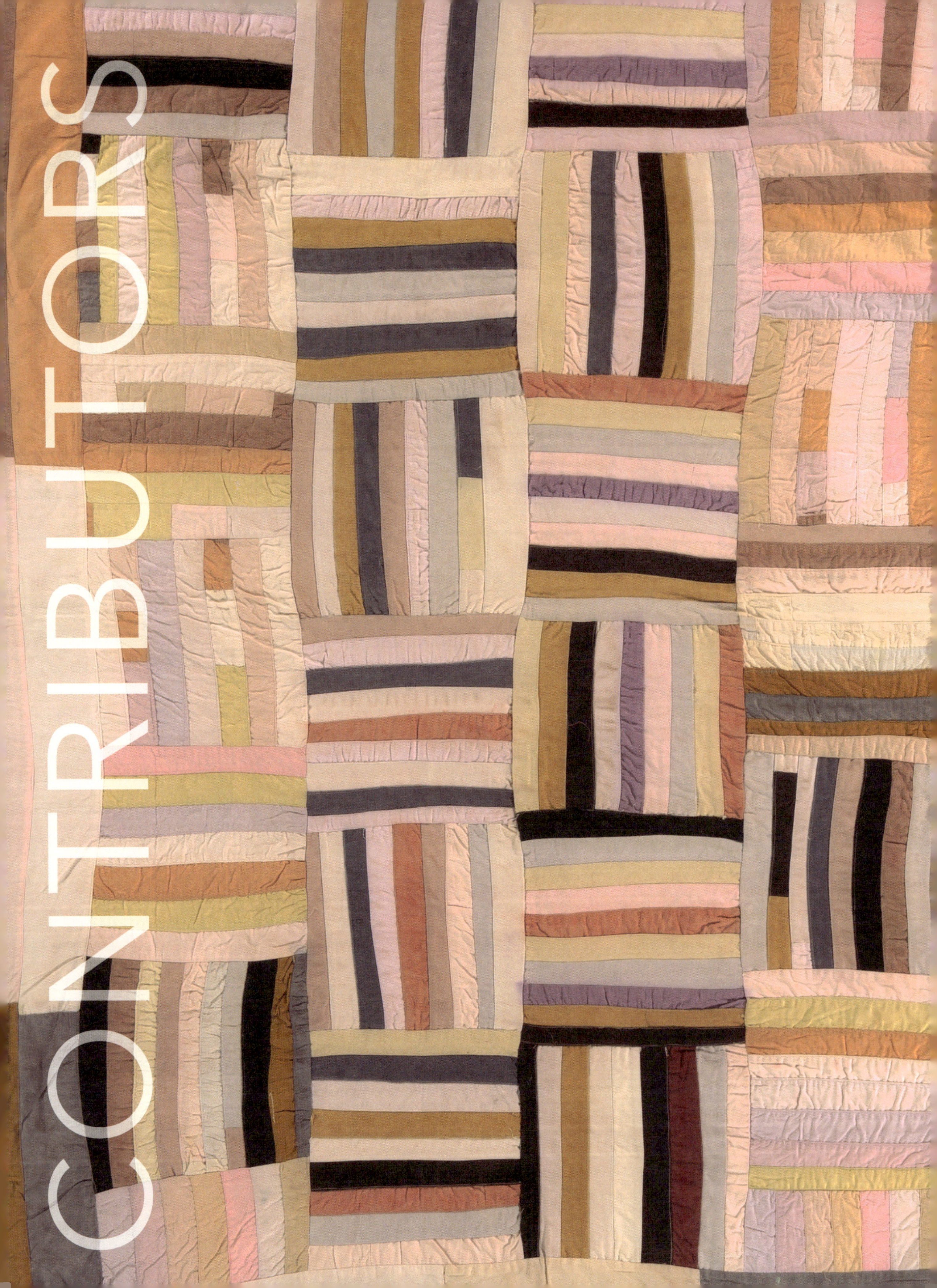

**CAROLYN DUCEY** is curator of collections at the International Quilt Museum (IQM), a position she has held since 1998. Ducey oversees acquisition and management of the IQM collection of more than 8,500 quilts. Ducey earned an MA in American Art History from Indiana University in 1998, and her PhD in Textiles, Clothing & Design, with an emphasis in Quilt Studies at the University of Nebraska-Lincoln in 2010. She is co-editor of *American Quilts in the Industrial Age 1760–1870* (2018) and co-author of *What's in a Name: Inscribed Quilts* (2012).

**JONATHAN GREGORY** earned an MA in Textile History and PhD in Human Sciences from the University of Nebraska-Lincoln. His research, curatorial work, and writing pursue twentieth-century American quiltmaking, particularly in relation to social engagement and meaning-making. Gregory is assistant curator of exhibitions at the IQM and oversees production of its many exhibition projects. He has contributed to several IQM publications including *American Quilts in the Modern Age, 1870–1940* (2009) and *American Quilts in the Industrial Age, 1760–1870* (2018), and to IQM's "World Quilts" website (worldquilts.quiltstudy.org).

**MARIN HANSON** is the IQM's curator of international collections and is responsible for building and interpreting the museum's non-Western collection. She earned an MA in Museum Studies and Textile History from the University of Nebraska-Lincoln and a PhD in Museum Studies from the University of Leicester (UK). Hanson has been a curator at the IQM since 2001 and is co-editor of its collections catalog, *American Quilts in the Modern Age, 1870–1940* (2009). She is project curator for the IQM's "World Quilts" website and contributor to several of its modules.

**JONATHAN HOLSTEIN** has been involved with the IQM since its inception and is currently a member of its Acquisition Committee. He is an art dealer and an independent curator in his fields of interest: quilts, Americana, and Native American art. He has a BA from Harvard, was an editor at McGraw-Hill in New York, then in the 1960s began to photograph art and artists for books and exhibition catalogs. In the late 1960s, he and his wife Gail van der Hoof began to collect American pieced quilts. This interest culminated in an initial quilt exhibition at the Whitney Museum of American Art, New York (1971) and subsequent similar exhibitions in many museums in the United States and abroad. He wrote the catalog for that first exhibition, *Abstract Design in American Quilts*, and the catalog for their European exhibitions, *American Pieced Quilts* (1972), followed by *The Pieced Quilt: An American Design Tradition* (1973). For a remounting of the Whitney exhibition on its 20th anniversary he wrote *Abstract Design in American Quilts: A Biography of an Exhibition*. He continues to write about quilts, advise museums and collectors in his areas of interest, and curate quilt exhibitions for museums.

**NAO NOMURA** is an associate professor in the Faculty of Liberal Arts at Saitama University, Japan. She earned her MA in Museum Studies and Textile History from the University of Nebraska-Lincoln and is working toward her PhD in American Studies from the University of Tokyo, Japan. Her current research examines the intersection of religious identity and consumer culture in the Old Order Amish of Lancaster County, Pennsylvania. She is also interested in exploring the US-Japan relationship through the lens of quiltmaking.

**SANDRA SIDER**, a New York quilt artist since the early 1980s, holds an MA in Art History from the Institute of Fine Arts, New York University. Sider has served as president of Studio Art Quilt Associates, and today she is Editor of *Art Quilt Quarterly* and Curator of the Texas Quilt Museum. She has written or edited more than a dozen books concerning contemporary quilt art, including *Art Quilts Unfolding: Fifty Years of Innovation*. She teaches the History of Textiles course in the MFA Textiles program at Parsons School of Design in New York and is a fabric designer for Benartex.